THE WONDERS
OF
LOURDES

Publisher: Pierre-Marie Dumont
Editor: Gerald Korson

Translator: John Pepino
Copy editor: Janet Chevrier
Assistant to the Editorial Staff: Aude Bertrand Desombre
Production: Marie Guibert
Concept, Design, and Cover Design: A Cappella
This book has been composed and created thanks to the precious help of the
Shrines Notre-Dame de Lourdes (NDL Editions).

Cover: *Madonna of the Rose Bush* (1440), Stephan Lochner (1410-1452),
Wallraf-Richartz Museum, Cologne, Germany. © Erich Lessing/akg-images.
Page 23: *The Apparition of the Virgin in Lourdes* (1858), attributed to Franz Xavier
Winterhalter (1805-1873), Private Collection © Photo Lionel Antoni.

ISBN: 978-0-9798086-1-6
Second edition: September 2008
© Magnificat USA LLC
© Mame-Paris, 2008

THE WONDERS
OF
LOURDES

MAGNIFICAT®

WE WOULD LIKE TO THANK FOR THEIR VALUABLE COLLABORATION:

Most Reverend Jacques Perrier, Bishop of Tarbes and Lourdes

LADIES

Marie-Élisabeth Aubry, documentalist
Chantal Touvet, historian of Lourdes
Thérèse Franque, archivist for the Lourdes shrine
Roselyne de Boisséson, documentalist
Martine Korpal, secretary of *Lourdes magazine*
Danielle Oribès, secretary of Canon Charriez
Maryline Plagnet, secretary of the Medical Bureau
Céline Bonnier, press attaché of NDL Editions
Cécile Jouanoulou, assistant to the editorial staff, NDL Editions
Madame Chaubon, director of the Blue Star Association
Maria de Faykod, sculptor
Chelo Feral
Danielle Hay and her son
Paola Montera, documentalist

GENTLEMEN

François Vayne, director of NDL Editions and of *Lourdes magazine*
Francis Dehaine, general director of the shrines
Pierre Adias, director of the communication service of the shrines
Jean-François Monnory, general secretary of the shrines
Francis Latour, director of the SEM-Accueil Notre-Dame
Patrick Theillier, director of the Medical Bureau
René Ricaud, technical director of NDL Editions
M. Tierny, president of Notre-Dame de Lourdes' Hospitality
Richard King, organizer of the HCPT Pilgrimage
Bertrand Galimard-Falvigny, Knight of Malta

Aymerick O'Neill, Bernadette of Marseille Community

Alain Marchio, hospitaller

Lucio Orsoni, mosaicist

Vincent Bourdier, assistant documentalist

Jean-Michel Feral

PRIESTS AND RELIGIOUS

Father Raymond Zambelli, rector of the Shrines Notre-Dame de Lourdes

Father Pierre-Marie Charriez, chaplain and archives director

Father Régis-Marie de la Teyssonnière

Father André Doze

Father René Point

Father José-Maria de Antonio

Father Wojciech Kowalewski

Father Horatio Brito

Father André Cabes

Father Pierre Leborgne

WORD FROM THE EDITOR

The one hundred and fifty stories in this book are based on historical documents from the Shrines of Notre-Dame de Lourdes' archives. The italicized quotations and phrases, when not used for emphasis, foreign terms, or to reflect one's interior thoughts, have been authenticated from these archives. Although some stories use fictionalized or composite characters and creative literary styles, the essential histories of Lourdes and the miraculous healings that have taken place there are true.

CONTENTS

CONTENTS

PREFACE

Should one say "the shrines of Lourdes" or "the shrine of Lourdes"? I am not posing the question for the love of quibbling, but because the two expressions are current and each is interesting in its own way. An explanation on this subject will serve as prologue to my preface.

"The shrine" is what used to be called "the domain," the complex of properties that Bishop Bertrand Laurence and his successors prudently acquired to protect the grotto's surroundings. In fact, there is the town on the one hand and the shrine on the other. The town, or at least the lower part of town, offers its hotels and businesses. For a hundred and fifty years now, they have been the subject of ridicule and scorn, called "merchants at the temple," even though they are not in the temple. It's a good thing they are there and that I do not have to manage thirty-five thousand beds and sell millions of Holy Virgin statues! The shrine is a space where you can stay all day, and no one will bother you for a nickel. You are in the shrine: You are safe, and you are free.

"The shrines" are a certain number of places, churches especially, within the domain. The plural number is interesting, for each of these places has its own character: The Ways of the Cross are not the waterway, the pools are not the Chapel of Reconciliation. In any case, the grotto is separate. As for the basilicas, churches and chapels, they are very diverse in size and style. This variety reflects different tastes but also different visions of the Church. Between the neo-Gothic upper basilica and Saint Pius X Basilica, which is shaped like a velodrome, much water has flowed under the bridges of the Gave River. And it is just as well: The Church belongs no more to one period than to another.

What I have just said about the shrines could apply to the wonders of Lourdes as well. One may speak of Lourdes in the singular or in the plural.

This place is unique in the world. Nowhere else has the Virgin called herself "the Immaculate Conception." Nowhere else have the sick come in greater numbers for a hundred and fifty years, and nowhere else have so many been healed. Several narratives in this book bear witness to the fact. Nowhere else do peoples and languages coexist on such terms of equality. Nowhere else do the armed forces of historically enemy countries come together to pray for peace. Yet Lourdes makes no claim to superiority: That would be ridiculous.

Every shrine in the world reflects a specific grace. Lourdes is therefore as unique as every other shrine. It is a marvel, in the sense that one speaks of the "marvel" of *Mont-Saint-Michel*, in Normandy.

Yet this marvel recurs in countless wonders. A hundred and fifty of them are recounted in this volume. There had to be a limit. They are spread across time. They deal with diverse aspects of the human condition. They are gifts from God in which the generosity, the faith, the boldness of men and women have their place. The editors' talent expresses all of this felicitously. This collection of wonders fits perfectly with the goal of the apparitions' sesquicentennial jubilee – to show how Lourdes, in her own way, contributes to the Church's essential missions in the present day, as she has done in the past and will continue to do in the future.

I am sure that Lourdes has not exhausted all its resources. Lourdes is more laboratory than conservatory. Fifty years from now, our successors will be able to write another book.

Most Reverend Jacques Perrier
Bishop of Tarbes and Lourdes

FOREWORD

The Lord Did Wonders for Us

A little town crowded around its church and its castle, Lourdes emerged from the shadows in the year 1858 to become the place of reference for a great many Christians.

Lourdes is the story of a very young girl, the poorest of the poor, illiterate, and in delicate health, who became the object of a favor from heaven; it is a child's personal history disrupting human history; it is the path proposed to a young girl who, by setting off upon it, would remind the world of the only path that leads to the source of all grace.

Bernadette offered herself to the gratuitousness of the gift of God, who reached out to her for her own sake, to be sure, but above all for the sake of the world. God always acts in the same way: The election of a single individual opens the torrents of his generosity toward all. Those who have heard God's call and answered, "Here I am, send me," have allowed God's plan to come to pass.

God chose Bernadette, and Mary came to indicate her specific mission to her – to be a witness to the call of the Gospel. When Mary says, "Come drink from the fountain and wash in it," she is saying nothing more than what Jesus has said. To do penance and to purify one's heart is the attitude that corresponds to the call to convert and believe in the Good News proclaimed by Christ.

In Lourdes, Bernadette turned completely to God. She passed the message of grace along and then buried herself in the silence of an ordinary religious life. She let Lourdes and the whole world turn, at the Church's own invitation, to Mary, whose words calling for penance keep bringing to Christ those who would draw near to the running water by making the step of a pilgrimage.

Bernadette grew in holiness by taking the Gospel seriously. In her own words, "Lourdes is not heaven." Lourdes is the place of discovery, the place of reminder, the place of deepening the truth of the Gospel. Heaven is what we await in faith, whose advent we hasten through charity; it is what holds us up in hope; it is the reign of Christ "all in all." That is why, when the Church gives us the feast of Our Lady of Lourdes, she squarely places us before the demand of the Gospel. So, in this jubilee year, let us take the time to be schooled in the liturgy so that it may teach us the path of a proper Marian devotion bearing fruits for the glory of God and the salvation of the world.

The liturgy of the feast of Our Lady of Lourdes opens with an entrance antiphon drawn from an image from the Apocalypse (Rv 21: 2): *I also saw the holy city, a new Jerusalem, coming down out of heaven from God, prepared as a bride adorned for her husband.*

The new Jerusalem is none other than the gathering of the holy people, the people of the saved among whom God establishes his dwelling place. Mary is a figure of this saved people, for she is the first to have accepted the Gospel message in its totality. Her "yes" to the Word of God makes her the model of the believer who is advancing along the path of life without refusing any of it – and who, in so doing, becomes the holy dwelling in which God delights.

At the opening prayer of the celebration, the liturgy orients our gaze toward the journey's end, though doing so without neglecting the truth

in daily life: *God of Mercy, we celebrate the feast of Mary, the sinless mother of God. May her prayers help us to rise above our human weakness.*

God loves us. Is there any greater and more felicitous truth than this? It is within this ceaselessly reaffirmed love that the Church finds the support of her forward march and the strength of her hope; it is within this primordial love that she places her confidence in the intercession of Mary who, as at Cana, never ceases to present the failures, weaknesses, and shortcomings of humanity to the Father and the Son. Yet what the Church awaits is the healing of sin, that is, salvation; she desires for the salvation brought about by Christ in his death and resurrection to be accomplished totally. That is what she celebrates in the Eucharist.

In celebrating the commemoration of the Immaculate Virgin we offer you, Lord, the sacrifice of praise: may it go up to you as a pleasing gift and bring us salvation in mind, spirit and in body (prayer over the gifts).

The liturgy makes us participants in the in the sacrifice of Christ; it does so through the sacrifice of praise that actualizes salvation for each individual. The Eucharist is the sacrament of healing *par excellence*; in it, Christ acts on the behalf of his gathered people; in it, "the work of our redemption is worked out."

Most holy Father, it is right to acknowledge your glory in the triumph of your elect, and, to celebrate the Virgin Mary, to take up her song of thanks: yes, you have spread your mercy to all ages and revealed your marvels to the whole world, choosing your humble handmaid to give a Savior to the world (preface of the Virgin Mary II).

Here the most beautiful prayer of thanksgiving, the eucharistic prayer, invites believers to have a heart like Mary's when she exulted with joy at the news of the salvation being achieved for the world through her. God chose a humble handmaid and granted her to sing the new canticle that still echoes in every Eucharist, when the Savior join us in his Word and gives himself as food so that our joy may be perfect.

Thou visitest the earth... Thou waterest its furrows abundantly, settling its ridges, softening it with showers, and blessing its growth (cf. Ps 65: 10-11). Mary, more than any other, is the symbol of this earth that is visited, watered, and abundantly fertile, but every baptized person communing in Christ is likewise visited by God, watered, and abundantly fertile in the riches of the world to come. That is why the prayer after communion implores the grace that this gift be not in vain:

You have fed us, Lord our God, by giving us the bread of the Kingdom: grant that this Eucharist, which we celebrate in joy, may be for us the sign of unity and the bond of charity (prayer after communion).

In Lourdes, the Eucharist is at the center of all pilgrimage-related activities. It alone gives meaning to the charity that is exercised in a special way toward the sick. The Eucharist sets Mary's visit to Lourdes in its proper place – the place indicated by the feast's Gospel reading on the wedding at Cana. Mary attentively is at her Son's side when she says, "They have no wine," the wine that gives a taste for life; she is thus at the side of all persons in distress. "Do whatever he tells you," she says, and you will taste abundantly of the wine of the joy of salvation.

Lourdes bears the particular mark of God's love, of which the Virgin Mary's luminous face is a sign, yet whose power manifests itself in the charity and the joy implemented and shared by the immense crowd of pilgrims from all nations pressing together in this blessed place. The wonderful news of Lourdes doesn't end at Mary's visit to this earth; it draws the pilgrims to rediscover the message that is more extraordinary yet and always new – namely, the Gospel of Christ. Saint John of the Cross warns that one who "would wish for a vision or a revelation, would not only commit a folly, but would insult God by failing to keep his eyes on Christ" (*The Ascent to Carmel*, § 22). The Church, in her prudence, has maintained this way of receiving the grace of the apparitions from the beginning.

In Lourdes, the Father's loving kindness for mankind passes through Mary's hands. In this jubilee book, it is that truth of Lourdes, into which the liturgy helps us to enter, that we have sought to bring out. This truth will reveal itself, taking flesh in real lives, along the thread of one hundred and fifty beautiful stories. They ought to be read in a spirit of contemplation, as one says the beads of a rosary. These are not only marvelous stories, but also truthful testimonies of the marvels that God performs in our lives through his Church, the sacrament of salvation, at Mary's invitation, the *betrothed adorned for her spouse* that prefigures her in God.

Dear reader, you are about to cover, in one hundred and fifty steps, one hundred and fifty years of Lourdes history. May this written pilgrimage cause your mind and heart to brim with the joy of the *Magnificat* and bear its fruit in your lives through love.

Through love, because devotion to the Virgin Mary makes sense in seeking to live the new commandment day in and day out. Bernadette said it with her customary simplicity: "All that's needed is love…"

Pierre-Marie DUMONT
Creator of *Magnificat*

HAIL MARY, FULL OF GRACE.
THE LORD IS WITH THEE.

BLESSED ART THOU AMONG WOMEN,
AND BLESSED IS THE FRUIT OF THY WOMB, JESUS.

HOLY MARY, MOTHER OF GOD,

PRAY FOR US SINNERS,
NOW AND AT THE HOUR OF OUR DEATH.

AMEN.

INCIPIT

The Song of the Rock

There is the grotto, an ancient thousand-year-old covering of rocks worn down by glacial waters, with its velvety blanket of grass that over-hangs and hides it. Its name, Masse-Vieille ("ancient mass"), has become Massabielle. Seen from the banks of the river Gave, it is nothing very remarkable. Set under a rocky mass sixty-five feet high, it is one of several granite shelters in the area that were thrust up from the moraines of the past. Neither broad nor deep, it protects bad, muddy, and humid soil where swine and wandering beasts have always come to graze. Six feet high, it is framed with ivy branches and wild rosebushes that stamp the ephemeral sweetness of flowers and plants upon this austere mineral dwelling.

Desolation, cold, and the strong smell of abandonment have taken up residence there as though the place were at the dusk of its life. It might have remained obscure and forgotten by men in this crisscrossing of wind, rain, and nothingness if the little Bernadette had not stopped there to pick up some firewood, and if the Lady had not appeared to the poorest of the poor, revealing a radiant light in this ordinary life. "*The grotto is my heaven*," Bernadette was to say later; and at the moment of her definitive departure for Nevers, in 1866, she would declare: "*That is where you will find me in spirit, bound to the foot of the rock that I love so.*"

"There" is not just any word in Bernadette Soubirous' mouth. It is the place where the hunger and thirst of innocence marries truth and abandons humiliation: *All you who are thirsty, come to the water!*[1] It is the place of encounter with Mary, that mother of signal goodness who sheds light upon humanity and conceals sorrow in the secret of her soul. Near the thick waters of the Gave, the grotto comes to life under the pilgrims' feet, and the granite warms those hands that linger there to give thanks and to touch a piece of heaven on earth. So many kisses have mingled the breath of man with the barren rock that in time it has acquired the polish and patina of obsidian.

Nothing is more astounding than a man kneeling with his back to the world in the silence of God. Yet did the world even exist to Bernadette before February 1858, on this immense prairie through which she came? The castle and the mill of Savy, which dominate the grotto, are two contrasting universes: Here is where grandeur encounters lowliness, and glory meets humility. And it is in this place, without any particular beauty, that the most important event in the life of Bernadette will play out. The land of the humble and the forgotten will become that of the overwhelmed and the amazed, a little more so after each apparition.

This meeting lights up the young girl's heart; it bears the repeated sweetness of a relished encounter, the incandescence of life, the ripple of hope. Those who follow Bernadette – the simple people of the area, the curious, and the undecided – are overcome with impatience and distraction before what their narrow hearts do not grasp, before what their eyes, with their impaired clarity, do not see. Meanwhile, the prayer is said as beads between fingers, as words within the silence of the heart: *Hail*

---

1. Is 55: 1.

Mary, full of grace. The muffled laughter of the sarcastic and the skeptical slides off the rock and falls back into the mud.

Then, suddenly, on February 25, a mystery would be revealed – a revelation and a gift without equal, like that of Christ to the Samaritan woman at Jacob's well.

The grotto conceals a hidden treasure, a source, or rather a muddy trickle. This muddy water, so invisible and so thick that one has to dig for it far beneath the leaves and twigs, is what Bernadette drinks and washes in. She eats the grass like an animal. Those who have confidently followed her are surprised and worried. But Bernadette Soubirous unwittingly opens the way. Before the amazed eyes of the three hundred fifty people who watch her, she surprises the intelligent and puts closed hearts to the test, abandoning all fear and pride. The young girl lets herself go and brings out of this nothingness the model of her obedience and the power of her faith.

From now on, nothing will be as before. The marvelous takes up residence here at the foot of the grotto in the smile of Mary that opens for each one of us, as in the book of Ezekiel, a path of light and purification. *"I will sprinkle clean water upon you to cleanse you from all your impurities, and from all your idols I will cleanse you. I will give you a new heart and place a new spirit within you, taking from your bodies your stony hearts and giving you natural hearts."*[1]

Renewed is he who stretches his hands toward God's holy waters, who lets the humble and soft prayer of the prodigal child rise up within him, who places his lips and palms on the rock that has become so smooth by the work of love and of faith that one may see the faces of all humanity upon it.

Like the ill-matched flowers of a winter bouquet, all these pilgrims of various backgrounds gather and mingle in the thin thread of the prayer

---

1. Ez 36: 25-26.

to Mary, who comforts and who fortifies: *Hail Mary, full of grace...* and the Lord is with us, and grace is there, weaving bright hope before our eyes.

Then it happens – the rustling of a cure, the brushing of a wing that passes by and leads us on with unexpected answers, spread amid the wax of the votive lights that unceasingly stand vigil.

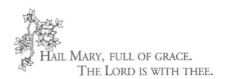

HAIL MARY, FULL OF GRACE.
THE LORD IS WITH THEE.

A BEAUTIFUL LADY DRESSED IN WHITE

First Apparition, February 11, 1858

18 58 In the fireplace of the Soubirous home, the fire was once again dying out. On that morning of February 11, 1858, the hearth had taken on a gloomy atmosphere, the feeling of days when the family was out of everything, even firewood. Without the flames' dance, the walls of the only room seemed even grayer, danker. The room deserved its nickname, "the dungeon," that dwelling where the six members of the family were crowded within a few square yards. Besides, the name was not even ironic: It was, in fact, an old prison, put out of commission because it had been deemed unsanitary. The Soubirous family had found asylum here thanks to a cousin's generosity.

Yet the Soubirouses were not the type to groan about their poverty, as obvious as it was. No wood? So what! Time to look for some on the outskirts of town. By making one's way as far as the Gave du Pau, the river that supplied water to Lourdes, surely one could gather enough to rekindle a good blaze and warm up the air in the dungeon.

Bernadette was the first to suggest going to look for a bundle of firewood. Toinette, her younger sister, immediately leaped toward the door: She wanted to tag along with her big sister.

"We'll gather animal bones while we're at it. The rag-and-bone woman[1] is bound to give us five *sous* for it!" Toinette suggested with enthusiasm.

Louise Soubirous, their mother, agreed with a smile. François, the father of the family, who had worked odd jobs as a day laborer since his mill went bankrupt, was out of work. A few small coins would come in handy! Still, Louise expressed a reservation: "Go alone with your friend Jeanne, Toinette. Bernadette must not catch cold!" The older sister, who suffered from chronic asthma, was so fragile at fourteen years of age.

"Oh, Mama," begged Bernadette, "let me go. I will bundle up!"

By relentlessly insisting, Bernadette won her case, and off she went in the drizzling rain with Toinette and Jeanne.

Once out of town, they walked up and down the foggy meadows, idling like three carefree girls. Having reached the sandy spit of land where the Gave River joined the canal of the mill at Savy, they stopped to observe the other bank. There, under the grotto of Massabielle, firewood and bones seemed plentiful!

In a flash, Jeanne and Toinette took off their clogs to cross the icy stream. Bernadette, for her part, hesitated. Had she not promised her mother that she would not catch cold?

"*Help me throw stones into the water, so that I can ford it!*" Bernadette cried.

"*Do what we did!*" answered the two younger girls, a mite annoyed by the adolescent affectation.

The two girls reached the other bank and started to busy themselves at the foot of the grotto.

Bernadette no longer had a choice. She took off one stocking. Suddenly, she heard the sound of a gust of wind, unexpected in that rainy fog in which nothing moved. The young girl glanced at the poplars

---

1. The rag-and-bone woman, in French *chiffonnière*, would pick up used objects to sell.

growing not far from the Gave, but their branches were motionless. Thinking she had imagined it, Bernadette continued to remove her shoes. Another gust of wind! This time, right in front of her, in one of the grotto's crevices, a wild rosebush bended under a slight breeze. It seemed to be playing in the wind at the feet of a magnificently beautiful young lady. Wearing a white dress, a rosary fixed to her blue belt, the stranger was in the hollow of a rock on which a sweet light shed its rays. She gave Bernadette a radiant smile.

Naturally, the youngster did not believe her eyes. She rubbed them and blinked several times, persuaded that they were deceiving her. But they did not lie. The stranger was still there, smiling peacefully!

By reflex, Bernadette's hand slipped deep into her pocket, grasped her familiar rosary, and brought it back out into the open to try to make the sign of the cross. Overcome by surprise, her hand was unable to reach her forehead and fell back trembling to her side.

At this point, the lady in the vision took the lead, making the sign of the cross herself. Bernadette tried once again, this time successfully. Her fear was replaced by a great peace. She got down on her knees and prayed an entire rosary. The stranger joined her, slipping the beads between her fingers without opening her lips. The rosary over, she invited Bernadette with a welcoming gesture to come closer to her. But the girl did not dare attempt a single step forward. The vision, without insisting, then disappeared as mysteriously as it had appeared.

Bernadette thought: *What am I to do? Go back to Jeanne and Toinette, who are a few paces downhill from the grotto, and pretend nothing is going on?* The youngster crossed the cold water without feeling any discomfort and found her companions busy with their bundles.

"*Did you see anything?*" Bernadette asked Jeanne and Toinette offhandedly.

"*No. How about you: What did you see?*"

Bernadette was evasive and changed the conversation. How could she speak of the unspeakable? Yet how heavy the secret was to bear – far heavier than the basket of bones she was carrying back toward the dungeon without even feeling its weight!

On the way back, she could bear it no longer. As Jeanne had gone ahead of the two sisters, she described the incredible apparition to Toinette under the most absolute seal of secrecy, her voice yet aquiver with a mix of stupor and excitement.

But the tongue of a twelve-year-old girl is prompt to loosen! They had barely returned home when, taking advantage of a moment when Bernadette was out, Toinette coughed a few times to attract her mother's attention. The signal was successful.

"*Why are you doing this? Are you ill?*" her mother asked.

"*No,*" replied Toinette, "*but I will tell you what Bernadette told me. She saw a girl in white in the grotto at Massabielle…*"

Mrs. Soubirous reacted strongly, and bluntly interrogated her eldest daughter. What was all this about? The Soubirouses had always been an honest family, but they had already had enough trouble back when the father was accused of stealing two bags of flour and was sent to jail. It was not going to start all over again, was it?

But Bernadette could only repeat in front of her mother what she had told Toinette. She saw what she saw, without any possible doubt or retraction.

Mrs. Soubirous' sentence was swift, the only reasonable sentence for a mortal mind, a maternal one at that, to formulate: "*You are not to go back to Massabielle.*"

François, the father, had heard everything. He agreed with his wife. He loved his daughter, in whom he had immense trust; among the Soubirouses, love and trust were the two riches that never ran out.

Bernadette had to be protected, and therefore she had to be barred from going to the grotto and its mirages.

"*Let us pray,*" he said. Prayer had always been the family's strength. Bernadette had been taught well from birth.

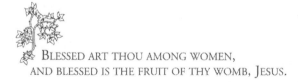

BLESSED ART THOU AMONG WOMEN,
AND BLESSED IS THE FRUIT OF THY WOMB, JESUS.

THE CALM OF A SMILE

Second Apparition, February 14, 1858

18
58
Leaning over a coarse notebook, Bernadette laboriously linked together lines of writing. The teacher, a religious from Nevers, walked to and fro between the silent rows, overseeing the dictation's progress. Singled out and exempted from so difficult an exercise, Bernadette copied out endless A's and B's.

What an unbelievable girl! thought the religious leaning over Bernadette's clumsy and labored penmanship. Bernadette, at fourteen years of age, was just barely acquainted with the school's blackboard and desks. In the mid-nineteenth century, despite government efforts, education was a rare luxury among the poor! Bernadette had been given a position with her former wet nurse for a few months: She would perform minor chores and watch the sheep in the hills a few miles from Lourdes. She had just returned to the town to be admitted among the sisters and to start going to school in the hope of making her First Communion that year. To be admitted to the Lord's table, one had to know more about him – which would require learning how to read, and in French, too, not in the local dialect!

Suddenly, Bernadette's pen was stopped in midair by the teacher's hand. The teacher looked at the unfinished B, then at the young girl whose black eyes were lost in the distance, far beyond the window. Cases of distraction were rare in this willing student. How could the religious suspect that, since this morning, Bernadette had been completely inattentive? The Gave, the grotto, the stranger, and her rosary: That was all the pupil could think about, and her mind was playing hooky. This morning, when she expressed her wish to go back to Massabielle, her mother had simply answered, "*Get to work, Bernadette!*"

Still at her desk, the young girl pulled herself together, took up the B where she had left off, finished her line of writing, and started a new one. She told herself: *Do not get noticed! Do not awaken the religious sisters' curiosity, less yet that of the pupils! Forget the Lady in White by blackening the notebook's pages with ink...*

But that was without counting on Toinette and Jeanne. At recess, the story spread and swelled: Bernadette was seeing friendly ghosts and was keeping it a secret! The girls' imaginations were running wild. On Sunday, February 14, after Mass, a small group of curious girls got it into their heads to convince François and Louise Soubirous that Bernadette must be allowed to go back to Massabielle – accompanied by a good crowd, of course!

Worn down by a barrage of so many shrill voices, the parents granted their consent. Their eldest didn't need to be told twice and dashed off to the grotto, dragging her chattering escorts behind her – not, however, without a prudent stop at the church to pick up a vial of holy water. Exploring the supernatural was a heady but dangerous thing: Best to arm oneself as well as possible!

Bernadette arrived at Massabielle, and the girls began to imitate the way she knelt, clasped their rosaries as she did, and together began a first decade – which the seer suddenly interrupted: "*She is there! She is smiling at us!*"

Every pair of eyes opened wide, focused on the spot, and wondered. Nothing. Nothing but a shady hole in a crack in the rock. And yet Bernadette got up with a leap, grabbed the holy water, and emptied it out upon the void.

"*If you come from God, stay. Otherwise, go away!*" she said loudly – or so she thought. But it was only the voice of her heart, for her companions heard nothing.

For her part, Bernadette intensely observed the magnificent young woman. Upon her mute lips, her unspeakable smile dawned as never before. It seemed to bloom like a flower under the dew of the holy water. Bernadette still did not know with whom she was dealing. At least it was not an evil spirit, or else the water surely would have put it to flight!

The Lady in White approached young Bernadette, who then fell on her knees. Deaf and dumb to what was playing out before them, the other girls saw only one thing: Bernadette's face had suddenly become as white as the hood that Mrs. Soubirous had made her wear to protect her from the cold.

"*She is going to die!*" moaned one of the onlookers, wringing her hands.

And suddenly, a scary moment: A big stone fell not far from the group. Jeanne, posted at the top of the cliff and impressed by the strange atmosphere that Bernadette had created around herself, got the idea of pelting the praying girls as a diversion.

But down below, the girls did not understand that the stone had been hurled by their friend. They thought the trouble originated from "it," from the ghost! There would be no gathering moss here: The onlookers had seen enough. They attempted to drag Bernadette, but she, unaware of the panic around her, kept her eyes affixed upon the grotto.

One might as well have attempted to lift one of the stone boulders that were strewn upon the ground. Bernadette, so frail one would have guessed her age was about four years less than it actually was, so small that she would never be taller than four feet, six-and-a-half inches, had taken on the inertia of rock. Sealed off from the world around her, she could not take her eyes off the stranger whose smile distilled a perfect peace into her heart.

Without wasting a second, the bevy of girls ran toward the mill of Savy nearby, pulled the miller by his sleeve, and forced him to leave his flour sacks to go to Bernadette's aid. Not understanding a bit of the girls' breathless explanations, he arrived at Massabielle quite confused. There he found Bernadette motionless, kneeling, and smiling. What was he to do?

"Get her away from there!" the girls kept telling him in an insistent refrain.

That was easier said than done. Though he was as strong as the millstone that ground his grain and was accustomed to handling flour by the scores of pounds, the miller nevertheless had all the trouble in the world hoisting Bernadette onto his shoulders and carrying her off to the mill. As for Bernadette, unaware of having given the miller so much grief, she kept smiling at the young woman, who followed her with her gaze from the grotto.

When Mrs. Soubirous, having been alerted by Bernadette's friends, reached the mill to fetch her daughter, her decision was irrevocable.

"This time it is over," she told Bernadette. "I forbid you ever to set foot again in that evil place."

HOLY MARY, MOTHER OF GOD,

The Promise

Third Apparition, February 18, 1858

1858 There was a knock at the door of the "dungeon." Leaving the corner of the hearth where she was darning the family's clothing, Mrs. Soubirous opened the door to her dwelling and saw a majestic tableau. In the doorway was an opulent crinoline above which reigned a well-fed face. All roundness and affable smiles, the wealthy Mrs. Milhet bowed her head to greet the mistress of the house, ringlets swaying about her plump cheeks.

Invited in, the visitor inspected the place with an approving and compassionate air. It was poor, but always as clean as possible at the Soubirous home, just as in the happy days when the family worked the mill at Boly. Mrs. Milhet remembered François Soubirous as one of the many millers who dotted the length of the Lapaca stream. He used to work fast and well. No complaints on the beautiful white flour that he used to draw from his mill! He was honest and never cheated with the grain measures. Yes, honest – and even too kind. His impoverished clients often had to postpone payments; François would wipe clean all debts. Never demanding money, he trustingly handed over sacks of flour. *Alas! His kindness lost him, poor man,* thought the visitor to herself as she stood at the dungeon entrance.

Mrs. Milhet entered in a rustling of silk, her dress's ample hoops creaking as she walked through the narrow door. Louise Soubirous did not know what to do with herself. Quick, a chair! No, two – for behind the august silhouette of Mrs. Milhet had appeared her humbler seamstress, Antoinette Peyret. The visitors had neither the same estate nor the same stature, but their piety was equal and they were rivals in devotions.

"Dear Mrs. Soubirous, let us get to the facts," declared Mrs. Milhet in her even voice. "Your Bernadette has apparitions."

"Well, the fact is…" Mrs. Soubirous interjected.

"No, please. I know how great your maternal humility is," said Mrs. Milhet. "But it is a fact: Your daughter is privileged by heaven. Now, let me ask you, who is this beautiful young woman?"

Mrs. Soubirous was speechless.

"Antoinette, here present, and I think the woman is Élisa Latapie," said Mrs. Milhet. "That poor dear, as you know, belonged to the Congregation of the Children of Mary. Her recent passing upset all of Lourdes. She requested a very simple outfit for her last voyage, wearing only the attributes of a Congregation member. Alas!"

Her emotions suppressed in a batiste handkerchief, the pious woman continued: "That white dress, that blue belt, those naked feet adorned with two roses… What if the visions described by your daughter were our lamented Élisa, returning to ask for prayers for her soul's repose?"

At a loss for an answer, Louise Soubirous nodded. Mrs. Milhet pursued her idea further.

"I am asking you to lend me your daughter," the visitor said. "Be so kind as to lift your wise ban on the grotto. We shall accompany Bernadette to Massabielle and shall ask the vision to reveal her identity. I take responsibility for your dear child's safety."

"But…"

"Thank you infinitely, my dear lady," said Mrs. Milhet. "I knew I could count on you!"

With these words, the wealthy visitor made a triumphant exit, dragging Antoinette Peyret in her wake.

That is how, at dawn on February 18, Bernadette returned to the grotto without disobeying her parents. By her side, kneeling on the uncomfortable earth-and-pebble prie-dieu, the two pious ladies begin a rosary. Antoinette had brought up to Massabielle a writing pad belonging to her father, the bailiff of Lourdes, so that the apparition might finally reveal its mystery.

A few *Aves* later, Bernadette's gaze was suddenly drawn to the beautiful young woman. Mrs. Milhet tapped Bernadette on the shoulder and put the writing case between her hands. The young girl's ecstasy was no reason to forget the essential.

"We want a name!" Mrs. Milhet said.

Bernadette obediently advanced to the back of the grotto. Still kneeling, her companions had never prayed with as much intensity! Moved by pious curiosity, they trembled with impatience and perked up their ears, only to hear a deep silence. Did that fool Bernadette already forget her mission? Not at all. She had given the Lady in White the pen and the writing board, pronouncing very loudly all the words that Mrs. Milhet had dictated to her.

"*Would you have the kindness of putting down your name in writing?*" she asked the Lady.

Her reply was a new amazement: For the first time, the stranger allowed the sound of her voice to be heard.

"*It is not necessary,*" she said.

The apparition spoke in the dialect of Lourdes, but Bernadette did not recognize her as Élisa Latapie. The Lady continued in the same singsong dialect: "*Would you have the grace of coming here for fifteen days?*"

The courtesy formula was perfect, echoing the polite request of Mrs. Milhet. But what sweetness in the quality of her voice, and what exquisite delicacy in the smile that accompanied it! The beautiful young woman did not speak authoritatively, but rather awaited Bernadette's free consent. In the face of such a gracious invitation, the little girl from Lourdes finally lost her inhibition. Forgotten were the obstacles that might prevent her from keeping such a commitment – human prudence, filial obedience, school duties.

"Yes!" was Bernadette's response.

The promise was made. As for keeping it, time would tell. Meanwhile, the vision having vanished, Bernadette returned to her companions, for whom the wait had been a difficult trial. The writing pad was blank. Clouds of disappointment gathered in the eyes of the two pious ladies. But Bernadette, whose own eyes sparkled, related her conversation with the enigma in white.

"*What if it were the Holy Virgin?*" whispered Mrs. Milhet. Her question was greeted with a great silence, as the humble Bernadette could not say for sure. All she knew was that the magnificent young woman brought her own heart and thoughts closer to God.

Mrs. Milhet's practical mind soon overcame all theological hypotheses.

"Well, then, since you have made a promise to this lady, you will have to come back every day," she told Bernadette. "Starting tonight, I am taking you as a boarder at my house. We shall be able to make the trip discreetly, without alerting the entire population. People are so nosy!"

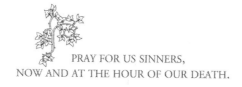

PRAY FOR US SINNERS,
NOW AND AT THE HOUR OF OUR DEATH.

IN THE HEART OF SILENCE

Fourth, Fifth, and Sixth Apparitions,
February 19, 20, 21, 1858

1858 The moonlight slipped between the brocade curtains. Reflected by the mirror on a dresser, it bathed the guest room where Mrs. Milhet had put up her "protégée" with all its elegant comforts. In her big bed with its fine sheets and soft mattress, Bernadette had trouble falling asleep. Her cautious eyes scanned about the room, stopping here on a gleaming piece of furniture, there on an engraving of His Majesty Napoleon III, then on a bookcase in which beautiful leather-bound volumes were neatly arranged.

But these wandering eyes always returned to fixate upon the only familiar object in this comfortable room – the crucifix that adorned the wall just above this decidedly too-beautiful bed. The corpus, though, was not disorientating, despite its ivory's flawless polish. Spreading his protective arms around Bernadette, the crucified Christ seemed to keep watch over her sleepless nights with tender care.

The young girl's jumbled thoughts turned once again to prayer. They escaped from the luxurious room to go back to the stark grotto where the radiant Lady had appeared to her that morning for the fourth time.

It was a short visit, at least according to the eight people who witnessed it, for Bernadette lost all sense of time whenever she was at Massabielle. It was also a silent visit, granted to the young girl from Lourdes perhaps so she would become accustomed to this incredible presence. The flame of the holy candle she had brought along shone in her eyes. But something even more luminous was reflected in them – the peerless smile of her visitor, a gleam of heaven in a cave's twilight.

Bernadette sighed. She turned over on this mattress whose comfort would not cease surprising her, closed her eyes, and begged Jesus to keep her heart simple, her soul as plain as the life of the poor. All that was in her strenuously refused to derive any glory from this extraordinary adventure. Without Bernadette's humility, the Lady would no longer come to honor her with her presence. That much was for certain.

The next day, Saturday, when Bernadette arrived at the grotto with Mrs. Milhet, her crinolined mentor sighed with dismay. About twenty people were already kneeling on the Gave's bank. The pious fifty-year-old's maneuver had failed: Lourdes was rustling with rumors, and discretion was no longer in play. From that day onward, the audience would gather and grow more numerous every day as they watched the young girl's face for a reflection of someone from beyond.

That evening, Bernadette returned home. Getting into the bed she shared with Toinette, she drew the rough blanket up to her chin and smiled happily. Would she fall asleep right away? No. Looking for the crude crucifix which had for many years received the family's prayers, she entered into conversation with God. Earlier that day, the grotto visitor had taught her a prayer to say every day without ever repeating it to anyone. This memory caused Bernadette to smile, as she remembered the desperate efforts of her nurse to teach her the rudiments of the catechism. Back then, the sentences would jostle together in her head and lose all meaning, so that the young girl could never put them back together again. Invariably, the catechism manual would be sent flying across the room.

"*Bah! You are too stupid,*" her nurse would say in exasperation. "*You will never be able to do your First Communion!*"

Yet this morning she had retained everything, word for word. Her soul had effortlessly memorized the new prayer that would accompany her until the hour of her death.

The next day, Sunday, a small crowd of a hundred people surrounded Bernadette when she arrived at Massabielle early that morning to meet the apparition. A "thing," that was the word! The youngster, unable to name her visitor, referred to her with the expression *Aquéro* ("that") in the dialect of Lourdes.

Within the audience, amid a crushing majority of peasant dresses, there was a man, and not the least of men – Dr. Dozous, one of the most distinguished and respected men of the town. He was not kneeling like the others. As a rational mind professing science as his sole religion, the doctor had decided to come and study this case of catalepsy that was causing such a sensation. His gaze scanned Bernadette's face, ready to fire off a diagnosis.

Like everybody else, he saw a young girl fall into ecstasy, her features lit up with a peaceful smile. What was it that could inspire such a smile? What was it that could suddenly clothe this sickly and common girl with such beauty? The doctor refused to allow his mind to wander beyond the limits of reason. He did not understand, and therefore he did not give a prognosis, except to say that it was not a case of catalepsy. Bernadette, to be sure, was no longer moving, but it was clear to the doctor's eyes that her motionlessness was not pathological: It was not due to a temporary paralysis of cerebral faculties.

The doctor decided to return over the next few days to refine his study and draw some conclusions. Meanwhile, he pensively watched Bernadette go back to the town, now that the grotto was empty of whatever she saw in it. Surrounded by the crowd, she answered the questions that the witnesses pressed upon her simply and gaily in her straightforward and artless dialect. It was quite obvious that this young girl had a sound head on her shoulders and was thinking straight; there were no hysterics or lies in her. Still, what a mystery...

AMEN.

FOR THE GOOD OF PUBLIC ORDER

Portrait of Police Chief Jacomet, February 21, 1858

1858 "A good police chief amounts to precise hearing, swift thumb-rings,[1] and a steady trigger" was a slogan that Police Chief Jacomet, an honorable civil servant who made it a point of honor to watch the slightest stirrings in his sleepy town of Lourdes, often repeated to himself. He personally took charge of all the cases. Last spring, for example, a baker had two sacks of flour stolen. The police chief received the plaintiff immediately and arrested a certain François Soubirous, whom the baker had employed six months before and whom he accused of this petty theft by reason of his notorious poverty. Yet the Soubirous case was never closed. The suspect's prints did not match the thief's. After a week, François Soubirous was released from his cell to be sent back to his family "dungeon."

The very professional police chief was never off duty, even on Sunday. On December 21, he had just heard an incredible story. A young town girl claimed she was a visionary. Her name? Bernadette Soubirous. Well, well...

Jacomet posted himself on the church square at the end of vespers. He had asked the county warden to point out the aforementioned

---

1. Ancestor of handcuffs, used until 1920.

Bernadette amid the gaggle of schoolgirls who would come twittering into the square. Once spotted, Bernadatte was led to the police chief's office with a firm yet clement hand. In reality, behind his uniform, Jacomet hid a good heart and a real care for the fate of poor people. In 1855, during the cholera epidemic that ravaged Lourdes, he gave of himself unstintingly to tend to the sick and to help wipe out the contagion at his own peril. It was therefore not an inflexible policeman who was about to interrogate Bernadette, but rather a man who considered himself to be the guarantor of public order in his county seat in the Pyrenees. As such, he was not about to put up with tall tales and reckless gossip.

As Bernadette stood before Jacomet's intimidating desk, she furtively took in the room while he prepared his pen. Books, portraits, a beautiful fireplace whose flames were reflected in the waxed floor, a dignified clock that marked the passage of time… It was yet another luxurious room to which she was not accustomed. Yet she was not too uncomfortable there, either. She was serene. She had only told the truth, so what could happen to her?

The interrogation began in the usual impersonal and routine way — surname, given name, age, names of father and mother… Bernadette answered carefully with an even tone of voice.

Suddenly, Jacomet set down his pen and interrogated Bernadette directly to throw off the young girl.

"*So tell me, Bernadette,*" he asked, "*you are seeing the Holy Virgin?*"

The young girl answered tit-for-tat, without batting an eyelid: "*I did not say it was the Holy Virgin.*"

Jacomet carried on with his strategy of rapid-fire questioning.

"*Right. So you did not see anything?*"

"*Yes, I did see something.*"

"*Something… or someone?*"

"*It had the shape of a little young lady,*" Bernadette replied.

The police chief, a little confused, asked Bernadette for an exact account of the events. The young girl complied without embellishment. From the very first account she had given to her sister, she had always wanted to stick to the simple facts – first, because her dialect was simple, like that of uneducated families, and second, because no superlative would add anything to the perfection of the stranger in white.

"*And your friends?*" interrogated Jacomet. "*They saw nothing?*"

"*No, sir.*"

"*You dreamt, then!*"

"*No, sir.*"

"*You saw a reflection!*"

"*I saw Aquéro several times. I am sure I did.*"

The police chief was becoming impatient. His pen grated on the report. The little bell on his uniform cap tinkled frantically. Bernadette snuck discreet glances at it, suppressing a mischievous smile with great difficulty. How funny this furious hat was!

The fact was that Jacomet did not know where to begin unpacking the story. Who put these ideas into the girl's head? The parents, to make some money? The thought had barely occurred to the police chief before he abandoned it for good. He knew that François Soubirous, the man, simple and honest as he was, did not have the profile of a hoaxer.

Yet this story had to be nipped in the bud before it covered Lourdes with ridicule. Supernatural phenomena no longer had their place in this century where all was order and progress! As he imagined the faces his regional or Parisian superiors would make when they heard these tall tales, the police chief felt ready to do anything to keep this story within the proportions of an everyday occurrence.

"*You are going to promise me never to return to the grotto,*" he told Bernadette.

"*I promised I would go back,*" she said.

Jacomet shifted from friendliness to anger and let out a few curses, accompanied by his headgear's jingling. Bernadette was not put out. The police chief reread his first drafts for her, changing certain passages to throw her off:

"*The Virgin smiles at me*," Jacomet read from the draft testimony.

"*I did not say 'the Virgin.' You changed everything!*" she corrected.

"*If you do not promise to give up your stories, I will send you to jail*," he threatened.

Bernadette held her ground. As for jail, she would get out as her father had, since she had done nothing wrong.

How could anyone untangle this inextricable situation? The solution was suddenly chanted by the crowd that had been gathering under Jacomet's windows since the beginning of the interrogation. "Soubirous, Soubirous! Go into the chief of police! He has no right to interrogate your daughter without you!" Alerted by some kind souls, Bernadette's father arrived to inquire about his daughter. Pushed forward by rough peasant hands, Mr. Soubirous knocked at the door to find himself face to face with Jacomet. He fiddled with the beret between his hands before the police chief's scolding demeanor and promised something that Bernadette had refused to promise: He made a commitment that his daughter would not return to the grotto.

He would not have to keep his word for long. By the next evening, Jacomet, in agreement with the other civil authorities of Lourdes, decided to lift the restriction. Public opinion supported Bernadette and considered the police chief's attitude to be unjust bullying.

One does not quarrel with public opinion. At best, one can only deplore its blindness.

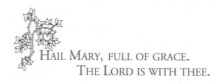

HAIL MARY, FULL OF GRACE.
THE LORD IS WITH THEE.

The Young Man and Grace

Seventh and Eighth Apparitions, February 23, 24, 1858

1858 Insistent knocks at the door of his bedroom roused Jean-Baptiste Estrade from a deep sleep. The young man awoke with a start, opened his eyes to the dark night, and mumbled a few questions.

"Eh? What? Who's there?"

His sister Emmanuélite's familiar and impatient voice answered him: "It's just me! Get up, Jean-Baptiste. You promised to walk me to the grotto this morning with my friends. Hurry up! It's already four o'clock!"

For a few seconds, he was speechless with indignation. Finally getting his voice back, he exploded with recriminations.

"Do you think this is a decent hour, Emmanuélite?" he said. "I need some rest. My days are very busy!"

"I know, Mister 'Deputy Tax-Collector on Horseback,'" Emmanuélite shot back with a measure of sarcasm. "But the apparitions do not wait. The little seer reaches Massabielle very early. We must head out there if we want to get good spots. There'll be a crowd, and the place is not set up as well as a theater."

A promise, however slight, remains a promise, and a well-bred young man does not let a string of young ladies go out alone, especially at such an ungodly hour. Estrade arose from his bed grumbling, hastily put on some warm clothes, and met his sister on the landing. Before leaving the building, he cast a glance toward the rooms of Police Chief Jacomet, who shared the house with him. On that side, all was dark and silent. Estrade smiled, amused, his mind suddenly clear. If Jacomet knew that his neighbor and friend was preparing to be in attendance at the little Lourdes girl's "ecstasy," his dismay regarding the Massabielle case would know no bounds!

Outside, the town was shrouded in darkness. Fifty yards away, the church's belltower stood out against the sky, darker still than the night. It was very cold. Emmanuélite's friends, who were awaiting their gentleman escort in the street, beat the pavement with their elegant soles, shivering under their shawls.

A short time later, as the group arrived at Massabielle, they found one hundred fifty people already gathered. Estrade's stovepipe hat and the ample crinolines following him had their effect: The little crowd parted to allow these new arrivals to pass. So Emmanuélite, her brother, and her friends were in an advantageous position when Bernadette arrived at half past five.

"My word," Estrade whispered to his sister. "We have ringside seats. But I am afraid I may be disappointed by the show."

Estrade prided himself on being a reasonable man and, therefore, of having a skeptical mind. He shared the prudence of his friend Dr. Dozous, who came this very morning to observe the grotto phenomenon in order to try to penetrate its mystery.

Attentive and doubting, Estrade saw Bernadette light her holy candle by the fire of a lamp. The immense shadow of this tiny adolescent started dancing upon the grotto's walls at the flame's whim. The onlookers did not make a sound. All one could hear was the Gave's lively waters endlessly rolling over the pebbles, indifferent to the events that the crowd awaited.

Suddenly, Estrade saw Bernadette lose herself in contemplation. The young man perceived in the candid black eyes a light that touched him to the depths of his soul. He, a man of levelheaded intelligence, allowed himself to be seized with emotion. He, the sneering spectator who a few moments earlier had mocked the ambient piety, no longer felt like laughing. For the entire time that Bernadette's visit lasted, he intensely observed those limpid eyes open onto the invisible…

On leaving Massabielle, however, it was most important for Estrade to keep a stoic front so as to avoid his companions' ridicule. How could he snap out of the religious sentiment that had bewitched his faculties of reason? By talking of the theater, of course! *"I saw Miss Rachel at the Bordeaux theatre,"* he stated casually. *"She is magnificent… but infinitely beneath Bernadette."*

Yet how these words rang untrue even to his own ears! Jean-Baptiste Estrade felt bound to admit the real impression that the spectacle of the grotto had made upon him.

"That child has before her a supernatural being," he said.

That day, at the Café Français where Estrade was a regular, there was a serious discussion over drinks. Besides Estrade and Dozous, a Mr. Dufo, lawyer and member of the town council, was present at Massabielle. Impressions were swapped; there were questions and disputes. The proud secular faction was now split: Estrade had been touched by grace. For him, the dawn of February 23 was the dawn of a brand-new faith.

The next day, the news of this conversion had spread throughout the town, and attendance at the grotto was even higher. Three hundred people could be counted along the shore with three hundred rosaries held between fervent hands to accompany Bernadette's prayer.

Suddenly, she made an unexpected move. Treading the grotto's ground on her knees, she advanced a few steps and fell down with her face in the pebbles! Her aunt Lucile – Louise Soubirous' younger sister, who was nearly the same age as Bernadette – shrieked with fright and fainted. Panic began to take hold of the crowd; the last rows, kneeling right on the edge of the Gave, ran the risk of being thrown into the river if the crowd's motion increased. But Bernadette, drawn out of contemplation by Lucile's cry, was contagiously calm. As soon as her aunt came around, Bernadette explained her behavior to her in a reassuring voice: The stranger in the grotto had asked her to kiss the grotto's ground as a gesture of penance for the conversion of sinners.

"*Be not afraid, dear aunt,*" concluded Bernadette as she took Lucile's hand between her own.

Bernadette's words spread and helped soothe the frazzled onlookers. The crowd dispersed with perfect calm that morning.

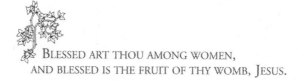

BLESSED ART THOU AMONG WOMEN,
AND BLESSED IS THE FRUIT OF THY WOMB, JESUS.

THE FOUNTAIN OF LIVING WATER

Ninth Apparition, February 25, 1858

1858 When Bernadette came out of her orans-like ecstasy of motionlessness, the first rows of bystanders stirred with dumbfounded murmurs. Immediately, questions and rumors ran through the crowd. Today, the bystanders numbered three hundred and fifty. The latecomers – those who arrived at Massabielle after two o'clock in the morning and had the misfortune of having to kneel far from the grotto – wanted to know more. What was Bernadette doing that so astonished the immediate witnesses?

Her strange behavior was described by word of mouth. The young girl handed her candle and her hood to her neighbor. She advanced on her knees toward the back of the grotto, kissing the ground several times. Then, just under the crevice where appeared the apparition that no one but her saw, Bernadette pronounced inaudible words; she was seen to move her lips, absorbed in an intense dialogue with her visitor. The murmurs ceased, and the first rows silently watched for what would happen next. They even forgot to relay the succession of events to the back of the crowd. But there was no need: Bernadette, who had turned on her knees back toward the Gave, suddenly stood up. All the way to the last rows, everyone saw her return to the back of the grotto, where she bowed toward the ground. She was once again withdrawn from the farthest gazes. The whispering started up worse than ever: "Where is Bernadette?" "What is she doing?" "What do these comings and goings mean?"

Suddenly, the first rows uttered small cries of astonishment and indignation. With her right hand, Bernadette had dug a hole in the earth. Between her fingers, the moisture-saturated soil had formed a reddish mud, which she smeared on her face and put to her mouth. Had she lost her mind?

When the apparition asked Bernadette to go drink the "fountain's" water and to wash in it, the adolescent first believed that she meant the Gave, the only visible water in the immediate surroundings – which was why she was going there on her knees. The young woman called her back and pointed to a spot at the back of the grotto, telling her that she had to dig. Indeed, water had come to the surface in this little hole in the ground. But what water! Nothing at all like the Gave's streams.

That didn't matter. A request from the young woman with the perfect smile could only be right and good. With a swift hand, Bernadette had "purified" her face with Massabielle's mud. But to drink this water? That was a different story. Bernadette made four attempts, so revolted was her tongue at the thought of tasting the muddy liquid. But she felt the magnificent gaze enveloping her, weighing up her hesitations and repugnance for what they were worth, yet awaiting her consent. And so she ended up obeying in complete freedom. As her lips parted in the hollow of her hand, Bernadette overcame her disgust and swallowed this strange fountain's water without worrying about the disapproving murmurs that rippled through the audience.

Within the audience, no one considered how much this incomprehensible gesture cost Bernadette – whose fragile stomach had since childhood rejected the crude food that sustained the poor, and whose parents ruined themselves financially buying white bread because she threw up the cornmeal dough that made up their everyday food. How could she so readily swallow the muddy water that welled up from the soil at Massabielle? But there was the beautiful young woman in white, who asked her to perform this gesture as a sign of penance, to save sinners, to touch the heart of God and attract his mercy.

The scandal was not over. As soon as this gesture of penance ended, Bernadette was off to pick up a few weeds growing at the back of the grotto and chew them under the crowd's dismayed gazes. Jean-Baptiste Estrade, yesterday's convert, felt an icy cloak fall upon the fire of his enthusiasm. His new faith was not snuffed out for all that, but he no longer understood a thing. He humbly admitted as much to a group of friends, still skeptics, whom he dragged to Massabielle, and whose sarcasm started to grate on him before the spectacle.

How many times would Bernadette be asked to explain herself regarding this baffling gesture? It would continue to surprise, even after the Church eventually admitted the authenticity of the apparitions by confirming the identity of the beautiful visitor. Eating grass? Really, was that a request worthy of the Holy Virgin? To scoffers, Bernadette would later answer with a mischievous smile: "*We eat salad, don't we?*"

That morning, however, her mind had not yet developed this light response designed to dispel unwelcome remarks. Once the stranger of Massabielle had disappeared, Bernadette was confronted with the perplexed comments of reasonable people. Nevertheless, she calmly explained to them, through her still mud-stained lips, that it was all for sinners.

Everyone went home with thoughts and questions. Hours passed without calming the emotion aroused by Bernadette's behavior. At breakfast in more than one Lourdes home, conversation centered on the strange "fountain" pointed out by the apparition – a source at Massabielle? No Lourdes resident, past or present, had ever found one before!

That afternoon, some people returned to the grotto to get to the bottom of it, to check the absence of running water under the cliff. In the little hole that Bernadette had dug, someone shoved a stick… which suddenly awakened a murmur of living water! Amazement ensued. The ground was scratched, the mud cleared out; the water surged, clearer and clearer. Hands began to draw water from this hole and repeat Bernadette's gesture. They sought to drink from this new fountain, to purify one's face, one's eyes, and one's heart at the contact of this unexpected water revealed by a mysterious young girl dressed in white! The first bottles of Massabielle water were brought back to town that day along with new rumors regarding this marvelous event. There would never be an end to the water drawn from that fountain.

HOLY MARY, MOTHER OF GOD,

THE FIRST MIRACLE

Tenth, Eleventh, and Twelfth Apparitions,
February 27, 28, March 1, 1858

18
58 The chilly winter sun was about to disappear behind the mountains. At the religious sisters' school, the bell rang to signal the end of classes for the day. The girls played in the courtyard and began the last "ring around the rosie" game of the day before going each her own way. They wheeled and spun around, their hair disheveled and carefree, in the waning late-afternoon light.

Bernadette did not require much begging to take her place among the little girls. Known as the class clown, she participated in every dance and reel. Despite her asthma and shortness of breath, despite the obvious frailty of her health, the young girl's vivaciousness always surprised her teachers.

But although Bernadette danced briskly that afternoon, her heart was not in it. That morning, her visitor in white had neglected their meeting at Massabielle. Kneeling before the empty grotto, surrounded by six hundred people, Bernadette said an entire rosary. Her prayer of intercession for sinners and for herself surely reached up to God, who rejects no supplication. But *Aquéro* did not come. All day long, acting as though nothing were the matter, Bernadette had borne her sorrow and her worry. What if the stranger had forgotten her?

The next morning, Bernadette began a rosary with beating heart. Very soon, a radiant smile lit up her face. The young woman was there. After this ordeal, she remembered the humble adolescent! She came to pay her a silent visit. But Bernadette now knew what she must do. Without a single question, without any word but her interior act of thanksgiving, she went to the fountain to drink its purifying water, on her knees, her candle in hand – for sinners.

The next day, February 28, at dawn on a Sunday, over a thousand people gathered to follow these gestures of penance. All these people prayed fervently under the perplexed gaze of Commander Renault, the Tarbes chief of police. The officer came to examine the danger that threatened this ever-increasing crowd, pressed against the Gave by the cliff's steep slope. The venue did not lend itself to big improvised gatherings. What measures ought to be taken to avoid accidents?

That day, at the end of Mass, a week after her interrogation by Police Chief Jacomet, Bernadette was brought before another Lourdes authority figure: Procurator Dutour wished to hear her and, if possible, to induce her to interrupt her visits to Massabielle. Like Jacomet, he tried persuasion and intimidation by turns. Like Jacomet, he suffered defeat before Bernadette's gentle stubbornness. A promise is a promise, fifteen days is fifteen days, and the adolescent fully expected to return every day to Massabielle until next Thursday! The magistrate did not refrain from expressing his dissatisfaction. But what could he do? He, a man of the law, had no legal means to counter this so-called seer's strange notions.

As he dismissed Bernadette, the citizens of Lourdes were already getting organized to attend the next apparition as near as possible to the grotto. Many of them were determined to have supper early and allow themselves a short time of rest before going to Massabielle about midnight. In the middle of the night, which in early March was hardly mild, a myriad of lamps and candles converged upon the grotto, and a common prayer rose toward the stars. When Bernadette arrived in the middle of these fifteen hundred people, the crowd had no trouble entering into meditation, for it had been there for hours already.

As simple and natural as usual, Bernadette knelt and started to pray. She did not even have the leisure to notice – an extraordinary fact that did not escape the crowd's notice – the presence of a priest right next to her. The pastor of Lourdes had forbidden any clergyman to venture out to Massabielle, but Father Désirat was a stranger to the town. He was ignorant of the prudent ban issuing from the rectory. At any rate, he did not claim to bring the clergy's guarantee to the grotto's strange phenomenon. He came only for prayer, a believer among others.

An even more extraordinary fact marked that night. Among the bystanders there was a certain Catherine Latapie, who had come to Massabielle with her two children and a belly swollen with a baby ready to be born. The young woman suffered from the aftereffects of an accident that had taken place a year and a half before. She had fallen from a tree where she had been knocking down nuts, and the accident had dislocated her arm and had injured her hand. Though the doctor was able to heal her arm, two fingers on one hand had remained paralyzed. Such a disability was a real obstacle for a poor housewife who earned her bread by working with her hands. Despite all of that, Latapie did not despair. It was precisely her hope – a mad and courageous hope – that had brought her to Massabielle.

Once Bernadette emerged from ecstasy, the young woman dragged the two children to the new fountain that murmured at the base of the grotto. She bathed her affected hand in it and immediately uttered a small cry of astonishment. As much as she believed, she dared not expect it: Her fingers had just regained their former mobility. Her prayer of praise was short-lived, however, as she began experiencing contractions indicating the onset of the labors of childbirth and an imminent delivery!

She went back home, a little more than four miles from Lourdes, as fast as her children's small legs and the intermittent cramps that seized her would allow. That would not keep her from revealing very quickly the favor she had received. Her hand's healing would become the first miracle that the Church and medical experts would credit to Massabielle.

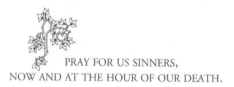

PRAY FOR US SINNERS,
NOW AND AT THE HOUR OF OUR DEATH.

The Shrine's Genesis

Thirteenth Apparition, March 2, 1858

1858 *"Go tell the priests that there must be a procession to this spot and that a chapel must be built here."* The morning's request, made in a voice as soft as heavenly music and accompanied with that now-familiar beautiful smile, penetrated Bernadette's mind without encountering resistance or surprise. She simply accepted this mission, proposed by a stranger whose identity she still did not know.

Once the marvelous vision had disappeared, once the brilliance that accompanied each one of her visits had faded, Bernadette awoke from her ecstasy. As usual, questions rained upon her. The sixteen hundred people who had accompanied her that morning wanted to know everything. Had the Lady spoken? What did she say?

Devout old ladies rushed to be the first to get information from Bernadette's mouth. She recited the terms of the request to them: *"Go tell the priests that there must be a procession to this spot..."* The pious women looked at one another, and a glint of enthusiasm lit up their eyes. Without waiting for the rest of the message, they drew up their skirts and ran down to the town. What a piece of good luck! One doesn't get a shot at being heaven's ambassador every day! They wanted first dibs on making the announcement. They figured they would be the first to receive the reaction from the deeply moved Father Peyramale, the first to see him make arrangements to honor the Lady's request.

Along their brisk walk, they battled shortness of breath to swap comments and prattle.

"I do love a procession!" one said.

"What banner do you think Father will deem appropriate for the head of the procession?" another asked.

"What a question! The Holy Virgin's, of course," the prattle went on... and on....

"But Bernadette said that she did not know the Lady's identity."

"Well, the child is modest. It's surely the Mother of God who comes and visits. Anyway, the newspapers are positive."

"What a shame it's early March! The gardens are hardly in bloom. I would have dreamt of a procession filled with yellow roses just like those that adorn the Lady's feet."

"The question is when the Virgin wants her procession. We could wait for spring."

"Excuse me? Obviously the ceremony must take place Thursday, at the end of the two weeks of apparitions."

"Jesus, Mary, and Joseph! That leaves us two days to organize everything!"

"Father will be so relieved that we are helping him."

The good wives finally arrived at the rectory's door, all atwitter with impatience and curiosity.

Alas! When they came out a few minutes later, it was under the shock of a sharp reprimand. Father was not easy to get along with, and they knew that better than anyone, living as they did in the pulpit's shadow. Still, they had not expected such a rage. Father Peyramale had flared up at them like never before. He told them in no uncertain terms not to involve themselves in the grotto business and rather to go back to church to pray for the salvation of their souls!

When Bernadette later knocked at Father's door, she did not know of the scene that had just pitted him against his devout and faithful laywomen. But she fared no better. It was one thing to receive a demand pronounced in the light of an irresistible smile; it was quite another to go and submit it to Father Peyramale, whose voice sometimes growled so loudly under the church's arches, like the sound of thunder rolling through the mountains!

Far more intimidated than when she faced the police chief or the judge, Bernadette surrounded herself with two aunts to meet with Father Peyramale. One of them was her godmother, Bernarde, her mother's eldest sister, a domineering woman whose authority reigned over the entire family. In fact, it was her name that the young girl bore: Bernadette is a diminutive of Bernarde.

So the youngster stood before Father Peyramale, but the priest left her no time to speak. *"Are you the one who goes to the grotto?"* he addressed her sternly.

"Yes, Father," Bernadette replied.

"And you say that you see the Holy Virgin?"

"I did not say that it was the Holy Virgin."

"So who is this Lady, then?" Father probed.

"I do not know."

"Liar!" he lashed out. *"All those you've got running about say it, and the newspaper prints it. You claim to see the Holy Virgin."*

Bernadette and her aunts bowed their heads at the outburst. Bernarde, so prompt to interrupt any and all conversations, fled the rectory without saying a word. Bernadette plucked up her courage to transmit the procession request to the pastor, not knowing that the good wives had already requested it, and for Thursday yet! Father Peyramale cut short this ill-fated interrogation by brusquely dismissing Bernadette and her aunt Basile.

Hardly had they departed than the youngster smacked her forehead: *"Mercy! Aunt Basile, I forgot to ask for the chapel!"*

But Basile would not so much as step back into the rectory for anything in the world. Bernadette, with much effort, convinced a friend to accompany her. Prudently allowing Father the time to cool down from his anger, they went back to see him that evening.

In the light of the lamps burning at Father Peyramale's, they were greeted this time by an imposing row of cassocks: The pastor had surrounded himself with his vicars to face this troublesome girl! So frail among all this black clothing, aware of her own ignorance before these fonts of wisdom who spoke French and Latin, Bernadette brought up the chapel to be built on the spot of the apparitions. The priests looked at each other, perplexed. Father Peyramale said neither yea nor nay. Until now, he had declined to compromise his priestly authority in the grotto business. But today's apparition placed him in a terrible dilemma, since the Lady seemed to want to involve his authority in this story. To believe or not to believe? A man endowed with solid common sense, Father Peyramale insisted on thinking twice before committing himself to a business that went beyond his understanding. His all-too-human reason would come in handy before this unreasonable mystery! So he ended the interview with neither a promise nor a refusal. For the time being, he opted to sidestep the issue.

AMEN.

A Child's Patience

Fourteenth, Fifteenth, and Sixteenth Apparitions,
March 3, 4, 25, 1858

18
58
Occupied by his thoughts, Father Peyramale let his altar boy help him put on his vestments. Beyond the sacristy window, the dawn light began to make the sky more pale. *The dawn of a great day,* thought the priest, sharing in spite of himself in the collective fervor that had overtaken Lourdes. That Thursday, March 4, would end the fifteen days of visits requested of Bernadette by the apparition. An immense crowd had already gathered at the grotto – at least eight thousand people, according to the police squads called in for reinforcement from the neighboring garrisons to maintain order.

Indeed, everyone expected a revelation that morning – something extraordinary, a miracle, a final burst of fireworks, so to speak. Actually, the "fireworks" metaphor applied: Police Chief Jacomet had checked the previous night to ensure there were no firework rockets near the Massabielle grotto in case hoaxers might have the idea of taking advantage of popular credulity!

For his part, Father Peyramale waited for only one thing – for the Lady finally to reveal her name. The previous night, Bernadette had gone back to the rectory.

"Father, the Lady still wants her chapel," she told the pastor.

"You asked her name?"

"Yes, but all she does is smile."

"She is making a fine fool out of you," Father Peyramale cautioned.

Yet the priest this time had an idea in his head to solve the enigma: *"Let her say her name and cause the grotto's rosebush to bloom. Then we will have a chapel built."*

Blackmail? No, prudence. And a respectful nod to the Virgin of Guadalupe, who had caused a Mexican hillock to bloom in the middle of December three centuries earlier.

That is why the pastor was pensive on that morning of March 4 as he prepared to celebrate the six thirty Mass. But returning to his immediate concerns, he whispered a quick prayer and, with a vigorous hand, rang the bell announcing his entrance into the nave.

Before going up to the altar, he cast a glance toward the assembly… and smiled. As for an assembly, there weren't many more than Bernadette accompanied by a cousin! The pews were empty. Even the most faithful devout ladies had deserted the church to take a spot before the Massabielle grotto.

Bernadette, as was her custom, had come to recollect herself in Christ's presence before going to find the stranger who spoke to her every day about him. Her First Communion was set for the month of June, and the youngster, who thought constantly of this wonderful date, regularly heard Mass to prepare herself for it.

The morning Masses were short. Just before seven o'clock, the *Ite missa est* echoed under the arches, carried aloft by the priest's firm and warm voice. Without taking an extra minute's time for prayer, the youngster and her cousin ran to the exit. The act of thanksgiving would get done in the grotto, in front of the apparition who elevated Bernadette's heart toward God so well.

Arriving at Massabielle, the young girl was glad for her foresight. She had asked Tarbès, Lourdes' wheelwright, to build her a wooden gangplank to allow her to reach her spot. The size of the crowd today went beyond all that she could have imagined!

After a few *Aves*, the Lady was there. Casting her luminous gaze upon the immense crowd that had been praying for some long hours, she entered into conversation with Bernadette, whose gaze would light up or be saddened depending on the words she heard. Police Chief Jacomet, who occupied a strategic spot right next to Bernadette, did not miss a single detail of this silent dialogue; in the notebook he brought with him, he tallied thirty-four smiles and twenty-four greetings toward the crevice where there was the invisible *Aquéro*.

Yet nothing spectacular took place. Three-quarters of an hour later, when Bernadette snuffed out her candle, the crowd had to face the facts: No miraculous sign had marked this ordinary day with splendor. No great revelation was made to the young seer – not even the visitor's identity.

When Bernadette knocked at the rectory door a few minutes later, the pastor was disappointed. He listened to Bernadette relate her attempts.

"*I asked her name, she smiled. I asked her to make the rosebush bloom, she smiled again,*" Bernadette explained. "*But she still wants her chapel.*"

"*Have you got any money to have it built?*" Father asked.

"*Oh, no, Father…*"

"*Well, neither do I. Tell the Lady to give you some!*"

Father Peyramale dismissed Bernadette with this bitter sarcasm, leaving her at the mercy of the long line of visitors that had established itself in front of the "dungeon" in hopes of seeing her, questioning her, making her touch holy objects – something the humble Bernadette was loathe to do. The quasi-devotion of which she was already an object was torture to her. She would so much love to see it turned directly toward God, his saints, or at least his priests.

"*I wear no stole. Have your rosaries blessed by the pastor,*" she invariably would answer.

She thought without ceasing of the Lady in White, whose name she had been unable to obtain and whom she would perhaps never see again.

And yet, three weeks later, on the feast of the Annunciation, Bernadette felt drawn toward the grotto by that irresistible force that she had grown to know so well. Rushing down the slopes, running through the grass greening in the spring, she arrived at Massabielle. By the time the candle was lit, the visitor was there. Her mad run and her emotions made her weak heart beat furiously. Regaining her breath with difficulty, she nevertheless bluntly asked: "*Miss, would you have the kindness of telling me who you are, please?*"

This time, she was determined to receive an answer. She was doubtlessly ignorant of the story, as old as the Old Testament, of Jacob struggling with the angel: "*I shall not let you go without your blessing me.*" And yet a similar determination was in her gaze: *I shall not let you go without your telling me your name.*

The stranger, still silent, smiled. Bernadette repeated her question three times. The fourth time, the young Lady in White slowly spread her hands and turned them toward the ground. In the musical dialect of Lourdes, she said: "*Que soy era Immaculada Counceptiou.*"

Bernadette had her answer. She did not understand these words, which to her were as complicated as a foreign tongue. That didn't matter; the pastor would surely know how to unravel their meaning. She quickly ran to bring the words to him, repeating them at every step in order not to forget them on the way.

HAIL MARY, FULL OF GRACE.
THE LORD IS WITH THEE.

The Mystery Revealed
to the Littlest Ones

The Dogma of the Immaculate Conception, March 25, 1858

1858 "This is no weather for the angels..." Father Peyramale said to himself as he stood in front of his rectory. That morning, March 25, 1858, the feast of the Annunciation, the sky was empty and gray. Suddenly, he saw Bernadette rushing toward him, shouting inaudibly. She ran toward him breathlessly, followed by an unruly group that was trying to keep up with her. She had barely arrived when, without catching her breath, she shouted to him: "*Que soy era... Immaculada Counceptiou!*"

Father Peyramale felt as though he had been struck in the face. He restrained his hand and the slap that quivered in it: How dare she?

"*No lady can bear that name!*" he said. "*You are mistaken! Do you know what it means?*"

Bernadette shook her head.

"*So how can you say it if you do not understand?*" he asked.

"*I kept repeating it along the way,*" Bernadette responded.

Father Peyramale felt his anger suddenly ebb; in its stead, sobs were welling up in his chest.

"*She still wants the chapel,*" Bernadette added timidly.

The pastor of Lourdes was dumbstruck. The little girl simply did not know what these words signified! But how could she know them? He had a little trouble understanding them himself when the dogma of the Immaculate Conception was proclaimed less than four years before, on December 8, 1854, in a bull of Pope Pius IX.

The pastor did not answer right away. Regaining his composure, he told her, "*Go back home. I will see you another day.*"

Thus dismissed, Bernadette went home, unable to take the full measure of what had just happened. She had repeated the words without distorting them; she had done her best. It was only that evening that Jean-Baptiste Estrade would explain to her what the words signified and teach her the fullness of the Lady's message... the Holy Virgin's message.

For his part, Father Peyramale locked himself in his room. After a moment of silence, he took up his pen to write to Bishop Laurence and warn him of what had just happened. To be sure, Bernadette may already have heard the words "Immaculate Conception" at Mass last December 8, but that was in French, not in the dialect. Besides, a little peasant child had no natural propensity for theology. Once his letter was mailed, Father Peyramale quickly got up, opened a cupboard, and drew from it a little book that he read avidly – *Ineffabilis Deus* ("Ineffable God"), the papal bull. A sense of religious awe began to seize him. This God, whom he thought he knew, and who had become a habitual and nearly ordinary presence, was now here next to him, unpredictable as ever, revealing himself again through Mary in his humble town!

Then, as he started reading the text, he found the dogma's formulation. Pius IX wrote: "*The doctrine which holds that the most Blessed Virgin Mary, in the first instance of her conception, by a singular grace and privilege granted by Almighty God, in view of the merits of Jesus Christ, the Savior of the human race, was preserved free from all stain of original sin, is a doctrine revealed by God.*"

The priest stopped reading. How could he explain all of this to Bernadette? It would rather be up to *her* to enlighten *him*! She did not need to know this dogma's Latin formulation; she had contemplated it in all its splendor! He had adhered to the dogma with a pious conviction, to be sure, but one that was full of questions. Did not God wish to come among sinners and become one of them, exempt from sin and yet a descendant of sinners? And if Mary did not know sin during her life, not even at the first instant of her conception, in what way would she have needed the salvation of God, and why does our Church go through so much trouble to defend the absolute universality of original sin?

The priest asked himself, *Do these questions not have a convincing answer today?* These words, "Immaculate Conception," took on a new luster in his eyes on this day. He got a little dizzy to think that God had waited for this moment for nearly two millennia.

Closing his eyes, Father Peyramale was overcome by the memory of the Scriptures and savored, one by one, the titles he recited – *Mary, New Ark… Burning bush… Impregnable tower… Closed garden… Temple of the Lord… Pure dove… House of eternal Wisdom*[1]*…* He also remembered the vision of the spouse in the Song of Songs, to whom the beloved says, "*You are all-beautiful, my beloved, and there is no blemish in you.*"[2]

The names given to Mary by the Fathers of the Church follow each other like the beads on a rosary: *Mary, lily among thorns! Mary, intact earth from which Jesus, the new Adam, was formed! Mary, new Eve crushing underfoot the serpent's head!*[3] At last, the eminent title confessed by the Church: *Mary, Mother of God, the Theotokos!*[4]

And so Father Peyramale, feeling his way through history, rediscovered the ultimate expression of faith in Mary Immaculate – the role of popular piety, the input of theologians, the decisions of popes.

And today, the priest thought to himself, *Mary herself has come to the assistance of his faith!* The angel's words, which he had just read on that

---

1. Gn 6-9; Ex 3: 2; Song 4: 4; Song 4: 12; Is 6: 1-4; Song 2: 14; Prv 9: 1.
2. Song 4: 7.
3. Song 2: 2; Gn 2: 7; 1 Cor 15: 45; Gn 3: 15.
4. Dogmatic expression approved by the Council of Ephesus in 431.

morning of the Annunciation, fully echoed in him: *"Hail, favored one!"*[1] As did Elizabeth's greeting: *"Most blessed are you among women, and blessed is the fruit of your womb!"*[2]

Yes, thought the priest, those words speak of abundant joy, of the overflowing and unique grace that binds the Savior to his mother. He saved her from all sin in advance; he made her fully free to say yes to God's love. He made her the model of humanity, the masterpiece of creation, and the first fulfillment of the Redemption, for the radical disappearance of all evil. Yes, Father Peyramale understood, our salvation is involved in Mary's unblemished conception, just as is God's omnipotence!

The priest now better comprehended Bernadette's mysterious gestures and the fountain's welling up in the grotto. These were indeed signs coming from God, who took on human nature, except for sin, to save it from the mud that had made it impure. Purity had sprung up from impurity, cleansing all things around it.

The rosebush, despite his wish, had not yet bloomed in the grotto, but in the priest's heart something had quivered. He felt it, for in the winter of his doubts as well as in his cut-and-dried certainties, green buds of faith blossomed anew.

Reading his book, the pastor was preparing to join Bernadette, who was waiting for him in the church. Like a soft slap, a cold and bracing gust smacked his face as he left the rectory, and tiny white flakes landed on his eyelids. As unexpected and silent as an angel, the snow slowly covered all things under its white coat.

BLESSED ART THOU AMONG WOMEN,
AND BLESSED IS THE FRUIT OF THY WOMB, JESUS.

1. Lk 1: 28.
2. Lk 1: 42.

A FLAME BETWEEN TWO HANDS

Seventeenth Apparition, April 7, 1858

1858 As lively and busy as Martha in her house, Antoinette Tardhivail, the sacristan's aide, toddled through the church, counting candles, emptying poor boxes, dusting a few statues, setting in good order the prie-dieus that had been moved during the Office of Vespers. From time to time, she walked the length of the line that was waiting at the confessional. Taking on a contrite look befitting this place of penance, she slyly observed the faces that had come for absolution.

A frail figure suddenly drew her gaze. That tiny bit of a girl wearing a small blue kerchief was Bernadette Soubirous without a doubt. Antoinette, perplexed, discreetly nodded. *Surely this child has a pure conscience... What can she possibly accuse herself of?* wondered the curious woman inwardly. Suddenly, her eyes started to shine in the church's twilight. *What if?*

What if the young girl had come to seek counsel from her confessor about a new visit to the grotto? The keen Antoinette had already linked Bernadette's confessions to the apparitions at Massabielle. More than once, while Bernadette was forbidden access to the grotto and nevertheless felt an irresistible desire to go there, she had come to seek out the priest to ask for his help in resolving this matter of conscience. The previous week, she appeared before the procurator who, to put an end to the four-hour-long interrogation, forbade her from returning to Massabielle. Bernadette proved obedient, since she thought that the Virgin would no longer appear to her. "But if...!"

But if the Virgin were to call her again?

While carrying on with her cleaning so as not to draw attention, Antoinette Tardhivail came closer to the pious wives, her friends, who were reciting their act of contrition in the church's front pew. She leaned over the kneeling figures:

"I would stake my life that Bernadette has once again been invited to Massabielle," she whispered. "Something is in the works for tomorrow morning!"

Cutting their prayer short, the ladies hastily went out to the church square to lie in wait for Bernadette. A few moments later, absolved and counseled, the youth also left the church. She greeted the pious wives with a joyous voice. That liveliness, that peaceful gaze... Antoinette was surely right. The confessor must have endorsed this case of civil disobedience.

"Above all, tell no one!" warned the sacristan's assistant, waving her duster. "We are not supposed to be in the know!"

"Of course, Antoinette," her friends replied. "You know you can count on our absolute discretion." So the devout ladies parted ways with conspiring looks.

The next day, at dawn, a thousand faces awaited the young seer when she arrived at Massabielle. The value of a secret! Bernadette smiled, amused to see rumors circulate so efficiently in her beloved town. She bore no one a grudge, of course. On this Easter Wednesday, in the light of the resurrection and in the expectation of a new visit from the Virgin, her heart sang. She rejoiced at the sight of this procession that had come to attend in faith her meeting with the Lady!

There was the Virgin, as beautiful as all the other times. She stood before a beaming Bernadette. The crowd prayed to her without seeing her, surrounding the youth with a cloud of fervor, sharing her joy in a silence spoiled only by the Gave's murmur.

Suddenly, the sound of rapid footsteps disturbed the widespread recollection. The crowd grudgingly parted, allowing the intruder through, displeased with this insult to the contemplative silence reigning before the grotto. The new arrival was none other than Dr. Dozous, who had been warned – a little later than everyone else – of this unexpected apparition. He stubbornly cut a swath up to Bernadette. He wanted to be able to examine the little girl's ecstasy. This was no doubt the last opportunity he would have to do so, and he had no intention of allowing it to pass him by. Up until then, he had not managed to draw any medical conclusions regarding the young girl. He did not yet share the faith of his friend Estrade, who had been convinced by the revelation of the Lady's name.

There, in the first row of onlookers, was Dozous, intensely observing the youthful face. Suddenly, murmurs rustled beside him, forcing him to shift his attention to Bernadette's hands. The young seer, as usual, had brought to the grotto a thick holy candle that she had planted in the ground. To keep the wind from blowing it out, she took the slender flame between her hands. Immersed in her contemplation, she did not notice that the fire was licking at her palms.

"Do something! The girl is going to get burned!" a witness implored.

With an imperious gesture, the doctor quieted the murmurs and kept the well-intentioned from intervening. Bernadette did not seem to suffer. The physician's heart beat wildly. Perhaps he had finally witnessed his supernatural phenomenon.

When the young Bernadette returned to consciousness, the doctor dashed ahead, took her two hands, and attentively scanned their palms. There was nothing. These little hands did not bear the slightest trace of a burn. Bernadette understood nothing of this examination, nor of the exclamations coursing through the crowd. She was told about what had happened without her awareness. She smiled, marveling in her turn, she who never thought herself worthy of a "miracle." Dozous, for his part, was already long gone. He had rushed to the Café Français to announce the event and to proclaim his conversion, the news of which soon traveled around the town.

 Holy Mary, Mother of God,

A Path to Christ

From Bartrès to First Communion, June 3, 1858

18 58 Joy, light, and astonishment swept through Bernadette's heart in marveling waves. That morning, the children of the First Communion class had been received at the altar. Now, kneeling and lost in prayer, Bernadette did not even seek to translate into her simple dialect the luminous sentiments that filled her. In order to greet Jesus Christ, her heart had bedecked itself with acts of thanksgiving. God had joined her in her fragility and had lowered himself to her lowliness. Her thoughts ran the gamut of the *Magnificat*.

At the end of Mass, having come out of the chapel of the Nevers sisters' hospice, Bernadette abandoned herself to the joy of gratitude. The youngster's gaze sought the mountains that spring had trimmed in fresh green in the distance and stopped in the familiar direction of Bartrès. That was where the imperious desire to make her First Communion initially grew in Bernadette. That was where began the path that led her to this glorious day on which, at last, she would receive Jesus' body.

It was in this tiny hamlet of Bartrès, located a few miles above Lourdes, that Bernadette arrived, still a baby, at the end of 1844. She was born on January 7 of the same year at the mill of Boly, in Lourdes, where her parents lived. Her mother, who nursed her, accidentally burned her bosom in November. No longer able to suckle her daughter, Louise Soubirous resolved to entrust her to Marie Laguës, a young woman of Bartrès who had just lost a baby. After Bernadette's return home, in March 1846, the Soubirous parents stayed in touch with the Laguës couple. Many years later, after they had fallen into deep poverty through a succession of unfortunate circumstances, Marie Laguës proposed to take Bernadette back in to have her keep her flock of sheep. The Soubirouses did not refuse. Besides the real financial relief that one fewer mouth to feed represented, they reckoned that mountain air would heal Bernadette's frail lungs.

In September 1857, the Soubirous' eldest daughter returned to her wet nurse. From sunup to sundown every day of the week, she fed the sheep and took care of the many chores around the house. This held true even on Thursdays, when the pastor of Bartrès gave his parish children their catechism lessons – alas, in French and not in the dialect! At first, Laguës had promised Bernadette that she would be allowed free time on that day so that she could attend the lessons, but Laguës immediately went back on her word. Sheep grazed on Thursdays, too.

Bernadette's thwarted desire ripened. It was like a throbbing pain. Faced with the youngster's implorings, Laguës decided to teach her the catechism herself – in the evening, by the fireside, once the sheep were locked in their fold. But the former wet nurse was not practiced in the subtleties of pedagogy, and the girl was not used to learning. The dry lessons taken from the catechism manual entered her ears like so many untranslatable formulas. She did not understand a thing. Laguës became more and more convinced that Bernadette would not be able to receive her First Communion. Once and for all, she put away the book that had been the object of so much exasperation.

Bernadette's hopes seemed even more dashed when the pastor of Bartrès went off to join a monastery one fine day. The catechism classes would no longer echo in the rectory's rooms! Yet the adolescent did not give up what had become the great preoccupation of her life. She saw but one way to reach her goal – to return to Lourdes to follow lessons there. Furthermore, she missed her family, even though her father came up to see her as often as he could.

Bernadette had no trouble winning over her parents. Despite their terrible poverty, François and Louise Soubirous wanted only to keep their brood about them. They had lost too many young children not to cherish those that life had spared them. In January 1858, Bernadette announced to her former wet nurse that she was going back to Lourdes to prepare for her First Communion. Without regret, she left the close-cropped meadows where the mist hangs a thousand cold droplets on the sheep's fleece.

She was admitted to the free school that the Sisters of Nevers ran. Before the austere blackboard that was overhung by a crucifix, she knew that she must "merit" her First Communion. She must learn to read, to write, and to retain her lessons. As time went by, thanks to the combined efforts of the sisters and of Father Pomian, the hospice's chaplain, she made notable progress. There was also the infinitely precious help of the Lady of Massabielle, whose teachings were worth all the manuals in the world.

The vision of the Virgin and the encounter with Christ at the altar were two favors that helped Bernadette progress on the path to sainthood. They also were two favors she absolutely refused to pit against each other. After her First Communion, she was asked, "*What made you happier? First Communion or the apparitions?*"

Bernadette's answer avoided any spectacular revelation. "*These are two things that go together but that cannot be compared,*" she said. "*I have been very happy in each of them.*"

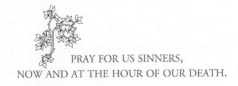

PRAY FOR US SINNERS,
NOW AND AT THE HOUR OF OUR DEATH.

AN ANGRY MAN

Portrait of Father Dominique Peyramale, June 4, 1858

1858 All along the road from Lourdes to Tarbes, Father Peyramale had felt welling up within him one of those boiling angers that so frightened his good parishioners. But his indignation that morning was not directed at a handful of church ladies. Rushing along the last streets that separated him from the prefecture, he headed straight for the office of Baron Oscar Massy, prefect of the Hautes-Pyrénées. In the clear June air, his cassock's folds seemed to raise a storm as he walked by.

"Father!" The call, given in a friendly voice, caused the "Peyramale squall" to turn on his heels. A passer-by, whom the pastor had just walked past without seeing him, firmly shook his hand, his jovial face split in a delighted grin.

"You don't remember me?" the man said as he stood at mock attention. "I was cared for here, at the military hospital, in the days when you were chaplain. Four years ago. By... um... gosh, what an impression you made on your patients! Always joking and kind, not too particular about our ignorance of prayers, always there to revive our spirits... Ah, Father, you can certainly say that you taught us to love the good Lord!"

For a moment, at the memory of that time, so close and yet so far, the pastor and dean of Lourdes forgot his anger. How he had loved that apostolate among rough men, whose tough shell sometimes hid a surprising spiritual thirst.

The man suddenly took on a confidential tone of voice.

"Father, it seemed that your heyday was with us," he told the priest. "Your posting in Lourdes sent you into a hell of... er... into quite a mess. The papers won't stop talking about that grotto!"

At these words, the priest once again felt indignation overtake him. He was back to business. Taking leave of his former patient with a final exchange of pleasantries, he hastened to the prefecture to call on the baron.

A few moments later, he stood before Prefect Massy. Before going in, he had dammed up his flood of anger with great difficulty, but his voice shook with quiet determination. The pastor of Lourdes had just found out about an unjust decision. Baron Massy was preparing to have Bernadette Soubirous confined to an insane asylum, a Machiavellian solution to put an end to the Massabielle business.

"Mister Prefect, as you know, since you had Bernadette examined by three mental disorder specialists, the girl is as sane as you," Father Peyramale told Baron Massy. "I gave her First Communion yesterday, and I confirm that her happy smile was that of a perfectly normal young girl."

"But Father," the prefect protested, "you have to admit that..."

"Nothing, Mister Prefect. I admit nothing," the priest interrupted. "Know that I have taken Bernadette under my personal protection. If you have her sent for to confine her, warn your men to come well armed. They will have to go over my dead body."

For a moment, Baron Massy was speechless. He stared at the patched cassock, the old shoes solidly anchored to his polished wood floor, the shapeless biretta the pastor was holding between his rough peasant hands. He remembered what his files had to say about this self-possessed priest, a man so kind as to distribute his meager revenue among the poor... A moral vigor as strong as can be... unimpeachable faithfulness, eloquence, a sense of responsibility, famous bouts of anger (the informants evidently had not exaggerated on that point!)... a solid common sense inherited from his parents, wealthy peasants in the small town of Momères. *What else?* thought the baron, searching through his memory. Oh, yes – humor, great spiritual subtlety. Under his rough-hewn looks, this priest was perfectly comfortable in all social milieus.

This summary was one that demanded respect. From the pinnacle of his imperial nobility, Baron Massy felt inclined to a certain sympathy toward Father Peyramale. Begging his guest to take a seat, he rang for refreshments and broached a reassuring conversation. "How do you mean, dear Father? God preserve me from offending this admirable solicitude of yours toward your young parishioner. I give you my word that Miss Soubirous will not be confined. I shall take other measures to put an end to this grotto scandal, which – and I make no secret of this – annoys me in the highest degree."

Leaving the county hall, Father Peyramale rubbed his hands together. A sly smile lit up his face. Readjusting the old biretta on his unkempt hair, he looked at the prefect's elegant windows. Once again, he gave thanks for his tendency for getting into these great bouts of anger that no one could resist. They were as good as any clever diplomatic maneuver.

From this time on, Father Peyramale took Bernadette under his wing. He was not through helping his protégée with all his moral resources. In 1860, to withdraw her from popular curiosity which had turned into harassment, he had her admitted to the hospice of Lourdes, run by the Sister of Nevers. Was it humor, wisdom, or pragmatism? It was as an "indigent patient" that the pastor had her taken in. With all due deference to Prefect Massy, asthma was not a form of mental illness.

Bernadette, then, lived at the hospice in relative peace until her departure from Lourdes to enter the novitiate in 1866. The pastor then undertook a regular correspondence with Bernadette, who would soon become Sister Marie-Bernard. This rock-solid priest, named a monsignor in 1874 by papal favor, had humbly asked the fragile religious sister for a daily prayer for his intentions. For her part, Bernadette would always acknowledge a certain spiritual fatherhood in Father Peyramale. When he died in 1877, he preceded her into the kingdom of heaven by two years.

AMEN.

The Farewell

Eighteenth and Last Apparition, July 16, 1858

1858 What a strange sentry duty for a soldier of the glorious French army! The corporal wasn't quite sure whether he ought to interpret this station at an empty and boarded-up grotto as a promise of promotion. Watching the Gave's surroundings with expressionless eyes, he tried to maintain a dignified and stiff appearance despite the afternoon heat that stifled him in his uniform.

Bah! All in all, better to be here than manning a cannon as during the terrible Crimean conflict that had ended two years before, thank God. The peaceful corporal preferred to be a policeman in peace to a hero in war. He didn't risk his life by mounting a guard at Massabielle. At worst, he was exposed to the catcalls and recriminations of the denizens of Lourdes, who had been denied "their" grotto. They can blame no one but themselves, those exalted Christians who've turned this spot into a venue for vast religious excesses!

That a little sprout of a girl claimed to have seen the Holy Virgin would not be so bad, thought the soldier. *Me, I don't care; maybe it's true, maybe it isn't. But for fifty children and mature ladies to claim, one after the other, to have seen her, too, that's pretty strong coffee. The authorities were right to intervene and barricade the grotto. And this habit of bringing dozens of sacred objects to Massabielle day in and day out!*

A month earlier, before the wooden barrier hid it, he had seen with his own two eyes this grotto cluttered with candles, statues, plaques, metal hearts. That was excessive for sure. So the corporal felt useful here where his superiors had sent him. What he was preserving here was once again public order in the service of France. Were he not here, along with a chum, the barrier would have been long gone. Already agitators had torn it down three times!

Ah! Here comes country warden Callet. He's just waking from his nap, lucky fellow, thought the corporal upon seeing the good civil servant's eyes still puffy with sleep. Smiling knowingly at the corporal, the country warden climbed up the high wooden barrier. His daily mission consisted of ridding the grotto of the illicit bouquets that were thrown into it. As he threw the colorful flower arrangements into the Gave and watched the poetic scene as they floated downstream, he was touched by a brief melancholy. Then he examined the grotto's slightest corners to see whether some clandestine believer was hiding there. So many fines had been meted out since the barrier had been erected in June!

Across the river, on the Gave's right bank in the Ribère meadow, small groups of people prayed silently on their knees. The country warden ogled them suspiciously in order to detect possible inclinations to mischief. These believers seemed calm, though. Callet could leave in peace after a cordial greeting to the two sentry guards. Nothing would happen today.

How could the poor man suspect the inner conflict tearing Bernadette apart at that very same moment? Bernadette, who had not returned to the grotto since the apparition on Easter Wednesday, who had done everything in her power to appease the minds of the people of Lourdes by encouraging them to obey the authorities, was now drawn to Massabielle by an imperious inner voice. To top off her misfortune, the bishop of Tarbes himself had intervened less than a week before to beg the faithful to remain reasonable. He severely denounced the abuses of fervor committed at the grotto. Bernadette listened to his proclamation as it was read from the pulpit by Father Peyramale, whose thundering voice vibrated throughout the church, causing heads to bow under his scolding. The youngster made herself the promise of not going against the bishop's will. And yet there she was, feeling invited to the grotto since that morning.

At sunset, light-footed and furtive under a plain borrowed headscarf, she escaped her home with her aunt Lucile, whom she had taken into her confidence. Two friends discreetly joined them. The four figures ran along toward the Ribère meadow, which was softly lit by the sunset's colors. On the other side of the Gave stood the long barrier under strict guard. The corporal breathed easier now that the sun had gone down, and he enjoyed the evening's cool air. He had no thoughts troubling his head, no thought to examine the faithful kneeling beyond the river. He did not know that among the shadows in the falling night was that of Bernadette. He did not know that the youngster was intensely staring at a point located just above him, a crevice that had been pointed out to him as the origin of all these troubles.

Once again, the Virgin was there. Bernadette spread her arms in a marveling greeting. She felt that the distance separating her from the grotto had been erased. The Lady seemed as close to her as ever, even more splendid than ever. Bernadette prayed a rosary that she wished would last for ever. The Virgin smiled at her without saying a word, a bright shining smile that would be her farewell. The next time Bernadette would contemplate that marvelous face would be in the next world, where the Lady promised to make her happy for ever.

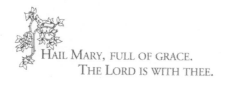

HAIL MARY, FULL OF GRACE.
THE LORD IS WITH THEE.

AN EMPRESS ON HER KNEES

Eugénie de Montijo and
the Decommissioning of the Grotto Barrier,
September 30, 1858

18 58 Through the window opened to the night air, the unceasing murmur of the Atlantic Ocean entered the luxuriously decorated room. But the surf's monotonous crashing was drowned out by a child's moans, accompanied by a rattling cough. In September 1858, while the imperial family was on vacation in Biarritz, little Napoléon-Louis, the only son of Napoléon III, was struck with a serious laryngitis. His life was in danger, and the dynasty's future was compromised.

Empress Eugénie didn't care a bit about the dynasty. Her thoughts did not go that far. She felt only the black distress of a mother who saw her two-year-old child in agony in her arms. Fatigue and despair had drawn deep rings under the eyes of her ravishing face so prized by court painters. For the first time in her life, the exceedingly coquettish empress had refused her chambermaids' care. Her loose bun, her make-up washed out with tears, her wrinkled crinoline – everything about her pointed to an unprecedented mental distraction.

By her side was Admiral Bruat's wife, the imperial prince's governess, who had maintained a delicate silence in respect for Eugénie's sorrow. Yet she had to speak. She had a suggestion to make. Coughing politely to gather the courage to interrupt the empress's confusion, she began: "Your Majesty, there is perhaps – who knows? – a non-medical way to save your son."

Eugénie eagerly looked at her. "Well then, Bruat, quick, speak?"

"As you know, your Majesty, I have just returned from Lourdes, and…"

"Lourdes! How could I fail to think of it!" exclaimed Eugénie.

The amusing account of the admiral's wife's trip immediately came to her mind. The governess had shown up at the grotto despite the barriers and therefore against the decree in force. Some pranksters alerted the country warden for the explicit purpose of getting him in trouble before so august an outlaw. Prudent and well-advised, the civil servant of course refrained from demanding the fine of five hundred francs and instead merely wrote the rebel's name in his notebook: *Admirall-wife Bruhat, widow, governoress o' the chillren of France*. Whereupon, at the lawbreaker's request, he promptly filled an elegant beaker with water from the forbidden source.

"Bruat, tell me," asked the empress, "do you have this water with you?"

"Alas no, your Majesty," replied the governess, "but one of your ladies-in-waiting possesses a tuft from one of the grotto's plants. She procured it from Father Peyramale, the pastor of Lourdes."

The empress dashed out of the room to awaken the young woman and immediately returned, victoriously brandishing a few blades of grass whose color had already faded.

Leaning over the crib in which the imperial child lay between life and death, she applied this strange remedy to his tiny lips and lost herself in ardent prayer, using her courtly French and native Spanish in disordered haste.

Death did not knock at the palace gates that night. As the hours progressed, the imperial prince's fever abated, and Eugénie recovered her *joie de vivre*. Early in the morning, as the sun cleared up that terrible night's shadows, Biarritz seemed to have recovered its charming colors. Leaving her son in the care of the faithful admiral's wife for a moment, the empress went out to take in the fresh air on the terrace. *My Lord, isn't the sea beautiful! Isn't this region sweet!* Until now, Eugénie liked the southwest of France for its spas that were so conducive to relaxation. On that morning, she started to cherish it for that obscure town, Lourdes, to which she may owe her son's recovery. The empress felt it: Napoléon-Louis' cure, whether a miracle or not, was something providential.

It now remained for her to fulfill a vow she had solemnly made before the little bed around which despair had lurked. The empress had promised the Virgin to have the barrier removed from the grotto if her child should survive.

Calling her chambermaids, so idle just yesterday, Eugénie focused on her make-up. Now resplendent, she found her husband and passionately explained to him the commitment she had made to heaven.

"*One word from you, Sir, and the unworthy barrier that bars entrance to the grotto will be taken down forevermore,*" she told her husband.

The emperor smoothed his mustache for awhile with a perplexed expression. He thought of the Hautes-Pyrénées' prefect's stupefaction upon finding out that the sovereign allowed himself to be swayed by a misplaced fervor. But he also thought of the crown's future, and of this past night that could well have proved fatal to it. Finally he thought of his wife's irresistible beauty: The vivacious Eugénie exerted a strong influence upon him.

His inner deliberations were short-lived. A few moments later, Prefect Oscar Massy received the order to restore access to the grotto at

Massabielle without any restrictions. The same day, the guards left, the barrier was destroyed by a joyous band of the faithful, and the country warden voided the recent tickets given out on the Gave's left bank.

BLESSED ART THOU AMONG WOMEN,
AND BLESSED IS THE FRUIT OF THY WOMB, JESUS.

THE BISHOP WHO REVEALED LOURDES
TO THE WORLD

Portrait of Bishop Laurence, December 7, 1860

18 60 She was so convincing. That afternoon, while the twelve members of the commission over which he presided were hearing Bernadette for the last time, His Excellency Bertrand-Sévère Laurence, bishop of Tarbes, was unable to keep two tears from running down his cheeks.

In his office at the chancery, he constantly thought of Bernadette's words and of her tone's forthrightness. Yes, he was now certain: This child was not telling stories. One by one, she had convinced the most reticent minds. Even if he had taken his time and exercised proper caution – concerned as he was with respect to his responsibility as bishop – today he knew that he would publicly announce the veracity of these apparitions. He had seen and heard children in his day, but this young girl had something special – disarming simplicity, astounding honesty, and humility. What was not to believe?

He thought over the visit of Bishop Thibaud of Montpellier. A year and a half before, he had stopped in Lourdes and had conducted a veritable investigation into the events at the grotto. He met with Father Peyramale and the principal witnesses of the apparitions, ecstasies, and healings. Above all, he listened to Bernadette as she told him what she saw and heard. After his investigation, Bishop Thibaud came to find Bishop Laurence in Tarbes to share his certainty with him. He told him what he said to the witnesses he had met: *"It was not my intention to stop at Tarbes, but today my conscience as a Bishop makes it my duty. If His Excellency the bishop of Tarbes still hesitates to believe in the apparitions of the grotto, I shall tell him to come here and to do what I have done. I challenge him to remain in disbelief."*

Bishop Thibaud was right. How could one still have doubts after hearing her and reading the report that his faithful confidant and adviser, the diocese's secretary general, Canon Antoine Fourcade, had handed to him? Bishop Laurence was preparing to write to the bishop of Grenoble to ask him how he went about the recognition of Our Lady of La Salette and the building of the first place of worship. Bishop Laurence wished to honor the Virgin's request: *Let a chapel be built here and let there be a procession here.*

He had also decided to purchase the land around the grotto, especially the meadow of Savy, from the city of Lourdes. He had excellent relations with the town; he initially had come as a priest, at the bishop's request, to celebrate Sunday Mass and holy days for nine months in 1831 in order to pacify a parish that had been profoundly scarred by division since the French Revolution.

Bishop Laurence had to send a letter to the mayor of Lourdes in the next few days. He knew that town hall would grant him the purchase of the land, but he sensed that things would go less smoothly with the prefect and the minister, who for several months had pressured him to take a stand against the grotto apparitions. Indeed, church-state relations were deteriorating. Nevertheless, Bishop Laurence was tenacious. Whatever the cost, he would stick it out to the end. Once all the formalities were settled, he would publish his recognition of the apparitions.

The old bishop's thoughts went back to little Bernadette, to whom he had listened that afternoon. Seeing her so simple and so frail, he remembered his own childhood in the little village of Oroix, at the border between the Bigorre and Béarn regions. The twelfth child of a very modest family, he understood this young girl who had not had the chance, as he did, of being taken in by the village priest to be educated. Who could have foretold that the young child born in a remote village on the heels of the Revolution would become bishop of Tarbes and be made a Roman count by Pope Pius IX? To be sure, God granted him gifts that allowed him to pursue brilliant studies at the minor seminary of Bétharram and then at the seminary of Aire before undertaking theological studies, all the while teaching grammar, the humanities, mathematics, and philosophy. He had been a priest for less than a year when, in 1822, the bishop of Bayonne entrusted him with the rectorship of a new minor seminary, in the former monastery of Saint-Pé in the Hautes-Pyrénées, which he had just bought back. Bishop Laurence remembered Bishop Double, head of the recently re-established Diocese of Tarbes, who had asked him to become vicar-general and superior of the major seminary.

Upon Bishop Double's death, Bishop Laurence was chosen to succeed him and to continue the pursuit of the great reforms that he had undertaken in the diocese. In the apparitions of Lourdes, Bishop Laurence saw his principal task as a bishop. All he had done until now had been but a preparation for this. He had reinforced the formation of priests and set up spiritual retreats for them; he had restored the Marian shrines of Garaison, Poueylaün, Héas, and Pietat, which he had committed to the care of the Fathers of Garaison, now known as the Fathers of the Immaculate Conception.

Leaning on his windowsill, Bishop Laurence gave thanks for this life already well accomplished in the service of his diocese. Little Bernadette's face continued to inhabit his mind. He inwardly knew that this child to whom the Virgin appeared was going to change his diocese's image and would bring to perfection in Lourdes the work he had undertaken when he first became bishop of Tarbes.

 HOLY MARY, MOTHER OF GOD,

THE FACE OF A SAINT

The Photographs of Bernadette, October 22, 1861

1861 The door softly opened a little, and there she was, this was it! Father Bernadou's heart beat faster as he took delight in his photo session that would capture Bernadette's profound gaze, the gaze that had beheld the Virgin. A few drops of sweat beaded the priest's face. He had already met Bernadette, and she had not refused being photographed by this good father, a professor of chemistry and draftsmanship at Saint-Pé minor seminary. Now he had to keep his promise to the pastor of Lourdes, to immortalize the moment of the encounter between the fourteen-year-old child and the Mother of the Lord, and to capture the traces the events had left on the still-childlike face of a young girl of sixteen now, who kept buried in her marveling heart the memory of those luminous encounters with the beautiful Lady. Bernadette had not declined, of course, but something deep within her did object; although she did not show it, it rose up inside her.

The priest was both patient and determined. He sought not to photograph the young girl, but *the one who saw.* To this end, he wished to set her on location, to recover elements of the décor, the grotto in its bareness, and that infinity of the inner gaze that weaves the soul's life and moves mountains. Bernadette, the receiver of divine mercy through the channel of Mary, was what moved the man and overwhelmed him. He had devoted his life to God and felt so unworthy of his mission. He was at a loss and nearly paralyzed by the weight of his responsibility.

Bernadette, for her part, peacefully waited, her arms crossed, as was her habit. Her fate was not played out here, but elsewhere, where the life of men was thoroughly submerged in God. In fact, something of this feeling of submersion would be reflected in the first photograph that Father Bernadou would take – the most famous one, the one that would go around the planet and serenely rest between the yellowed pages of forgotten missals. This first photo was like a blessing. Bernadette had done her best, yet how difficult it was to find in it the inner feeling that had inhabited her then! She often balked when the priest insisted again and again that she resit the pose, with that gaze that cuts through one's heart like tears of fire. She was getting a little annoyed. *Eh! what do you expect, she's not there anymore!* Then she resumed patiently and made efforts to pose properly. In the 1860s, collodion snapshots required long poses. But she who had seen must seize us in her turn with her vision, and Bernadette was now learning the long-suffering obedience of the saints and of the humble in heart whom the goodness of God had touched with his radiant wing.

After this first session, six official "seer of Lourdes" photography campaigns would take place with other photographers. None would do more than fix in an image a fleeting reflection of the encounter, as though life in Mary's intimacy resisted the profanation of staring eyes to reserve itself for the purification of silence and for the friendship of prayerful souls. Meanwhile, at a country girl's peaceful rhythm, Bernadette was changing. She was inwardly growing and escaping from what the photographers wanted their successive snapshots to convey: holy images, like those of Billard-Perrin, that sacralized the place with strewn dead leaves; narrative pictures like Paul Dufour's, made between February and

March 1864, that touched up Bernadette's face and invented a levitation scenario before the grotto; or iconic pictures, like Philippe Viron's, made in July 1866, in which Bernadette seemed so inordinately frozen by the apparition that nothing divine quivers in her any longer.

Yet in this all-for-God attitude and in all this obedience, it sometimes happened that the young girl was too accommodating. At the age of twenty-four, she accepted one last series of photos to assist the construction of the church the Virgin had requested. She posed in her religious habit, with a crucifix in her hand, even though she was only a novice and her congregation's statutes disallowed it. Then Father Peyramale, who had been watching over her from the beginning, got angry in a letter of November 9, 1868, in which he lectured her for having posed in such an outfit and with such a tired look that she seemed unhappy and quite alone: *You have been punished for this obligingness, for this portrait is so unlike you that I failed to recognize you.*

Her heart was no longer in it. Bernadette slowly withdrew from the world of appearances. Long gone were the days of Father Bernadou's purely pastoral joy! She who had seen no longer wished to be seen; she was now in silence's humble keep, in the secret of sainthood's mystery. Hidden now from our gaze was she who had said these words: *The Virgin was so good, so beautiful, that after seeing her once, one would like to die in order not to leave her.* Indeed, Bernadette abandoned herself in order not to leave her, having become what she contemplated with the reverence of the simple, which consists in saying nothing, in doing nothing, simply in being.

The crucifix that had been thrust into her hand had joined her deeply with Mary in an invisible *Stabat Mater* that she had exemplified her entire life and that she had written down in her private notebook: *I have nothing any longer, I have nothing but Jesus, neither place, nor thing, nor people, nor ideas, nor feelings, nor honors, nor sufferings that could turn me against Jesus.*

So the pictures of Bernadette had become, in time, the refreshing well at which our desire stops to see and to be seen by the one who did not shrink from showing herself and from showing the way of grace to a simple and peaceful child.

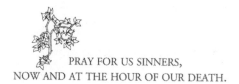

PRAY FOR US SINNERS,
NOW AND AT THE HOUR OF OUR DEATH.

MIRABILIA ET MIRACULA

The First Seven Miracles, Acknowledged on January 18, 1862

1862 "What, again?!"

This exclamation leapt from the lips of Croisine Bouhort who, on the morning of June 27, 1860, opened her front door to find herself face to face with Dr. Dozous and an unknown colleague. She did not know whether she should laugh or sigh in resignation: She had never seen so many doctors march through her house – until her son's recovery!

Croisine Bouhort used to consider doctors' house calls useless. Justin, a frail little two-year-old, was dying of tuberculosis. Sickly from birth, he never even learned to walk. A physician, Dr. Peyrus, had looked into his case, but he had left his mother no hope. Croisine Bouhort could read it in every pitiful glance she would encounter: Her child was destined to a very early death.

Anticipating the good woman's sentiments, Dozous begged her pardon with a broad smile. Yes, once again, Justin will have to be torn away from his toys to be examined.

"My colleague is Dr. Henri Vergez, professor at the University of Montpellier and water inspector in Barèges," Dozous said in introduction.

Upon hearing all these flashy titles, a sheepish Croisine Bouhort respectfully bowed and expressed regret for her exclamation, but it was too late to take it back. In any event, the professor smiled, too, and presented his apologies to the lady of the house. He would try to work fast but well. The stakes were high: Bishop Laurence of Tarbes had charged him with examining all cases of mysterious healings that had occurred after the use of water from Massabielle.

Justin was one of these "miracle-healed." During the first days of July 1858, while his state was becoming critical, his mother, hoping against hope, decided to act. There was so much talk at that time of the new water source in Lourdes. Taking in her arms the nearly half-dead child, Croisine rushed to the grotto. Taking no notice of the public authorities, she walked straight to the basin that the quarrymen had just laid out to gather the source's water. Astonished witnesses saw her dunk her child in this icy bath. Protestations, shrieks of anguish, and entreaties from the disapproving onlookers did nothing to stop her. Croisine Bouhort held her child in the basin for a very long time. When she finally drew him back out, he was still breathing. As far as the witnesses were concerned, that was the first miracle in itself! But the true mystery was yet to come: once back at home, Justin finally awakened to life again, recouped his strength and his complexion, and started to walk.

Professor Vergez had already examined the file of this case in advance of this house visit. It remained for him to ascertain it for himself: The boy, rosy and alert, was now as stout as a child bursting with health!

Taking his leave from the Bouhorts, the professor presented himself at the house of Louis Bourriette, only to be received with yet another incredulous exclamation. Here again, a verification was needed. An old quarryman, Bourriette had been struck in the right eye by a mine shard in 1839. With advancing years, his eyesight had only worsened. Nineteen years after the accident, in 1858, he had become, for all intents and purposes, blind in one eye.

In early March, when Bernadette had first dug the earth at the behest of the Lady in White, he had a little of this mysterious water brought back to him. He washed his eye a few times… and recovered his eyesight completely! Filled with excitement, he rushed to the office of Dozous, ran like the wind through the waiting room, and erupted into the practice to proclaim his miracle.

Miracle? In the eyes of the Church, one cannot leap to such a conclusion. Warned of several similar healings, Bishop Laurence adopted a policy of prudence. He established an investigative commission and charged it with assessing these cases under rigorous medical scrutiny. The commission members, after examination, determined there were twelve healings whose cause might be supernatural. Nevertheless, *might* was the operative word, and the investigation continued. In March 1860, Bishop Laurence decided to entrust the study of these delicate files to the well-known Professor Vergez. That is why he went to Lourdes to conduct his own cross-examination of the results of his colleagues' investigation.

Back home in Barèges, Vergez settled down to a new selection of alleged miracles. Among the cases that the commission had retained, he examined a few, added a new one, weighed the evidence, and developed his own conclusions. He was careful to allow some time to pass after the formerly sick patients reported healing. Is a miraculous healing not supposed to be definitive? Then he sent the results of his work to the Diocese of Tarbes.

Never did a bishop study a medical file with such care. Bishop Laurence, who had already annotated the commission's first report, gave this new assessment his most meticulous discernment.

In January 1862, the bishop finally decided he was able to commit the Church's magisterium in the case of the unexplained healings. In a solemn *mandamus* (a bishop's letter) relying on science and reason as much as on faith, he declared seven of these healings to be "works of God." Catherine Latapie, Louis Bouriette, Blaisette Cazenave, Henri

Busquet, Justin Bouhort, Madelaine Rizan, and Marie Moreau were the first seven persons whose healings at Massabielle were determined to be miraculous.

At the same time, another episcopal investigation, one to which Bernadette herself had long been subjected, came to an end: the determination of whether the apparitions themselves were genuine. The last objection that Bishop Laurence's caution had raised up had fallen. So he declared in the same mandamus: "*It is Our judgment that the Immaculate Mother of God has truly appeared to Bernadette.*"

Amen.

THE LIGHT SHINES IN THE DARKNESS

The Torchlight Procession and Father Marie-Antoine, November 10, 1863

18 63 *For the redemption of man lost through pride, the Son of God had to make Himself small. For the confusion of Satan, the king, the type of the prideful, the immaculate Virgin had to choose what was smallest: the little Bernadette. The divine plan is maintained to the end: the choice of the weak instrument who has just written these pages is proof of it: a poor mendicant Religious. There is nothing smaller in the Church and in humanity.*

Father Marie-Antoine lifted his pen and distractedly contemplated the sheet before him. He had promised this book on Lourdes and Bernadette to so many pilgrims. He had been going to Lourdes for over fifteen years to preach, to confess, to celebrate, and to pray. Between a retreat here and a mission there in the region of Toulouse, where he founded the Capuchin convent, the grotto's domain had become his second home. Simple words that inspire faith – that is what he must put into his book to speak to the heart of pilgrims and of the faithful.

He recalled the event that so influenced him and of which he thought about so often. During one of his last pilgrimages to Lourdes, a terrible storm had struck and the pilgrims, filled with sadness, said that there would be no torchlight procession that evening. This procession was something that was appreciated by every pilgrim, an occasion that allowed everyone to pray and sing before the grotto in the candles' festive light. Just as they had seemed to have resigned themselves to the procession's cancellation, a voice in the crowd had shouted out: "*No, no, have trust! Have trust! Let us invoke Mary.*" Father Marie-Antoine had prayed with the pilgrims when suddenly, as happened in the Gospels on Lake Gennesaret, calm had followed the storm. Thousands of voices had then greeted the immaculate Virgin, and thousands of torches had lit up her image. Before this had happened, Father Marie-Antoine had given up the idea of preaching. Propped up by the trembling of all these hearts, he had instead sung a canticle inspired by the words of Job: "*The Almighty said to the raging ocean one day, pointing with His finger to the sand on the shore: 'Thus far you shall come but no farther, and here shall your proud waves be stilled.'*"[1]

In the second half of the nineteenth century, the tide of the times, the rage of disbelief and of blasphemy, had broken – of this the priest was sure – upon the grain of sand that was Bernadette, upon this flower fallen from heaven from the very heart of Mary. He remembered his first stay in Lourdes, his first meeting with little Bernadette. She was fourteen and had just made her First Communion. It was July 1858, and he was coming back from a thirty-day retreat preached in Saint-Gaudens. She had had an apparition on Easter Wednesday and was to see the Virgin for the last time a few days later, July 16. She had come to his Mass, and he had given her communion. What a thrill when he saw this poor child kneeling before him! He remembered the young seer's tale when he later asked her to reproduce the Virgin's gestures. Her sincerity, her expression, her attitude… He had had the impression of being in Mary's presence himself. Time appeared to have stopped. She

---

1. Jb 38: 10.

seemed transfigured. He, the big, bearded man in his rough wool robe, had found himself to be so small before the mystery enveloping the young girl. How could he doubt this story? The glory of God *par excellence* is to do what is greatest with what is close to nothing.

Bernadette was a divine light on earth. In the image of Genevieve, Joan of Arc, Germaine – illustrious shepherdesses all – she made the Lamb's light shine in the midst of the faithful. These sparks of faith, like so many torches, formed a fiery procession that started up the march of the people of God toward him who awaits them, a people who sing and pray to the Virgin in the light of faith. Such is the meaning of the torchlight procession of which the pilgrims were so fond.

Father Marie-Antoine was the founder of this procession. He had established it in Rocamadour. Then, one day in 1863 when, as was his habit, he was praying at the grotto about nine in the evening, his intuition had prevailed upon him to process in this way. There must have been about twenty pilgrims praying there that day. At the foot of Mary's statue, candles glittered. *These candles have to go on the move*, he had thought to himself. *These pilgrims' faith must sing and dance to God; it must light up the world. The Virgin's message must come alive, so that its announcement may be visible to heaven and earth. The night must shine with the light of Mary, so that the darkness may shine with the light of Christ!* He had walked toward the pilgrims and had asked them each to take a candle and to form a semicircle before the grotto. Then they had prayed to the Virgin together and had sung the *Ave Maris Stella*. The lights danced in the dusk like it was Easter night and answered to the heavenly luminaries to celebrate God's perfect creation.

How great his joy had been to see this show of faith taken up the next day by a hundred people, then in the following months by thousands of pilgrims, praying at the grotto and then spreading out in a joyful procession. A new song to Mary had been composed, which, like the procession, had filled out: Down the years, it had gone from eight couplets to sixty!

Father Marie-Antoine picked up his pen. *Give us the grace of bringing us back here again more than once!* He wrote, as if echoing the Virgin's request to Bernadette: *Would you have the grace of coming here for fifteen days?*

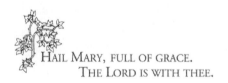

Hail Mary, full of grace.
The Lord is with thee.

THE HISTORIAN OF LOURDES

Henri Lasserre, December 4, 1863

1863 For a while now, Father Peyramale had been pensive. His eyes remained fixed on the signature at the bottom of the letter he was holding in his hand: *Henri Lasserre*. Little by little, his memory gathered together what he knew of this man – his reputation as a lawyer, his Christian journalist's fiery pen... The priest remembered the first letter that Lasserre wrote to him over a year before in which the journalist poured out his dismay. He found himself suffering from a serious eye infection that no physician had succeeded in healing. Within a few months, his eyesight had dramatically deteriorated to the point that he could no longer read nor write. A Parisian friend who, like all in high society at the time, had gone to take the waters in the Pyrenees over the summer had mentioned the miraculous healings of Lourdes to him and had convinced him to obtain Massabielle's source water. That is why he had turned to Father Peyramale.

The priest remembered that letter. He, of course, had sent the requested water and, as was the case for all who made this request, he had prayed a long time for Lasserre. And this morning he was holding an answer to his prayers in his hands. The letter's tone was enthusiastic; the miracle had taken place. Lasserre told of how, on October 10, 1862, after praying fervently, he had rubbed his eyes with a towel soaked in Lourdes water and found himself instantly cured.

The priest thoughtfully reread this account in which journalistic acumen was allied to faith. Could this pen, which told of the miracles so well, tell of even more? After a few hesitations, the decision was made: He would ask Lasserre to write the history of the apparitions of Lourdes.

Once contacted, the journalist hastily accepted. To be sure, there already existed an account of the apparitions which, in fact, the pastor had attached to his letter. However, Father Peyramale, with the approval of Bishop Laurence, wished to give more widespread recognition to this supernatural event. Lasserre went down to Lourdes and envisioned a grandiose work on the spot... but wrote nothing. Indeed, this man, a rising star in the Parisian journalistic milieu, led a hectic life that didn't leave him much time to undertake the research necessary to his work. Sick and tired of all the delays, his confessor, who had a profound admiration for the Virgin Mary and earnestly desired to see this book written and published, ordered him to get to work that very day in August 1867.

Being a good penitent, Lasserre left for Nevers, interviewed Bernadette in her convent, and went to Lourdes, where he spoke with Father Peyramale and the first eyewitnesses. In Pau, the prefecture, he attempted to consult the official sources, but he was denied access to the files. Since Father Peyramale's memory was somewhat sketchy, the journalist lacked the elements to assign precise dates to each of the eighteen apparitions. Neither could he retrace the pastor's or the administration's reactions precisely. Nevertheless, he took the plunge and published, in the *Revue du Monde Catholique*, an account of the first apparitions, for which his documentation was reliable. It was an immense success.

Pressed by his readers, he resolved a few months later to continue his publication despite his sources, which this time were patchy. In June 1868, ten years after the apparitions, the last installment was published. The work was produced as a single volume in 1869 under the title *Notre-Dame de Lourdes.*

The book became the nineteenth century's greatest publishing success. Continuously republished, translated into eighty-one languages, and distributed throughout the world, it contributed to making Lourdes the premiere pilgrimage destination after Rome, and earned a fortune for its author. Lasserre, working this goldmine, published other works on Lourdes with his publisher's blessing, and despite Bishop Laurence's reservations.

The bishop had had the articles examined by Father Sempé before their compilation into a single work and had addressed to the author some precise observations, notably denouncing the caricatures he had made of official personages. Indeed, Lasserre felt no hesitation in exaggerating to heighten the narrative's evocative force. Under his pen, Baron Massy, the department's prefect and a staunch Catholic, became a mediocre and mulish civil servant. The imperial administration, from the chief of police all the way to the secretary for religions, he presented as stuffed shirts, which he contrasted with faith and openness to miracles. The history of the apparitions thus was portrayed as a struggle between good and evil, between little Bernadette's faith and an obtuse and meddling bureaucracy's contempt. Far from producing a work of history, Lasserre wrote a thoroughly romanticized work, all the while assuring in his preface that *I have intended to make this an exhaustive study.* This he proclaimed with a fine self-assurance, refusing to take the bishop's observations into account. For him, modifying his stylistic effects at the peril of dulling the work was out of the question.

How, then, are we to explain the success of a work that was judged severely by witnesses closest to the events? The polemical tone adopted by the author, the epic character of his descriptions, and the account of the first miracles were far more impressive than a faithful account of the events. Furthermore, Lasserre, who was also a lawyer, knew how to defend himself. He summoned his supporters to counter the criticisms of the bishop of Tarbes and to keep up his publications. His work had dubbed him "the Historian of Lourdes," even though the epic sweep of his personal faith often brushed aside historical accuracy.

BLESSED ART THOU AMONG WOMEN, AND BLESSED IS THE FRUIT OF THY WOMB, JESUS.

The Sculptor of the Impossible

Fabisch's Sculpted Virgin, April 4, 1864

1864 Stretching his legs numbed by an interminable journey, the sculptor Joseph Fabisch got off his stagecoach and, with a severe expression, examined the little town of Lourdes, which was in the caress of a warm September sun. Despite the medieval castle overlooking the town, the spot lacked the bucolic charm of Italian Renaissance landscapes. Nor were the mountains that dominated the country as grandiose as the Alps. In short, the sculptor, accustomed to referring everything to the arts, was hardly overcome by this modest town.

An engaging voice cut his critical examination short. Dominiquette Cazenave, the postmaster's sister, gaily approached this stranger she had never seen before.

"Where are you going, Sir? Can I help you?" she asked.

"Joseph Fabisch, sculptor, member of the Academy of Sciences, Fine Letters and Arts of Lyons," Fabisch introduced himself. "I am expected at the pastor's house. If you would be so kind as to point out the rectory…"

"Oh! Isn't it you who is going to make the statue of the Virgin for the grotto at Massabielle?"

"It is I."

"Boy, what a challenge!" replied Cazenave. "Fortunately you'll have Bernadette's directions to guide you. She's a great friend of mine, just so you know. If it isn't too indiscreet, Sir, how much will it cost – the statue, I mean?"

"It is indiscreet, madam," Fabisch answered stiffly. "Yet I shall answer you. The Misses Lacour, my honorable backers in Lyons, are disbursing seven thousand gold francs, not counting traveling expenses."

Upon hearing of this fantastic sum, Cazenave's eyes popped out of their sockets.

"You have to take into account that I shall be working on Carrara marble, alone worthy of representing the perfection of the Most Holy Virgin," added the sculptor.

Under his stilted manners, Fabisch felt intimidated. This is not to say that he was a mere journeyman of his art! He had already made the statue on the spire of the Basilica of Fourvière in Lyons as well as the one adorning the sanctuary of La Salette. All modesty aside, representing the Queen of Heaven in the splendor of her glory seemed to be a worthy challenge for him. And yet Cazenave had just reminded him of this assignment's novelty. His contract stipulated that he must conform himself in every detail to the descriptions Bernadette was to give him...

So the sculptor found himself in the young girl's presence. Torn away from the games she was playing with the little children in the yard of the hospice, she hastily rearranged her wild hair under her kerchief and replaced her carefree face with an appropriately serious expression. Once again, she was asked the everlasting description of her heavenly visitor. The stakes were high today! Bernadette forced herself to erase from her memory the five years since the apparitions to evoke the Virgin as though she had seen her only the day before. Furthermore, Fabisch's investigation compelled her to meticulous precision. "*Was the body* straight? Did the head bend? How did she join her hands to say 'I am the Immaculate Conception'? Of what cloth was her dress cut?"

At this question, Bernadette suppressed a light laugh. A memory came back. She remembered the visit of a commercial salesman who had brought along every sample from his millinery store. Among the countless pieces of cloth, she did not see the kind the Virgin wore. The salesman watched her, disappointed and disbelieving. She concluded in a mischievous tone: "*The Holy Virgin did not dress at your store.*"

At the end of his interview with the young Lourdes girl, the sculptor was satisfied. He had understood and written down everything.

"*When you see my statue, I want you to say, 'It's her!*" he stated with a hint of conceit, sending Bernadette back to her interrupted recess.

Back at his workshop in Lyons, the sculptor took the sketches he had outlined out of his trunk. He examined the over four-and-a-half-foot-tall paper silhouette that he had refined in Bernadette's presence. So small, so young, so frail a Virgin? This did not tally with the canons imprinted on Fabisch's mind in indelible characters. The sculptor surreptitiously took liberties with his plaster trials. The Lady grew nearly fourteen inches and took on a stylized pose befitting the sovereign of angels. Though smiling less than Bernadette had indicated, the Lady would be more eloquent. And as to the constantly indicated infinite simplicity? Surely the child, ignorant of the arts and of the sublime, had been a poor observer, so Fabisch added folds to the dress, breadth to the veil, and soft forms to the figure. He was so sure of his discernment that he shipped the rough plaster model off to Lourdes and immediately began the definitive execution in marble.

Alas! A few days later, a letter from Father Peyramale interrupted his work. Laying aside his chisel before the majestic feet adorned with roses, the artist scanned Bernadette's comments with a furrowed brow. Gaiety, sobriety, youth – none of these was there, not even the rosary which, in the impetuosity of his interpretation, Fabisch had forgotten!

The sculptor struggled to acquiesce to representing the Virgin as she was suggested to him, yet he had to force himself to do so. He rectified and transformed the marble directly without achieving the childlike and gracious purity for which Bernadette so ardently wished. Perhaps the challenge was too difficult for a sculptor imprisoned in the artistic criteria of his time.

On April 4, 1864, Fabisch's statue was blessed with much pomp. Father Peyramale suggested that Bernadette should not be present at the inauguration, for she had said with regret, as she looked at the finished statue, "*That's not it...*" The youngster stayed alone at the hospice that day. She reflected upon the memory of the marvelous vision, humble and pure, from then on replaced in the grotto with the majesty of a marble statue.

HOLY MARY, MOTHER OF GOD,

The Very First Pilgrimage at Massabielle

The Loubajac Procession, July 25, 1864

1864 Leaning on his cane, Étienne watched the procession arrive with a sly smile.

"Go ahead, say your pious claptrap at the grotto!" he mumbled into his beard.

The citizens of Loubajac who were passing by the field paid no attention to the old growler Étienne. They were accustomed to hearing him carry on all day long. Since the death of his wife, Jeannette, Étienne had been embittered and unhappy. Nothing moved him, especially not "pious claptrap," as he called it.

"Jeannette strongly believed in the Virgin Mary, and see where it landed her!" he would answer those who reproved him for not coming to Mass on Sunday.

On this beautiful morning, however, the inhabitants of Loubajac did not wish to spoil their pleasure with Étienne's lamentations. They were entirely given over to the joy of having received authorization from the bishop of Tarbes to go on pilgrimage to Lourdes, a little more than four miles away. They were heading to pray to the Holy Virgin, to thank her for all the graces she had granted them – the healings of Marie Vignette, the Capdevieille woman, Jeanne Pomiès, and, above all, Catherine

Latapie, whose cure was recognized by the Church as an authentic miracle on January 18, 1862! Her paralyzed arm had recovered all of its flexibility after she dipped it in the water of the Massabielle grotto.

"Well, well, you've brought out the whole fancy outfit!" Étienne mocked.

Colored banners and golden pennants fluttered in the warm morning breeze as the pilgrims raised their bright colors in the already harsh light. The stately flag bearers advanced in two rows at the head of the procession.

"Look at Marcel – he's taken off his cap!" added the shepherd disdainfully.

Within the procession, all the men walked slowly, bareheaded, despite the sun that already was beating down hard on the valley.

"Why, they've all turned themselves out dandy!"

The old shepherd continued his uncivil comments on principle, as he watched the procession stretching out before his eyes. Yet, his heart already was no longer in it. Even he had trouble remaining completely insensitive to the beauty of what he saw. Women advanced, rosaries in hand, reciting their prayers. Girls brightened the train with their *Ave Marias*. Children ran about here and there, joining their little high voices to the chorus. Even for the skeptical old man, the sight was moving.

"Hey, Mister Mayor! You're going, too?" Étienne called out.

Indeed, the mayor closed the march along with the council members. With his tricolor sash, he gave the procession an unexpected official dimension. With him, it was the entire small municipality of the Hautes-Pyrénées that went to render homage to the Virgin. By his side, the timid pastor of Loubajac, Father Latapie, walked, breviary in hand. He was proud of his parishioners, who so insisted on organizing this pilgrimage. It was they who obtained the bishop's authorization, they again who contacted the pastor of Lourdes to propose their day's schedule – procession, crossing through Lourdes, a stop at the parish church, devotions and prayers at the grotto where, since April, a statue in the image of the apparition had been set up.

But once the procession had passed, Étienne found himself alone, leaning on his cane, at the edge of his field. A terrible feeling of loneliness came over him. In the village, the bells had fallen silent. They would soon be relayed by those of Lourdes' church that would welcome the pilgrims from Loubajac. And so, without fully understanding what was happening to him, Étienne started walking, then faster and faster, nearly running despite his advanced age. Finally, he, too, wished to be part of the trip, to see Lourdes and that famous grotto where the Holy Virgin appeared six years before. He, too, wished to venerate Mary, to recite prayers to her, to sing of her. Was this not the best way of remaining faithful to Jeannette, his dear wife, of once again feeling close to her?

"Wait! Wait for me!"

Upon hearing the call at his back, Father Latapie turned around. The voice was weak and out of breath. Étienne was well past the age for running down mountain paths. The priest stopped to await the old man. Seeing the grouchy shepherd smile despite the effort he had just made, the pastor of Loubajac told himself that this pilgrimage requested by his parishioners was decidedly a good thing, a very good thing. If it had managed to bring a man back to the faith, that was already wonderful.

The inhabitants of Lourdes must have felt the importance of that very first pilgrimage. They had come out in great numbers to welcome the pastor, mayor, and all the pilgrims from Loubajac on that day of July 25, 1864. The town's schoolgirls were posted along the way. The families, too, the merchants, even the police, all were there to greet the procession effusively.

Among the onlookers there was one person whom the sight of this pious march especially moved. It was shy Bernadette. Upon hearing the chants and prayers of these men, women, children, and old people, the young seer could not help but think of that morning of March 2, 1858, the thirteenth time the Virgin had appeared to her. The beautiful Lady had then asked her: "*Go and tell the priests that there must be a procession here and that a chapel must be built here.*"

These very first pilgrims would open the way to all the countless others who would succeed each other at the Lourdes shrine, coming from Loubajac at first, then from Poueyferré, from Nay or from Bayonne, and soon from Bordeaux, Paris, Italy, Spain, Mexico, the United States, Africa, America, or Asia...

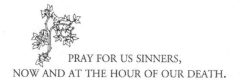

PRAY FOR US SINNERS,
NOW AND AT THE HOUR OF OUR DEATH.

Four Men for a Shrine

The Arrival of the Garaison Fathers, May 17, 1866

1866 "*I have always believed, without mentioning it, that you and the other Fathers would be in charge of the Lourdes chapel.*" Father Peydessus folded the letter that Bishop Laurence of Tarbes had just sent him on this April 19, 1866. He leaned his head on his seat's headrest and closed his eyes. To say that this correspondence had caught him by surprise would have been an untruth. It was not the first time that the Garaison Fathers were solicited to take charge of a Marian shrine. Besides, was that not their *raison d'être*? Since December 8, 1848, the date of their foundation, they had been entrusted with the delicate mission of managing Marian shrines and of reviving those that had fallen into oblivion, starting with the shrine of Garaison, barely forty-three miles from Lourdes. For the bishop to ask them to take care of the brand-new pilgrimage site of Lourdes was therefore nothing surprising.

Bishop Laurence wanted two chaplains to arrive in Lourdes by Pentecost – that is, within a month. Although that was too short notice, Father Peydessus knew that the Fathers of Garaison were committed to *go at any time and on any occasion wherever the Bishop judges it to be appropriate.* He would not go back on that vow. Yet one detail bothered the superior of the Missionaries of the Immaculate Conception a little.

"Are two chaplains enough?" he wondered, even as he ran the gamut of the fathers he might be able to send there. "The work that awaits them is immense. The chapel is not yet completed. Pilgrimages have barely begun, and already the crowds are thronging Lourdes. This shrine is surely going to surpass all others."

Father Peydessus knew the men of his congregation. Many were solid mountain men like himself. They did not spare their efforts and worked with admirable energy. Still, that wouldn't be enough. What the bishop required for Lourdes were not foremen. Bishop Laurence wanted people capable of overseeing all of the shrine's construction, but more importantly, he also sought men who were able to walk spiritually with the pilgrims flocking to the little grotto of Massabielle. He needed priests to teach, to preach, to hear confessions, and to convert.

Father Peydessus straightened himself up in his seat and looked straight at the crucifix before him. "All in thy service, Lord," he thought before he entered into a long prayer.

When he left his office, he knew what he had to do. He had four chaplains called in from among those he deemed most capable. The good fathers would soon arrive.

"Father Sempé, Father Duboé, Father Fourcade, and Father Dimbarre, I am sending you to Lourdes," announced Father Peydessus, who was not one for beating around the bush.

The four men nodded in assent. Humility and obedience were the hallmark of their commitment.

"You will need to take charge of the new shrine by next month," he told them.

He spoke in a clear and strong voice that left no room for opposition.

"I shall accompany you for the first weeks so that we may undertake the work that awaits you there together," Father Peydessus explained.

"The Lord will guide you in your responsibilities. He will show you what to do. The bishop, too, will help you. Father Sempé?"

"Yes," answered the oldest of the four.

"I am naming you head of this mission. Father Duboé shall be your right hand. I have only one recommendation for you, dear brethren," ended Father Peydessus on a suddenly softened tone. "Be good... Be saints!"

The meeting was over.

On the way out of the room, Fathers Sempé and Duboé looked at each other, smiling. So this was what the Lord was calling them to! Both were glad to be assigned to this new mission. They had already had the opportunity of going to Lourdes, and Father Sempé had even met Bernadette. They liked the place. The little seer moved them.

"We'll do great things over there, I hope," said Father Sempé.

"With God's help," piped in Father Duboé, who would become his faithful assistant for years.

On Thursday, May 17, 1866, when the four chaplains, accompanied by their superior, arrived in Lourdes, there was nothing, or rather next to nothing. Only a crypt was being built, near the grotto, to receive pilgrims. All the rest had yet to be done! The size of the task was immense, but the four Fathers of Garaison undertook it with faith and courage. When they were not hearing confessions, greeting pilgrims, or preaching at Mass, they would watch over the countless construction sites that would crop up over twenty years of faith, courage, and work in the service of Our Lady of Lourdes.

Amen.

AQUÉRO'S WISH

The First Mass at the Crypt, May 19, 1866

18 66 The bells of Lourdes' parochial church had just chimed five o'clock, and morning was just beginning to break in the east. Turning his back on the rising sun, a man in dark clothing, bearing a flickering lantern that barely lit his feet, walked quickly toward what still resembled a construction site. Above the Massabielle grotto, architect Hippolyte Durand, one of Viollet-le-Duc's talented students, had the audacity of building, overhanging the Gave, sheer foundations and a platform upon which to erect the chapel the Virgin had requested of Bernadette. It was a simple crypt to be completed during the following five years and intended to lead to the building of the upper basilica. The architect, confronted with grave technical difficulties, enjoyed the full support of Bishop Laurence, who wanted to accede to the apparition's wish. On that feast day, barricades, brackets, cranes, and tools had been set aside, but some of the materials, sand, and bricks were still stored here and there, revealing an interruption of a construction site rather than its completion.

The man, none other than the shrine's first sacristan, stepped around these heaps and made his way toward a large wooden double door that gave access to the level façade. Raising a huge wrought-iron key toward the lock, and aware that his gestures would inaugurate the first of the countless days that would be devoted to our Lady, he "officially" opened the door for the first time.

The sacristan, in fact, was coming to set up the crypt to be blessed. He also was preparing for the celebration of the first Mass over which Bishop Laurence himself would preside as bishop of Tarbes and Lourdes and in which the Fathers of Garaison, recently appointed to the upkeep of the shrine, would assist.

The man – who knew his job well, having long assisted the parish priests – was moved, proud of his responsibility, and aware that the eyes of a missionary community, of a bishop, of Catholics the world over, and of the Mother of God herself, would see to it that not the slightest incident would happen that might tarnish such a moment!

The sacristan entered the building. Dimly lit by his lamp, the many columns supporting its vault seemed to greet this first pilgrim's passage briefly before sinking into the cold darkness. The slightly oppressive silence was broken only by the creaking of his heavy leather soles on the smooth stone. Having reached the nave's threshold, he took out a wick, applied it to his lantern's flame, and then began the long ritual of lighting candles and luminaries. As he progressed in his task, the forest of columns, the capitals, the vaults, and their ribs slowly emerged from the night, their shadows dancing at the whim of the movements of the air that stirred dozens of tiny flames.

He proceeded in this manner through the crypt's five chapels, first giving life to the statue of Mary bearing her Son, then to Saint Peter, the first of the Church's leaders; Saint Joseph, who watched over Mary and her Son; and Saint John, who protected her. Seeing them illuminate from the darkness like this, the sacristan could nearly imagine that all these residents of the crypt were waiting for him.

It was getting late, and the time was fast approaching to set up for Mass, prepare the vestments, and ready the lectionary. The sacristan had duly accomplished all these duties when Bishop Laurence and the Fathers of Garaison arrived in silent procession through the long corridor. The religious took their places in their stalls. The moment was marked with the solemnity of an inauguration and of a consecration, but also with jubilation, with the inner joy of having accomplished a vital mission.

Bernadette was there in the prayerful crowd, but almost no one knew it. For a long time, she had been very discreet, and in April she had written a request to enter the novitiate. Bishop Laurence, who was in charge of approving such requests, had insisted on her presence for the first Mass in the crypt, since it was she who had communicated the Virgin's wish that would be accomplished that day. Bernadette entered among the rows of the Children of Mary, wearing their uniform so as to blend in without attracting attention.

During Mass on that day, many questions ran through the minds of the faithful. Emotion was intense, comprising fervor for many, doubts for a few. What would the site become? Won't it all fall into oblivion with time? Were not the plans for a future church too grand, too presumptuous? Did Mary truly desire such a display? What about those miracles, which had begun to be spoken of everywhere and which enthralled the crowds? What were the odds that they might, in fact, have been hoaxes? Many prayers ascended to the vaults and mingled in the wispy plumes of incense.

Once the crypt was again empty and the sacristan slowly snuffed out the candles, he knew that the celebration had dispelled the doubt in the hearts of men, just as his own breath had put out the flames.

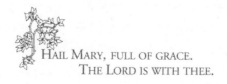

HAIL MARY, FULL OF GRACE.
THE LORD IS WITH THEE.

BERNADETTE IS BURIED AWAY

The Departure from Lourdes, July 8, 1866

1866 It was one o'clock on a summer's Sunday, and the windows were wide open at the novitiate of Saint-Gildard's convent in Nevers. Heated by the noonday sun, the air entering the hall blanketed its swelter upon the three hundred religious sisters crammed together on the polished wood benches. Dressed in their black habits and confined in their white wimples ending in two spotless bands on either side of the chin, the sisters felt the cruel effects of the summer temperatures, but their attention was undimmed despite the discomfort. Silent and curious, their gaze was fixed upon an unusual figure set in the middle of the hall. There was a tiny peasant girl, standing straight, intimidated and blushing under her white kerchief. Her traditional Bigorre costume was not ordinarily worn in Nevers, yet it seemed familiar to the sisters, for they had seen many photographs of the famous Bernadette before her arrival at the convent.

The young Lourdes girl had passed through the new residents' grille the previous evening. Despite her intense fatigue brought on by four days' journey by train, she had hardly been able to sleep that night. All the commotion of these last few days, all the pain of separation that she went through during her departure from Lourdes, jostled about in her mind. The farewell to parents, to friends, to Father Peyramale, to the grotto of Massabielle, to the beloved mountains. The infinite sadness at the moment of taking responsibility for a choice, as free as it was. The unfamiliarity of a trip marked by the rhythm of the steam engine's din. The visit to the immense Bordeaux with its august monuments, and that pond in which swam fish of such incredible colors, red, black, and white! Next to Bernadette, a swarm of children had crowded about the water to contemplate these masterpieces of strangeness. This gathering reminded the young Lourdes girl of all those people clustered before the hospice's cloister these past six years, hoping to catch a glimpse of her. Bernadette smiled at these harassed fish with fraternal sympathy, glad she was not, at least this time, the target of all the curious.

That day, though, in the novitiate hall, she was once again in the crosshairs. The superior general had asked her for an account of the apparitions for the community. Bernadette knew that this would be the last imposition on her in the matter. Then she would be able to slip into a much-desired and well-deserved silence. She therefore complied. Was she shy, nostalgic? She started her address in her dialect without noticing. Very soon she segued into French, a language with which she was now comfortable, all the more now that her story, which she had told more than a thousand times, had taken on the form of a recitation.

During the course of her recitation, Bernadette's voice turned mechanical. It was not that her encounters with the Lady of Massabielle had lost any of their luster. It was enough to see her make the sign of the cross as the Virgin had taught her to grasp the ineffable depth that the apparitions had given to her prayers. That day, however, she was too tired, too sad, too busy becoming familiar with that new place that smelled of wax polish and monastic austerity.

Reaching the point in her account of the birth of the miraculous spring, Bernadette spoke of the blackish water, specifying that she had to really force herself to drink it. With that, a dry voice rose in the novitiate hall – the superior's: "Sisters, *by this you can judge her lack of mortification.*"

The novice mistress followed up like an echo: "*You were not mortified, Bernadette.*"

"*Well, the water was dirty, Mother,*" Bernadette answered softly, feeling her heart sink.

She had just undergone one of those reprimands that the superiors of the time expertly used to crush all pride in the young religious. That would be neither her first nor her last vexation. The key words of nineteenth-century conventual pedagogy were *humility* and *discipline.* Faced with a story as exceptional as Bernadette's, the superiors, though they felt great affection for this naïve and frail young girl, had resolved to make no allowances. For the salvation of her soul…

At the end of her account, it was time for Bernadette to leave the Lourdes clothing that had been left her for the purposes of this very last story. She doffed her hot kerchief with relief. Then she excitedly put on the white crimped bonnet that was the distinctive sign of postulants in Nevers. She donned the uniform cape over her Bigorre dress. She was then fit to join the anonymous crowd of young religious sisters. Even if the news of her coming had arrived in town far ahead of her, the curious would have had much trouble picking her out among her companions. Her small size might have betrayed her – if people were informed. No one imagined that the "great" privileged recipient of the apparitions could have been so tiny!

"That?" exclaimed one of the religious sisters when Bernadette was pointed out to her.

"You're right, Miss: That's it!" Bernadette would answer friendlily.

Fortunately, Bernadette did not arrive alone. A friend from Lourdes, Léontine Mouret, was also postulating in Nevers, as was Marie Larrotés, a young girl from Bagnères. Together they gave free rein to their tears under the expressionless eyes of the older sisters, who told them that they recognized in this sorrow the sure sign of a good vocation.

The three girls paced the convent's garden, their eyes brimming with tears, when Bernadette came to a sudden halt with a slight cry of surprise. Before her stood a statue of the Virgin, gleaming white in the summer sun with a smiling countenance, her arms open in a welcoming gesture. Bernadette contemplated her for a long while, overcome with the feeling of a distant yet peaceful resemblance.

Here, at last, was a salutary link between Lourdes and her new life.

BLESSED ART THOU AMONG WOMEN,
AND BLESSED IS THE FRUIT OF THY WOMB, JESUS.

"*LET A CHAPEL BE BUILT*"

The Upper Basilica's Birth, December 13, 1868

1868 In the winter's north wind blowing between the Gave valley's hillsides, work on the Massabielle chapel was difficult. Sand had to be loaded in large shovelfuls into a creaking wheelbarrow, whose handles then had to be grasped in a quick forward thrust requiring the force of the entire body; the wheelbarrow then had to be extricated from the wet mud of the construction site without spilling its contents. Then someone had to throw himself into the demanding climb on the furrowed clay path that led to the level area above the grotto. New foundations were already emerging from the roof of the crypt that had been dedicated two years earlier. The distance covered was barely a hundred yards, but it was a steep incline; one could not stop at any cost if one was to avoid having to go all the way back down to gather sufficient momentum again.

The wheelbarrow rattled about and endlessly tried to escape its driver's iron fist by getting stuck in the deep ruts that had been forged in the path by heavy carts transporting building stones.

François Soubirous held on tight. His stubbornness, his unrelenting will, and his former miller's pride, rather than his constitution, overcame the cart and the steep rise. Once at the top, he was bathed in sweat despite the cold. He was short of breath, and his heart hammered away at his chest at an insistent pace, but he did not take the time to catch his breath. Emptying his load, he quickly went back down the hill. The sand heap had to be brought up to the upper level by nightfall, but the work evidently was not moving fast enough for the foreman.

Having arrived back down, François noticed a small gathering. Two or three religious – among whom he recognized Father Sempé, who was in charge of the site; Bishop Laurence, with whom he had already had dealings; the foreman, and a "civilian" whose arms were loaded with paper scrolls. When they noticed him, the foreman stretched out an arm in his direction, uttered one or two words, and turned back to his business. "What do they want this time?" grumbled François to himself, long accustomed to curious stares and the interest that he elicited.

Having reached the smiling group that awaited him, François let go of his empty wheelbarrow and straightened up, discreetly rubbing his lower back. Father Sempé drew near, took him gently by the arm, and pointed out the man with the paper scrolls.

"François, allow me to introduce Hippolyte Durand, the architect of the church you are building," said Father Sempé. "Mr. Durand, this is François Soubirous, our Bernadette's father."

François was quietly annoyed at the words "the church you are building," knowing full well that he had been hired out of kindness, at one and a half francs per day, to push a wheelbarrow, not to build a church. But he liked the rector and was quick to forgive him his excessive kindness.

"Mr. Durand, of course, knows your story and your family's," Father Sempé continued. "He also knows, since we have spoken of it, that you think that this church is out of proportion with the simple "chapel" that the Virgin requested. We were thinking that presenting the project to you might remove your doubts. Would you, with the foreman's permission, spend some time studying it? It might relieve your back, too," the good priest added with a knowing smile.

Why not? thought François, none too upset to take a break. *These people seem committed to doing good, and perhaps they're right.*

"I'm listening, Mr. Durand," François replied.

"Mr. Soubirous, it is indeed a chapel we're building," Durand explained. "A chapel in the proper sense of the term – a place dedicated to Mary, Mother of Jesus, who paid your daughter a visit. The recently built crypt was but the beginning of the project. See the enthusiasm this encounter has elicited: Hundreds, thousands of people have already come here, and millions more will follow in the centuries to come. Bishop Laurence is right: They will have to be fittingly welcomed, and we must provide now for the crowds to come. Here is my project."

The architect unrolled one of his drafting scrolls to reveal a drawing representing the façade of a narrow and tall church, with a slender bell tower and spire, all grace and distinction.

"The whole thing will reach a height of about one hundred yards above the Gave, but less than seventy-five yards above the entrance portico. The nave and chancel will measure fifty-six yards, and the greatest width will be twenty-two yards. The interior height, from ground to vault, will be twenty yards. So you see, we are far from a cathedral's dimensions. So much for figures."

Durand continued: "But that is not the main point. What will correspond, I am sure, to the Virgin's request communicated through your daughter are the symbols that this church will offer to pilgrims on a search for visible signs. The chancel will be located directly above the very spot of the apparitions, for the grotto lies right underneath. This will add to the fervor of the celebrations, the emotion of knowing that the Virgin stood there, right underneath, and that she has remained there, though she cannot be seen.

"All around the nave we shall set up small chapels, which may perhaps match your idea; each one will be outfitted with an altar allowing the many pilgrim priests to say their Masses there. This, then, fulfills Mary's wish: to build a chapel so that many may come."

The architect's enthusiasm was contagious: François' interest was aroused, and he soon understood that this church was absolutely necessary. He willingly listened to the detailed presentation of Mr. Durand, who was obviously enthusiastic about his subject.

François knew, in the depths of his heart, that the intimate relationship his daughter had with *Aquéro* no longer belonged to Bernadette alone. Now it must rather be given to all of humanity.

HOLY MARY, MOTHER OF GOD,

A THOUSAND COLORS IN THE SKY

The Banner Procession, October 6, 1872

18
72

What was happening? Since dawn that morning, a strange fervor had taken over the town of Lourdes – a phenomenon unseen since the shrine's creation a few years before, and even since the first trains arrived in town in 1866.

Since even before the first light of day, the candles of thirty-two altars improvised around the unfinished basilica – it was only one year old, and its spire was unfinished – had begun to gleam on the mountainside. Chants rose, and Masses were celebrated in the Pyrenees' purple shadows. There were neither chimes nor bells, since the basilica had not yet been endowed with any. There was not even a clock to count the hours or prayer beads; only the psalms of the faithful and of the fifty thousand pilgrims who arrived on that evening, right on time. When, at about eight o'clock, the dawn's first rays finally broke over the peaks of the pass, the spectacle was magnificent: At the bottom, the Gave rolled and took with it the deluge of the evening's rains; above, on top of the steep cliff, stood the white walls of the Immaculate Conception, sparkling in the rising sun; and, in front of the esplanade, an immense deep green meadow, resplendent with its dewy grass, stretched out. With neither ramp, belvedere, nor accommodations, Lourdes was home to only about five thousand residents – a small town. Yet, in its mountain's folds, a rock crevice attracted a crowd that swelled with every hour as the day went by – the Massabielle grotto.

About noon, the sun, now bleak and chilly, was drying the muddy paths and the meadow's grass. A movement began throughout the shrine. The crowd of fifty thousand pilgrims converged toward the town and gathered around the parish church. There was a crush for over an hour and a half. What was happening? At two o'clock, all was ready. In an explosion of colors, two hundred fifty-two banners rose to heaven all around the space in front of the church. Each one represented a diocese of France, a town, a parish... Big and colorful, they bore the arms of their respective towns and their provinces' titular virgins on silk or velvet. Madonnas in needlepoint or painted right onto the material, silver cloth with woven roses, motifs borrowed from Flemish artists, crude designs of local coats of arms, tapestries both rough and fine surged forward, propelled by the same spirit. The spectacle was arresting. Reporters sent by the great national newspapers gaped at the sight. They had never witnessed such an event.

Once the procession began, it streamed for an hour down the town's only street and over the old bridge crossing the Gave toward the esplanade. Banners went by in successive waves, accompanied by the chants' rising surge. Fervor kept increasing – a sprightly, simple fervor, fed by each region's peculiar jargon and accent. There stood the banner of Lille, held at arm's length by six strapping lads in the northern tradition of popular church fairs and processions of giants. There, the sea virgins of Brittany, the delicate Madonnas of Burgundy, the Marys of the Provençal scrubland billowed in the wind. At the head of the procession, the velvet banners of Alsace and the Moselle stood out, veiled in black crepe as a sign of national mourning, since the two provinces had been granted to Germany in 1871 after Napoleon III's defeat. Finally, the procession emptied into the meadow. The banners gathered around the high platform bedecked with garlands and streamers, where the bishop of Tarbes intoned his blessing. When the archbishop of Auch took the floor, there was silence. In the wind, in which only the flags fluttered, he celebrated in an historical speech this first *manifestation of France's Faith and Hope in Our Lady of Lourdes.*

His words echoed in the pilgrims' hearts, which had been struck with a certain renewal of faith. For although in these latter years of the nineteenth century the notion of "hope" caused many to snicker – especially intellectuals, politicians, and scientists – for twenty-odd years now the need for a horizon beyond that proposed by the factories had emerged among the people. Mary's successive apparitions – to Catherine Labouré in Paris in 1830, then to the two little shepherds in La Salette in 1846, and lastly to Bernadette in Lourdes – gave birth to a new form of piety, a faith simpler than that preached by the clerical hierarchy – a rejuvenated, immediate faith, modeled after the faith cultivated by these children seers, these humble and innocent souls to whom the Virgin spoke. The people saw the sign of a renewed hope in it. Everywhere in France, small local pilgrimages organized spontaneously, but none had reached the national level yet.

Some religious, such as the Augustinians of the Assumption, noticed the emergence of this new movement of fervor and sought ways of giving it a fuller expression. In 1871, events rushed forward: While France was being vanquished by Germany and losing its eastern provinces, the Virgin appeared again in Pontmain, near Laval. At the same time, a project for a shrine dedicated to the Sacred Heart was proposed in Paris; and in Lyons, the Basilica of Our Lady of Fourvière rose from the ground. In January 1872, two Assumptionists decided to found the Association of Our Lady of Salvation to encourage the organization of national pilgrimages. The first took place the following August 22 in La Salette, but it gathered only five hundred pilgrims for three hundred seventy-five priests. They took the opportunity to establish the General

Council of Pilgrimages, but it remained to set up a real project, a cere-mony that would give full sway to popular devotion.

On this point, a little parish priest from Beaune, Father Victor Chocarne, had his own idea: to organize a pilgrimage representing all the dioceses of France, and to an exceptional place – Lourdes. He immedi-ately set to work on it with the assistance of a committee of ladies, among whom Mrs. de Blique, who gave of herself unstintingly to organ-izing, sending close to four hundred thousand invitation letters all throughout France. Two months later, on October 6, 1872, to everyone's surprise, fifty thousand pilgrims answered the call.

This "banner pilgrimage" ushered in the era of the great pilgrimages. Father Chocarne's report to Rome permitted the creation of a "pilgrimage month" every summer, with the pope's permission. A year later, the first "national pilgrimage" to Lourdes began. The banner pilgrimage was the ancestor of all the others, the one that allowed the shrine in Lourdes to become what it is today. Since 1872, its two hundred fifty-two banners have adorned the vaults and walls of the Basilica of the Immaculate Conception, providing visible signs of an immense movement of faith of which Lourdes was the beating heart.

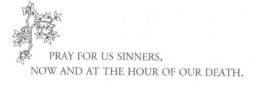

PRAY FOR US SINNERS,
NOW AND AT THE HOUR OF OUR DEATH.

THIRTEEN YEARS OF INTRANSIGENCE

Bernadette at the Convent of Nevers, November 5, 1873

1873 Mother Marie-Thérèse Vauzou leaned over Bernadette's face, which lay exhausted and so pale against the stark white pillow.

"Sister Marie-Bernard, I ask you not to take ill what I am about to announce to you," Mother said. "From today on, you are no longer in charge of the infirmary. How can one reconcile the employment of a perpetual patient with that of infirmarian? Sister Gabriel will replace you. You can always assist her within the limits of your feeble strength."

Bernadette looked at the novice mistress, seeking out in vain the slightest trace of solicitude in her gaze. How often had she thus begged alms of kindness over the seven years she had been at Saint-Gildard? It was comfort she had never been granted. Mother Marie-Thérèse Vauzou and Mother Joséphine Imbert, the superior general, had agreed to treat this illustrious young religious without any special regard to spare her from pride, the greatest of sins.

Sister Marie-Bernard stifled a sigh, forced herself to smile, and wordlessly acquiesced. Still, she felt capably efficient in her employment as infirmarian. She knew how to dose the medicines, prepare poultices, and dress wounds delicately. Above all, she knew how to comfort the sick sisters, to elicit light laughter that spread from bed to bed as so many challenges to fever and suffering. Perhaps her example as a chronically ill patient helped the infirmary's inmates to accept more readily their own temporary ills. Is a fragile nurse's perpetual smile not the best tonic?

And so, on that November 5, 1873, Bernadette, now twenty-nine, was relegated to the role of simple assistant infirmarian. True, that of assistant sacristan would soon be added. Yet she sadly thought of her novitiate mates, now professed nuns like herself, who had swarmed all over France to put their talents at the service of the poor, the children, or the sick. Alone to remain within the motherhouse walls, Bernadette was confined to the position of "good for nothing," to quote the very words of Mother Joséphine Imbert.

"My Lord, she is good for nothing," she had told Bishop Forcade of Nevers, who had come to preside over the sisters' ceremony of departure to their assignments.

"Well then, Sister Marie-Bernard, I give you the employment of prayer," answered the bishop.

In his smile, at least, Bernadette had read a great kindness.

That was a mission to which Bernadette devoted herself wholeheartedly. Whether healthy or bedridden in her "white chapel" – her sick bed, outfitted with white curtains – the young religious led a life of prayer. Mother Vauzou could see it and approved from the depths of her being. But there was too much that separated her from Bernadette for her truly to appreciate her. First of all, there was the humble origins of the little Lourdes girl, this "shepherdess" whose education gave so much trouble to the sisters. In her big black habit, under her stiff wimple, Sister Marie-Bernard had stayed as rustic as the little Bernadette who, dressed in her clogs, would run in the meadows of Lourdes. Mother Marie-Thérèse Vauzou could not help but harbor a preference for a more elitist representation of the religious. In the presence of chosen witnesses, she expressed her surprise at heaven's choices.

"If the Holy Virgin wished to appear somewhere on earth," she wondered aloud, *"why would she choose a crude and illiterate peasant girl instead of a virtuous and well-educated religious?"*

The apparitions of Lourdes! That was the inscrutable mystery on which Mother Vauzou's reason stumbled. A competent novice mistress recognized for her great human qualities and her natural authority, Mother Vauzou had been elected superior general of the congregation by plebiscite in 1881. She was far from being a heartless woman; she simply was a woman with doubts. Her solid faith accepted the mysteries of the Catholic faith, especially those regarding Jesus Christ, but the Marian apparitions left her skeptical. She resisted the movement of fervor that had come about in Bernadette's wake. So long as she was superior general, from 1881 to 1899, she would always oppose the introduction of the dead Bernadette's cause for beatification in Rome. Even after she was replaced, the aged religious would tell her successor, *"Wait till I'm dead for that."*

That was the source of her strictness toward Bernadette. The young religious, for her part, had given up on garnering her superior's sympathy. Their incompatibility of character was a secret wound that she had resigned herself to bear for ever. It had been quite some time since she had stopped confiding her joys and sorrows in the novice mistress, and a long time since she began opening up only to simple and guileless sisters like herself. This reserve did not help their relationship, for Mother Vauzou liked transparency, "openness of soul," among novices and young professed nuns. Bernadette's interior life remained a troubling secret, a place of silence from which she knew she was excluded. Did Bernadette not bear in her soul, inaccessible to all, a number of revelations the Virgin made to her over the course of her apparitions? *"They concern only me,"* the young religious would repeat obstinately whenever an attempt was made to know more.

Inflexible personality, very touchy, Mother Vauzou wrote in her confidential files, annoyed that Sister Marie-Bernard remained so aloof. She reproached her for drawing her veil too far over her face, as if seeking to hide from sight, to disappear in that black cloth chapel! And although the novice mistress was also capable of laudatory remarks on Bernadette's piety, modesty, and sense of service, she concluded in her notes that *she's an ordinary religious,* with a shrug that was discernible even in her pen.

Yet throughout the thirteen years of common life, down to Bernadette's painful death throes in April 1879, the novice mistress's sentiments were too complex to be taxed with gratuitous harshness or injustice. These last words uttered by Mother Vauzou at the hour of her own death are proof: *"Our Lady of Lourdes, protect my agony…"*

Amen.

OUR LADY OF SORROWS

Portrait of Marie Saint-Frai, April 6, 1874

1874 The sun inundated the convent infirmary of Saint-Gildard in Nevers. Distracted from her service to the sick for a moment, the infirmarian's frail silhouette drew near to the window and started to dream of her native land. One must not think about it. Sister Marie-Bernard knew that she would never again see her native Bigorre. By her own admission, she would have gladly returned to the grotto. Oh, if only she could become a bird to fly over the area around Massabielle... Since that was not possible, she preferred to live her hidden life as a religious, a servant, an infirmarian, very far from the town where her celebrity had kept her from living in peace.

Bernadette thought of the pealing bells on the feast of the Resurrection, joyfully stirring the Pyrenees sky on that Easter Monday 1874, and she returned to her business going to and fro among the rows of beds. She came to the bed of Mother Anne-Marie Lescure, who was blind and so old that she was beyond age. Under the lay clothes that her state compelled her to wear, a horrific wound was slowly killing her. Bernadette was the only one to be able to bear its sight serenely. Her soft and expert little hands busied themselves about the dressing. In the twinkling of an eye, the wound was washed and dressed anew. Bernadette had not stopped smiling and speaking to Mother Anne-Marie in the tone of voice one uses with a beloved grandmother. There was also infinite respect added to it: The suffering old religious must be cared for "*as though she were the Good Lord*," Bernadette told her companions.

At the same moment, in that faraway town of Lourdes whose memory the infirmarian avoided, another religious was thinking of her. Marie Saint-Frai, now Mother Marie de Saint-Jean-Baptiste, had founded the congregation of the Daughters of Our Lady of Sorrows in 1860. They devoted themselves to the care of the sick, the poor, and the elderly. The shelter she created in Tarbes, in her own family house, was a place of welcome to all wretchedness. Bernadette's devotedness at Saint-Gildard, her calm when confronted with the gravest diseases, her absolute availability were qualities that the Daughters of Our Lady of Sorrows practiced all day long.

On Easter Monday 1874, the bishop of Tarbes and Lourdes, smiling broadly, stood before Marie Saint-Frai and her sisters. Between them there was a large stone, the cause of a joy shared by Father Ribes, co-founder of the congregation, Mother Marie de Saint-Jean-Baptiste's friend and spiritual director, who was present at the ceremony. On that occasion, Bishop Langénieux blessed the first stone of an immense building, Our Lady of Sorrows Hospital, which was destined to receive hundreds of patients. Indeed, already at that time and from then on, the pilgrimages brought to Lourdes hordes of distressed people. To contribute to their alleviation, the religious of Our Lady of Sorrows had already established their quarters in town, first in a barn and later in a chalet. But such a venue was laughably small when compared to the throng of so many sick people at the grotto!

With this stone's blessing, Mother Marie de Saint-Jean-Baptiste's dream finally rested on larger foundations. She thought of Bernadette with emotion. Like everybody else there, she knew the smallest detail of the seer's life at the time of the apparitions. Like everybody else, she did not know much of her present life except that Bernadette, despite her weak health, devoted herself without respite to the care of the sick. Today, Marie Saint-Frai felt close to the infirmarian of Nevers!

Four years later, in 1878, the immense hospital had risen from the ground. During the national pilgrimage that summer, it opened its barely finished halls to three hundred patients. For lack of space, since construction was still ongoing, the pilgrims even slept in the chapel! The hospital's high walls and its chapel's Romanesque rose window were now part of Lourdes' landscape.

Marie Saint-Frai died on April 9, 1894, twenty years after the solemn blessing of the hospital's first stone. But the Daughters of Our Lady of Sorrows continued their foundress's work. Year after year, they entrusted their patients to Our Lady of Sorrows, who suffered, who stood at the foot of the cross, who beheld her Son, dead on her knees. Since 1878, how many pilgrims, before going to Massabielle, had prayed before the Pietà adorning the hospital chapel? This Mary, whose heart was forged by distress and hope, could understand all wretchedness, receive all doubt, comfort all despair. Our Lady of Sorrows Hospital, so well named, led its patients from sorrow to trust.

Down through the years, thanks to the gifts of grateful patients, the hospital grew to meet increasing demands. It would welcome up to seven hundred patients at a time! But, in 1997, the truth had to be faced: the hundred-and-twenty-year-old structures were no longer up to code. Should the institution, then better known under the name of Marie Saint-Frai Welcoming Center in honor of its foundress, be closed? It was out of the question. Instead, a new ceremony, recalling that of 1874, took place when Bishop Sahuquet blessed the first stone of the future building. Completely renovated by 1998, the hospital welcomed four hundred patients who make use of the most modern equipment for the handicapped. But the same welcome awaited them, the same availability, the same care. For more than a hundred and fifty years now, Bernadette's torch of hospitality and heritage of kindness have been handed down without wavering.

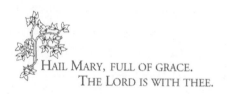

HAIL MARY, FULL OF GRACE.
THE LORD IS WITH THEE.

THE VIRGIN OF FLANDERS

Pierre de Rudder, Eighth Miraculous Healing, April 7, 1875

1875 On a beautiful April day, Pierre de Rudder, leaning on his two crutches, approached the Château of Jabbeke with great difficulty. The former squire, who believed only in science, had twice refused to allow his disabled worker to go on a pilgrimage to Oostacker, near Ghent. Today, however, Pierre hoped to convince the new viscount of Bus to let him go. Nothing would keep him from going to pray at the exact replica of the grotto of Massabielle, which devout Belgian Catholics had just built in eastern Flanders. Who knows? A miracle is always possible. Gangrenous wounds and the absolute necessity of never setting his diseased foot on the ground had been Pierre's daily lot since his accident.

It happened seven years earlier. Listening only to his kind heart, he was helping a couple of woodsmen to drag back on the road one of the trees that had accidentally fallen into a neighboring field. As Pierre was busying himself with the branches of a bush that was interfering with their work, the raised tree fell back on him, crushing his left leg in one fell swoop. The result was an open fracture of both leg bones, the tibia and the fibula. No cast allowed the fragments to heal. On the contrary, the harm only worsened: The infected sores threatened gangrene. The powerless doctors proposed amputation. Pierre refused, preferring to remain bedridden for a whole year at the cost of atrocious pains. Although he could walk by leaning upon his two crutches, he had to wash his sores several times a day and take care never to bump his leg if he was to avoid terrible suffering.

Pierre knocked at the château's door. A servant girl came to open it for him. When he went into the parlor, he immediately noticed the benevolent smile of an engaging young lady, the future viscountess of Bus. Throughout the conversation, she took an interest in him, going so far as to ask him to undo the bandages on his legs so that she could take a look at the damage for herself. The viscount smiled slightly as he saw his fiancée repress a gesture of disgust at the odor of his workman's sores.

"It's agreed, Pierre," the future viscountess said. "As a reward for your good and loyal services to the castle, I grant you what my uncle, who believed only in medicine, denied you: You may go to Oostacker. May God be with you."

Two days later, a hopeful Pierre went on his way. Nothing scared him – not the trying trip nor the curious and rude stares of the people around him. To the signalman who, while helping him get into the car, recommended that he stay at home, he answered: "*Others have been healed at Oostacker. Why couldn't I?*" He kindly smiled at the driver of the Ghent-Oostacker omnibus who, in helping him down, exclaimed at the sight of his broken leg bending in a strange way: "*Say, here's one who is losing his leg!*" It was true, though, that the lower part of his leg sometimes took on angles that did not fail to puzzle.

At the end of all these trials, Pierre was finally at the blessed grotto for which he had been pining with all his heart for the past seven years. Pierre's hope was at its height. He prayerfully turned to the Virgin: "Our Lady of Lourdes, forgive me all my sins. Grant me the grace of being able to work. Help me to earn a living and no longer to depend upon charity. Restore my honor and my dignity to me." Scarcely had he finished his prayer that, forgetting the crutches he had never let go of for the past seven years, he got up as though outside of himself. The incredulous crowd saw him go toward and kneel before the replica of the statue of Lourdes. Suddenly, he regained his senses. *What is going on? Where am I?* Almost immediately, without responding to the solicitations of his wife who was also wondering what was going on, he once again got up to walk around the grotto. Two days later, faithful to his promise, Pierre got back to work at the castle, handling spade and rake. The evening before, the doctors were able to observe that the bones had knit within a few minutes without the leg presenting any deformation. Smooth at the point of the fracture, it looked like a child's leg.

Confronted with such a prodigy, several doctors began to believe: One acknowledged that *the miracle of Pierre de Rudder has opened his eyes;* another that *what doctors cannot do, Mary can.* These conversions were to continue after Pierre's death, over twenty years later. In fact, fourteen months after his death, on May 24, 1899, his body was exhumed for the examination of his legs. This was the first autopsy of a miracle. The radiographs – invented just four years before – revealed the reality of the lesion and its extraordinary union. On October 21, 1901, a medical report affirmed that "*the bony union, revealed in the autopsy, cannot have occurred by natural means. The signatories therefore think that the fact must be considered as supernatural and miraculous.*" To this day, photos of the bones that can be seen in the church of Oostacker bear witness to the calvary that was Pierre de Rudder's life.

Officially recognized as the eighth miracle of Our Lady of Lourdes by the bishop of Bruges on July 25, 1908, Pierre de Rudder was a simple and honest man, always ready to pray for his fellow men. He was rarely ever seen without a rosary in his hands. After traveling on pilgrimage to Lourdes on May 9, 1879, he went on pilgrimage to Oostacker on his healed legs about four hundred times.

Blessed art thou among women,
and blessed is the fruit of thy womb, Jesus.

THE CROWNING OF THE VIRGIN

Portrait of Bishop Jourdan, February 1, 1876

1876 Bishop César Victor Jourdan, visibly feverish, entered his office with a letter bearing the coat of arms of the Holy See in his hands and unfolded the thick ivory paper. A few moments later, in a mild state of shock, Bishop Jourdan let the envelope slip from his fingers. Pope Pius IX had just given him his full and complete authorization to go ahead with the crowning of Our Lady of Lourdes. The bishop of Tarbes remembered the day when, just four months before, he had written to Rome. It was always intimidating, even for a bishop, to write to the Pope. It was even more staggering to receive a positive answer, especially so quickly.

Emotion was soon replaced with a kind of panic: Work on the Basilica of the Immaculate Conception was in its last phase, but was not quite finished. As for the statue of the Virgin itself, it existed only in the mind of the bishop and of the solicited artists. Bishop Jourdan ran out of his office to the surprise of his personal secretary and hastily announced to him that the papal brief received just a few moments before had authorized the crowning. Without a moment's delay, he asked his secretary to make urgent appointments with Hippolyte Durand, the architect; Cabuchet and Raffl, the sculptors; and the

Parisian goldsmith Mellerio. Indeed, the bishop was not thinking of one Virgin, but two. He wished to crown the big Virgin on the exterior, on the esplanade, and another one inside the basilica upon the high altar. The two men prepared to face the excellent but urgent news from Rome.

On June 3, 1876, Bishop Jourdan was dismayed. Raffl had only been able to create sketches and rough drafts. The crowning was to take place within the month, but the esplanade's sculpture was still not ready. Cabuchet was not much further along but proposed to offer a plaster model for the basilica. It would not be the finished product, but it would be close enough. Mellerio was the only one to promise to meet the deadline. In his workshop, goldsmiths were working on two crowns, one of gilded bronze for the great Virgin and the other made of gold and diamonds for the basilica. The artist was a passionate admirer of Enguerrand Quarton, that fifteenth-century painter who created the masterly reredos of the crowning of the Virgin of the Villeneuve-lès-Avignon church. Mellerio was particularly moved by this commission and did not shrink from extending the stone-setting work deep into the night.

Faced with Bishop Jourdan's dejection, his hands clenched with fatigue and anxiety on his desk's leather blotter, the secretary dared to propose an idea: One of the Fathers of Garaison had some talent in sculpture, and perhaps he could help them resolve the situation. Bishop Jourdan's eyes brightened a little; indeed, he had seen creations by Father Pibou, the kindly shrine chaplain. Be that as it may – with courage and faith, he must urgently create a representation of Our Lady.

By July 3, 1876, Bishop Jourdan no longer felt the effects of fatigue biting at his muscles. He was in the midst of the last day of an unusual triduum. On Saturday, July 1, the various prelates in attendance blessed the "Gregorian water" reserved for the blessing of churches and altars, made up of salt (symbolic of health, fertility, and preservation), ash (a sign of humility), and wine (a symbol of spiritual abundance and joy). On the next day – Sunday, July 2, the feast of the Visitation – Cardinal

Guibert, archbishop of Paris, consecrated the Basilica of the Immaculate Conception in the name of Pope Pius IX and in the presence of three thousand priests.

That Monday morning, the sun was soaking the esplanade at the foot of the basilica. The preaching of Bishop Pie of Poitiers had set the congregation ablaze: "*The crowning of Mary Immaculate, which is about to occur just now on this Pyrenees plateau, will resound through all ages and up to the heights of heaven as one of the most magnificent echoes of the words that were sung, nearly nineteen centuries ago, on the mountain of Judah,*" Bishop Pie had proclaimed.

Bishop Jourdan could not help but tremble at his words. For months, he had known the importance of this event and had desired it with all the ardor of his soul, yet he could not keep his heart from beating like a drum. When Bishop Meglia, apostolic nuncio to France, who was delegated by the Pope to "*give to all of France a great and precious token of his paternal care,*" started climbing the steps of the great wooden scaffolding erected behind the Virgin, the bishop of Tarbes felt that his heart was about to burst. It was finally the moment when Mary would be revealed to the world just as God had wished her to be, as an ocean of kindness and queen of heaven. But her pure, white forehead had barely been adorned with the bronze crown than the procession of bishops started moving again to present the golden crown to the grotto and to offer it symbolically to Our Lady of Lourdes at the very spot of her apparitions. Going up the hairpin turns, the procession entered the basilica and adorned the second Virgin with the royal diadem.

For Bishop Jourdan, this unusual celebration's five hours only seemed like a few moments. In the sacristy, where the bishops were laying down their vestments, he exchanged a few words with the nuncio and told him how the wonderful gift received from Rome had caused the shrine to put in several wonderful but exhausting weeks of work in an effort to prepare itself to respond to the gift as worthily as possible. He also disclosed his regret that the sculptures were only rough drafts and shared with the nuncio his feeling of guilt regarding the "provisional" crowning that had just taken place. In the now-deserted sacristy, the nuncio fraternally touched his shoulder and softly told him that, on the contrary, he found it marvelous that a simple chaplain had worked with such courage to offer the crowds such a celebration. After a short moment of silence, he whispered to him, with a smile, that the Virgin herself would surely not be upset that a humble man contributed to her representation, if only to remind men to be far more attached to the mystery than to its images.

HOLY MARY, MOTHER OF GOD,

IN THE POPE'S PRIVATE ORATORY

*Pope Pius IX and Bernadette Soubirous' Letter,
December 19, 1876*

1876 Pope Pius IX returned to his rooms. He had just left the French bishops on their *ad limina* visits and held in his hand the mail that Bishop de Ladoue of Nevers had delivered to him – a letter from little Bernadette of Lourdes. He was eager to read it, even though the bishop had already indicated its content to him. Between this young lady and him, there was more than a common understanding: There was, entirely lived out, the mystery of Mary. He wished to read her letter in his private oratory, where he had placed the superb cloisonné enamel picture portraying the March 25 apparition to Bernadette, presented to him by Bishop Langénieux of Tarbes in 1874. Crossing a drawing room, he stopped for a moment before a terra cotta reproduction of the grotto that Mr. Hispa, of Toulouse, had sent him. That, he thought, was where she confirmed to Bernadette the dogma of the Immaculate Conception that he had promulgated a few years before.

Pope Pius IX pushed his oratory door open, genuflected before the Blessed Sacrament, then knelt before the apparition's representation. He particularly liked this enamel whose undeniable aesthetic value was now invested for him with a great spiritual value – as if the Virgin, through this work of art, had made herself available to his prayer. He repeated it once again to the French bishops, speaking of Lourdes to them: *"If my soul is despondent, if I feel that God is deaf to our voice, I raise my eyes toward the Immaculate, she will pray with us, she will pray for us."*

He pulled out of his wide sash the letter that the bishop gave him, unsealed it, and began reading. *Most Holy Father, I would never have dared pick up my pen to write to Your Holiness, poor little sister than I am...* Poor little sister... There are at least two of them, he thought, to be infinitely richer than he – Catherine Labouré and she. Both received the message of the Immaculate Conception – one of them in a prefiguration of the dogma, the other, so to speak, to confirm its revealed truth. From the miraculous medal and the prayer (*"O Mary conceived without sin, pray for us to have recourse to thee"*) to the pronouncement made to Bernadette (*"I am the Immaculate Conception"*), it was the Virgin herself who had fully revealed her mystery through the humblest voices of the Church. He, too, simple vicar of Christ, felt the supernatural presence at the moment of the dogma's promulgation in the Vatican. He remembered with what difficulty his voice rose above the noise of the immense multitude that had thronged Saint Peter's to hear him. Suddenly, an immense and divine strength had overtaken him. God had lent strength to his voice so that all might hear and receive the Marian dogma. This proclaimed utterance had overpowered him; the mystery of Mary had inhabited and transfigured him for ever.

The Pope thanked the Lord for having preserved two pure hearts in this century of sorrows in which the spirit of the Enlightenment had obscured the truth and in which the Church was under attack from all sides, assaulted by both weapons and modern theories.

In this century's darkness, as in the day of darkness of Christ's death, two women had received the grace of an apparition. Like the two Marys at the tomb, Catherine and Bernadette had been dazzled by the shining light of Truth and had received the commission of offering it to the world.

The Pope remembered the letters he had received from his brother bishops after the encyclical *Ubi Primum* requesting their opinion on the manner of defining the Immaculate Conception. They had comforted him in the Church's fidelity to the Word of God: The path to conversion is the Immaculate Conception, the promise that sin will not prevail over the world. Like the empty tomb showing Christ's resurrection and the victory of good over evil, the Virgin's apparitions recalled, in a disturbed century, that through grace and a singular favor, God almighty had preserved Mary, from the first instant of her conception, from all stain of original sin. She is the land of Galilee to which all Christians can turn to make the light triumph. She is the one who can lead them to her Son while preserving them from snares. The Church must pray to her according to the message given to Catherine Labouré; she must announce her according to the request made to Bernadette Soubirous. The millions of miraculous medals distributed in the world, just as the millions of pilgrims coming to Lourdes seeking the grace of faith, were a sign of the renewal possible within the Church. Missionary expansion as well as the young Churches of Australia, of Canada, and of the United States were full of promise. The action of laymen, which the sovereign pontiff had been encouraging since 1866 to defend the Catholic faith, also seemed to be bearing fruit.

Yes, as Bernadette wrote, he was, despite his doubts, certain that *this good Mother will take pity on her children, and that she will once again graciously set her foot on the head of the cursed serpent, and thus put an end to the Church's cruel trials and to the sorrows of her August and beloved Pontiff.*

Pope Pius IX set the letter on his prie-dieu. His face was moved by the contagious simplicity of Bernadette's faith. He contemplated the figure of the Virgin and prayed to her that she might intercede before her Son in favor of the young religious to whom he had very gladly granted the blessing requested by the bishop of Nevers.

PRAY FOR US SINNERS,
NOW AND AT THE HOUR OF OUR DEATH.

THE *PÈLERIN*

The Birth of Le Pèlerin Magazine,
January 3, 1877

18
77
The mission of Pèlerin *is to take the lead and to proceed with a certain boldness like the poor who have nothing to fear because they have nothing to lose. The whole world is our field of action because the whole world is Christ's field of action. Human politics alone is forbidden to it; he knows of only one politics: to know, love, and serve God, and through this means to attain eternal life.*

"Well! They're certainly not pulling their punches! It's no longer a pious weekly, it's a political newspaper!"

In his dining room, Dr. Émile Bellevue puffed on his pipe while leafing through the latest issue of *Pèlerin*. He knew that the Assumptionist weekly needed a makeover, but he did not have this change of tone in mind. He wondered what his father's friend, Father Emmanuel d'Alzon – the congregation's founder, whom he often used to meet in Nîmes when he was that diocese's vicar-general – must think of this. The doctor had a taste for action, but he preferred in-depth texts to the powerful articles of this new and improved *Pèlerin*.

"What did you say, my dear?"

His wife walked into the room, still covered in her kitchen apron, wearing her hair hastily tied up in a bun and beaming with a smile. Their son should arrive any minute to introduce to them the one who was to become Mrs. Ernest Bellevue. The doctor and his wife were intrigued. Their son, who had just been admitted to the École Polytechnique, was immersed in the dominant ideas of his day. Like the parliament, which had tilted to the left the year before, he had embraced the theses of a political program hostile to the Church – an end to religious instruction at school, expulsion of the great congregations, and an end to the Concordat. Although he was an anti-clerical left-winger, he was enamored with a charming young lady, the neighborhood pharmacist's daughter, who, for her part, had remained very much attached to religion. The two lovebirds hoped this difference would not cloud their radiant idyll and their relations with their parents, who had remained practicing Catholics.

Émile Bellevue was about to answer his wife when the front door bell rang to announce the children's arrival. He got up to greet them.

"Hello Papa, hello Mama," their son greeted them. "May I introduce Émilie who, I hope, will become my wife?"

"Welcome, young lady, please feel at home here," Dr. Bellevue said. "I am delighted that my son has announced this good news. How is your father?"

Mrs. Bellevue took advantage of the developing conversation to go back to the kitchen, take off her apron, tie up her bun again, and bring out glasses and a bottle of wine to celebrate this joyful occasion.

"Ah! You have bought this bad publication," Ernest observed as he noticed the copy of the *Pèlerin*. "No offense, dear parents, but it isn't the virulence of your friends' words that will hold back the march of progress. With the working class, your Church is losing the bulk of its parishioners. It is high time for us to remove from your priests the last privileges they enjoy. They are a danger to our society and to man in general."

"Actually, Ernest, I was just telling your mother that I thought the new and improved *Pèlerin*'s editorial a little virulent," Dr. Bellevue replied. "But after hearing your words, I find that it's fair enough after all. Father Vincent de Paul Bailly will have much grist for his polemical mill if your words are so lacking in nuance."

Émilie, visibly somewhat bothered by her fiancé's attitude, intervened with a broad smile and an ever-so-slightly mundane voice.

"Do you know Father Vincent de Paul? I have met him several times on the national pilgrimage organized by the Assumptionists," Émilie said. "I was in the second one, in Lourdes, in 1873. It was in fact then that the *Pèlerin* was founded, I believe, but by another priest who was in charge of the pilgrimage."

"Yes, by Father François Picard," the doctor said in response. "He is the one in charge of pilgrimages. We owe the Lourdes pilgrimage to him, but also many other pious public events in all of France and even in Rome. That is why he had founded the *Pèlerin*, to organize and promote all these events. But of course, confronted with the permanent attacks of your fiancé's friends, the tone evidently must change. And it is Father Vincent de Paul who has undertaken the task. And even though he was only admitted to the École Polytechnique, I believe he is very talented. At any rate, he writes very well!"

"He will need more than pretty phrases to bring the workers back to the Church," his son interjected. "They know where their interests lie."

"You are right. But Father Vincent de Paul's insight consists precisely in using other means of communication," Dr. Bellevue explained. "Look through the paper: it has doubled in volume, changed format, its tone is combative and humorous, nearly irreverent. Throw in the illustrations, the caricatures… The *Pèlerin* has truly become a popular paper and I believe that many will be won back. Especially since the price has not changed, six francs per year! And besides – an argument that will leave you cold – it is not impossible that they will find their interest in salvation. After all, grace can also play a role."

Mrs. Bellevue saw an occasion to break up the discussion. "Come on, gentlemen! We're not here to speak of politics or religion, but of human love," she said. "Émilie, welcome to the family."

The two couples raised their glasses to the wedding that was taking shape and the conversation turned to all these promises of future happiness, leaving aside the issue of the *Pèlerin* – which, from the dining room table where they had left it, nearly seemed to look at them with bemusement.

Dr. Émile Bellevue was not mistaken; the efforts of Father Vincent de Paul Bailly would pay off, since two years later the paper would circulate eighty thousand copies. This little publication, created on the occasion of the first pilgrimages, more particularly of the national pilgrimage in Lourdes, soon would have a circulation in excess of one hundred thousand and, eventually, five hundred thousand copies.

Amen.

A MOTHER AMONG OTHERS

The Pilgrimage of Zélie Martin, June 11, 1877

18 77 On the compartment's folding table, two well-bred lady travelers set up one of those "spirit stoves" that were cutting-edge technology in the 1870s. The ladies busied themselves about this portable marvel, and with gestures as cautious as the jolts of the train tracks permitted, they prepared coffee for six. Every so often, they discreetly cast glances toward their compartment companions, a mother and three girls who, like them, were bound for Lourdes.

From the very beginning of the trip, with a practiced eye, the two friends judged the family to be within the honorable ranks of the lower middle class. Their judgment was confirmed when the mother, Mrs. Louis Martin, indicated to them that she worked as a seamstress specializing in the Alençon stitch, typical of the town where her family lived and where her husband was a watchmaker. Simple and well-dressed, the girls had very proper manners. They had listened to their mother answer the two travelers' questions, without interrupting that conversation among grown-ups. Now here was company that one could keep without risk! So the two ladies had taken Mrs. Martin and her daughters under their wing, with all the more concern as this poor mother seemed exhausted. Indeed, she was seriously ill and had undertaken a pilgrimage to Lourdes in hopes of a cure, taking three of her daughters with her.

"You have others, then, Madam?" one of the ladies asked.

"Yes," came the reply. "Thérèse and Céline stayed with their father. They were too little to undertake such a journey."

Neither of the two women reacted to the name of Thérèse. How could their piety guess that this unknown four-year-old girl was the future Thérèse of the Child Jesus, a Carmelite, whose statue would someday adorn the altars of so many churches?

So they were charitably busied with the preparation of a fragrant coffee with a view to enliven this poor Mrs. Martin, to treat her daughters, and to savor for themselves a tasty pleasure.

Suddenly, in one of the railroad's fits, an unusually strong jolt shook the compartment. The two good Samaritans both gave out a little cry of fright, and the girls rushed to their mother. The coffee pot was thrown from the stove, pouring its contents upon the travelers' dresses, the provisions, and on the Martin family's linen!

The good women were so manifestly sorry that Zélie Martin tried to put a good face on it. These were the risks of traveling, she said… Fortunately, the girls were dressed in black, so the coffee would not show… No, have no fear, we were not scalded… How lucky the stove did not start a fire! The reassuring words piled one on top of the other without quite managing to hide Mrs. Martin's interior dismay. She was already worried about her daughters' future should she pass away. She was very vulnerable, and the slightest upset could overwhelm her. Add to this the fatigue of the journey, and she was beginning to wonder whether it had been a good idea to venture on this pilgrimage in the first place.

Yet when she set foot on the platform in the Lourdes railway station at dawn on the next day, Zélie Martin had regained her composure. A meager smile brightened up her tired face as she explored this little town, which was already familiar thanks to the photographs she had seen. Without delay, she set out to find lodging. This search caused her more stress: The first inn in which she settled was not the one where she was expected, so she had to pack up her bags again and carry them, with tired steps, to a new destination. Little did these last-minute contingencies matter. Soon her family would be able to pray before the rock whose crevice bore the Mother of God. Soon she would be able to bathe in the saving water of Massabielle.

Later, at the moment of plunging into the pool, Mrs. Martin shivered with all her limbs. How icy the marble seemed! How hostile this clear water seemed despite the warmth of a June afternoon! With great effort of will, she closed her eyes and plunged into the basin over her shoulders. Lost in the crowd of pilgrims, an anonymous mother of a future illustrious saint, Zélie abandoned herself to the hope of a physical healing for which her daughters prayed with all their might by her side. In the Martin family, prayer was as essential to the soul as oxygen is to the lungs.

No miracle that day would strengthen Zélie Martin's fragile health. Further baths on the following days, more Masses, and additional novenas also failed to produce the hoped-for healing. When Mrs. Martin and her daughters boarded the train again three days later, taking a few liters of Lourdes water home in their luggage, Zélie struggled not to yield to a great inner sadness. She did not regret this pilgrimage of last hope, for had she not attempted it, she would have blamed herself for her lack of faith. But she now felt herself very near death. What would happen to her daughters?

"Our Lady of Lourdes, protect them, watch over them," she prayed.

Our Lady and her Son would see to it. They would have all these free and happy young women enter convents where they would be able to devote their lives to prayer, in keeping with their wishes.

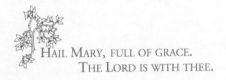

HAIL MARY, FULL OF GRACE.
THE LORD IS WITH THEE.

The Last Triduum

Bernadette's Death, April 16, 1879

18 79 *"There was in him no stately bearing to make us look at him, nor appearance that would attract us to him. He was spurned and avoided by men, a man of suffering, accustomed to infirmity. One of those from whom men hide their faces, spurned, and we held him in no esteem."*[1]

In the chapel of Saint-Gildard's convent, the sisters listened in grave silence to the words of the prophet Isaiah depicting the features of the Suffering Servant. In the grip of the anguish of the passion, they were thinking of the infirmary's only patient who alone, on this Good Friday, had been unable to come down to the Office.

On the convent's second floor, Bernadette, in her sickbed, had but a few days left to live. All the sisters sensed it: This time, it was truly the end. Bernadette was living the torments of Christ crucified in her flesh; like him, her spirit was engulfed in the darkness of anguish. All of her sisters had occasion to observe this distress but were powerless to alleviate it.

---

1. Is 53: 2-3.

"Because of his affliction he shall see the light in fullness of days."[1] Bernadette, upstairs, read the canticle of Isaiah in unison with her companions.
A slender smile brightened her face, soon effaced by the unbearable
shooting pains caused by her right leg. For a few months, she had
suffered from a bone deficiency that had swollen her knee. Compared to
this atrocious pain, her asthma attacks and expectoration of blood had
nearly seemed innocuous.

Sister Marie-Bernard turned the pages of her Bible. She did not need
to look far for the passion of Christ. Marked by frequently repeated
reading, the book opened to the last chapters of the Gospels on its own.
Once again, Bernadette immersed herself. With all her being, she
followed Christ up to Calvary; with Mary, she suffered at the foot of the
cross. But wasn't she rather nailed to it herself?

Having finished her reading, she raised her eyes from the Bible. For
several days, her "white chapel's" curtain had been absolutely bare. She
had asked her sisters to remove the multitude of holy cards that had been
pinned there: a portrait of Saint Bernard, an engraving showing a priest
at the altar during the elevation… For Bernadette, the hour of stripping
down had come. She had wished to keep only her crucifix. God alone
suffices…

By Holy Saturday, Sister Marie-Bernard was still suffering. She
suffered and she awaited, as does the entire Church, the day of the resurrection. Day broke on Easter Sunday morning. In Saint-Gildard's
church, a triumphant Alleluia burst forth; in the infirmary, the young
religious fruitlessly asked the Lord for five minutes of respite during
communion. In her case, the suffering of Good Friday would last a few
days longer, until the risen Christ deigned to grant her the grace of
calling her home at last!

---

1. Is 53: 11.

In her mind, very old images arose. There she was, as a small girl, at the mill of Boly, in the arms of her mother, who had been waiting for her in heaven since 1866. She heard the millstone's familiar creaking, crushing the wheat under the supervision of her father, who had died in 1871.

"*I am crushed like a grain of wheat,*" she murmured to Sister Léontine, who was watching over her.

Days passed. Hour after endless hour, Father Febvre, the convent's young chaplain, regularly visited the infirmary. He, better than anyone, perceived the work of the Spirit in Bernadette. He had never forced himself to be severe toward her the way the congregation's superiors had. Ever since he came into the house, he had witnessed in wonderment the work of grace in the young religious's heart. So he accompanied her as best he could in those last trials. To Bernadette, his visits were moments of peace wrenched from the darkness.

The religious, too, took turns at the patient's bedside to comfort her as much as possible. The fact is that Bernadette was prey to an insurmountable fear. To Sister Nathalie, who was so warm and so supportive to her, she confided: "*My dear Sister, I am afraid. I have been given so many graces and have taken so little advantage of them.*"

With a heavy heart, Sister Nathalie forced a smile. Taking the dying sister's hand, she promised to help her give thanks to the end.

On Wednesday, April 16, in the middle of Easter week, Bernadette was at the very end. Shortly before noon, she asked to be placed in one of the infirmary's chairs, her legs stretched out on a stool. There she was seated amid her sisters, who supported her with all their spiritual strength. Though the mealtime bell was ringing at full swing, it took a while for the refectory to fill: At Saint-Gildard's that day, no one was really hungry.

Gathering what energy she yet had, Sister Marie-Bernard grasped her crucifix and pressed it to her heart: "*My Jesus, oh how I love Him!*"

The religious then had the idea of tying it around her neck with a string to spare her the trouble of holding it in her too-weak fingers. Soon after, Bernadette emerged from her prostration for a moment. Her gaze suddenly riveted to a fixed point, her face stamped with an inexplicable serenity. She put her left hand to her forehead, whispering, "*Oh, oh, oh…*"

What did she see? Her companions would never know. This relief was the prelude to the end. About three o'clock in the afternoon, Bernadette uttered for the last time the words that she had said so often in her life, from Lourdes to Nevers, from Massabielle to Saint-Gildard: "*Holy Mary, Mother of God, pray for me, a sinner…*"

The attending sisters looked attentively at the dying Bernadette, surprised by her tone's vigor. A few moments later, Bernadette asked for a drink. Barely was her thirst slaked that she nodded and quietly breathed her last. The religious looked intensely at her finally peaceful face. Their Sister Marie-Bernard had just found eternal peace. At this moment, several remembered one of the Virgin's utterances to Bernadette: "*I do not promise to make you happy in this world, but in the next…*"

BLESSED ART THOU AMONG WOMEN,
AND BLESSED IS THE FRUIT OF THY WOMB, JESUS.

A WITNESS'S PERSONAL RECOLLECTIONS

Portrait of Jean-Baptiste Estrade, December 2, 1888

1888

Sitting at his desk, Jean-Baptiste Estrade was writing with a hesitant pen. Not that his right hand was experiencing tremors, for in that year of 1888, Estrade was barely sixty-seven. To be sure, he had been retired for twenty years because the revenue service, which had employed him first in Lourdes and then in Bordeaux, had granted him an early retirement. Yet the old man was still alert and bursting with health.

The reason his pen was not swiftly scratching the white pages was that Estrade was having trouble organizing his narrative. He had undertaken an apparently obvious task – to relate his personal recollections of the apparitions in Lourdes. As one who was touched by grace on his very first visit to the grotto and was present at Bernadette's side on several occasions in those blessed days, was he not in a better position than anyone else to publish his memoirs?

Many persons – and personalities – had approached him on the subject. For years, Estrade was reticent. Though he was a willing oral witness who would answer the inquiries of specialist historians, he could not bring himself to write a book. The former civil servant, like many of his contemporaries, had a noble idea of literature. It must be magnificent or not be at all, and Estrade did not feel that he was made of the same stuff as, for instance, Victor Hugo.

Only recently had he finally overcome these aesthetic scruples. Cardinal Langénieux of Reims gave an interview to the potential author during a stay in Lourdes. He led him to understand that the writing of such a book would be an act of filial devotion toward the Virgin – a duty, nearly. That is why Estrade, back home in Bazas, had begun to work on the book.

The only thing was that in thirty years so much water had flowed between the Gave's riverbanks! So many details had been effaced from the witness's memory! Estrade had *the heart's memory*, as Father Laurentin said. The atmosphere of the prayers at the grotto, the piety surrounding Bernadette, the clearness of the gaze fixed on the Virgin – these he remembered as though they were yesterday. But dates, the order of the anecdotes that struck the crowd, all the precise details that a rigorous public would expect – all of that was muddled in his mind.

Estrade sighed, set down his pen, and opened a desk drawer. Once again he reread the few pages of the statement he had redacted in 1858, at the very time of the events. He knew them by heart, yet they were of nearly no help to him. To a recent convert filled with faith and wonder, the essential point was quite elsewhere than in calendar details! Out of the eighteen apparitions, he had described only six, of which one lacked a date and another was wrongly dated.

To help him gather his memories, Estrade turned to a familiar helper. His sister, Emmanuélite, unmarried like him, had always lived by his side. She now lived in his house in Bazas just as she had dwelled with him in 1858, at a time when they had been witnesses of the apparitions. Emmanuélite and Jean-Baptiste spent long conversations together to bring back to life those timeless moments. The writer's sister had a far more reliable memory. Alas, this was still not enough.

That is why Estrade made up his mind to use crutches to support his deficient memory. Only these were dangerous crutches: He knew that they might turn into sticks with which to pummel him! They were the works of the historians, authorities in the matter of the apparitions, Lasserre and Cros. How much polemic had surrounded the conflicting research of these two scholars! Jealous researchers had crossed swords over Bernadette's luminous story. Estrade had always been leery of these quarrels. He, so eager to relate his memories, had shrunk from an 1869 request of Lasserre's to condemn the *Petite Histoire des Apparitions*, undertaken by Father Sempé and continued by Father Cros.

Now he was compelled to have recourse to these critical studies at the risk of being accused of plagiarism – he, the direct spectator of the 1858 events! Father Sempé, Estrade's mentor and advisor, had sent him the works of Father Cros, with whom he had shared a long collaboration. He reckoned that he had a measure of "author's rights" to these works in proportion to his contributions. But those boundaries were ill-defined, and Father Cros, alerted to the undertaking, jealously kept an eye on the work's progress, as did Lasserre's friends! The eyewitness, anxious to give thanks for the graces he received in 1858, therefore had to write under the cover of the deepest secrecy, cleverly foiling the historian's suspicions with every line. He knew that they would have no mercy if they were to detect the many sections he had lifted from their research!

But the paradox did not end there. Completed in 1893, Estrade's much-anticipated manuscript was buried in the archives like a sensitive and highly confidential document. Despite these precautions, the clandestine writer was vigorously taken to task. Through an indiscretion, a Catholic journal obtained and published long passages of this litigious work. Father Cros' reaction was not long in coming: He inveighed against *A Witness's Personal Recollections* with raging remarks on the literary theft of which he was the victim!

Only in 1906 could Estrade's memoirs arise from the catacombs. By that date, Lasserre was dead, and the touchy Father Cros no longer fulminated. Time had passed, passions had quieted. It was left to an historian's meticulous work on Estrade's memoirs to sort out its imprecisions and to explain the truth of the matter. That would be the work of Father Laurentin fifty years later.

 HOLY MARY, MOTHER OF GOD,

A Life Spent in the Shrine's Service

Father Sempé's Final Days, August 31, 1889

1889 A bright late-summer sun warmed the mountains. The night's rain had chased away the dull weather, and the luminous fresh air and blue sky promised a beautiful day, the kind the Pyrenees can present this time of year. The shrines were all the more splendid, and the crowd that already had begun to swarm was all the more cheerful.

These were the favorite conditions for Father Sempé, superior of the chaplains of Lourdes, as he went on his daily rounds. Although this time, an unusual weariness momentarily tempted him to cancel them. Yet this walk was vitally important for him; this intimate, nearly carnal contact with the holy place gave him physical exercise, mental rest, and spiritual serenity all at once. It also kept him from losing sight of the essential point of his mission – to organize the pilgrims' welcome and the spiritual service they counted upon.

The first stop on his circuit – all in all, a rather long one, since the domain had increased over the previous few years – was at the grotto and the statue of Mary, which made her seem so present, so alive. When Bishop Laurence entrusted the shrine's organization to him, the prelate expressed his wish that the place be preserved according to its original appearance, just as Bernadette Soubirous had known it. But notable additions had become necessary for the pilgrims to be able to pray there in the requisite serenity: Among them, a rerouting of the Gave's riverbed in order to enlarge the path between the water and the rock face to facilitate the installation of the altar and sacristy so that the Eucharist could be celebrated on the very spot of the apparitions. Father Sempé often recalled with a smile the Lourdes mayor's bewildered expression when he announced that he wished to modify the raging river's course!

Already feeling fatigued from his rounds, Father Sempé directed his steps along the Gave, passed alongside the pools toward the esplanade, then made his way into the upper basilica whose construction he had spent five years supervising. The *Ave Maria* had just been rung by the bells, which were perched two hundred thirty feet above the grotto. In Father Sempé's heart, they echoed as a permanent reminder that faith must remain anchored in reality: The chimes' melody lifted the soul up to heaven, yet the clear sound of the bells reminded him that one's feet, on the other hand, must remain planted on the ground and that there was still much to do before one could enjoy the promised eternal rest. A moment of prayer, seated among the dozens of pilgrims already gathered in the church, allowed him to recoup some of his strength, but this tiredness worried him.

Despite his lack of stamina, which he hoped was temporary, Father Sempé left the church to admire once again the dome of the Basilica of Our Lady of the Rosary, on which a few workmen, entrusted with the final touches of the building whose dedication had taken place barely three weeks earlier, were still busy. It certainly fit well into the landscape that extended from the Basilica of the Immaculate Conception to Saint Michael's Bridge across this immense esplanade. Furthermore, the fact that it was regularly filled with pilgrims seeking to meditate, rest, pray, or, more trivially, to take shelter from the rain amply justified the enormous investment that its construction had required.

Further along, he also noticed the grotto boulevard. As his present fatigue made his usual walk there inadvisable, he contented himself with admiring the view and observing the crowd that was beginning to swell and distribute itself here and there in a cheerful and prayerful mood. It was a crowd that now could easily make its way from the train station to the shrines, thanks precisely to this new boulevard that had been opened up despite the opposition of the majority of inhabitants and merchants. Yielding to this secret pride, he noted that at the time he had stood nearly alone – in opposition to the local residents, town leaders, and public officials – in his prediction of the imminent development of the Lourdes pilgrimage and in his claim that the town would soon have to adapt. No one regretted these inspired works of urban planning that had largely facilitated the traffic of pilgrims through the city.

Father Sempé found himself extremely tired after his rounds, despite curtailing his normal route. With slow steps, a little out of breath, he made his way to the chaplains' residence to take up again, he hoped, his daily work. This functional, beautiful, and welcoming residence – whose contract, which he had drawn up with the architects, had been faithfully kept – had greatly assisted the chaplains' work since its dedication.

It was with a serene eye that, on that day of August 31, 1889, Father Sempé contemplated the site to which he had devoted his natural life. The Virgin Mary clearly had expressed the desire that people come to meet her in Lourdes in large numbers. The warm welcoming of the countless pilgrims, now possible thanks to all these additions, constituted an edifying token of respect and obedience. Interiorly, the dedicated Father Sempé suddenly realized on this gentle morning that his earthly mission was accomplished. The emotion that gripped him marked the end of the work he had to do for Mary. His strength would leave him the next day, allowing him to reach heaven, a glimpse of which he had so long sought to offer to the pilgrims of Lourdes here on earth.

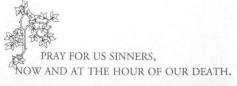

PRAY FOR US SINNERS,
NOW AND AT THE HOUR OF OUR DEATH.

THE RELIGIOUS SISTER OF BRIVE

Sister Julienne, Twelfth Miraculous Healing,
September 1, 1889

1889 "But Doctor, has the Virgin ever saved a native of the region?"

At dinner, all gazes converged upon Dr. Gustav Boissarie. The question was posed by Mrs. Dubrulle, the notary's young wife, who was known throughout Sarlat for her devotion to the Virgin and the charity she exhibited every day by helping the most indigent. On this day late in September 1889, a soft light still brightened the dining room of Sarlat's mayor, who was entertaining, as was his habit every Thursday, a few of the town's leading men and their wives. Tonight, he had invited Boissarie who, after brilliant studies in Paris, chose to practice medicine in this charming town of the Dordogne; Robert Dubrulle, who came from a family of notaries dating back to the reign of the Bourbons; and the schoolmaster, Jean Balou, a freethinker who never missed an opportunity for a dig at the clergy.

The mayor smiled. His wife fidgeted nervously, sensing the schoolmaster's reaction. Boissarie, who was familiar with Balou, hastened to answer with a wink all around.

"Yes, that's right, my dear Jean, we are going to speak about miracles," he began in playful condescension. "Oh, I beg your pardon – about these *so-called* miracles, fit only to comfort pious ladies in their antiquated faith, but unworthy of enlightened and scientific minds such as your own."

Everyone guffawed as Balou feigned taking offense.

"Never, Doctor, would I permit myself to speak thus, and Mrs. Dubrulle is well aware of it," Balou said in reply. "I simply think that your religion, as socially necessary as it is, sometimes tries to make us swallow some rather queer ideas."

"Dear friends, to answer the question posed to me, I shall relate a story that is not a month old," Boissarie continued. "Do you remember little Julienne, at the hospice orphanage?"

"The religious sister of Brive?" cried out Mrs. Dubrulle. "She came to spend a few days at the hospice two years ago, I believe. She suffered from pulmonary tuberculosis, but her youth and our town's healthy air finally overcame the disease."

"That is the one," the doctor went on. "Coming from a very poor family, she had been placed in that orphanage at the age of eleven. When the doctor of Brive wished her to spend a few calm days with her family to rest, she naturally went back. Indeed, Julienne had a chest complaint, but her stay in Sarlat did not cure her. I met her doctor in Brive, Dr. Pomarel. He related her illness's progress to me. The poor girl must have suffered a lot."

For a few minutes, the conversation digressed to Sarlat's orphanage and the construction that the city intended for it. Mrs. Dubrulle continued to fidget in her seat, like a child eager to learn the rest of the story. No longer able to contain herself, she begged Boissarie to be so kind as to resume his tale.

"Back in her convent in Brive, Julienne had about ten months' respite, but in October 1887, the illness started up again and she began to spit up blood," the doctor said. "After a second remission, the illness reappeared in May 1888, but it did not keep her from making her profession in July of the same year. I think her doctor gave a favorable opinion so as to allow her to become a sister before she died. Ever since her First Communion, Julienne had dreamed of entering the convent."

"So young, yet so sure of wanting to become a religious sister!" Mrs. Dubrulle interjected.

"This reminds me of a certain religious sister of Rousseau," muttered the cynical schoolmaster, a remark that earned him a withering glare from Mrs. Dubrulle.

"Her vocation was somewhat impeded, dear friends," continued the doctor. "Indeed, as the community did not have an extern sister, the bishop asked her to give up the cloister and to devote herself to being the link between the community and the rest of the world. That is why Sister Julienne is so well known in Brive. Everybody has passed her on the street."

"Giving up the cloister, living in the world in contact with sinners and suffering in one's body," said Mrs. Dubrulle. "God wanted to make her share in his Son's suffering."

It was now the schoolmaster's turn to glare with annoyance at Mrs. Dubrulle, and, if it were not for his wife's swift knee to his right thigh, the dinner might have taken a far more ugly and combative turn. Fortunately, by the time Balou had rubbed his leg and silently rebelled against his wife's methods, the mayor's wife had had time once again to propose her steaming bean stew to her guests.

Boissarie resumed his story. "In January 1889, the illness worsened from day to day. There was talk of raging tuberculosis, and heat acupuncture points were applied by the hundreds. Starting in the month of July, the poor sister never stopped spitting up blood from her purulent lungs."

"Doctor! We are eating," one of the women protested at the distasteful reference.

"Excuse me, Madam," the doctor apologized. "But really, her condition was in an absolute state of collapse, and no medical means were able to curb the illness's progress. Sister Julienne could only take broth and milk. She was visibly wasting away."

"And then she went to Lourdes," Balou piped in. "She took a dip in the pool and was healed. Now Doctor, you are a scientist. A pulmonary lesion does not disappear like that in a bath of ice water!"

"That's right, my dear schoolmaster," Boissarie responded. "But, you see, that is what happened! Against her doctor's recommendations, she made the trip to Lourdes at the end of August with two friends, including a religious from the convent of Brive. Throughout the trip, those who saw her, the bishop of Albi in particular, thought that she would not make it to the shrines. At the pools themselves, the two ladies who were supposed to bathe her refused at first; that is how close to death's door she appeared to be. It was up to the two ladies who had come along with her to assure them of Julienne's will and to stay by her side. And at that point, believe it or not, the miracle took place. She came out of the water and was able to walk all the way to the grotto, where she prayed on her knees before the pilgrims' captivated and happy eyes. If you do not believe me, go and meet her in Brive!"

"Mr. Boissarie, you're a doctor!" Balou repeated.

Boissarie stood his ground. "Yes, just like the doctor of Saint-Maclou who is the founding president of the Bureau of Medical Authentication. I have been his assistant for three years now in his scientific work of verifying that the Lourdes healings termed 'miracles' cannot otherwise be explained. We appeal to many physicians, sometimes unbelievers. There is a veritable investigation, and we never draw frivolous conclusions."

"Go see Dr. Pomarel," he challenged the schoolmaster. "Go to Lourdes... and see!"

The dinner having ended, the men retired to the town hall's drawing room to smoke cigars and continue the conversation about the scientific work of the Bureau of Medical Authentication. Gathered among themselves, the women promised each other to go to Brive soon to visit Sister Julienne.

AMEN.

Our Lady's Valiant Soldier

General de Sonis and the Virgin of Lourdes,
December 2, 1890

1890 The cemetery of Loigny was strewn with misty wisps this winter morning as a young French officer, his sword at his side, crunched the gravel of the sleepy pathways under his confident stride. Having just received his gold braids, he wished immediately to go on a pilgrimage to the tomb of General de Sonis, the man of legendary bravery who had inspired his vocation. To his great surprise, although the cemetery was deserted, an old Papal Zouave, in a uniform both flamboyant and out of date, stood at attention before the headstone.

After many long minutes of silence, the young officer, sure that in this old man he was seeing one of de Sonis' comrades in arms, could no longer restrain himself from asking him some questions. The man's steel-blue gaze slowly turned away from the tomb and, his body still stiffly at attention, the old Zouave brought de Sonis, who was none other than Baron Athanase Charles-Marie Charette de la Contrie, back to life from his impeccable memory.

"Terrible. There is no other word to describe that year 1870, with its icy winter turning earth to rock and its battles staining fields red with men's blood," he began. "Terrible was every minute that played out on that December 2, 1870, twenty years ago to the day. Just as General de Sonis committed his brigade to an assault on a German position near Loigny, he was told that his center was withdrawing!

"'*Forward!*' he shouted to them. '*Are you afraid?*'

"But the 51st Infantry continued to sound the retreat. The general rushed to me and my Papal Zouaves, posted with the artillery reserves.

"'*Colonel de Charrette, my friend, give me one of your two battalions,*' he asked. '*Let's show them the worth of men of strong mettle and of Christian soldiers!*'

"At the head of three hundred men, the fine flower of French nobility and chivalry, I could see unfurling the banner of the Sacred Heart, trying to rally the cowards to their duty: '*Here is honor's flag. Follow it!*'

"A magnificent idea, if ever there was one! Over recent months, the Sacred Heart had gathered the masses. The bishop of Nantes had blown upon the embers of faith to counter the ambient despair. God had abandoned France to defeat because France had abandoned the Church to face the threats that hung over the Pope's temporal authority, and it was up to us to turn the situation round. The bishop's appeal had the effect of a spark, and a multitude of dioceses had been consecrated to the Sacred Heart. This was the impetus that de Sonis was counting on, persuaded as he was that it would be contagious, if it was channeled by the more enthusiastic – the Papal Zouaves. De Sonis wished to turn it to his advantage to awaken his troops, achieve victory, and obtain national reparation through the Sacred Heart.

"But the banner did not have the anticipated result. Aware that we were throwing ourselves to the lions, we shouted a last hurrah: '*Long live France! Long live Pius IX!*'

"We were greeted with a violent volley of musket fire. The general fell among the first, his leg splintered into pieces. Our flag, disfigured with bullets and blood, strewed its golden embroidery on the battlefield, trodden underfoot by enemy boots. The spectacle that followed was worthy of a painting by Detaille: One hundred ninety-eight Zouaves and ten officers laid on the ground.

"De Sonis was stretched out on the ground with his head resting on his saddle, thanks to the care of Brugère, his aide-de-camp. From this spot, he saw the Prussians combing the field of the vanquished, finishing off our war comrades with the butts of their rifles. From this spot, too, he felt the snow fall upon his face and the ground freeze his feet. From this spot, he could see only an immense white sheet stained in red.

"This was where the image appeared to him, drawing him out of his despondency. It was an image from a pre-war pilgrimage, that of the Immaculate Mother, that he had seen in statue form in the grotto of Massabielle. Kind, serene, radiant… He clung to this vision and drew his strength from it. He even managed to speak to the Zouaves who had dragged themselves up to him: '*We are at the threshold of those eternal hopes that form, as it were, the prize of this great combat we call life. On this threshold, the Church has placed Mary, to inspire trust in those who must cross it.*'

"Absorbed in his contemplation of the Virgin, the general forgot his pains. His body went through icy hours, yet he felt an immense inner consolation.

"'*I have, after all, offered my suffering for the salvation of our poor country,*' he let out when he was received at the rectory of Loigny and had a leg amputated.

"De Sonis was certain that Loigny was a glorious defeat – redemption through a bloody sacrifice, a spiritual and patriotic act that redeemed a France that had lost her way and must toll the war's end! For us, the Zouaves, *Loigny is Joan of Arc in Rouen*. A brilliant action by martyrs. The general attributed his blessed fate to his blessed Queen: *This December 2, he has invoked Mary only under the name and figure of*

Our Lady of Lourdes. This Virgin, who is inseparable from the Sacred Heart for whose honor we fight, is the heart of his life: 'May the Lord graciously allow me always to be faithful to It and to know none other!'

"Some time later, his battered body bowed before the grotto of Massabielle where he had come on pilgrimage, he laid his officer's cross and that of commander of the Legion of Honor at the Virgin's feet. Next to the banners, notes of testimony, swords, and metal hearts, these objects have only one function – to shine with gratitude in the gleaming décor of the reliquary chapel.

"He was to preserve this joyful submission to Our Lady all his life, even when his prayers for healing found no answer after a riding accident that left him pinned in a wheelchair. His stays in Lourdes and his baths in its holy waters remained without issue, but he did obtain, as at Loigny, a deep peace. His heart lives on in Lourdes.

"In an impenetrable coincidence, he left us on the feast of the Assumption in 1887. There was a national outpouring of emotion. I wanted to offer this incomparable friend half of the vault I had reserved for myself here in Loigny, *but I am not worthy to rest by the side of this saint, unless he takes me up to heaven just as he led me on the battlefield.* The bishop of Angers agrees with me on this point: *His tomb will be the pilgrimage of military devotion and virtue. I do not know whether God will deign to cause the miraculous to grow on this forever blessed spot, but the memory of General de Sonis will go down the generations* for eternity.

"So, Lieutenant, you who came, as I did, to kneel before this *miles Christi*, soldier of Christ, to implore strength, light, and health, know this: You will be heard, for de Sonis was great before God and men. He found his salvation in Our Lady: Imitate him and entrust yourself to her."

The old Zouave gave one last salute and walked away, leaving the young officer there, his eyes brimming with tears and hope.

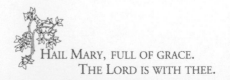

HAIL MARY, FULL OF GRACE.
THE LORD IS WITH THEE.

THE PRODIGAL SON

An Anarchist Doctor's Conversion, July 11, 1894

1894 On a hot July day in Lourdes, many pilgrims meandered among the shrines, looking for tree shade and a little coolness inside the Basilica of the Rosary. For once, it was not raining. Yet in the reception hall of the Bureau of Medical Authentication, the conversation was far from the indolent torpor blanketing the sun-weary pilgrims.

"Look here! How can one, from being a rebellious anarchist, with neither god nor master, suddenly turn into a practicing Christian with a devotion to the Virgin Mary?"

The question was posed point-blank by the old and somewhat surly priest in charge of reception. The young man before him claimed to be a doctor and sought to lend his assistance to those who authenticate miraculous events occurring in Lourdes.

"What is truly extraordinary, Father, is that I have been so long influenced by anarchism," the young man replied. "That hopeless movement, whose only effect is to exacerbate man's pride and self-sufficiency! But in truth, there is nothing surprising. Ever since childhood, I have been unable to stomach the illness, suffering, and injustice that reign over the world. That is why I embraced the medical profession."

"Precisely, that's it!" the priest shot back. "I cannot understand this enormous contradiction: The anarchist is the man who destroys, undoes, pulls apart. The doctor, on the contrary, heals, mends, puts things back together! How have you been able, in conscience, to reconcile these two antitheses?"

The young doctor was not disconcerted by this challenge. He got the impression that convincing this priest of his good faith and sincerity would be no walk in the park! But he also knew that through this servant of God, he was addressing himself to the Creator, to ask for the absolution of his past sins and to give thanks to the Blessed Virgin, who helped him during his conversion.

"Father, it is indeed contradictory," he admitted. "Deep down, the rebel we call an anarchist has only one desire – to eradicate the evils of this world, to build a new one without affliction and without calamity. It is not in his purpose that the anarchist is wrong; rather, it is in his judgment of fact. He is convinced that all of society is evil, that it corrupts everything. He has no hope, no trust. So he thinks he must act, and destroy everything, just as one must destroy an old and excessively unstable house to build another on new and solid foundations. In a like manner, he seeks the end of an old and depraved world in order to allow another one, virginal and pure, to rise up in its place."

The young man continued: "The doctor I once was believed that his role was to heal and comfort individual wounds, all the while working for the alienating collectivity's destruction. That is how I behaved, without committing any violence myself, but without condemning it either."

"Thank God for that!" replied the priest. "What kept you back?"

"I told you," repeated the man. "I considered that my mission, within the anarchist movement, was to alleviate suffering. Also, I received a good Christian education, and, as a child, I had much tenderness for Mary. My family often entrusted itself to her intercession. It remained engraved somewhere in a corner of my heart, and though my mind ardently wished for a general disaster, my soul, for its part, remained dedicated to caring and consoling."

The old priest, surprised and caught off guard by this confession, stared at his interlocutor for a few long seconds, plumbing his gaze for some sly glimmer that might betray a ruse or insincerity. But the candor of the doctor's gaze acquitted him better than any speech. The priest's curiosity was piqued; he wanted to know a little more.

"Why have you come back to place yourself under God's wing?" he asked the young doctor. "What event can have set you back on the right course?"

"It did not happen overnight, as you doubtless suspect, Father," he replied. "Still, it went rather quickly, because my mind has always remained open. I often wondered about life, death, what comes before and after. Answers to these questions are only to be found in the religions, for science refuses to consider these 'hereafters.' The miracle is that I perceived, amid my reflections, an essential fact: Man is unique, but not alone. The anarchist believes that the individual alone can evolve, and that society prevents this. He ends up believing that his combat alone will be able to save the world, and that nothing and no one can make him change his resolution. Religion, the Catholic religion in particular, puts the good of each at the service of all.

"As for the event," he went on, "there is not any one in particular. As I told you, the Virgin Mary had much importance in my youth. It was on May 24, 1894, that I acquired the certainty that God existed. May, the month of Mary. It was during the month of October that I felt the imperious need to go to Mass, then to go to confession. October, the month of the rosary. It is here, in Lourdes, that I have come to strengthen my conviction that God lives among men… I believe that Mary has always had particular graces for me, and in the end, it may be to thank her that I am here!"

The old priest was visibly impressed.

"My son! Give thanks to God, who causes a font of infinite hope and mercy to spring up here. Would you like us to go to the grotto together? It would be a pleasure as well as an honor for me to accompany a prodigal son on his way back to the Father's house!"

BLESSED ART THOU AMONG WOMEN,
AND BLESSED IS THE FRUIT OF THY WOMB, JESUS.

The Battle between Faith and Reason
Émile Zola and Lourdes, November 21, 1894

1894 On this autumn evening, the *Cercle Catholique du Luxembourg* (Luxembourg Catholics Club) in Paris had a full house: The doors were unhinged so that the crowd, which overflowed all the way into the hallways, might hear the lecture of a physician, a certain Dr. Boissarie, straight from the Pyrenees countryside. This huge audience had come to witness the continued unfolding of events arising from the polemic caused by Émile Zola's last novel, *Lourdes*.

A few years earlier, while on a trip to the Cauterets spa, the famous writer had made a stop in Lourdes. His positivist convictions could only predispose him against the Massabielle phenomena. Nevertheless, Zola was vividly struck by what he saw at this pilgrimage site, a pro-clerical venue if ever there was one. The crowd's fervor, the exalted faith of the sick, the impassioned expectation of miracles – all of this fascinated him. Toward the end of that century, a religious revival had placed itself in opposition to the triumphant scientism of which Émile Zola was a proponent. The idea of observing this phenomenon through the microscope of naturalism was, for this writer, a bracing challenge. Zola decided to return to Lourdes in 1892 at the time of the national pilgrimage, sensing that this event might well nourish his inspiration as he brought to an end the immense Rougon-Macquart series upon which he had been working for the past twenty years.

And so, in August 1892, the writer was in Lourdes. He would have preferred to vanish into the crowd of pilgrims, but his cover was quickly blown. As soon as he was recognized, all doors opened up to him. He was given a tour of the shrines, of the pools, and of the "dungeon" where Bernadette used to live. Boissarie, director of the Bureau of Medical Authentication, benevolently received him into the offices where the healings that occurred at the grotto were examined. During the two hours he spent there among twenty physicians, the novelist had occasion to observe the doctors as they scrutinized an astonishing case: Marie Lebranchu, in the last stages of pulmonary tuberculosis, had just undergone a perfect remission.

Based on what he had seen in Lourdes, Zola blackened with ink over two hundred pages of his travel notebook and undertook the construction of his novel. In Catholic circles, the result of his inspiration was awaited with bated breath. The atheist writer seemed to be moved by the atmosphere in Lourdes. Could he have been conquered by grace?

When *Lourdes* was published in 1894, it was thought, Zola would have to face the truth of the matter. Sadly, however, such was not the case – far from it, in fact. Upon their becoming aware of Zola's novel, Boissarie and his confreres were overcome with a limitless indignation. Far from admitting the fruits of grace that he had glimpsed, Zola denied the truth of the grotto miracles throughout his work. Marie Lebranchu in particular, the novel's "la Grivotte" (literally, "the saucy one"), undergoes under his pen a deadly relapse at the end of the pilgrimage: She who, in reality, had left Lourdes healed for ever.

Deeply wounded, Boissarie intended to respond to what he considered to be an outrage committed not only against himself, but also and especially against Our Lady of Lourdes. That is why he made the journey all the way to Paris to give a lecture at the *Cercle Catholique du Luxembourg*. Before an audience of reporters, students, doctors, and people from all walks of life, he slowly shred to pieces the novel's assertions and insinuations in order to re-establish the truth. Sometimes to booing and hissing, and other times to applause, he proclaimed the hypocrisy of the novelist who had displayed so much affable courtesy to win over the doctors' trust, and he condemned Zola's rank materialist prejudices. His indictment of Zola was no less comprehensive and pointed than would be *J'accuse*, which the evening's accused party would publish four years later charging French military leaders with anti-Semitism and obstruction of justice in the well-known Dreyfus affair!

After this tempestuous lecture, Louis Borrel, one of the audience's many students, who in fact was preparing for a career in medicine, walked aimlessly in the Latin Quarter. He ambled along the thoroughfares and quiet side streets, absorbed in an intense interior debate: *Did Zola lie? At the very least he certainly bent the truth, using his talent as a novelist in a field in which fiction perhaps had no place. Why did he do this?* The question tormented Borrel. As one who admired the novelist, he could not bring himself to settle this business by appealing to bad faith alone.

While lost in his thoughts, Borrel's gaze fell on the streets as he walked. Claude Bernard, Jean-Martin Charcot, Louis Pasteur, and many other scientific geniuses lived and worked not far from here. At the thought of these prestigious names, the student glimpsed the shadow of an answer: More than anyone, Zola's mind had been struck by the impassioned medical research of this half-century. In Claude Bernard's minute experiments, the supernatural, of course, had no place. In Charcot's conclusions, a hysterical patient could be cured through auto-suggestion, or hypnosis. As for Pasteur, the tireless promoter of strict hygiene, his precepts had influenced the severe judgment that Zola had passed on the pools of Lourdes, whose water was changed only twice a day.

The student nodded. He recalled the clear gaze of a young woman healed at the grotto who, from the top of the stand, surveyed the audience at the *Cercle Catholique du Luxembourg* with a smile. No hint of hysteria shone in her eyes. In the face of such limpidity, Borrel could not doubt. In Lourdes, the unexplainable was not due to gaps in medical knowledge, as Zola claimed; instead, the unexplainable bore the fingerprint of God.

But such a thought was too disturbing to gain admission to the positivist philosophy to which Zola was the heir, a philosophy that postulates science's capacity to explain everything. That is why the novelist preferred to study the supernatural on naturalism's own dissection table! In doing so, he had reduced it to naught. A lie? A fear of the vertigo that grips the mind when it confronts the immeasurable? Or a sincere conviction that faith and reason can never be reconciled?

Louis ended his walk in the falling dusk. On his way, he promised himself to become a physician responsive to the progress of knowledge... as well as the mysteries of God.

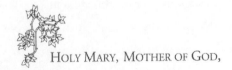 HOLY MARY, MOTHER OF GOD,

WHY NOT ME?

Esther Brachmann, Twenty-Second Miraculous Healing,
August 21, 1896

1896 "Why not me?" In the train taking her to Lourdes with so many other sick people, a young Parisian girl of fifteen maintained a tenacious hope.

And yet, according to the doctors' opinion, her case was desperate. At the Hospital de la Charité in Villepinte, where she had been living at death's door, no one had been able to do anything at all for the tuberculous peritonitis that threatened the most horrific of deaths.

Esther Brachmann had an angel's face, with fine and marked eyebrows under thick ebony hair. Her clear voice, her lively and deep eyes were full of ravishing youth – were it not for the wheelchair, that casket where already she lies... were it not for the growth, not of her adolescent body, but of her belly, a spectacular, monstrous, inhuman swelling that she could no longer hide from those bold enough to look at her. Beauty and horror: The atrocious contrast does not elicit pity at first. It does, however, elicit queasy disgust.

Just over two years ago, she was in bloom, barely awakened from life's great dreaminess. Then she started to cough a little, and then a little too much. In no time, tuberculosis took everything from her – her dreams, her life, her very body. A momentary torture, far from passing, changed into an unyieldingly constant agony.

And medicine? Worse yet than the illness – repeated, interminable punctures, revulsive treatments as violent as they were inoperative, useless eviscerations. Everything had been tried. The case was incurable, and the prognosis was imminent death.

"Why not me?" Oh, the relief, at the departure, of feeling the jostle of the Pyrenees-Express! She knew, with a feeling of liberation mixed with ominous apprehension, that she was at last on her way, that she was leaving her prison, whatever her final destination. Seeing the landscape drift by and feeling the speed of the coach gave her a very lively excitement that pain, cold sweats, and skin irritation soon snuffed out. The numbing metallic rhythm of the wheels squealing on the rails became a source of migraine and nausea. Esther then remembered that many of the sick died like this, in one of the jolts of the very car that was to save them. She started to doubt the wisdom of this trip and wondered if she was foolish to undertake it. At last, the coolness of the evening lessened the extreme discomfort that the priest and two nursing sisters, who dedicated themselves at her side to her care, powerlessly tried to remedy. Then there was the night journey. Esther did not really sleep; if she did nod off, her sleep was poor at best. The coughs and moans of her companions of misfortune punctuated the interminable journey just as her own did. Ten hours after departure, the fleeting outline of the trees began to take shape through the third-class car's windows. The day was finally about to break!

"Why not me?" Once again, Esther thought of all the miraculously healed people about whom she had heard these last few years. A place had been reserved for her and her Villepinte companions on one of those pilgrimage trains for the sick. Sometimes there was a yearlong wait, besides the expenses that many, outside of hospital institutions, could not afford. When they were told of their upcoming departure for Lourdes only a few weeks after her request had been made, it was already a little miracle for her. She firmly believed in the Holy Virgin's intercession. Mary, she thought to herself, was perhaps fifteen, too, when the angel Gabriel appeared to her. All things are possible with God. Often, she would strike the wood of her chair in despair; often, too, she would join her raised hands in prayer to implore him who had known the wood of the cross. She found in the wooden fibers of her chair an unexpected intimacy with the Crucified. She guessed that, in her own way, she was participating in his suffering; may hers be useful and have some meaning! She wanted at least to offer it up for someone, to be happy as he was happy. Yes, she was sure of it, he was happy to give his life, even unto death, for those whom he loves. And she knew he loved her, for she accompanied him on the cross like the good thief. Then she told herself: "Why not me? Why wouldn't he heal me?"

The sun had barely risen when the train entered the station. No time to tarry; others were following behind, transporting hundreds of other passengers. The dozen patients from Villepinte were soon pushed out of the station and immediately led to the grotto. Half an hour later, the sick passed the security line and were finally parked in front of the spot of the apparitions, in the first row, while an Assumptionist priest, at a pulpit to the right, welcomed them and exhorted them to prayer.

Esther did not see the Virgin. She did not notice the rosebush and the ivy running up the rock face, nor the crutches lining the grotto's ceiling as so many offerings from those who had been healed. She did not hear the fountain trickling to the left; she did not smell the scent of wax wafting off the countless candles burning on prickets. She was not even praying. She was no longer doing anything. She had just entrusted her entire being to the mercy of God.

It was in the pool to which she was soon carried that the unexplained occurred. Esther re-emerged from the water nearly by herself, saying that she no longer felt any pain, that her stomach had flattened and that she was hungry. And there she was, walking… "I am healed!"

That afternoon, she participated in the pilgrimage's functions and, on the next day, in the Stations of the Cross. Having reached the cross itself, she spent a long time kissing its wood that was so familiar to her.

In reality, her path had just begun. Two days later, the physicians of the Bureau of Medical Authentication confirmed the healing, while those in Villepinte kept her under observation for a whole year. It was only twelve years later, on June 6, 1908, that Archbishop Amette of Paris officially recognized the miracle.

One question never left her, a question that guided each of her days, each of her prayers to the Crucified: *Why me, Lord, why me?*

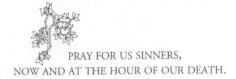

PRAY FOR US SINNERS,
NOW AND AT THE HOUR OF OUR DEATH.

HEALED, BODY AND SOUL

Gabriel Gargam, June 20, 1901

19 01 "I won't go. No use insisting. For fifteen years now, I haven't darkened a church's door, so what makes you think I would feel like going to Lourdes?!"

"But Gabriel, in the state you're in, God is your only hope. Don't turn your back on him."

"No, no, and again no. Lourdes is just yet another superstition. Me? I want to get better or die, not to believe."

Annoyed, Gabriel turned over in his hospital bed to shun the entreaties of the hospital chaplain who was getting on his nerves. *Let him sleep,* the chaplain thought, *since that's the only way he is not in pain...*

It was December 17, 1899, half past ten in the evening. Gabriel Gargam, a railroad postal worker, began his shift on the fast train leaving Bordeaux. Soon after departure, the train, because of a technical difficulty, came to a halt. Suddenly, a terrifying rumble was heard. In a flash, Gabriel understood that the express train from Bordeaux was hurtling toward them at high speed. Before he was able to make a move, he found himself crumpled at the bottom of an embankment, buried in the snow. One of his co-workers died on impact; two others hung between life and death. It would be seven hours before Gabriel was found and taken to the hospital. The diagnosis was final – paralysis from the waist down. Fed through a tube to his stomach, he soon weighed no more than eighty pounds. Before long, purulent sores covered his feet. His condition worsened daily. Though doctors disagreed about the particulars of his case – one concluding he had a bone marrow disease, the other suggesting paralysis due to crushed bone marrow, a third claiming it was traumatic hysteria – all were in accord that the infirmity was incurable and that death would be soon and inevitable.

Gabriel awoke from his sleep in a sweat. That cursed dream again! Would he ever stop reliving the accident? The two people paid to take care of him thanks to the indemnities granted by the railroad company were conversing with a doctor at his bedside. When will he ever be left alone?

"Mr. Gargam, in light of your condition, we have decided to operate on you by trepanning your vertebrae," one of the doctors said. "It's the only way of loosening the boney marrow."

"No, a thousand times no," Gabriel resisted. "I forbid any desperate assaults on my body. I want to go. Let me die at home."

"The decision has been made, Mr. Gargam. You'll be operated on within the week."

A prisoner! "Help me leave," Gabriel begged his visiting cousin a little later. "I can't take it any more."

His cousin's answer was unequivocal. "Sign up for the national Lourdes pilgrimage," he told Gabriel. "They can't keep you from going. I see no other solution."

Between the chaplain, his mother, and his cousin, everyone was decidedly working on him. This time, however, under the threat of an operation, the argument became convincing: He finally agreed that he must go to Lourdes. Any means would be good if it got him out of that cursed hospital.

On June 20, 1901, after a Homeric journey that left him exhausted from so much suffering, Gabriel reached Lourdes. When his mother pointed out the great image of Christ at Calvary and suggested that they pray, Gabriel pretended not to hear and turned his head. He was not falling for that! Having not yet broken the eucharistic fast, he was carried to the grotto, where he received communion, more out of respect for the institution than out of belief.

A tingling sensation in his legs fleetingly attracted his attention first. He was not about to believe this nonsense, not he! But after communion, with tears choking him up, he had to face the facts: Faith had caught up with him, a salvific faith that moves and liberates. His future took on the gleam of hope.

Though his soul was born again and took flight, his body was on its way back to the hospital. When he was dipped into the pool a few hours later, a very calm Gabriel fervently prayed. Come what may, he thanked the Lord for these moments of grace. Alas, he was soon lying prostrate along the path of the procession of the Blessed Sacrament, worse off than ever. Everyone around him was positive: This was the end for Gabriel. Fortunately, an orderly kept people from taking him away. Suddenly, Gabriel came around. Sad at first for having missed the procession, he regained his hope when he heard the acclamations. Moved, he wanted to get up and see. Someone restrained him, but he insisted. They tried to reason with him. Firm in his resolve, he refused to obey.

"Let me walk!" he shouted in an otherworldly voice. In an instant, he was up on his bare feet. Like Lazarus coming out of the tomb in a shroud, he joined the procession and followed after the Blessed Sacrament. But he was soon put back on his stretcher. That didn't matter; he was healed, healed in his soul returned to God, healed in his body given back to life.

Gabriel, who could again walk normally, very soon gained weight. His sores disappeared. Now an extraordinarily sweet man, he graciously submitted to the examination of incredulous doctors for hours on end. This sudden resurrection turned the realm of science on its head. To those who, to explain the unexplainable, did not hesitate to say that his paralysis must have been nervous in origin, the examining physician answered that, try as he might to find *a reactive strong enough to restore suddenly a completely ruined nervous system, he has knowledge of none.* For him, there could be no doubt: It was God who delivered him from evil. To thank him, Gabriel would return to join the hospital staff of Lourdes for fifty-one years. Only a slight lameness and a certain weakness of the back would bear witness, until his death, of what he had lived through.

As scientific clarity and certitude could not be established definitely in his case, the Church, in her prudence, did not recognize him as miraculously healed. This would not prevent grace from shining through this man until his death at ninety-two.

Amen.

A RESURRECTION

Marie Savoye, Twenty-Eighth Miraculous Healing,
September 20, 1901

19 01 *"There is no hope for this little girl. I give her at most fifteen days to live."* The doctor's verdict coldly echoed in the hospital room. Mrs. Savoye, standing, doubled over for a moment in shock at the news. Then she straightened up and looked the doctor in the eye.

"There is hope yet," Mrs. Savoye affirmed. "I have contacted the nursing sisters of the Lourdes hospital. Marie will take part in the next pilgrimage. She's leaving in a few days."

"Madam," replied the doctor, "look at your daughter: She's twenty-four and weighs fifty-five pounds. She's all skin and bones! She's been lying in this bed for six years now. She no longer has the strength to move, eat, or even speak. Not only is she suffering from infectious rheumatism, but also of cardiopathy: Her heart is affected. The fatigue of the trip will only hasten her demise… What are you hoping for, a miracle?"

"Yes!" the mother told him. "I've looked into it. Ever since the Blessed Sacrament processions were established, cures have been multiplying in Lourdes."

"But Madam, these cures are the fruit of the autosuggestion of patients suffering from nervous illness," the doctor responded. "Your daughter's case is different: It is a strictly physical condition."

"But there are miraculous cures, few, but there are," she explained. "What else do you propose – to wait here, doing nothing, for her to die before my eyes?"

"I understand," sighed the doctor. "Listen, I am not going to oppose this trip. I just wanted to guard you against excessive optimism."

A few days later, in the violet-colored train from Cambrai, Mrs. Savoye, with a heavy heart, recalled the physician's negative words. Marie was stretched out on a berth in one of the cars reserved for the sick. Would she survive the trip, the train's jolts, the nurses' handling? Mrs. Savoye doubted it. Before her, newspaper clippings were strewn, as well as the book by Dr. Boissarie, director of the Bureau of Medical Authentication, published the year before in 1900: *The Great Cures of Lourdes* (*Les Grandes Guérisons de Lourdes*). In it, the doctor spoke of the phenomenal multiplication of healing cases and especially of the first eucharistic miracles. Indeed, since 1888, the daily ceremonies at the grotto had been followed by a great eucharistic benediction in which the priests in procession showed the Blessed Sacrament to the sick on their stretchers near the fountains and pools. The crowd of pilgrims would invoke the Lord by repeating the words of the Gospel: "*Lord, save me! Lord, help me! Jesus, son of David, have pity on us!...*" Astounding miracles had already taken place, like the case of a young twenty-two-year-old woman, Nina Kin, who had one leg burned to the nerves by an acid spill; she had arisen from her stretcher as the Eucharist went by. Twenty-two was nearly Marie's age, and Mrs. Savoye wanted to hope still. As the northern plains streamed by outside the dull windows, she prayed amid the din of the train's progress.

As they arrived in Lourdes, Marie's state was critical. Pale and voiceless, she was spitting up blood. Bloodless, bones protruding, motionless – she already looked like a corpse. Even the doctors dared not touch her! Mrs. Savoye answered questions mechanically: "No, she has not gotten up from bed in six years." "No, she takes no solid foods, she doesn't have the strength." "No, she doesn't have tuberculosis, but she spits up blood because of the lesion in her heart." "Yes, she also suffers from a large sore on her back, a scab due to lack of exercise." One of the physicians, Dr. Perisson, told her that because she was in such a state, Marie absolutely could not be undressed and dipped into the pools. On the other hand, she would be able to participate in the eucharistic procession at the grotto the following day.

On September 20, 1901, at nine o'clock in the morning, Marie was placed in front of the grotto on her stretcher. Her mother was at her side. She had heard everything these last few days: The doctors had predicted her daughter's imminent death at least ten times. She also knew that Marie, too, had heard them. Yet her drawn little face did not betray fear, but only a sort of intense concentration. Perhaps she continued to believe in all this. Who knows? Mrs. Savoye closed her eyes to pray and clutched the stretcher's handles with all her strength. An acclamation made her open her eyes again. Some of the sick lifted themselves up on their stretchers, eyes wide open. Then came the priests. One of them, in the middle under a canopy, showed the Blessed Sacrament to the crowd. He walked by each of the sick, elevating the body of Christ. The priest was coming closer. Suddenly, he was there, in front of Marie's stretcher, and he elevated the host. Mrs. Savoye shook, a fog covered her eyes, yet she saw... yes, she saw all that took place then, as if in slow motion... the shudder, minute at first, under the stretcher's sheets... then, a terrible convulsion: Her daughter's body was violently hurled forward, bounding like a spring, and she fell on her knees at the foot of the stretcher, three feet away. Her frail figure got up and walked – yes, walked – toward the priest without any support. And her voice, her lovely youthful voice that she hadn't heard for so many years, said: "*I am healed.*"

Mrs. Savoye dashed to her daughter. Marie turned around and took her hands: "*I am healed!*" The crowd cheered; the priest made the sign of the cross. Marie joined the procession.

Some hours later, she entered the door of the Bureau of Medical Authentication on her own two feet. The doctors stared at her, dumbfounded. Her vital functions seemed wholly restored. To be sure, she was weak, pale, and thin, but a new fire shined in her eyes. "*This is no miracle, it's a resurrection!*" exclaimed Perisson.

In a few months, Marie would grow three inches and gain seventy-seven pounds. The doctors who examined her in her native Nord concluded one after the other that this was *a complete and definitive healing attributable to no natural cause.* Seven years later, Marie was an active young woman, dedicated to the sick in order to provide them with the same care she had received during her own long illness. On August 15, 1908, Archbishop Delamaire of Cambrai rendered his canonical judgment after examination and investigation: Marie Savoye was declared miraculously healed.

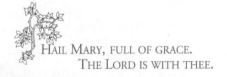

HAIL MARY, FULL OF GRACE.
THE LORD IS WITH THEE.

"THE MUZZLE OF A PISTOL OR THE FOOT OF THE CROSS"

Portrait of the Writer Joris-Karl Huysmans, December 1, 1905

19 05 Bitten by the frost that was seeping in through the windows, Joris-Karl Huysmans laboriously buttoned up his jacket. His valet, handing him an overcoat, noted with irritation how much his master's clothes had suffered from the humidity. It had been three days since Huysmans took up residence in Lourdes, and it had been raining cloudbursts of icy water without respite. From his window, the writer saw hordes of pilgrims marching by, converging upon the grotto and singing. But his weak condition and the journey's fatigue had, until then, kept him from setting foot outdoors. His gaze lost on the horizon, he told his valet: "Look at them, Jean. The rain doesn't stop them. Though their feet are in the mud, they still have the heart to sing! Let's go and take a closer look."

But he was interrupted by a violent fit of coughing, and Jean, annoyed at having to accompany him, muttered, "Let's go and seek your miracle."

Huysmans was not expecting a miracle. His wavering health was the result of a long nervous degeneration from which he did not expect to recover. It was a voracious faith that had brought him to Lourdes, a faith that sought to discover, to see everything. His recent conversion had left him somewhat obsessed by a curiosity and a hunger for the supernatural that led him to the grotto, to the mystery of the apparitions and the repeated reports of miracles. After years of perdition and decadence, he had done the rounds of unbridled pleasures and had grown weary of a painful freedom. Worn down by the vicious circle of his life, his world suddenly opened up. The grandeur of a dialogue with God, in all its purity and boundlessness, abruptly lightened his sorrow and loneliness. He then thought back on Jules Barbey d'Aurevilly's words as he finished reading his novel, *Against the Grain*: "*After such a book, the author is left with the choice between the muzzle of a pistol and the foot of the Cross.*"

He wished, by merging into the swarm of pilgrims, to witness the miracles, to become submerged in the power of God. He therefore swelled the flow of Christians flocking toward the grotto. The lame and the faltering hastened their pace to join the cartloads of the infirm. Huysmans' fascinated eyes beheld the crowd packed around the Virgin's statue. The sick returning from long hours of suffering, their well-meaning and devoted kin, and Catholics with their beatific faces formed an assembly enveloped in a spirit of hope and surrender. The writer saw in these lives of pain the very principle of his own life. All these beings belong, with him, to nature, which is the very will of God.

As his gaze scanned the procession of believers, he suddenly was knocked down by a religious trinket vendor. Just as he was collapsing into the mud, he caught himself on the merchant's basket and his face fell into a sundry mix of dusty baubles bearing the garish effigy of the Virgin. The fragile balance of his constitution was upset by this incident. The grandiloquent emotion that the scene had elicited from him just a few minutes before was shattered in an attack of nerves. Huysmans felt faint; suffocating in his drenched clothes, he now saw only ugliness and vulgarity. This tatty mass of broken and supplicant bodies revolted him, and he reproached himself for leaving the serene solitude of his Parisian apartment.

He then remembered why, for years on end, he had locked himself up there, tolerating only the sweet company of books, of the ancient authors who soothed him and the intellectual stimulation of medieval mystical quests for answers. Considering this rabble in its rags and tatters and hearing its wailing, he found he had nothing in common with these creatures who had come to demand of a grotesque statue the healing of their withered bodies! He now felt only repugnance for these puny souls whose faith was reduced to rules of behavior and to the habit of dull collective practices. Jean came near, worried at seeing him so pale, but Huysmans, overtaken by panic, fled without a backward glance.

He knew he must recover that breath of Being and of the Spirit that had inebriated him to the point of conversion. The writer hastened his pace and, to escape from the Lourdes basilica's artificial and imposing stature, he plunged into the crypt's long hallway lined with *ex votos*, those testimonials of thanksgiving for prayers answered.

The place's silence and intimacy had a calming effect on him. The pews were empty, and the soberness of the whole presented a sharp contrast to the other places of devotion in Lourdes. There was, in this starkness, in the purity of the red luminaries gently lighting the chancel's worn stones, an incredible consolation. Huysmans saw a little chaplain, pudgy and smiling, approach, his alb silently gliding over the central aisle's flagstones. Having reached him, the man whispered: "Some of the choristers need to practice for the Office. We expected to find the crypt empty... Would it trouble your prayers?"

But Huysmans was not listening to him. Three pure and crystalline voices had burst forth from the choir. He leaned forward and managed to glimpse the singers' silhouettes, but then turned away. Eyes shut, he abandoned himself to these luminous harmonies. He at last savored the soul's elevation. These notes, nearly supernatural in their transparency and beauty, unfurled about him a halo that enveloped him and healed his wounds. He then swore that his heart was capable of the deepest and most humble love. The blending of the voices saved him from back-sliding. It was indeed God who inspires this eternity in man, this absolute beauty. And it was God who was speaking to him, opening his heart and elevating his spirit.

The last note fell, but Huysmans remained dazed. His faith had resonated there in the crypt and in the ineffable beauty of Gregorian chant. Irresistibly, he had to return to Paris to put his pen to the test of this sublime and recovered faith.

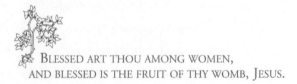

BLESSED ART THOU AMONG WOMEN,
AND BLESSED IS THE FRUIT OF THY WOMB, JESUS.

A FAMILY OF ARTISTS
IN LOURDES' SERVICE

The Orsoni Mosaicists, June 3, 1906

1906 Day was just breaking at the *Corte dei Vedei*, in the Cannaregio neighborhood of Venice. Since May 1888, a beautiful two-story building had been home to the Orsoni firm, a famous glassworks specialized in the manufacture and creation of mosaics.

Angelo Orsoni, the master of the house, was preparing to remove a viscous glass paste from the kiln to check its color. It took a whole night to create this incandescent ball, fruit of a centuries-old recipe. This operation, so familiar to him, produced ever-new effects on Angelo's sensitivity. On that day, he saw in the bright red that nearly seemed to breathe through the kiln's mouth the last glowing flashes of the sun setting on the lagoon.

The master mosaicist was tired. The work in hand that had been occupying him for several years already was very demanding on him, but it was so magnificent – the Basilica of the Rosary in Lourdes. Angelo provided the mosaicist Facchina with millions of shimmering tesserae to adorn the structure's various chapels. Once assembled, its colored sparks would take on the features of Mary, Joseph, and the angels. He was particularly attached to this great work, and a veritable fervor overcame him a little more every day.

As morning dawned, the household gently awakened. The master recognized the clicking of glass being set on work benches, cut into squares, and reduced to tesserae by means of tiny hammers; and on the first story the sound of shovels scraping the floor to load the sand that comprises glass paste. And, always, there was the fire's hum from the furnace. *That noise is so familiar to me that I would nearly think it to be silence*, Angelo thought with a nostalgic smile. He remembered that by the age of seven he was lending a hand to the workmen in a glassworks in Murano. Hypnotized by the changing colors of the *fritta* in the kiln, the smells of silica and of soda, the song of broken glass fragments, he had started experimenting with his first mixtures at a young age. Most importantly, Angelo – who learned to read and write by himself – acquired, by experience, the magic of colors and the all-consuming devotion to the secret of color shade creation.

"Be careful, Giovanni, for this hue of turquoise, you'll need a good spoonful of cobalt less next time," Angelo advised. It was one instruction among many others, for Angelo, patiently and precisely, was transmitting his knowledge to his son, to whom he would hand over the enterprise's management in 1911, ten years before his death.

Fast forward to Cannaregio, June 2002. While the liquid Sunday peace cloaked the city, Ruggero Orsoni was locked in his laboratory. As often happened on Sunday, he was carrying out trials in color composition. This time, a particularly intense shade of blue that did not figure in the catalog had been ordered, and Ruggero was having fun changing the doses of cobalt to obtain the desired shade, using the very spoon his great-grandfather had used. It had clocked up so many years of service that it was slightly blackened with oxidization, but it remained steady and resistant, like the succession of generations in the Orsoni business.

Today, as it has been since 1969, in this same two-story building, it is Ruggero and his brother Lucio, Angelo's great-grandsons, who carry on mosaic creation and manufacture in the footsteps of the ancestor who invented the gold tessera.

Ruggero seems to have inherited Angelo's alchemical talent. Lucio, on the other hand, is a mosaicist, and his abstract compositions have made his fame. Their talents are perfectly complementary – the artist and the technician, the body and the soul of this expertise that is as unassailable by time as a well-made tessera. In the workshop, nothing has changed; the palette of colors available in the "library of color" is just as extraordinary as a century ago. The ranges of blues and reds, greens and golds are stacked up in a multitude of gradations with labels such as "lemon," "orange," and "skin." The *souls*[1] to be mixed with *bodies* to obtain multiple color gradations are the same. Just like Angelo Orsoni's precious recipes, they are carefully preserved in the little black-bound books that Ruggero uses, repeating exactly the chemical compositions used in past projects in order to create "historical" shades.

We move now to Lourdes, the Basilica of Our Lady of the Rosary, September 2003. *What an emotion to see and touch the mosaics my great-grandfather made!* thought Lucio Orsoni. Stopped in the middle of the center aisle before the representation of the Annunciation, he had tears in his eyes. Damaged by time and by the elements, his ancestor's mosaics had come to need restoration. Naturally, the shrine called upon the Orsoni family. Lucio contemplated the result on the fifteen mosaics adorning the basilica's five chapels. He was proud of having coordinated the mosaic artists' work with the help of Francis Latour, who managed the work in the shrine's name. It was not just a work of art that was recovering all its splendor; it was the mosaic of a family at the service of the Basilica of the Rosary. Lucio smiled as he watched the pilgrims and

---

1. The basic components.

thought of Angelo Orsoni, who so dedicated himself to this work, to this place, so that the gold-leaf tesserae might allow a glimmer of God's beauty to enter into the pilgrim's eyes.

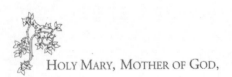

HOLY MARY, MOTHER OF GOD,

A GREAT SURGE OF FAITH

The Apparitions' Fiftieth Anniversary, August 23, 1908

1908 Fifty years… It has been fifty years since the Holy Virgin deigned to appear in the grotto at Massabielle, in Lourdes. Fifty years that miracles had made of this land a haven of salvation and hope for Christians the world over.

All the newspapers of France and Navarre had a duty to cover the shrine's jubilee. No news could supplant it in this year 1908. The editor-in-chief had asked me to go along with him to cover the great events of this fiftieth anniversary. As I was a young reporter just starting out, there is no need for me to point out how much honor this represented for me. This was one of the greatest events of the year and of the beginning century's religious history!

The festivities began on February 11, anniversary of the first apparition to Bernadette Soubirous; they continued on March 25, the day the Holy Virgin told her, "I am the Immaculate Conception"; then they went on to July 16, the date of the last apparition. These three celebrations had an extraordinary effect: Tens of thousands of pilgrims poured in from all over the country to meditate and pray to Mary. Rarely, perhaps never, had anyone seen so many faithful gather in France. The celebrations continued on October 4 with the dedication of the two turrets on the basilica's upper part, and climaxed on February 11, 1909, the last day of the jubilee year.

Before these last two events, we once again went down to Lourdes with Jean, the editor-in-chief, on Sunday, August 23, to cover a special celebration for the miraculously healed.

The weather forecasts of the previous day were correct: Rain had lashed at my windows since early morning. I was having trouble imagining the Offices unfolding under this deluge. When Jean came to fetch me, I was taken aback: "What? The processions haven't been canceled?"

He cut me off with an enormous laugh, and said: "Do you really think that a few raindrops, a storm, or even a tempest could stop these pilgrims? The miraculously healed people we are going to meet have already had a brush with death, and believe me, their faith could hardly consider a bad weather forecast an obstacle. Come on, hurry up, and don't bother with an umbrella; it's useless. You need to be like them and with them, to test your body's limits. You'll be in a better position to talk about it later, you'll see."

The Mass in the basilica was remarkable in intensity. When we left for the procession, the driving rain and mud were already less of a bother. We joined the procession. In front of us, three hundred twenty-five healed people – miraculously and otherwise – carried a banner aloft, and each had five witnesses around them. We slowly moved forward toward the grotto, drenched to the bone. Around us was a seemingly limitless crowd of forty-, fifty-, sixty-thousand people… who could say? Once there, Father Picart, head of the General Council of Pilgrimages, was awaiting us to say a few words. But hardly had he uttered his first sentences when a *Magnificat* burst out. All eyes turned at the same time toward a patient who had just come out of one of the pools, without his crutches.

This moving scene swelled our hearts with an ardor and a joy I would not otherwise have been able to imagine. When we resumed the procession to the foot of the basilica, we no longer were bothered by the rain; although it was of a rare intensity, we forgot about it. The hymns and prayers surrounded us with such power that they literally enveloped us. Gestures of hope multiplied. One miraculously healed woman proudly brandished her crutches, the symbols of her bygone infirmity; another delicately pushed away the arms that were supporting her.

The immense crowd was of one heart when the *Tantum ergo* resounded but, even more surprisingly, it became absolutely quiet in seconds at Bishop Bouvier's request as it entered into prayer. Then Father Picart took the floor again to exhort the sick to imitate their miraculously healed brothers and sisters, who bear upon themselves the reality of the divine miracle: "*Rise, brethren, and walk!*"

We all were looking at these infirm, motionless people, nailed to their chairs, to their stretchers. Not too far away, a sick lady stood up and approached the altar, fragile but revivified. Praise was heard everywhere. Another young woman made an effort to rise, then another. The crowd was emboldened and cheered these marvels with all its heart; *Magnificats* arose on all sides; curiosity, happiness, prayer, praise mingled together in a deep bliss. We were transported as the celebration ended in a peace and a joy I had never felt before. The sick, very dignified, returned to the welcoming areas. Most had not budged from their chairs or their stretchers, of course, but their souls were saturated with hope.

When I returned to the hotel, I was still shaken by all that I had just experienced. I wondered whether my article would mention inner healings or miracles in the strict sense, and whether the Church would validate them as such... I did not know. On the other hand, I knew its title: "The Day of the Miraculously Healed," the day when over fifty thousand people accompanied three hundred twenty-five miraculously healed people to pray and, in an unimagined communion, to thank the

Holy Virgin Mary for the marvels and blessings she has been lavishing here for fifty years now.

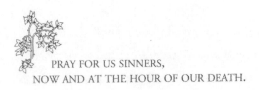

PRAY FOR US SINNERS,
NOW AND AT THE HOUR OF OUR DEATH.

THE QUEEN OF PEACE

Marian Piety during World War I,
October 1, 1914

19 14 Battle was raging in Ramscapelle, Belgium. German artillery was setting its sights on the parish church. When the smoke cleared, the French and Belgian troops who had defended the village could do nothing more than verify the extent of the destruction. Though the walls still stood in a prodigious balancing act, the roof no longer existed. The inside was all dust, rubble, and ash. Once again, the madness of mankind had leveled a monument consecrated to God – a fate the whole village shared!

As they passed before the bell tower destroyed by the shells, the soldiers stared incredulously. A gracious feminine figure stood very erect amid the ruins. All dressed in white, she was wearing a dazzling blue sash, and the yellow roses on her bare feet had not lost a single plaster petal! Unharmed and smiling, the Virgin of Lourdes was the only survivor among the now-vanished church furnishings.

That evening, over cold soup brought in by the kitchen wagon, comments abounded. Miracle? Chance? Among the French, it did not take much to reignite the discussions common before the war that pitted "church mice" against "coffeehouse miscreants" – that is, those who, sitting at a table across from the church, would sneer at the faithful after Mass. Yet times had changed, and the debate had become nearly brotherly. The "sacred union" had worked a reconciliation between the two camps. Confronted with a common enemy, secularists and Catholics stood shoulder to shoulder; in the mud of the trenches, military chaplains and schoolteachers of the Republic shook hands!

That evening, although some did let an easy joke fly – "Hey guys, we've got an apparition!" – most soldiers kept a respectful reserve. Some, stuffing their hands deep into their pockets, discreetly fingered a rosary they had brought to the battlefield. Others wore around their necks a miraculous medal bearing the image that the Virgin had shown to Catherine Labouré in 1830. Marian devotion was widespread among the grunts. In the midst of their daily hell, they often invoked the Mother of God, image of grace, icon of eternal peace. For the time that a few *Aves* take, she helped them to forget the machine-gun fire, the vermin, even the Hun.

In order to respond to this piety, a Belgian chaplain proposed that the men join the Living Rosary Association.[1] Its six hundred members were committed to praying a decade every day – a demanding requirement in this ceaseless war in which time was not the soldier's own. Bishop Schoepfer of Tarbes and Lourdes personally laid the list of these volunteers in the grotto under the Virgin's statue.

Marian piety existed even at the top of the French general staff. Ferdinand Foch, who would earn his marshal's baton in 1918, was a native of Tarbes. His mother – as he liked to relate – once accompanied Bernadette to the grotto. He was not at all an intransigent anticlericalist like Georges Clemenceau! In the midst of his strategic deliberations, Foch indulged the luxury of a daily rosary. In his eyes, prayer was a weapon that was easily as powerful as any gun or sword used in battle. In villages they passed through, he enjoyed gathering the children for a short prayer

---

1. Founded in 1826 by a young woman from Lyons, Pauline Jaricot, for the propagation of the faith.

in the church. Fortified by these privileged moments, he felt better prepared for resuming the pursuit of military objectives.

Did he believe, as so many others did, that Mary would secure victory for France? He surely had heard thousands of far-fetched propaganda stories and did not consider credible the fantastic rumors that sometimes ran through the French army. They said, for example, that Mary appeared to sixty thousand Germans as they were about to invade Paris, an intervention that halted their advance and changed the course of the war.

Though Mary's hand may not have been as visible as some claimed in the twists and turns of this bloody war, she did remain the Queen of Peace, the mother of all these soldiers sent to the meat grinder by their respective governments. It was by this title that many of them sought refuge under her protection on either side of the lines. "Over there" among the Germans as well as among the Austrians, there were many rosaries tucked deep inside the pockets of their uniforms. In the office of Marshal Hindenburg, a Lutheran if ever there was one, a statue of the Virgin leaned over the ordnance survey maps! Among the enemies of World War I, too, how many were yesterday's pilgrims, welcomed as brothers in Lourdes, like Countess Berchold, the wife of the Austrian minister of foreign affairs, who had participated in the great Eucharistic Congress of July 1914?

Four years later, in 1918, the "fields of honor" were finally made peaceful once again by the armistice. Marshal Foch could return to see the landscapes of his native Bigorre. On his way home, he stopped in Lourdes to give thanks. His armies' victory, the fragile peace that the diplomats had established – *this is not peace, it is a twenty-year armistice*, he lucidly predicted – he wished to lay at Mary's feet.

Amen.

The Virgin of Lourdes in the Streets of London

A Procession for Peace, May 26, 1918

19 18 *"Hail Mary, full of grace, the Lord is with thee..."* In London, within the Catholic Westminster Cathedral's brand-new walls, a large crowd had recited the ancient prayer to the Virgin. Their prayer echoed throughout the immense rectangle formed by the sanctuary built on the model of Roman basilicas; it filled the side chapels whose walls were covered in luminous mosaics; it rose in its majesty up to the immense vaults, where it burst into supplication.

It was three o'clock in the afternoon on May 26, 1918, the day celebrated by the Church as the feast of the Holy Trinity. Cardinal Francis Bourne of London had chosen this day to lead a procession in honor of someone close to his heart. A few moments later, the crowd of faithful left the cathedral to follow the statue of Our Lady of Lourdes as it was carried through the capital's streets under a heavy gray sky.

Like all bishops, all clergy, and all the laity of Europe, Cardinal Bourne called in his prayers for the end of the Great War. May this fourth year of the conflict be the last! Pope Benedict XV's wish to put an end to this *horrible butchery that dishonors Europe* was on the mind of the prelate as he prepared to exit the cathedral at the head of the faithful.

How to put an end to this abominable war? How to defeat the German and Austro-Hungarian powers that the cardinal, as well as all the people united under the Triple Entente, considered to be guilty of this bloodbath? Cardinal Bourne had the idea of this procession in honor of the Pyrenees Virgin. A great Francophile, he had already been to Lourdes in 1912 to solemnly consecrate his country to Our Lady. On the day of the procession, he asked the Virgin of Massabielle to intervene before God for the triumph of the allied armies.

The cardinal, no doubt, had not considered Bernadette's attitude some fifty years earlier during the Franco-Prussian War of 1870. The young religious was approached by many visitors who had come to find her in Nevers. The inquisitive wanted to extract from her hypothetical revelations about the Prussians, the French, and the conflict's outcome. Bernadette, however, had no spectacular secret to reveal as fodder for these patriots. The Virgin of Massabielle had never broached political or strategic matters!

In 1918, however, such neutrality was unthinkable. Ardently convinced of their own cause's loftiness, the Catholics of the alliance could not imagine that God might refuse them his support. That was the hope that opened wide the cathedral's great doors to the procession that took place that May 26. The orderly crowd massed behind the Lady in white with a blue sash, the familiar figure imported from a faraway town in southwestern France. Leaving behind the immense cathedral whose red bricks and Byzantine cupolas blazed against London's sky, the procession started to travel through the capital's streets lined with those sturdier new metal-and-concrete buildings that were an offshoot of the war, an architecture with a promising future. This unexpected procession elicited various comments as it went by.

"Look at those Catholics! They still don't understand that it's better to pray to God directly rather than to his saints."

"To God? Let's rather put our trust in our prime minister, Lloyd George; he knows about conducting war…"

"Mind you, he has capable advisors. Did you know that Sir Winston Churchill is having revolutionary machines built, *tanks*? They're armored vehicles on treads, unassailable, indestructible… To face the Germans, I put my faith in these technical advances rather than in the arm of God!"

"Especially considering that the Austro-Hungarians are also Catholic. Who knows? Emperor Franz Joseph may have ordered a procession in honor of the Virgin of Lourdes in the streets of Vienna!"

Upon catching sight of the procession, a few women drew near and shouted out an unexpected exclamation: "*Votes for women!*"

Policemen fell upon these disruptive women and dragged them to the nearest station. During these war years, the suffragettes' fight was an ongoing struggle. Any opportunity was worth seizing if it meant a chance to be heard by the crowds and eventually to obtain political equality! As they were dragged away by the police, the protesters continued: "These gentlemen place a lady on their altars and yet still refuse us the right to vote!"

The procession continued on its way to the rhythm of chanted prayers to the Virgin. As it advanced, it slowly swelled; passers-by recognized Cardinal Bourne, who was universally admired for his vigor and his social work. An archbishop at forty-two and a cardinal fewer than ten years later, this energetic young prelate had always been committed to putting into practice what at the time was a very novel idea – the closer association of lay people in the life of the Church. The crowd of London Catholics had an appreciative affection for him in return.

On the same day, a thousand miles from the paved streets of the British capital, all the Catholics of Lourdes had begun praying in unison with London. This was significant, for although the resident population of Lourdes was just four thousand, the little town had welcomed six thousand refugees since the beginning of the war. From Belgium, Picardy, or Lorraine, these displaced people fled their lands that had been rutted with trenches for battle. Where could one find a better refuge than in this Pyrenees town for which so many held fond memories of their pilgrimages there of previous years? That was why the number of resident families in Lourdes had more than doubled within a just a few months' time.

On that May 26, an article in the *Journal de la Grotte* announced the distant procession led by Cardinal Bourne in London in honor of the Virgin of Massabielle. Bishop Schoepfer joined the undertaking in thought and prayer. Originally from Alsace, he had long thrown all of his spiritual energies into the battle, personally presiding at a rosary for an end to the conflict each day at five o'clock in the afternoon.

So in London and Lourdes, great metropolis and modest hamlet, the faithful assailed heaven together, lifting their eyes to the Virgin's peaceful face in hope for peace and reconciliation.

Hail Mary, full of grace.
The Lord is with thee.

An Unforgettable Summer

A Curious Young Man's Pilgrimage, August 24, 1918

19 18 Dear Jean,

You'll forgive my cramped handwriting, but I have so much to tell you that I wouldn't want to waste the least square inch of paper. As you know, paper is getting scarce over here. Bread, too, for that matter, and I have to jump through all sorts of hoops to get some for our group of pilgrims. I hope that you, on the front, are wanting for nothing and that you are getting enough to eat.

Since I left Le Bugue and our beautiful region of Dordogne for Lourdes, so much has happened that I don't know where to begin. I'll try to be as detailed as possible so that you can clearly picture what I see, what I hear, and what I feel, too.

To tell you the truth, Lourdes is a small, dirty, and muddy town, as it often rains here. But that is not important. What counts is the shrine. And as for that, I must confess that I was shaken. When we first arrived, we participated in the torchlight procession. You may not recognize your brother when I tell you that I wept like a child at the final *Credo*! It was so beautiful – the basilica's magnificent lines shining in the glare of a thousand torches, a sea of fire proceeding, blazing the path as the air reverberated with countless voices praying in unison. The sight is enough to convert the most obdurate of souls. But wait, the best is yet to come.

Ever since I arrived here, I have profited intensely with every day. I have, of course, visited Lourdes, but also Pau, Cauterets, and Bagnères-de-Bigorre. Cauterets is a pretty, modern town. The castle in Pau is also worth the detour. But it is especially the Pyrenees landscapes that enchant me. I could describe them to you at length, but I doubt it would interest you as much as other things. So back to Lourdes.

As you can imagine, I have walked the shrine in all directions – the Basilica of the Immaculate Conception, that of the Rosary, the esplanade and, above all, the grotto! It is formed of three excavations dug out in a triangular pattern. The lower one, closed off with a grille, contains a little altar and two candlesticks. The upper right excavation, where Our Lady appeared, shelters a very beautiful white marble statue surrounded by two rosebush branches. The grotto walls and part of the cliff are covered in crutches.

That is where I took Berthe, our neighbor in Le Bugue, this afternoon. Since the beginning of our pilgrimage, I have taken her wherever she wants, pulling her in her little cart. I don't know whether you recall Berthe. The poor thing has been afflicted for twenty years now with an incurable disease that forces her to walk in horrible pain, even with a walking stick. Her left leg is three or four inches shorter than the right. I wrote "has been afflicted," but it would have been more accurate to write "used to be afflicted"! For when I came back to the hotel just now, she opened the door suddenly and fell on my neck, crying, "*Master Henri, what a joy, I am healed!*" Believe it or not, I wasn't all that surprised, because I had given it a lot of thought since my departure. Berthe, who is thirty-two, has come here for the ninth time to pray for healing. Still, I am very happy and I have asked her to tell me what she felt in detail.

As I told you, I had taken Berthe before the grotto and had left her there in another pilgrim's care. About half an hour later, at about six twenty, she felt a deep uneasiness. A great shiver ran through her. She even felt she might die. And then, she felt an invincible force urging her to rise and get on her knees, which she did. Yet for the past twenty years, she had been unable to kneel!

Needless to say, the news has created quite a stir over here. At the hotel, everybody is on the lookout for the least of her movements, and they acclaim the Virgin Mary and Our Lord. When Berthe goes about, people respectfully touch her. She is kissed and applauded. Chants are sung: "*Laudate, Laudate, Laudate Mariam...*" God has heard this poor lady who has suffered terribly. Berthe even claims that her eyesight, which had been poor, has also improved. And it is plain to see that her shorter leg has returned to a normal size!

To be witness to such a healing overwhelms me. Since I arrived here, a paralyzed young girl and another woman also have been healed. What is especially fascinating is to see, with one's own eyes, a healed person who is still astonished by what has happened even though she never lost hope. And as for hope, Berthe had plenty to spare, I assure you!

Dear brother, it is getting late now, and I confess that this day has rather tired me out. What emotions! This pilgrimage is one of the highlights of my life. I have telegraphed the good news to Le Bugue. I expect our arrival there will be a triumph. When you are on furlough, we'll pay a visit to Berthe together so that you can see the miracle for yourself.

Take good care of yourself and come home soon. I am praying for you.

Your brother, Henri.

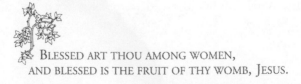

BLESSED ART THOU AMONG WOMEN,
AND BLESSED IS THE FRUIT OF THY WOMB, JESUS.

A MAN STANDING

The Unexplained Healing of John Traynor,
July 25, 1923

19 23 Shells exploded on the ground in a pitiless rhythm. Amid a rain of iron and fire, an English battalion, badly outmaneuvered, struggled mightily to conduct an orderly retreat. Withdrawal of the troops back toward Antwerp was its only chance for survival. The officers encouraged their men by shouting rallying cries, but their screams were drowned out by the din of German artillery. The battalion's progress was slow, its successful escape far from assured.

Nearly blinded by the dense smoke, John Traynor ran, forging his way across the bombarded terrain along with his companions, terrified that the next German shell might be for him. With every yard's advance he drew closer to safety, though it was like crossing through hell. Suddenly, a whistle tore through the darkened air just above him. The poor man shouted out… and then opened his eyes.

The peaceful hoot of a screech owl had taken the place of the cannons' rumbling. Through the open window, John Traynor glimpsed the mountains of Lourdes outlined against the summer sky, their shape illuminated by moonlight. The nightmare was over; the fields of death belonged to a different world from this serene landscape.

The man sighed, then rolled over in his bed with difficulty. October 8, 1914, returned every night to haunt him. And other even more terrible images were superimposed on those of the plain of Antwerp. Indeed, after undergoing brain surgery to remove the shrapnel shard he had received that day, Traynor chose to return to the front. He was reassigned to the Dardanelles expeditionary force. Landing in Egypt, he broadened his horizons, witnessing desolate open stretches, a land of sand and rock where the war continued its implacable work of human butchery. In April 1915, his unit was thrust up against the Seddul Bahr fortress, which was held by the Turkish army. During the siege, as he was rushing to the assistance of a wounded and unconscious officer, he was felled to the ground by a hail of machine-gun fire.

Immediately operated on in Alexandria and then repatriated to England, Traynor was examined by quite a few doctors, all of whom judged his case to be desperate. His right arm and both legs were paralyzed, and his lungs were affected; his brain remained damaged by his first injury. The veteran soldier had taken his place in a wheelchair typical of a Great War invalid. Surgical interventions attempted on him had all failed, one after the other, causing even further irreversible damage along the way, the most serious being total incontinence.

John Traynor sighed once again. With his left arm, he removed the overly warm blanket that enveloped his pain-racked body. He thought of his forthcoming admission to the Mossley Hill Hospice for Incurables in England. A few days before his final admission to that last refuge of the desperate, he moved heaven and earth to obtain permission to travel to Lourdes with the Liverpool pilgrimage. His doctors were opposed to it; but the trip's organizers were willing to receive him despite the violent epileptic seizures he suffered every day. That was how he had come to find himself under the Lourdes sky on this tranquil night of July 24 to

25, 1923, brought here by a hope as great as it was unreasonable. Already the day before he had been dipped into the pool filled from the source once revealed to Bernadette by the Virgin. Immersed in the clear water, John Traynor prayed intensely, his faith riveted firmly in his heart. To God the Father, nothing is impossible... or to the Son, who made a bedridden man rise... or to the Holy Spirit, who heals souls within bodies. No, nothing is impossible, especially in this place where so many graces have flourished under the Virgin's gaze.

The next day, Traynor had himself carried to the pool once again. Confident, he looked at his useless legs and his paralyzed arm on which the water's reflections played. A smile began to form on his lips during an *Ave*. Distracted for a moment, he thought of the pair of shoes he had bought in Liverpool before his departure. He had declared to the astonished clerk: "*I shall come back to see you on my return from France. I'll be wearing these shoes, and I'll be standing!*" The merchant nodded, hesitating between compassion for his patron's physical suffering and commiseration for his overactive imagination.

Suddenly, Traynor's legs thrashed in the pool. The stretcher-bearers hastily drew the paralytic out of the water, fearing one of those spectacular epileptic seizures they had already witnessed. Yet nothing happened – no convulsion, no shriek. Fully in possession of his mental faculties, Traynor was brought to the esplanade to participate in the Blessed Sacrament procession with the other sick pilgrims.

A few moments later, the welcoming committee members saw a man who was walking with some difficulty as he entered their office. It was John Traynor! With typical British understatement, he had come to announce that he was healed of his infirmities. The doctors, who were called at once, verified his ability to stand upright. They compared it to the voluminous medical file that their English colleagues had drawn up. As the hours passed, the healing became more striking. Just before he departed Lourdes, the veteran was examined one last time. His gait was flawless. His right arm now only presented, as an aftereffect of the past, a slight atrophy of the hand muscles. The specter of epileptic seizures had apparently disappeared.

The most thunderstruck reaction would be that of the shoe salesman in Liverpool – who, early in August, would see a very upright and solid fellow walk into his shop wearing a new pair of shoes!

Traynor's name was added to the list of unexplained healings verified in Lourdes. Among some seven thousand stories of healings, only sixty-seven would be officially recognized by the Church; that of the English soldier would not be among them. Nevertheless, John Traynor's life was transformed by this overwhelming grace, for which he would return to thank the Virgin every year as a stretcher-bearer in the service of other sick pilgrims.

Holy Mary, Mother of God,

THE RELIGIOUS WHO DID NOT RETURN TO DUST

Bernadette's Body, April 18, 1925

1925 The thick hand of Dr. Comte, expert in handling the scalpel, was resting respectfully on the New Testament. In a firm voice, the surgeon pronounced the oath set before him:

"I swear and promise to carry out faithfully what is requested of me, and to tell the truth both in the answers I shall give to the questions posed to me and in my written reports regarding the examination of Sister Marie-Bernard Soubirous' body, so help me God with these holy Gospels."

The echo of his oath reverberated for a few moments in the Saint Joseph Chapel in Nevers where Bernadette's tomb is located. Once it died down, it was followed by the warm voice of Dr. Talon, a colleague of Comte's, who enunciated each syllable of the same promise with restrained emotion. Next it was the turn of the workmen charged with opening the vault. A bit intimidated by so much solemnity, they also swore to perform their task rigorously and honestly.

On that April 18, 1925, the civil and ecclesiastical authorities had decided to proceed to the third examination of the body of the young woman of Lourdes who had passed away here, in an exile of her choosing, forty-six years earlier. Indeed, over a thousand miles from the peaceful convent of Nevers, within the imposing walls of his papal palace, Pope Pius XI was attentively considering Bernadette's file.

Already in 1913, Pius X had given his permission for the opening of beatification proceedings. The awful war that broke out the following year absorbed all of the energy and eloquence of his successor, Benedict XV. Concentrating his efforts on putting an end to this nightmare, the Pope placed a moratorium on peacetime projects. The process really began in 1918. It had progressed with the measured pace and prudence that the Church required before proposing a model of holiness to believers.

In 1925, the Church asked that Bernadette's mortal body be examined. That is why workmen and two doctors entrusted with this examination were gathered at her vault.

While waiting for the masons and carpenters to open Bernadette's casket, Comte and Talon recalled the memory of the exhumation they had already done in 1919, which itself came after a first examination of the body conducted in 1909. These had been legal formalities called for by canon law as a prerequisite to the beatification process. In 1919, the two physicians had been able only to confirm the reports established by their colleagues ten years before. Bernadette's body had undergone no decomposition: The young Religious appeared as though she was mummified in her ample black habit, her intact hands clutching the rosary beads she had so often prayed in honor of the apparition at Massabielle.

When the workmen broke the seals and carefully uncovered the body, the two physicians came forward simultaneously. What they observed moved them but did not surprise them: Bernadette's mortal remains were still intact.

Yet the two doctors did not proclaim it a miracle. They knew that certain human bodies, in a rare biological phenomenon, escape post-mortem decomposition. To be sure, they were surprised that such an exception might have taken place in a humid tomb, and for so fragile a body as that of this young woman, exhausted by chronic health problems. Yet the doctors were careful to refrain from drawing a definite conclusion. They could only observe and examine the body in order to draw up an impartial report separately. Comte, the surgeon, removed a few bone fragments, future relics destined for the Vatican and for Lourdes. After this operation followed the molding of face and hands to have a thin wax film made to affix onto Bernadette's face to protect it from the ambient air. Indeed, Bernadette was going to leave her tomb to be placed instead in a glass case before which the faithful would be able to pray. She is visible to this day in a chapel of the Saint-Gildard convent in Nevers.

PRAY FOR US SINNERS,
NOW AND AT THE HOUR OF OUR DEATH.

GOD'S ADVENTURESS

Marie-Thérèse Noblet, Thirty-Second Miraculous Healing,
November 22, 1929

19 29 There was the mountain before her – infinite, reaching beyond the clouds that stretched over it and veiled it. The giant pandanus forest smelled humid. The convoy halted. Mother Marie-Thérèse suffered and said nothing. On her delicate face she had that eternal smile of self-surrender that her Papuan sisters, the Handmaids of the Lord, knew well. Soon the travelers would be in the straw hut village in this lost district of Mafulu, in the depths of New Guinea, which even the coastal natives dared not risk traveling through. Mother Marie-Thérèse's mission was to bring the Lord's mercy where nobody went, to aid her native sisters in their tasks, to comfort them and watch over them like a mother. Her body shouted and wept in the chaos of the footpath. But here in the mountains, one had to persevere in one's journey to avoid being caught in the night's storm.

Perseverance! She knew the meaning of the word, this Mother Marie-Thérèse Noblet, who was born on September 30, 1859, in Signy-l'Abbaye, in the Ardennes, France. Born to a good provincial family, she had been destined to set up a simple and peaceful household. Yet her life was soon marked by pain and illness. Her body, devoured by Pott's disease, made her suffer atrociously and should have proved fatal.

She was again suffering on this journey, but she had already lived many extraordinary years. Perched on her uncomfortable mount, she had to reach the village before the fall of the long, humid, star-drenched southern hemisphere night. Louis the Kanak, who led the small group, was fast. Shadows already were lengthening, and the gold of the declining light hemmed the high-perched leaves hanging off the tall pandanus like fine hair. Suddenly, the rush of water was heard, and the native bridge crossing the river appeared, with its crisscrossed branches for railings. It seemed so precariously balanced.

Mother Marie-Thérèse was tense: Every time she crossed this bridge, her heart beat faster. Large knotty branches overhung the torrent's loud flow. The flood of rumbling fresh water reminded her of the Gave and of the blessing of Lourdes' waters, that bath for the sick that had raised up her bruised and paralyzed body.

Go there! These were the marching orders of someone who owed everything to the Virgin, someone who was the last of the twenty-two Lourdes healings in 1907! How could she forget that August 31, 1905, when, returning from the Blessed Sacrament procession on her stretcher, she was lifted up and straightened by the Lord at the doorstep of the Hospital of Our Lady of Sorrows? She was sixteen and, deep in her heart, was in that twilight of the condemned that only faith can enlighten with the glimmer of hope. That healing was not only a gift made to her body, which would always remain nervous and fragile, but also a serenade to her soul, which from that moment would gradually grow in the Lord. What love, what trust she had to have to reach this forest at dusk, after so many renouncements! She remembered this new grace in her life, her meeting with Father Jullien, the missionary Jesuit, who gave her a taste for great causes and distant horizons. On December 8, 1921, in response to the work of God in her healing, she made her vows at the age of thirty-two in the monastery of Koubouna, named Florival by the bishop because of the flowers that the rain and the scented breeze caused to fall like so much snow onto the valley slopes. Bishop de Boismenu, Vicar Apostolic of New Guinea and founder of the Handmaids of the Lord, was to appoint the little miracle girl of Lourdes their superior.

Ecce ancilla Domini, as says saint Luke (Lk 1:38): Handmaid of the Lord is what Mother Marie-Thérèse was with all her being. "*I am the little missionary of the Lord,*" she often said when she spoke to those who met her and were surprised at her courage, her gentle firmness with these simple girls whose hearts she had won and whose language she had been able to master. This inclination to serve and to give of herself came with great humility as she stooped to the smallest of needs. As befits a true missionary, her feet were here and there, always on the go, like the apostles', despite her advancing age and the wretched body that carried her as best it could. The mission was there, infinite and seething like the water of the monsoon floods. She had allowed herself to be inhabited by the gestures that comfort and heal and by a lusterless life on the other side of the world. Marie-Thérèse had become the adventuress of God, going around to unknown lands to teach mothers to bathe their children in those dented tin basins that sing in the rain, and to lavish the love of God on these wild souls that are as beautiful and rough as tree bark.

In the Futu village that welcomed an exhausted Mother Marie-Thérèse at nightfall, no one could guess that it would be the last time she would be coming. Soon, she who was affectionately known there as Mamé Teresa would let her bright soul fly away among the jasmine flowers. On January 15, 1930, she joined for ever the God who covered her sick girl's cross with a mantle of light, whom she gratefully followed with a handmaid's comforting hands.

Ecce ancilla Domini were her last words.

Amen.

TO KNOW HER WHO SAID YES

The Marian Congresses, July 27, 1930

1930 Bishop Pierre-Marie Gerlier, who became head of the diocese of Tarbes and Lourdes in 1929, was not a native of Bigorre. He was born in Versailles, very far from the Gave and the Pyrenees mountains. Yet, in a moment of unbridled enthusiasm, he spoke flawlessly in the dialect of Lourdes: "*Lourdés, que soy countent de bous!*" (*Lourdes, how happy I am, thanks to you!*)

The crowd cheered him for a long time, aflutter with the same joy as he. Along with the bishop, they thanked the citizens of Lourdes for their welcome – once again, exemplary – on that day of July 27, 1930. It was the closing ceremony of a four-day Marian congress that had drawn thousands of attendees. Pilgrims became students as men and women from all walks of life gathered in the basilica pews and the meeting rooms to hear lectures by specialists in Mariology.

A Marian congress, several Marian congresses… the plural form was appropriate, too, for the event that was drawing to an end that day was not unique in history. It was not the first time that the Church had organized study sessions devoted to the Mother of God. Nevertheless, for the previous three years, these encounters had taken on a more systematic form in France. During a congress in Chartres in 1927, it was decided that such congresses would take place every four years. Upon his appointment to Tarbes, Bishop Gerlier claimed the honor of hosting the next congress of 1930 in his diocese. Bishop Harscouët of Chartres, president of the brand-new French National Committee for Marian Congresses, granted his permission without a moment's hesitation. While Chartres had been, since the Middle Ages, a great center of Marian devotion with its cathedral whose spires rise up to heaven in homage to Our Lady, Lourdes could certainly boast a great intimacy with the Virgin, too.

That is why, in the year 1930, those who wished to know more about the Virgin Mary had poured into Lourdes. Great French theologians had come to answer this fervent curiosity under the authority of Cardinal Verdier, archbishop of Paris, whom Pope Pius XI had named pontifical legate for the congress.

Every Marian congress must have a theme, and it did not take the event's organizers long to find one. In Lourdes, one subject, the Immaculate Conception, was a foregone conclusion. For four days, the invited orators tried to shed light on the Marian dogma proclaimed in 1854. They specified its content, traced the history of its definition, and highlighted its place in theology. Finally, they underscored the "practical" lesson it applied to all Christians – the call to interior purity, the abandonment of oneself to the will of God, an abandonment of which the Virgin had given the most perfect example.

These teachers met with obvious success. Wherever open or closed sessions were held – the crowd being split into several working groups every afternoon – the participants were eagerly heard and cheered many times with thunderous applause. Each presenter in his own way was able to shed light on some aspect of this peerless figure of human history, the Virgin full of grace, born without sin and fully free. From one meeting to the next, the participants' understanding opened up more and more to this mystery.

And what joy to be able to kneel at the grotto between two meetings to speak to the one whose form Bernadette had had the privilege of beholding! In Lourdes, more than anywhere else, Mariology had a face.

That was the reason why the small Pyrenees town would become a frequent host of these Marian congresses. A little under thirty years later, in 1958, it was once again in Lourdes that Marian theologians would gather amid festivities marking the apparitions' hundred-year anniversary. "Mary and the Church" was the theme that time. The latter congress had an added dimension that the 1930 one did not: It was proclaimed to be an "international" Marian congress – just like the multitude of pilgrims who came from all parts of the world to gather in Lourdes, and just as the devotion to the Virgin Mary knew no national boundaries of latitude or longitude. This second Lourdes congress was attended by a crowd that was even larger than usual because the Pope had earnestly encouraged Christians to visit Bernadette's town that year.

With another anniversary on the horizon, Lourdes once again is preparing to welcome the third Marian congress in its history in September 2008, for the one hundred and fifty years of its privileged relationship with Our Lady. "The Apparitions of the Virgin Mary: History, Faith and Theology" will be the theme of this event. Now organized by the International Pontifical Marian Academy, these congresses continue to feature theologians from the four corners of the world. The 2008 session – the twenty-second of these worldwide gatherings – will be no exception to this universality, since about three hundred experts from all cultures will be gathered there by a common passion – the devotion they have for the Virgin and their desire to go ever forward into the mystery of the one who said "yes."

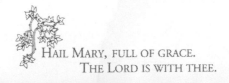

HAIL MARY, FULL OF GRACE.
THE LORD IS WITH THEE.

HEADLONG INTO SCRIPTURE

Portrait of the Writer François Mauriac, January 15, 1932

19 32 Yet another page, furiously crumpled, sank into the fireplace, crackling. François Mauriac looked at it for a long time as it twisted, reddened, and collapsed in the ashes. He was driven to distraction. For weeks now, he had not written a single worthwhile line. Yet he had come to Lourdes to compose the majority of his next book. This place – a pure consecration of divine grace for some, a vast theater of paganist processions to others – seemed to crystallize contradictory aspects of the faith to him. He had thought he might unfold this contrast across the breadth of a novel. Nearly fifty years old, he no longer had enough enthusiasm or objectivity to take sides. His faith had been alternately tortured by instinctive misgivings, which multiplied tenfold in adolescence, and consumed by the inhumanity of certain churchmen. Then, as time went on, tired of fighting these battles, he waited for peace to return to his heart. He was reconciled with the radical and rigorous faith of his childhood, that imposed passion that so often took the face of maternal love.

The day after Christmas 1931, he decided to accept one of his cousin's proposals and had taken up residence for awhile in a beautiful middle-class house near Lourdes. He lived there with a few distant relatives. A young cousin joined them a few weeks later. Lost in thought, he watched as she returned piously from daily Mass.

Mauriac found inspiration only in the company of others. He had hoped, in Lourdes' immediate surroundings, to immerse himself in the movements and rhythms that enlivened the grotto. He needed to observe people and their behavior, to feel their emotions, to sketch out in silence the spiritual places that seemed out of his reach. Yet for days he had walked in circles around his room thick with the acrid smells of the fireplace. He paced about in his robe, going from his bed to his desk without succeeding in touching upon his characters, without recovering the rhythm of his writing. He felt distracted, insensitive to the tensions that normally tormented him when he was shaping his prose. Despite his efforts, the lines he wrote remained bland and overwrought. All these scratched-out pages desperately lacked empathy and truthfulness. He feared he may have lost his power of clarity, that biting precision that eluded him.

And yet, he said to himself, head in hands, *I did see those marching believers. I was able to hear them! Why am I incapable of writing?* He plummeted into the memory of the long hours spent in vain among the pilgrims and beside the prayerfully devout. He had failed to penetrate the hearts of men. François Mauriac felt quite remote from his work. He raised his saddened eyes toward the window and glimpsed his young cousin who, as she did every Saturday, accompanied her aunt to the foot of the grotto. With her wrinkled skirts always fluttering in the whirlwind created by her quick gait, she suddenly beamed like a Madonna. And, for the writer, it was a true light: He seemed suddenly to look at her in an entirely new light. He noticed her slightly unkempt hair framing her tired face. He then realized how much she was dedicated, day and night, to her family, to the house, and, in her few moments of respite, to the sick she supported and accompanied to the Office. During these weeks of living under the same roof, he had simply overlooked the abnegation of this young woman who never complained or rested.

Holding his pen above a blank page, Mauriac felt incapable of lending his physical strength or of coming to the assistance of the most helpless as simply as his young cousin did. Entrenched behind a foggy window, he sat enthroned at his desk to produce abstract literature. Is a man of letters but a useless character? Do words truly comfort old age and illness? His heart beat nervously, gripped with shame – the shame of having glimpsed his cowardice, the shame of knowing to his depths that he was delighting in this inaction.

Furious at having admitted to his weakness, he laboriously got to work pushing forward on his novel about Lourdes, daring neither to go out nor to cast a glance outside for fear of catching sight of his cousin. He tirelessly wrote and edited by imagining two characters espousing opposing theses regarding Lourdes. One of them granted it the charms of divine grace, while the other saw in it the place of a cult debased and profaned by hordes of religious tourists. François Mauriac was bent on understanding the shrine, on capturing the charity expended there in uncommon acts. "*Pèlerins de Lourdes*" slowly emerged to become one of his least popular novels. And yet, as he spun out these somewhat bland paragraphs and gave life to his little puppets whose story had to be told to the end, he gradually became reconciled with his vocation as a writer. This exercise purged him of his sorrow and bitterness. He could be neither priest nor nurse, but all his life dwelt in that experience of humanity that constituted writing. Throughout his existence, he had devoted himself, whatever the sorrows or joys, to looking at men in their truth, their grandeur, and their torments. This mystery of man was so close to, so intimately bound with that of God, that all his work was marked with a profound humility, the same humility that enlightened his cousin's unwearied activity. Solitary, curled up in rooms littered with scratched-out paper, Mauriac had always sought to inspire in men a tender forbearance toward their neighbor.

BLESSED ART THOU AMONG WOMEN, AND BLESSED IS THE FRUIT OF THY WOMB, JESUS.

SAINT BERNADETTE

Bernadette's Canonization, December 8, 1933

19 33 The elderly gentleman, dazzled, did not know where to rest his gaze among the marbles and golds of Saint Peter's Basilica. Never before had he felt as far from home as he did among these monumental splendors. Yet Justin Bouhort had put on his Sunday best: His brand-new clothes and shiny shoes indicated as much! That was because his presence in Rome, on December 8, 1933, had a single cause. Today, in a Vatican ceremony, Pope Pius XI was to canonize Bernadette Soubirous. Justin Bouhort, who was healed in 1858 by the water of Massabielle when he was but a small child at death's door, considered it his duty and his joy to endure the tiring journey to participate in the ceremony. Even at seventy-seven years of age, his robust health permitted him to travel.

As he awaited the arrival of the papal procession, however, the old man felt somewhat out of place in this magnificent basilica. The new beret he was so proud of suddenly looked ridiculous, nearly indecent in its simplicity. He crushed it in his rough workman's hands to give himself a better appearance and instinctively drew near to the Soubirous family members, his compatriots. They didn't seem much more at ease. Old Maria, widow of Bernadette's brother, looked the most intimidated.

When she married Jean-Marie in 1890, her famous sister-in-law had long since passed away in Nevers. She never knew her. But family ties are what they are, and Maria felt for Bernadette a devotion nourished by the stories recounted throughout her entire married life.

Lourdes, its fields, its mountains, the murmur of the Gave, and the silence of the grotto where Bernadette would pray on those extraordinary days in the winter of 1858... How far from here all of that seemed! In the days before the apparitions, the Soubrious name was synonymous with poverty. On this day it would echo under the baldachino of Saint Peter's in Rome, pronounced by a pope's lips – enough to make Bernadette's sister-in-law and nephews dizzy! Their emotional gazes ended up looking steadily at the only small group of faithful who seemed familiar to them in the crowd of fifty thousand pilgrims who had come to witness the canonization. Not far from them, the "Bernadettes"[1] of Bigorre wore, with the Pope's authorization, the white kerchief their saintly kinswoman had rendered immortal instead of the usual mantilla!

A trumpet blast suddenly burst in the basilica. Thousands of lamps lit up in that instant under the golden vaults of Saint Peter's. Everything seemed brighter yet as Pope Pius XI solemnly entered the nave. A little bit later, he was seated on his throne in the back of the apse. In the crowd, every member of the faithful stood on tiptoe to catch a better glimpse of him. The members of the Soubirous family, the thousand Lourdes citizens around them, the other seven thousand French pilgrims, and the multitudes from the entire world all have focused their attention upon Pope Pius XI's majestic silhouette. In the section reserved for them, the many Nevers sisters who were present watched the Pope just as intently.

---

1. Name given to the young girls of the Jeunesse Féminine Catholique, a Catholic young women's association.

The Rome house superior directed a happy smile to the congregation's superior general, who returned it right away. Both women had closely followed the twists and turns of the three trials in succession that were required for canonization. The first opened in 1907 in Nevers under the aegis of the diocesan bishop. It would have taken place sooner if Mother Marie-Thérèse Vauzou – Bernadette's former novice mistress, who at the time was superior general – had not been firmly opposed to it in life.

The next two processes were conducted at the Holy See by the Congregation for Rites under the supreme supervision of the Pope himself. Throughout their course, the mother superior of Rome had spared no effort to support the "postulators," the men charged with promoting Bernadette's cause to the pontifical authorities. Her pressure, however, had only pushed wider those doors that were already open. Pope Pius XI made no secret of his fervor for Lourdes. After beatifying Bernadette in 1925, he had only been waiting for the bureaucratic delays of the process to be cleared before finally doing the honors of canonizing the visionary.

Even after the seemingly interminable procedure had been completed, the faithful of Lourdes still had to wait until the end of the year 1933 because a specific date was needed to honor Bernadette. December 8 was the feast of the Immaculate Conception. What better day to canonize the young girl who had unwittingly proclaimed, in her Béarn dialect, the dogma established in 1854 by Pope Pius IX?

At ten o'clock in the morning, December 8, 1933, the long-awaited formula finally echoed: "*We declare and define as a Saint the Blessed Marie-Bernard Soubirous and inscribe her in the catalog of Saints, ruling that her memory shall be piously celebrated in the Church Universal on*

April 16th every year, the day of her birth to Heaven."[1] A triumphal *Te Deum* then resounded in the basilica, born aloft by thousands of voices.

Far from the Vatican, in the town of Lourdes, all the churches' bells started to peal. Through the magic of radio, the residents of Lourdes who stayed home were able to hear the papal declaration on the airwaves. They were united with all their hearts to the prayers that went up in Saint Peter's in Rome. Their "little" Bernadette had become great among the greats of the Church. She was declared a saint, and her glory shed abundant light on her native town that day!

HOLY MARY, MOTHER OF GOD,

---

1. The feast of Our Lady of Lourdes is celebrated on February 11, the anniversary day of the first apparition. In France, the feast of Saint Bernadette is celebrated on February 18, the date of the third apparition, during which the Virgin spoke to her for the first time; the rest of the world observes her feast on April 16, the date of her death.

The Sun before the Storm

The Closing Ceremonies of the Year of Redemption,
April 28, 1935

19
35
Exuberance was not really in the nature of Cardinal
Eugenio Pacelli, Vatican secretary of state. Yet on this
particular day, an untrammeled joy shone in his gaze
behind his round metal-rimmed glasses.

The sun that had risen above the world in general and
above Lourdes in particular brightened an exceptional day. That Sunday
marked the close of the Year of Redemption, the end of the jubilee celebrated by the Church to mark the nineteenth centennial of Christ's
victory over death!

During this year of grace, Pope Pius XI had often mentioned the
happy coincidence that Lourdes celebrated in that precise year the
seventy-fifth anniversary of the 1858 apparitions. He had wished that the
jubilee's closing ceremonies would take place at Massabielle! That was
why he sent his secretary of state, appointed papal legate for the event, to
Lourdes.

At three o'clock in the afternoon, Cardinal Pacelli went to the grotto.
A radiant smile lit up his fine-featured face with its hooked nose.
Though he had put on his most elegant priestly vestments, his heart was

humble when it was time to say Mass, and his prayer was one entirely of thanksgiving!

As the *Introit* was sung, he approached the altar, which he kissed with particular respect. There had been uninterrupted Masses on the grotto altar for three consecutive days. One hundred and thirty-nine times in a row, in the successive priests' hands, bread and wine had become the body and blood of Christ. The honor of celebrating the hundred and fortieth Mass of this triduum belonged to Cardinal Pacelli. At the dismissal, when he pronounced the *Ite missa est*, the jubilee year would be completed.

In the first row of priests assisting at this last celebration, Bishop Pierre-Marie Gerlier felt as much happiness as did the Roman cardinal. He thought that ever since the apparitions to Bernadette, Lourdes had never known such perfect moments as these. Three days of grace and light. Three days outside of time. Three days snatched from the present in which the shadow of war was already being cast on Europe despite all the efforts of the optimists to ignore it.

Like Cardinal Pacelli, Bishop Gerlier let his gaze wander around the crowd that had come to participate in this jubilee closure. A countless crowd, but one that the security detail had nevertheless managed to esti-mate: Over two hundred and fifty thousand people were gathered along the Gave and on the Ribère meadow on the other side of the Gave! This crowd was as universal as the Church itself, and the multitude of its spoken languages evoked the polyphony of Pentecost. Indeed, Pope Pius XI had asked all peoples to send representatives to this *"corner of Heaven in the Pyrenees"* that is Bernadette's town! So pilgrims had come from the four corners of Europe, and also from Africa, North and South America, Asia, and Oceania. Still marveling at being here, the assembled faithful listened in reverent silence to the long closing speech that the legate gave.

Born to Roman aristocracy, Cardinal Pacelli expressed himself in flawless French. As usual, he spoke without notes, developing clear and convincing reflections on the redemption for the faithful. Though many foreign pilgrims did not understand a word of it, they nevertheless did not feel excluded from the celebration. Redemption is perfectly universal: All felt touched by the graces lived out during the jubilee year, and especially on these days spent in Lourdes! Attentive to the orator's warm tone, they watched him speak, not knowing that they had the future pope before their eyes: Upon the death of Pope Pius XI in 1939, Cardinal Eugenio Pacelli would be elected pontiff and would take the name of Pope Pius XII.

Bishop Gerlier, too, took the floor. His speech was a thanks to all who made the celebration possible – the Pope, the legate, the ceremony organizers, the pilgrims from every geographic and social horizon on earth – without forgetting the recently canonized Bernadette, to whom he gave a vibrant homage.

The jubilee had a beautiful ending. The cardinal-legate boarded the train to return to Rome. He had to return to the cares of the world, those of the secretariat of state, which were far from light on his shoulders. That year, 1935, the Vatican witnessed with dismay the turn that international relations were taking. Two years later, Pope Pius XI would denounce, in two thundering encyclicals, the dangers of Nazism and Communism. In this tense context, the redemption was a more comforting thought than ever before. As he watched the French countryside roll by, as he inched by the platforms where the crowds had come to greet him, Cardinal Pacelli attempted to think only of that. He would soon enough return to face the diplomatic problems. Meanwhile, the beneficial images of Lourdes crossed his mind, as if to illustrate Saint Paul's exclamation in his first Epistle to the Corinthians: *"Death, where is thy sting?"*

THE MIRACLE OF THE DANCER

Edeltraud Fulda, Fifty-Fifth Miraculous Healing,
June 29, 1937

19 37 *"Signori e signore, les sisters X!"* Two ravishing Austrians had burst on the variety theatre scene in Rome. Except for a leotard, they had only a simple swath of cloth wrapped around their chest. With their baggy trousers and a fez on their head, they strung together pirouettes, jumps, shoulder stands, and various acrobatic moves to the applause of the spectators. Backstage, their Italian manager was rubbing his hands. Ursula, the blonde, and Edeltraud, the brunette, were well on their way to success. The year was 1937. Mussolini's Blackshirts had long since brought Italy to its knees, but "Uschi" and "Traude" were barely twenty and thought only of dancing, swept up in the gaiety of the madcap thirties.

Once backstage, Traude suddenly and violently doubled over, hands on her abdomen. *"Magen"* ("my stomach"), she whispered to her sister in German. This pain, which every so often for three years had been shooting through her like a dagger, had overcome her again. Ursula watched her, worried and incredulous all at once. The physicians that Traude had already consulted in Vienna had spoken of nerves, of cramps due to her acrobatics, of overwork. They had operated on her for appendicitis, but could find no cause for these intermittent pains. Hints were made about a possible venereal disease. She's a dancing-girl, don't you know?

But at the Roman hospital where Traude had been taken, the doctor who examined her took on a far more serious expression. Traude was operated on urgently and was given the last sacraments to be safe.

In the summer humidity of Rome, the young Austrian's calvary began. It would last thirteen years. Two-thirds of her stomach had been removed because it was perforated from end to end. A persistent fever never left her. Flown back to Vienna, she had to undergo a second operation. A kidney abscess had put her life in jeopardy. Though her days were said to be numbered, she survived. "It's a miracle!" exclaimed her doctor.

Unfortunately, Edeltraud's convalescence seemed endless. She was able neither to feed herself nor to get out of bed, for her abdominal pains would pick up again and her skin would become strangely tan in places. In the new hospital to which she was taken, Drs. Krebs and Zloty finally diagnosed her as having Addison's disease. This deterioration of the kidney glands prevents the formation of hormones. Those suffering from it, like Traude, undergo permanent exhaustion with intense abdominal pain and have great difficulty digesting food.

In 1938, in the first days of March, Hitler's airplanes buzzed over the Austrian capital. Germany's annexation of Austria and the unleashing of anti-Semitic passions soon followed. "Aren't you afraid, what with Jewish doctors treating you?" Traude was asked. Yet it was those Jewish doctors who saved her from the grip of the Nazis. Zloty was careful to avoid noting in her file that she had Addison's disease. He simply mentioned a kidney-gland insufficiency and prescribed daily hormone shots. He was only too aware of what the Third Reich did with reputedly incurable patients.

Edeltraud spent the war years with her mother by her bedside, obstinately refusing hospitalization despite the Nazi doctors' insidious recommendations. The hormones she took kept her alive, but she couldn't walk and barely ate. Her mother watched over her day and night without the young woman ever drifting into the morbid complacency that sometimes tempts the suffering. She hated her illness with all her might, and she wanted to get better. When the country warden of the small Upper-Styria village – where she had found refuge to escape from the bombardments in Vienna – lent her Henri Lasserre's work on Our Lady of Lourdes, she was dazzled. Miracles were taking place over there, and she did not know it! Her decision was made immediately: She, too, would go to Lourdes to be healed like these miraculously cured people. With her deep and sincere faith, she did not doubt for an instant the Virgin Mary's power of intercession. She already saw herself as recovered!

At long last, the war was over. From the couch that kept her prisoner, Traude wrote to join the first German national pilgrimage. It was to take place on the feast of the Assumption in 1950. Thanks to the money given by priest friends, she could go with her mother. They were the only Austrians on the convoy. The prayers of the hundred people who shared in her perfect hope went with her.

The intrepid Traude even showed up at the Lourdes Medical Bureau on the eve of her first bath at the grotto. She simply wished to be examined in order to be able later to have her cure verified! Without discouraging her, the doctor who received her prescribed with a smile the usual remedies in Lourdes – a bath in the pool, prayer, and the Blessed Sacrament procession.

The next day, the young woman slowly made her way into the pool's ice-cold water. Two women held her firmly on either side. She prayed with an intense fervor despite the fear that gripped her. She who no longer walked wished to go to the end of the pool: She made the three necessary little steps, sank up to her neck, and returned, shivering with cold. As the ladies dressed her and returned her to her stretcher-bearer, Traude suddenly felt better, as if relaxed. The warmth that filled her body relieved her infinitely. Was she going to start walking and running, like one miraculously cured? No – she collapsed, exhausted yet beaming, into her wheelchair.

Back at the hotel, Traude ate enough for four people under the alarmed look of her mother, who feared terrible digestive pains. Yet her daughter spent a peaceful night for the first time in thirteen years. On the day of the Assumption, she voluntarily put an end to all hormone shots, and on August 17 she once again showed up before the commission to have her cure verified! The medical tribunal was doubtful at the sight of the skinny young girl: Was she not in the clutches of a sincere but misplaced enthusiasm? The young Austrian, however, had come prepared with x-rays, hospitalization reports, and especially the diagnosis of Addison's disease. The doctors, suddenly, began paying close attention.

She would have to wait five years for the Church to proclaim the miracle officially. After her cure, Edeltraud Fulda walked, ate, and worked like everybody else without any medicines. Too old anymore to dance in cabarets, she went into the manufacture of knit clothing, a novelty at the time. She married, and she was happy. Her prayer went up to heaven in an immense surge of gratitude.

AMEN.

In Bartimaeus' Footsteps

The Winding Way of the Cross, August 2, 1937

1937 A tall woman with a dark and thick head of hair gracefully strolled along the streets of Lourdes. She brushed against groups of passers-by as she stared at the horizon. She seemed lost. Sometimes she appeared to be oppressed or worried, and then would suddenly seem happy and at peace as though her burdens had been lifted from her. She meandered among the sick and the pilgrims. Often, she stopped to place her hands on the stones of the houses, to breathe in the Pyrenees breeze, to touch the wooden rosaries sold everywhere, as though these sensations somehow nourished her.

This fragile and sensual woman was an Italian. She was a sculptor, or rather, she had been a sculptor. Something in the fluidity of her movements betrayed her long years spent working with the raw materials of her art. At this point, however, she no longer wanted anything to do with the weight of clay in her arms because she no longer had the strength to lift it, to model it. Her eyes no longer were willing to scan space, waiting for a form to appear. A few months before, she had decided to drop every aspect of the practice of her art.

In the small town of Lourdes that she was busily discovering in the summer heat, she had just seen one of her old statues, a votive offering she had created some years ago for an astonishing woman named Maria Budini Cattai. Maria had come calling on the artist in her house one morning in tears. With much emotion, Maria had explained to the artist how God had given back her faith. Before even beginning her story, she had handed a text to the artist. It was a Gospel passage, the story of that blind man to whom Jesus gave back his sight at the entrance to Jericho. Maria recognized her own blindness in this man to such an extent that she wanted to have a bronze statue of him made. The light in the aged woman's eyes had touched the artist's heart so much so that she consented to hear Maria's entire story.

As she recalled these moments, the Italian woman followed the rhythmic flow of believers toward the grotto. Looking at them objectively, she discovered the diversity of their faces, the masks of sorrow and of joy. Lourdes…

Maria, too, had come here out of curiosity. At the time, she had just taken a long vacation in Biarritz with several of her friends. Since the terrible loss of her husband, she had renounced her childhood faith, cursed the doorsteps of churches, and embraced a life of pleasure. Her life had become an existence dictated by debauchery and a certain destructive madness. Along with her friends, Maria now knew only one rule – to shrink at no license, no excess, no experience. She had lived at night in a place where artificial light and alcohol deformed features to the point of monstrosity. She had revered that carefree attitude that claims to be unconditional freedom – but found only despair. Because she had touched only bodies, she had lost sight of the soul.

One day, she came to Lourdes. With bravado and mockery, she had followed the path of the processions. And, without in any way seeking the light of God, without a thought for her faith – which she believed to be dead – she fell on her knees before the grotto. Under her friends' astounded and jeering eyes, she remained there in prayer, her head in her hands, for hours. Her heart was unraveling. And suddenly, her past life weighed on her like a burden. In those few hours, she regained her faith, and her life of debauchery appeared to her as an abyss she no longer understood. She no longer knew why she had let herself become mired in the narrow trap of selfishness. Submerged in God's mercy, Maria learned to forgive herself, to give herself totally to this divine revelation.

Then she got up and wandered for hours in the streets of Lourdes, near the grotto, in the winding switchbacks, completely abandoned by her companions. It seemed to her that her soul and all the fibers in her body had finally freed themselves, that she finally saw love and light. She was filled with this joyous humility when eventually she had come to knock at the sculptor's door. She had told the tale of her return to the faith. On the pedestal of the statue she had asked the artist to create, Maria insisted that there be engraved the revelation that had lit up her life: "*To recover Faith is better than to recover sight!*"

At the time, in the whirlwind of her work, the sculptor had delivered the statue without bothering about its placement. She only knew that it had to be transported to Lourdes. As she walked the streets of the town that afternoon, her memories compelled her to find where her statue had been placed. Near the grotto, she looked for someone to direct her. A religious in charge of giving tours and directions to pilgrims pointed her to the winding Way of the Cross. She peacefully entered this narrow and rocky path and took in the cool shade of the trees.

Suddenly, in the bend of a turn wider than the others, she was struck by the sight of the bronze statue just a few yards away. She immediately felt its curves and its angles. She looked at the figure of this kneeling man leaning on a cross. She knew intuitively that he was her creation, but he was now strangely foreign to her. His lines moved her, touched her, and rejected her a little.

She saw a priest accompanying a weeping woman to the statue. He murmured a few words as he pointed out the inscription on the bronze. After several minutes, the woman's features became peaceful. Very calm, she began to pray, and the priest left her quietly. Slowly, the Italian woman also withdrew, leaving her statue to the privacy and faith of the pilgrims of the winding Way of the Cross to whom it now belonged.

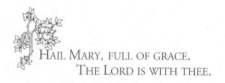

HAIL MARY, FULL OF GRACE.
THE LORD IS WITH THEE.

THE SECRET GUEST AT THE BISHOP'S CHALET

The Polish Primate's Exile in Lourdes, June 9, 1940

1940 A car left the Vatican in a squeal of wet tires on a humid June night. Inside, Cardinal August Hlond, primate of Poland and regent of the Polish state since the government fled the Nazis, clenched his jaw. He looked away from one of the palace's narrow windows at which the Sovereign Pontiff, a distant and pale figure, appeared to express a discreet farewell. The primate would have liked to have stayed with his compatriots at the worst of times, when Poland was occupied by the Germans, but he could not bring himself to do business with the Nazis. Never could he have accepted the compromises they had demanded. To consent to deal with them would have been the first step toward total submission.

For his refusal, Adolf Hitler's lieutenants had set a price on the primate's head, and so he chose to leave Poland to go to the Holy See. There, he had tirelessly made Pope Pius XII aware of the Polish people's painful fate. The Pope had gradually come around to the opinion of this cardinal who was renowned for the dedication and sound reason of his political positions. Unfortunately, Mussolini had abruptly shown the first signs of allying himself to Hitler. Worried that he might no longer be able to protect the primate, Pope Pius XII organized his departure for

Lourdes. Over there, in the French Free Zone, he would be sheltered from the Germans in the quiet of a peaceful sanctuary.

Squeezed into the back seat between the chaplain and the secretary accompanying him, the cardinal scanned every nook and cranny of the streets he crossed, as though his gaze could melt away possible informers. He resigned himself to fleeing rather than run the risk of being manipulated by his people's jailers. Every so often, he held his breath as if not to add to the engine's noise; at every checkpoint, the sound of every passing truck made him flinch.

It was already well into the day when the men, exhausted, finally caught sight of the promising Pyrenees heights. They arrived in Lourdes without a hitch and were driven to the bishop's chalet. Tucked away at a bend in the road, partly hidden from view by tall trees, the residence was surrounded by a spacious garden. At last the cardinal allowed himself a certain relief. He always had a feeling of well-being when he found himself surrounded by the beauty of nature. The vast mountain range all around, these lush pastures, the warmth of his host, Bishop Choquet – everything led him to an unexpected serenity.

Cardinal Hlond peacefully settled into the chalet and accepted his new circumstances without making any assumptions as to the length of his sojourn in Lourdes. His new way of life was punctuated by reading, the Masses he celebrated in the chapel on the house's second floor, and the long philosophical conversations he kept up with the bishop and the two clergymen who accompanied him. Two young sisters watched over the secret little community. The cardinal's chaplain and secretary, however, allowed themselves to go out in public. They paced up and down the streets of Lourdes, rubbing shoulders with pilgrims and churchmen. They often made their way to the grotto to give thanks to the Virgin for this unanticipated freedom.

For his part, the Polish primate considered himself a willing prisoner and resolutely put up with his seclusion. His physical activity was limited to a single walk each day in the chalet's garden, far from any wide-open spot. Though he tolerated this furtive escapade, Bishop Choquet regularly repeated his principal instruction, "*Keep the doors shut*," lest anyone catch sight of the primate's august silhouette and suspect his exile. But Cardinal Hlond was not the type to fade away. Protected by his hosts' good will and discretion, his patriotic feelings were keenly alive in Lourdes. Since taking up his forced residence, he had done everything possible to offer material and spiritual support to the Polish communities. The Poles of France relied on his determination to take the edge off their exile. In him they perceived the authenticity of their faith and the cradle of their culture. For all his prudence, the primate's intellectual activity echoed far beyond the silence of the bishop's chalet. He kept up regular communications in France and abroad thanks to an abundant correspondence. He secretly drew up strategic plans to free Poland from the German yoke. Lastly, he edited a clandestine newspaper that was passed around in the city of Toulouse. His heart and his mind remained focused on his country's destiny.

At the end of 1942, the Germans invaded the free zone. Consequently, the primate of Poland's residence was exposed to German house searches, and his safety was threatened. In April 1943, he decided to leave the little chalet nestled at the foot of the Pyrenees where he had spent nearly three years in order to take refuge in the Benedictine convent in Hautecombe. But a little under a year later, his anonymity was betrayed and he was arrested and taken to Paris. The Germans unsuccessfully urged him to cooperate. Faithful to his native Poland, the cardinal refused to compromise – and paid with his freedom. It was only in 1945 that he returned to a Poland mutilated by war to find his people deep in utter destitution. Until the end of his life, the primate devoted himself to relieving the distress of his fellow Poles.

Blessed art thou among women, and blessed is the fruit of thy womb, Jesus.

THE RESTITUTION OF THE GROTTO'S DOMAIN

Pétain and Bishop Choquet, April 1, 1941

1941 "My efforts have paid off!" At his desk, Bishop Choquet of Lourdes could have wept for joy. He reread the letter that Marshal Pétain had sent him to announce his arrival on April 20, 1941, for a visit during which he officially would return the domain of the grotto to the Diocesan Association of Tarbes and Lourdes. Finally, the domain would become the Church's property once again, the property of the bishops of Lourdes!

Though the matter had been settled for a few days already, this letter sealed it definitively. The marshal's journey to Lourdes would close the sad episode during which the state had confiscated from the Church the ownership of this domain where so many Christians came every day in ever-growing numbers to pray to Mary Immaculate. The bishop thought of his predecessor, Bishop Schoepfer. How happy he would have been to have received this letter! He had fought so hard to keep ownership of the domain. Like his predecessors, Bishop Schoepfer considered himself to be the grotto's protector – like Bishop Billière, whose motto was, "*She set me as her Guardian.*"

It was during the episcopate of Bishop Schoepfer that the Catholic Church of France suffered so much in the early years of this century. As early as 1901, with the law on the dissolution of religious congregations, the bishop saw the Fathers of Garaison, who had taken charge of the construction of the shrine, forced to leave. The government wished to become the proprietor of the grotto's goods immediately. The bishop had initiated a lawsuit to prove that this domain was not the property of the Mission Fathers Congregation but rather was indeed that of the diocese. The tribunal of Bagnères-de-Bigorre ruled in his favor in January 1904, as did the court of appeals in Pau on February 1905. A few months later, however, a new law pertaining to the separation of church and state annulled this victory. The domain of the grotto thus became "national property."

Bishop Schoepfer fought to prevent this law from causing any undesirable consequences for Lourdes and her pilgrims. To avoid nationalization, he first ceded the grotto to the shrine's faithful for a nine-year lease under the executorship of Messrs. Christophe and de Beauchamp, the president and general secretary of the Hospitality of Our Lady of Lourdes.

In April 1908, though, a law attributed to municipalities the properties devoted to religious uses. On April 7, 1910, Aristide Briand, president of the council and minister of the interior and of religious cults, and Armand Fallières, president of the Republic, signed a decree handing the grotto properties to the city of Lourdes and to its welfare office. The city council of Lourdes unanimously accepted this grant but immediately declared that it considerd it as *"an untouchable deposit that the municipality will continue to leave at the disposal of the diocesan authority, freely there to exercise the Catholic cult and to organize the various pilgrimages' religious events."* Bishop Schoepfer, for his part, recalled in a pastoral letter that *"these properties will remain, whatever may be said and done, the property of the Church's representatives, and they can never*

— barring the agreement of the bishop with the Pope's authority — legitimately be owned by their new possessors."

With the Pope's approval, the bishop agreed to hold the rented lands for an eighteen-year lease in order to continue the pilgrimages. The minister of the interior, in a letter of March 20, 1912, said that *"these buildings should, in principle, be used for a public service by their very nature, but that this use does not, in fact, seem able to be assigned to them."* He then declared that *"by reason of this quite extraordinary circumstance, I have no objection to raise against these leases."*

In 1940, Monsignor Méricq, rector of the shrines, terminated the lease. Shortly thereafter, Bishop Choquet himself decided to take up the fight over the grotto's ownership. He did this with an eye toward the new policy of Paul Reynaud's government, which was favorable to a revision of the 1905 law on the separation of church and state. On April 23, he registered at Lourdes the statutes of the Massabielle Association, among whose purposes was to gather together all properties acquired in the domain's name by private individuals to protect the grotto.

But the French army's rout in June 1940 led to the government's downfall and its replacement by Marshal Pétain. Bishop Choquet wrote to Pétain on July 18 to ask that the domain be restored to the diocese. Anxious to be reconciled to the Church, the state granted its permission and transmitted its request to Lourdes' municipal council which, in the October 12 session, accepted the restoration of these properties to the diocesan association. The head of state then ratified the decision in a decree signed in Vichy on February 10, 1941.

The bishop's right hand played with his pectoral cross while his left hand tapped out on his wooden desk the *Te Deum* his heart was singing to God. He knew that the difficulties of recent years had been like so many trials sent to remind him that the Father alone gives and takes away in his own good time. The bishop knew he did not owe today's victory to his own determination; rather, it was due to God's will that the Massabielle domain be returned to the Church's ownership. Still, he did not begrudge himself happiness over the victory. Already he was thinking about the land he would continue to purchase in order to protect the grotto and accommodate the pilgrims.

HOLY MARY, MOTHER OF GOD,

LOURDES, CITY OF PEACE

The Institution of Pax Christi, *December 10, 1944*

1944 In the chill of Saint Caprais' Cathedral in Agen, France, a woman prayed for a long time at Mass after receiving communion. A teacher of classics at the city girls' high school, married, and mother of a large family, Marthe Dortel-Claudot also had an intense spiritual life. For two months an imperious necessity had been growing in her, becoming stronger still with every communion received: *Germany must be rebuilt. Christ died for them as well as for others.*

In her silent prayer, day after day, Marthe received the deep conviction from God that she must pray – and convince others to pray – for Germany. That took a certain audacity: Everywhere in Europe, as 1944 drew to a close, Germany was considered the enemy. Armies fought her, the Allied Air Forces pounded its territory without respite, and everyone seemingly wished to annihilate the country responsible for Nazi atrocities. Pray for the enemy? Marthe refused with all her being. Republican by conviction, she joined the Resistance by her husband's side. Both organized networks that sought to hide all those whom the Germans tracked down – escaped prisoners, Jews, those avoiding forced labor in

Germany. To pray for those whom they fought so valiantly in the shadows… No, that would be asking the impossible.

Yet the more Marthe prayed, the more her conviction grew – so much so that she decided to confide the matter to her pastor, Father Dessorbès, who was also her spiritual director. For him, the young woman's repugnance was very important. It guaranteed that her inspiration was genuine. His advice was simple: "*Go and find others with whom to pray.*" Marthe convinced two women whose spiritual fervor matched hers. One was a war widow; the other was the daughter of a deported person! Along with Marthe, they fervently prayed that Germany be healed of the *moral and religious distress* caused by twelve years of Nazism.

Father Dessorbès closely followed the first steps of this movement. He advised Marthe to solicit the prayers of the Carmelites in Agen. So Marthe fortified herself with courage to present her project to Mother Anne-Marie of the Sacred Heart. The latter gave her a rather cold reception at first; however, impressed as she was with the young woman's conviction, she reconsidered the request. Not only would the Carmelites join their prayers to her intention, but Marthe would also receive permission to ask the prioress to solicit all the Carmels of France. "*It is you who have grace,*" Mother Anne-Marie explained to Marthe, who was surprised at this sudden reversal of perspective. Like Father Dessorbès, the prioress recognized the genuine action of the Holy Spirit.

The priest encouraged the young woman to place an ecclesiastical authority at the head of the movement to give it a greater official endorsement. Eventually, Bishop Théas of Montauban agreed to head the apostolate on March 13, 1945. He, too, had personally experienced forgiveness by celebrating Mass for the Germans while he was a war prisoner in Compiègne. As she left him, Marthe heard these sentiments expressed once again: "*It is the Holy Ghost who sent you.*"

Marthe was in the habit of presenting the project as a *"crusade of prayers for Germany."* Now that it was expanding its scope, however, she felt it should have its own name. Marthe grappled with the question in her head during a stay with her family in Montaubon, but in vain. The uncle with whom she was staying provided the solution: He suggested *Pax Christi* ("the peace of Christ"). The proposal was accepted by all who heard it.

From that point on, *Pax Christi's* growth was rapid. Marthe and her family produced a quarterly bulletin, and children were assigned to stamp and mail the issues as they piled up in the apartment. The number of subscribers soared. The first issue in 1945 circulated two thousand copies; by All Saints' Day, there were already sixty thousand subscribers! *La Croix*, which gave an account of the movement in June 1945, provided great publicity along with the silent, prayerful support of the Carmelites.

On the other side of the English Channel, the initiative made waves, prompting the archbishop of Westminster to write to Marthe. Belgium, Switzerland, and soon Germany joined in this communion of international prayer. The archbishop of Freiburg declared in November 1946: *"How we, in Germany, need the whole world's prayers! True, we are a very poor and beaten people; yet the vigor of our faith lives on."* Success was such that, beginning in 1947, the bulletin was published at the same time in both countries.

In August of the same year, *Pax Christi* was established in Lourdes. Nothing could be more natural, since Bishop Théas, who was in charge of the movement, had just been named Lourdes' bishop. What better town than Lourdes, a place of prayer and assembly open to all peoples, to give the young movement a permanent home?

In 1948, the first *Pax Christi* pilgrimage was organized at the Marian shrine; it brought together thirty thousand people. Ten thousand of these represented twenty-six different nations. There were Spaniards, Italians,

Englishmen, and Germans, but also Moravians, Ukrainians, and Poles who had recently escaped to West Germany. Bishop Théas' welcome message spoke of the equality of all in the face of the task to be accomplished in the aftermath of a merciless war: "*All nations are guilty; humanity is sinful and it is, in part, our own fault for we are all united to each other.*" Cardinal Frings, bishop of Cologne, acknowledged the unspeakable: "*After the horrible war, the Germans seemed to bear on their foreheads the mark of Cain and to have lost all right to human dignity. They were hated and despised.*"

Lourdes became the movement's bedrock. In 1953, while the movement was still broadening, a permanent office was opened there to bring all warring nations to prayer. Its nongovernmental-organization status also allowed it to participate in the United Nations as well as on the European Council. Motions and conferences gave voice to its cause, supported by the prayer of sixty thousand members in fifty countries. In the Saint Pius X Basilica in Lourdes, a chapel was reserved for *Pax Christi.* Every day in summer, pilgrims were invited to a time of prayer so that the movement might bear true peace both within self and throughout the world.

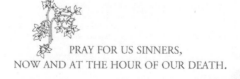

PRAY FOR US SINNERS,
NOW AND AT THE HOUR OF OUR DEATH.

OUR LADY OF PEACE

History of the International Military Pilgrimage,
December 10, 1944

19
44
In the morning of December 10, 1944, a hundred and twenty wounded soldiers prayed before the grotto in Lourdes. They were there courtesy of Father Besombes, a military chaplain in Toulouse. With the blessing of his ordinary, Bishop Saliège, and the assistance of the eighty enlisted men accompanying them, he took this initiative in the hope of bringing peace to the hearts, bodies, and souls of the handful of men entrusted to him.

The task was not easy. In the region, liberation committees confronted Gaullist prefects in an atmosphere close to civil war while the German forces were still fighting the Allies. War was everywhere, among peoples, between brothers.

The French Forces of the Interior were incorporated into the free French armed forces, but grudges died hard and divisions were real. *"We'll have to come back with the French military as a whole,"* sighed Bishop Saliège to Father Besombes after the first military pilgrimage. "To be a ferment of unity in a military torn apart by years of war, that is a fine goal for a military pilgrimage," said Father Besombes, who stayed behind alone at the grotto for a long night of prayer.

Three years later, thanks to Father Besombes' unfailing and fervent energy, the military pilgrimage to Lourdes drew ten thousand soldiers from all regions, along with their chaplains. The first truly national military pilgrimage was finally born.

Very soon, this pilgrimage became a formidable gathering with international appeal – which was the vision from the very beginning. In 1945, Father Besombes had invited the chaplains of the American troops who were stationed on the Atlantic coast. More boldly yet, he also had invited Father Steger, a German prisoner-of-war and chaplain at the prisoners' camp. These contacts had strengthened through subsequent years and led naturally to the decision to broaden the military pilgrimage into a vast international gathering. Thus was born the "*Pèlerinage militaire international*," or PMI.

In 1958, on the centennial of the grotto apparitions, the French military chaplain invited to Lourdes the chaplaincies of the foreign delegations present in France as a part of the North Atlantic Treaty Organization (NATO). Thirty thousand soldiers and officers, each in his own military uniform and with flag and trumpet blast to match, marched side by side and prayed for peace. What more splendid way was there to celebrate the miracle of Lourdes? "*We shall pray for the reconciliation of the peoples of the world*," declared Marshal Juin, French chief of staff, when he arrived in Lourdes for the event.

His speech echoed prophetically in 1958 when the Algerian war – the "operations," as official communications called it then – mobilized French recruits by the thousands. Several of these arrived in Lourdes directly from Algeria, exhausted and running late. They were greeted at the station by German soldiers who carried their bags to the camp set up for the occasion. Less than twenty years after the armistice, that kind of international cooperation was no common event. After years of war,

German and French soldiers finally met face to face. The young federal German army, which joined NATO in 1955, thus took its place in Lourdes alongside the Belgian, Canadian, British, Dutch, Italian, Luxembourgian, Portuguese, and American armies. They were not really comfortable, these German soldiers who, for the first time since the war, were outside of their country! Nor was the Lourdes population, which had not seen German soldiers in uniform since the occupation.

On the evening of the first day of the pilgrimage, some Germans en route to the military camp passed some French paratroopers coming up the street. Having reached the German colonel, the French colonel stopped the march, saluted, and then asked that all his men do likewise. Our Lady of Peace had begun her work... Another diplomatic miracle took place at about the same time. Austrian soldiers, who no longer were expected, had obtained authorization at the last minute from the Soviet troops stationed in Austria to go to Lourdes. Their van arrived right in the middle of the ceremonies!

As the years went by, the PMI followed the evolution of ever-changing politics of international relations. As soon as the Berlin Wall fell, Poland and Hungary began to participate in the event. In 1996, Ukraine, freed from Russian rule, joined in.

Today about fifteen thousand soldiers from over thirty different armed forces peacefully rub shoulders in the streets of Lourdes every year. Three traditional events mark the weekend – the Friday night welcoming celebration with a salute to all the flags, the next day's procession through town to the grotto, and the international High Mass on Sunday. The military camp, pitched above the grotto on the city heights, has also become a unique venue for mingling and friendship among young soldiers from different countries.

The PMI has progressively changed. Soldiers today often come with their wives and children. The growing secularization of participating countries also colors the ceremonies differently, and many baptisms and first communions are celebrated there. The sick – often wounded in war – are always treated with particular care. Father Besombes' vision today remains at the heart of the international military pilgrimage – to gather under Mary's one flag those who have committed themselves to peace at the risk of their very lives.

Amen.

ALMA MATER

Portrait of the Writer Franz Werfel, August 26, 1945

19 45 A dusty and golden beam of light crossed the living room in an opulent Beverly Hills residence. Seated in a wicker chair, Franz Werfel stroked with his fingertips a few books arranged on a low table near him. The dust jackets, of which some are a bit yellowed, were translucent in the late-afternoon summer sun, almost as brittle as fallen leaves. He had gathered the first editions of each of his books – in other words, his entire life's work. His fingers glided from one to the next; in turn, they alighted upon a drama, a novel on the Armenian genocide, and a science-fiction novel completed just recently. His fingers then clutched one of the volumes a little more closely – a text on Bernadette Soubirous. Then, they let go.

Franz Werfel was tired. He felt vaguely that he was sapped of his strength and would no longer have sufficient energy to leave, to travel again. And yet his entire life had been nothing but a movement, one of quest and of exile. Even as a youth in Prague, he had wished to escape from his father's bourgeois life and his glove store. He had longed to develop his talent for writing – how much talent he did not know, but he was sure of its existence. Austria soon smiled on him: Mobilized in

1914, he was assigned to the army's press service in Vienna. He wrote, and both publishers and literary circles opened their doors to him. His plays were produced, and he received in his dressing room both admirers and sycophants with a feeling of pride mixed with a carefully disguised surprise.

One evening, the publisher Jakob Hegner announced to him the arrival of the architect Walter Gropius. Werfel was happy to make the acquaintance of the colossus with a mind of fire and a body of stone, the future founder of Bauhaus.[1] Gropius made a strong impression on Werfel. Every time the master was mentioned, the conversation never failed to turn to his wife, Alma, widow of the great composer Gustav Mahler and mistress of the painter Oskar Kokoschka. But Werfel was more deeply interested in architecture than in women. Nevertheless, when he first heard that growling and smooth voice, he instinctively knew it was Alma. Werfel turned around and noticed, among the rustle of dresses and small talk, the stormy blue eyes of a motionless woman staring at him.

It was Alma who wanted it. She who would become his mistress within a few weeks was a woman of brutal and unconditional desire. She saw in Werfel a robust young man with quiet talent. Alma lived only through and for art, but was weary of the torments that came with it. The nervous Mahler and taciturn Gropius muzzled her own musical creativity. As long as she was deprived of her talent, she wished only to seduce and to shine on the arm of an intelligent and solid man. Werfel was the ideal man, and so she married him, her third husband, on July 8, 1929.

The Werfels were travelers. They went to Egypt, Venice, and Lebanon. While in Vienna, Alma hosted all that the town had by way of

---

1. German school of architecture and applied arts that revolutionized those fields between the wars.

intellectuals, artists, and personalities, from Richard Strauss to Arnold Schönberg, including the apostolic nuncio. The era between the wars, however, did not lend itself to protracted quiet. Europe's political unbalance was obvious, and Nazi youths conducted a reign of terror in Vienna. Franz was Jewish. His "degenerate" works were burned in the public square in Germany. In 1938, the Anschluss pushed Austria into Hitler's camp. Fortunately, Franz was in Italy at the time. The couple's comfortable life vanished with one fell swoop. Alma had time to return to Vienna, a town she no longer recognized. Franz, however, never went back there again. The Werfels fled – to Zurich, Paris, London, and to Sanary-sur-Mer in the south of France. When Germany invaded France, they attempted to reach Bordeaux, the provisional government seat, but were diverted to Biarritz, then to Pau.

In November 1940, Franz and Alma, bereft of everything, including their luggage, and waylaid during a transfer in Marseilles, ended up in Lourdes. The weeks of flight by train, motorcar, and sometimes on foot had left them shell-shocked. Alma slept while Franz went out in the Pyrenees drizzle to try to exercise his muscles, which exhaustion and fear had made tense. As he wandered in the dark blue Lourdes night, Werfel found himself attracted like a butterfly to the damp light of the few religious shops that were still open. Right next door, the sanctuary gate was ajar. His steps led him on the path that wound up to a large empty esplanade. Dazed, he did not know where to go from there. He remembered a few articles he had read before the war about a shepherdess and her visions. He did not even have the strength for sarcasm.

The sound of *Ave Marias* being prayed drew him to the edge of a long shadow that must have been cast by the basilica. The last pilgrims dispersed, driven away by the cold and damp. Werfel found himself at the foot of a rock face lit up by a few candles and grimy with soot. He was alone with a statue that wasn't beautiful yet was surprisingly pleasant in the middle of the dark grotto that echoed with the Gave's rolling waters. He stood still awhile as the cramps and terror of the last few days imperceptibly dwindled. With what strength and clarity of thought he had left, he tried to remind himself that such a simple statue could hardly constitute a source of enlightenment for his soul, the soul of an unbeliever. A marble statue by Praxiteles would more likely have moved him than this pious work, and yet emotion began to fill him. From this pit of darkness rose a light that warmed him to the depths of his being. Brutally, shamelessly, and wordlessly, Franz Werfel fell on his knees. If Alma saw him…? No matter. His desire to live, to escape from this turmoil, came pouring out in this place, and his voice rose above the silence: "Save me, and I shall write of thy mystery!"

The grotto did not have time to return even an echo of this prayer. Werfel was gone, still burning with this unknown warmth.

A few days later, the Lourdes hotel-keeper in whose establishment the Werfels had found refuge brought them unexpected news: Their luggage had been found! The man rejoiced for them without even knowing that the bags contained two precious manuscripts saved from chaos – Mahler's Tenth Symphony and Brückner's Third Symphony. Alma had snatched them from a covetous Hitler who had personally expressed his interest in them. It was while clutching these two irreplaceable compositions that Alma dragged Franz over the back roads to cross over into Spain and then into Portugal.

In the golden light, Franz Werfel's hand once again clutched *The Song of Bernadette*. He seemed still to experience that feeling of deliverance on the boat that took his wife and him to the United States. The young girl of Lourdes, the light under the grotto's mud, the Virgin's luminous smile… All these marvels recounted in the novel, the fruit of a vow in the midst of distress, filled the eyes of the man whom Alma found, that afternoon, at teatime, struck down by a heart attack.

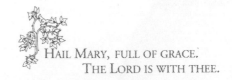

HAIL MARY, FULL OF GRACE.
THE LORD IS WITH THEE.

A Voice in the Night

The Deportees' Pilgrimage, September 10, 1946

1946 The train cars slowly swayed without waking their passengers. The rudimentary comfort of the seventeen trains specially commissioned for the pilgrimage of the repatriated, war prisoners, and displaced persons of the war of 1939-1945 did not seem to bother anyone on that return trip from Lourdes. Peace and serenity reigned on the rails.

It was four o'clock in the morning. In a car filled with dozing passengers, Marcel, from Nord-Pas-de-Calais, approached Father Beloin, his parish priest, and touched his shoulder.

"May I speak with you, Father?" he asked.

"Yes," answered Father Beloin sleepily. "What can I do for you at" – he glanced at his watch – "four in the morning?"

"You remember when you came to announce that you would pay for our trip to Lourdes?" Marcel asked. "You wished to invite all the repatriated in your parish, without exception, to the greatest pilgrimage in history? You cheerfully called out to us, with a young man's enthusiasm: 'A hundred thousand participants are expected on September 6 to 10, 1946, and, gentlemen, I'm taking you with me!' We didn't believe it at the time. We, communists, in Lourdes... I might as well tell you that we had a good laugh that day!"

"And I gave you my word that you would all come to thank the Holy Virgin for your return from this horrible war," the priest replied with a smile. "If necessary, I would have put the reluctant on the train myself."

"Oh! You know, at first, God, Lourdes – we were pretty skeptical," said Marcel. "I mean to say, you were over there, in Germany, you worked there, you sustained those who needed it. You even had to hide the fact that you were a priest."

Marcel, getting carried away in the moment, continued. "After such things, there no longer are any feuds over the cassock, politics, the red triangles[1] used to identify 'enemies of the state', whatever... We're all the same now. So for this pilgrimage, why, we wouldn't have let you go by yourself, end of story! And then gathering all those who've suffered during these years – prisoners, the deported, whether for political reasons or forced labor – strong stuff."

"But you wanted to tell me about yourself?" interjected Father Beloin.

"Yes. With all that has happened these past few days, I'm digressing," Marcel responded apologetically. "On the way down, with the whole gang, we were acting up, like at least this pilgrimage would be a free excursion, at any rate. We were feeling pretty full of ourselves!"

Marcel paused momentarily as he remembered the trip toward Lourdes. "In fact, I think we were afraid. We were wondering what kind of reception we'd get."

"I know," said Father Beloin. "You were laying it on a bit thick with all your bravado."

"Well," Marcel went on, "when we arrived at the station, something had changed. Fear had disappeared. I couldn't tell you why. The poster on the platform greeting those who had made the vow of coming to

---

1. The badge used by the Nazis to designate political prisoners.

thank the Virgin: '*Here, since the day of your promise, Our Lady awaits you...*' Whether you're a believer or not, it'll warm the heart. And that atmosphere, that silence... No one felt the need to speak. Time stood still. We could sense a fraternal bond in it. Words would have been useless. And frankly, what more was there for us to say? No one was there to tell his terrible memories, even though we'll never be able to forget what we lived through, you know as well as I do."

This last sentence, and all that it brought to mind, revived bad memories for the two men. Marcel changed the subject.

"Later, going into Lourdes, we were really able to measure the magnitude of the event," he recalled. "The immense podium built in front of the Basilica of the Rosary, the three bridges built over the Gave to the meadow. And all the chums... The ceremonies hadn't yet begun, and already we were moved."

"It's Father Rodhain, general chaplain of war prisoners, who originated the gathering," interrupted Father Beloin. "His wish was to abolish all difference among individuals – for example, by putting all the hotels and boarding houses at the same price. He was seconded by several deportees, such as the poet Patrice de la Tour du Pin, who wrote *The Way of the Cross*, and Father Primi, former Auflag choirmaster, who composed the pilgrimage hymn. Faith can move mountains, don't you agree?"

"Yes, certainly," answered Marcel. "You know, I followed you all day on Sunday. At first, without really believing much, just out of curiosity. Already by the Pontifical Mass, though, I was moved by the prayers for the dead. Sixty thousand comrades receiving communion, seventeen priests served by deportees in striped or khaki outfits...Who would have believed it early last year? I was listening, watching, remembering. This peace was like a balm on our war wounds. Coming together like this gives us all strength, and hope, too. How can I say this – I'll confide in you because I know you understand – it made me want to love, to believe."

"I know," offered Father Beloin, who felt in Marcel an intense and immediate need to have an honest discussion.

"Then, we crossed the Gave to reach the meadow where the 'Camp of the Return' had been reconstituted," Marcel continued. "Discovering this map of Germany on the ground and those gigantic signs with the numbers of the stalags, oflags[1], and camps where we had been held; seeing each man return to his former prison and his companions in misery, those faces… We looked at each other, and we held each other tight, without a word. We felt a little bit guilty. We didn't deserve to find ourselves here any more than the others who didn't come back. Remember, right after that ceremony, the confessionals were so full that the priests heard confessions in public, on benches, sidewalks, everywhere."

Marcel took a deep breath and continued.

"After what we had lived through, we needed to be at peace at last, to finish with our painful past once and for all! That evening, after Mass in the grotto, we followed the procession toward the meadow. A murmur arose: Men were on their knees, saying their beads. Hundreds of torches lit up one after the other, coming down from the Carmel. And the shrine flared up amid the shouts, 'Christ is risen!'"

Marcel hesitated for a moment, looked around at the sleeping passengers, and shifted into a firmer tone. "I sang, too. It's hard to explain."

He paused again. "I believe that, at that moment, I loved those present, those absent, but also all those who were suffering or who had suffered. I felt my heart stir. I wept. Finally, when Father Rodhain

---

1. A German prisoner-of-war camp for captured Allied officers, who generally received better treatment than non-officers.

announced that he was closing down the prisoner-of-war chaplaincy to open the Catholic Services Office, I told myself that it was really over, that we could close this dark chapter of our lives. Now I know why Lourdes is a unique shrine. All this fervor, this communion with all, this intimacy with God, whereas there were thousands of us – all that would have been impossible elsewhere."

Marcel became a bit more self-conscious.

"Actually, if I awoke you just now, it was to talk to you, indeed," he told his pastor. "To tell you… thank you."

BLESSED ART THOU AMONG WOMEN,
AND BLESSED IS THE FRUIT OF THY WOMB, JESUS.

THE SONG OF HOPE

Jeanne Gestas, Forty-Ninth Miraculous Healing,
August 22, 1947

1947 For two months I had not left my bed. Two months that the robins at my window had been singing a cheerful tune that gave me headaches. Two months that I felt far away from all joy. The third operation, intended to rid me of my adhesive peritonitis, had had as much effect as water on a duck's back. Yes, I did experience the more intense pains and health crises less frequently, but one could hardly have considered that an improvement when I had to remain bedridden in my room and endure frequent fainting spells. Fortunately, my friends visited me regularly, and that helped to sustain me.

On one such day, my neighbor came around again to give my morale a boost.

"Jeanne, I have seen you suffer for three years now," she told me. "It hurts me to see you in such a state. Allow me to make a suggestion: *Why wouldn't you go to Lourdes?* It isn't that far from Bègles."

The answer was obvious: Above my bed, there was a watercolor of sunflowers – not a portrait of the Virgin Mary.

"To tell you the truth, it's been quite a while since I last prayed," I told my friend.

"Well, here's the opportunity to start up again!" she suggested.

So in the month of August, because of my neighbor's insistence, I packed my suitcase and headed for the shrine. A non-practicing Catholic like myself, going to Lourdes – imagine that! I made my way to the grotto filled with doubt. Candles burned there without ceasing, dressing the great candelabra with a cloak of wax. There was a crowd, but by some magic the silence of the place was maintained. With tiny steps, I walked to the esplanade of the Basilica of the Rosary. It was as though I was in a movie with special effects: I felt myself move slowly, but all around everyone else in the crowd was moving at high speed. I tried to get a grip on what was happening to me. Perhaps an irrational hope had overtaken me. With my hands clasped, I began to pray. I prayed in Lourdes. I prayed on the return trip. I prayed back home again in Bègles.

I had barely returned home, but I could not resist telling my neighbor of my experiences.

"I have rediscovered the path to faith!" I told her. "My medical condition still isn't the best, but my heart has irresistibly turned to the Virgin."

My neighbor shared in my enthusiasm. From time to time, my joy lost some of its intensity as more and more dizzy spells made the world seem like a spinning top. Dr. Dubourg tried treating me with infiltrations, but in vain. A year after my visit to Lourdes, I took a second trip with the National Our Lady of Salvation Pilgrimage.

When I went to bathe in the pools, I suddenly felt like something was tearing in my abdomen. The pain slowly subsided. I thought maybe I was dreaming. Could it be a miracle? Could I relinquish all skepticism and abandon myself to the robins' cheery song?

The next day, I went back to the pools. I felt very cold in the water. When I came out, I had a wonderful feeling of well-being. I felt completely healed. At noon, I had a meal of broth, beans, a little wine, and some grapes. I hadn't had such an appetite in a long while.

The physicians of the Lourdes Medical Bureau consider the case of Jeanne Gestas:

It was August 19, 1948, and Jeanne Gestas had just exited the examination room. The twenty-five doctors of the Lourdes Medical Bureau looked at each other, incredulous, and spoke in amazement among themselves.

"She's been back in Bègles a year now. Her intestinal troubles resisted all treatment, and she had three operations in four years, but since her bath at the pools, she has not had a relapse."

"*From a clinical point of view, no pathological sign is to be found.*"

"The liver is in good condition."

"The spleen, too."

"No ganglions, no pains."

"Nothing wrong with the heart. Normal pulse."

"In fact, dear colleagues, we have to face facts: Jeanne Gestas' healing is a miraculous case."

Professor Mauriac, a Bordeaux doctor who was in charge of the investigation, suggested a waiting period to allow more time to confirm this healing.

On August 19, 1950, Jeanne Gestas again completed a round of questions and examinations. Eleven doctors of the Lourdes Medical Bureau look at each other, just as perplexed as before.

"The waiting period has been conclusive. There is not a trace a illness!"

"Let us hand the case over to the National Medical Committee."

Forward to February 10, 1951. For a third time, Jeanne Gestas was tested and gave testimony. Mauriac hastened to write his report. "*I find no trace of neurovegetative trouble. If it ever existed, it has been healed along with all the adhesive peritonitis lesions that tormented this patient for four years. The case seems inexplicable to me today!*"

Nearly a year and a half later, on July 13, 1952, Jeanne Gestas opened her bedroom window and set a few seeds on the sill, humming. The news she had just received filled her with joy. Archbishop Richaud of Bordeaux had just published a ruling. The instantaneous healing of all her troubles, the archbishop said, was "*inexplicable naturally.*" Her cure, he stated, was henceforth to be considered as "*a miraculous intervention that must be attributed to the Blessed Virgin Mary.*"

In April 1981, after thirty-five years of good health free of relapses, the miraculously healed Jeanne Gestas, in her eighty-fifth year, flew away like a robin toward heaven…

HOLY MARY, MOTHER OF GOD,

APPETITE FOR LIFE

Maddalena Carini, Fifty-First Miraculous Healing, August 15, 1948

1948 Lying in the train that was bringing me home to Italy, I suddenly felt like I could eat a horse!

"Nurse... Nurse!" I cried.

"Yes, Miss Maddalena," hastily answered the young woman in charge of the car's sick people.

"I'm hungry!"

The nurse smiled compassionately at me.

"I'll bring you some sugar water right away!" she said after a short silence.

"No, no, I'm ravenous!" I insisted. "I'd like to eat what the others are eating."

The nurse ran her hand across my forehead to check my temperature. Everyone in this car was well aware that I was very ill and could absorb nothing but liquids. I understood this young lady, her perplexity and her pity, too. I could read her mind: *Maddalena's delirious... the end is near!* But whatever she thought, I was hungry. Really hungry! I stubbornly pressed on.

"I would like to eat like the others, please!"

The nurse sighed and walked off with a look of resignation. How could she refuse to accede to one of a dying woman's last wishes?

A few moments later, a delicious smell tickled my nostrils. The meal, at last!

I let the caregiver straighten me out gingerly as I dug into the lunch she had set upon my knees. Under her stunned and watchful eye, I ate. What am I saying? I devoured! I had fed solely on sugar water for so long that this meal was a veritable feast. Hors d'œuvre, entrée, dessert! I ate it all without leaving as much as a crumb. If my upbringing hadn't forbidden it, I might have even licked the plate clean!

Seated next to my cot, the nurse suddenly got up and left with hurried steps, probably to fetch the pilgrimage's doctor.

I rested my head on the pillow and smiled, sated and happy. I knew that in a few minutes' time I would have to explain what was happening to me. Since yesterday I had been keeping this secret to myself. I did not want to cry "miracle" too soon and risk shaking the faith of the other sick people in case it turned out to be an illusion. But, after this good meal, I was certain that the Virgin Mary had healed me! From then on, I could speak.

It wasn't a long wait. The doctor, trailed by the young woman and a stretcher-bearer, came to the side of my cot.

"You're coming to see me, Doctor?" I asked him playfully.

The doctor coughed in embarrassment. "The nurse tells me you had a good lunch today. That hasn't happened in a while, I think?"

"She's right," I said with a smile. "Except for one detail: I didn't eat well, I devoured! I think, Doctor, that something extraordinary has been happening since yesterday."

"Tell me everything," he encouraged me as he sat by my bedside.

"I don't understand anything of it myself," I confessed. "It's inexplicable..."

"Go on!" he urged, anxious to hear the account.

"You know as well as I do, Doctor, that I made it to Lourdes in a deplorable condition," I told him. "In fact, I think the term 'critical' would fit better. The different seats of bony and pulmonary tuberculosis didn't leave me much chance of survival, did they?"

The doctor, uneasy, looked at me. He had not suspected that I, a young woman who was racked with pain and a high fever when I arrived, understood so clearly the gravity of my own condition.

"It doesn't matter. I was but a suffering body, half-paralyzed and boiling with fever. If it wasn't for my dear mother's perseverance and the kindness of my doctor, who finally agreed to issue the certificate allowing me to come to Lourdes, I ought never to have made this trip," I admitted. "It was pure madness. A dying woman's last whim! At any rate, I didn't see much during the pilgrimage. I spent it in my room, bedridden with fever and pain. Except yesterday…"

I stopped for a moment as my voice broke abruptly. I had just realized that the Virgin had flooded me with her graces on the last day of the pilgrimage, the only day I was able to pray before the grotto. She had waited for me until the last moment.

I continued more softly.

"Yesterday I went before the grotto to pray: 'Holy Mary, I thank you for having helped me to come and see you at last. I entrust my friends, parents, and physicians to you.' That's when I felt like I was on pins and needles and sensed a diffuse heat in my chest as my heart began to beat like a drum. I feared cardiac arrest. I wasn't far from one when I got here, I think. I told myself, 'I'm dying, I'm dying!'"

I stopped once more, overcome with emotion. The doctor listened attentively. Behind him, the nurse and the stretcher-bearer had tears in their eyes.

"But, while I thought I was dying, I suddenly had the impression of being very light and incredibly well," I said. "When the Blessed Sacrament came near me, my heart again went crazy. Yet I was no longer afraid. I figured I was feeling well because I was about to die. But my time had not yet come – and, far from dying, I had the feeling of coming back to life. The pain was gone. I could at last move my right leg without feeling pain."

The Lourdes train doctor looked at me with emotion. All that I had said was beyond him, too. I continued, happy to share my secret with him.

"I started shaking for joy. Yet I did not dare cry out, 'Miracle! Miracle!' so that I wouldn't hurt the Virgin if it wasn't for real. I didn't want to take that risk," I said. "But now, Doctor, I want to cry 'Miracle!' and go see the Medical Bureau of Lourdes to have my condition verified, to bear witness to my healing. And, above all, I believe I want to give thanks every day of my life!"

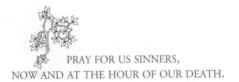

PRAY FOR US SINNERS,
NOW AND AT THE HOUR OF OUR DEATH.

The Saracen and the Queen of Heaven

The Origins of the City of Lourdes, January 18, 1949

1949 Today more than ever, the frozen January wind in the Gave valley has cut me to the heart. It followed me in the deserted alleys of the Lourdes cemetery as I walked behind my grandmother's little casket, a woman so beloved who has just left me an orphan. Going back to the silent house, Prosper, the fat cat, sadly rubs against my legs with a look that seems to say that I am now his guardian. The kettle whistles as I sit in my grandmother's soft stuffed chair. I think back on all the summers I spent here, reading and laughing with that wonderful woman. It seems so far away to me now. It was well before the war.

Prosper – who is clearly set on adopting me as his new master – rubs his nose among the publications heaped up about my feet. Among these I seem to recognize a magazine, which I carefully extract from the pile. The yellowed paper, the faded colors do not keep me from recognizing one of my favorite books from my childhood, the history of Charlemagne and the origins of Lourdes. As my tea cools, I immerse myself anew in this deliciously old-fashioned story that was so dear to us.

At the monastery of Lavedan, Bishop Turpin of Puy-en-Velay, chaplain to Charlemagne, and the monk Marfin, both illustrated in the book as wearing medieval costumes, are wiling away the endless langor of the summer of 778 in conversation.

"What I am about to tell you, Brother Marfin, you are under no obligation to believe", said Bishop Turpin. "But please, listen to me with your heart and your faith."

The bishop pauses. "The Mirambelle citadel[1] is an extraordinary edifice. Its builders were divinely inspired, as the ability and intelligence with which they conceived it render it a nearly impregnable strategic stronghold. Thanks to it, a simple prince, Mirat the Saracen, was able to resist for months the terrible attacks of Charlemagne's mighty army, of which I was a member. Truly, Marfin, that siege seemed to have lasted for ever. And since the imposing rock made it impossible to undermine the foundations, the catapults' springs and cords were in full swing, hurling rocks, beams, and carrion over the thick ramparts. But no war machine was able to get the better of this powerful fortification. Now, this Saracen prince was probably not the miscreant we imagined, a man capable of pushing himself to the limits of the bearable, of securing the unwavering support of his men, of inspiring in them the strength and courage to fight one against ten. Do you think him that far removed from God?"

"To be sure, the man has mettle. But from that to making of him a man of faith, I don't think so," answers Marfin, his eyebrows arched with skepticism. "Why did he not pledge allegiance to Charlemagne? Why did he stubbornly fly his own flag and inflict on his men the horrors caused by his pride?"

"I thought as you do," replies the bishop, "until a rather singular event, which I witnessed, came along and shook my certainties."

---

1. Medieval fortress in the Bigorre region, ancestor of the castle of Lourdes.

Marfin, who had heard of the incident and understood the reference, studied the bishop's face with a doubtful look.

"For a majestic eagle to fly over the fortress and lay a living salmon at this infidel's feet is a disconcerting event, is it not?" continues Bishop Turpin. "When Mirat picked it up, his attention instinctively turned to the source of the incident. Was he seeking a trace of this generous eagle? No. His gaze was fixed. He was staring at the sky. An indescribable smile formed on his face. From the top of the ramparts he looked at the tent of our august king and shouted: 'How could I leave this bountiful land? All around me I see nothing but abundance and fruitfulness. This salmon is splendid! Yet it is only one among hundreds. Take it, nature seems to have been less charitable to you!' And he threw the fish in our direction.

"For the Frankish soldiers, suffering in body, tired of an endless siege, this was the coup de grace. In our king, too, doubt started to take shape. All began thinking about beating a retreat.

"That's the very point when I decided to go to this Mirat, who was claiming that he possessed abundance and might. Several details, which were imperceptible to my companions, led me to believe in the presence of God within the fortifications. I only had to speak, and God would do the rest. Of this I was convinced.

"I then asked our king to let me attempt one last maneuver. The successive failures and the intolerable idea of a retreat were enough to persuade him. I soon went in alone to meet this Saracen prince.

"Faced with the state of neglect of his famished, exhausted, sick troops, I understood that I would get out of there alive only if my intuition had been correct, for never would Mirat let me reveal his weakness outside his camp. He was waiting for me.

"I spoke to him thus: 'Prince Mirat, just like my king, I admire the courage and loyalty you inspire in your men. You have given warning that you would never submit to a mortal, whoever he is, and you have kept your word. I therefore have not come to talk of that, but to speak to you on matters of chance. This morning, an eagle laid a superb salmon at your feet…'

"Mirat, eerily serene, interrupted me: 'That is right. Yet I did not see chance at work. I saw a sign in it. That eagle, whose talons dropped so beautiful a salmon… Salmons swim upstream to perpetuate their race and die shortly thereafter. Why don't they stay at sea? There is infinite room for freedom, the food is abundant. It is as though the focal point, the meaning of their entire existence, consisted in this – to suffer by going against the stream, and at last to give life. All of us here suffer, but to what can we give birth that is more important than our very existence? Do you know?'

"'Yes,' I answered. 'To a city free from all earthly allegiance, a city subject only to the noblest Lady that ever was: Saint Mary du Puy, Mother of God, to whom even Charlemagne, the most illustrious of mortals, submits. Become her knight and offer the most glorious and just governance to Bigorre. History will remember you as the founder of a divine city that belongs only to the Queen of Heaven.'

"For the second time on this extraordinary day, Mirat smiled. You know the rest of the story, Brother Marfin. Mirat, baptized, is now called Lorus. The city, the scene of this genuine miracle, would soon bear his name, Lourdes, and would become the exclusive and heavenly land of the Virgin Mary, the Holy Mother of God, for ever."

As I close the old picture book, I can see my grandmother's shining eyes as she proudly explains to me that this town that she so loved had already been chosen by the Virgin to be the setting for her grace over a thousand years before the apparitions to Bernadette. I recall our pilgrimages to the shrine, the rosewood rosary she nearly always had in her hand and that I laid by her today for the last time. I know that the

Virgin awaits her, just as she awaited Mirat, Bernadette, and millions of others to gather them under the mildness of her mantle. I smile at Prosper, at the magazine's yellowed paper, and at that dear woman who gave me the faith.

 AMEN.

ALIVE AGAIN

Thea Angele, Fifty-Third Miraculous Healing,
May 20, 1950

19 50 "Miss Doctor... I'm terribly hungry..."

For several months, not a word had passed Thea's motionless lips, frozen in the grimace that illness had etched on her waxen face. As a young stenographer, thousands of words had cascaded from her virtuoso fingertips. Then her hands inexorably stiffened. Soon, both arms, too, and then her legs, then her smile. Her ability to form words left her while other words, barbarous words, invaded her daily life with that terrible diagnosis of 1944, the year she turned twenty-three – multiple sclerosis. These were the first words of a chilling litany – paralysis, cephalgia, diplopia... What these words meant to her was that her life would slowly desert her body as it slowly would be overtaken by a living rigor mortis.

When, therefore, these recaptured and childish words of hunger escaped from Thea Angele's mouth as she came out of the pools – words spoken plainly with a shy smile that had just returned to her face – Miss Wimmer, the doctor, could not believe her ears: Thea was hungry! It had been a year since she last could feed herself, for her body was so tensed up with pain that she no longer had the strength for it. Thea, with a simple request and friendly gesture, smiled again to express her newfound appetite.

When she had joined the *Pax Christi* pilgrimage four days before, on May 15, 1950, Thea was nearly dying. Her last remaining energy seemed about to abandon her en route to Lourdes, and Wimmer, as the pilgrimage physician, was not in favor of this trip. The trouble was that, before the final assaults of the disease plunged her in a critical state very close to death, she had her friends and relatives promise something – that she would go to Lourdes to bathe in the waters that Mary, a century before, had made appear.

The journey was painful and endless, adding new sufferings for Thea, who for some time had no longer paid attention to her condition. Fate had hounded her so! In 1945, when the disease had first appeared, she had found herself buried alive during an air raid – for a time, a prisoner to fallen rubble as well as to her own tomb of a body to which her illness already had condemned her at barely twenty-four years of age.

As the train cars passed through the night, Wimmer seemed to be the most affected, fearing she might not be able to fulfill her patient's last wish. Before departing for Lourdes, she thought to herself: *How can one send a dying woman abroad like this, with nearly thirty hours by train?* At the young woman's bedside, she stiffened in imitation of Thea's para-lyzed body, knocked about by the jolts of the train. Far from the shrine, she had given no thought to the grotto's potential for miracles. She only prayed to get Thea there safely.

On the afternoon of May 17, the convoy reached Lourdes. Thea had survived the trip. Bringing her to the grotto or to the eucharistic proces-sion was out of the question. She couldn't take it. Her incurably vacant eyes betrayed the exhaustion of the last hours. The furrows that hollowed her ashen face seemed to foretell imminent death. At the end of the day, she received the sacrament of anointing. Wimmer then returned to her bedside for another night of pain, thinking it might be Thea's last.

However, at dawn the next day, May 18, the doctor emerged from a fitful sleep to see what for a moment she thought was the young woman's rather lively face. She could have sworn that Thea was trying to smile at her from behind her stony mask. She had no idea that a genuine smile would grace this face just two days later.

Accompanied by Maria Rude – Thea's friend, who accompanied her from the Cologne station – the doctor led the sick woman to the pools for the first time. Patiently bathing the spindly body and carefully immersing the bruised extremities, Wimmer felt a measure of relief that she could at least carry out her patient's last wish. At least her soul would have some respite, if not her body. Yet while lifting her out of the bath, Wimmer read a kind of peacefulness in Thea's face, as though the smile she had imagined that morning was slowly taking shape.

The next day, still with Maria, Wimmer brought her patient to the pools twice. Thea's paralyzed body seemed to grow lighter. It seemed to be casting off, in this purifying water, some of the ballast that had held Thea captive for six years. While observing Thea's thin hands gently drifting in the bath's water and seeing the hint of a smile from the day before forming on her patient's face more vividly, the doctor realized that the miracle, this improbable miracle, was taking place before her every eyes.

That evening, Thea was able to drink a little water with some orange and lemon juice. On the bed where, just the night before, the doctor had watched her lie motionless, her legs and hands slowly and haltingly were coming back to life. The strength that had deserted her gradually was being restored, and it was now the good doctor who could no longer utter a word.

On May 20, Thea was led to the pools for the fourth time. Upon leaving the bath, she realized all her pains were gone. The grip of the disease was visibly loosening, freeing her facial features and her frozen mask. She turned her head with assurance and, with this gesture that had been unthinkable the night before, she smiled. "Miss Doctor…"

Speechless at having witnessed Thea's incredible metamorphosis, her doctor was unable to answer right away. For a moment, she was elsewhere, grappling with her troubled memory of the dying woman she had watched over on the train, the patient she no longer recognized in the young, smiling woman before her. This young woman, who soon would be acknowledged as the fifty-third miraculously healed person in Lourdes, would decide never to leave the place where she came back to life, choosing instead to enter the convent of the Immaculate Conception in Lourdes. But for now, the doctor would have to get a grip on herself and get to work: Her patient was terribly hungry!

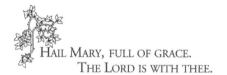

Hail Mary, full of grace.
The Lord is with thee.

THE END OF CALVARY

Evasio Ganora, Fifty-Fourth Miraculous Healing,
June 2, 1950

**19
50** Deep in prayer, Evasio did not see the young woman, a stretcher-bearer, who was watching him closely. Fervently kneeling before the twelfth Station of the Cross of Espélugues in Lourdes, the Italian farmer wept with gratitude as he looked at the statue of Christ hanging dead on the cross. Long, interminable minutes passed, and still Evasio did not move. Standing a short distance from him, the young woman continued to look at him.

Then, suddenly, Evasio got up and confidently walked to the thirteenth station. His feet sometimes slipped on the inclined path cut into the mountain, but that only made him begin again all the more determined. Though the path was steep, the pilgrim didn't seem to notice. Behind him, the stretcher-bearer struggled to keep up with him and was slightly winded from the effort. The young woman liked doing the Espélugues Way of the Cross because the location was so calm, so far from the hustle and bustle of the shrine below. Every time, however, she would forget that the mountainside was steep and that its mile-long hike required a degree of stamina.

As the Way of the Cross neared its end, Evasio was getting ready to go home. It was now or never: The stretcher-bearer had to speak to him to know for sure.

"Excuse me, Sir," she cried out to Evasio as he nimbly headed back down toward the sanctuary.

The man stopped and turned toward her. "Me?" he asked.

"Pardon me for bothering you," the stretcher-bearer apologized.

Evasio smiled at her pleasantly. "Yes?"

"I am Isabella Rosi," said the young woman, extending her hand.

"How do you do?" he answered, shaking her hand. "Evasio Ganora. What can I do for you?"

"Forgive my indiscretion, Sir," continued a blushing Isabella. "But I saw you two days ago in the train. Well, I think…"

A broad smile lit up the pilgrim's face.

"In what train were you, Miss?" he asked.

"I come from the region of Casale, in Italy," she said.

"We were in the same train, that's right," he replied.

"But you seemed so badly off…" insisted the young lady.

Evasio smiled even more. "You're right," he said in a whisper. "I was bedridden by a strong fever and a filthy disease – lymphoma. My physician didn't want to tell me anything, but I believed I didn't have much longer to live."

"But then," exclaimed an astonished Isabella, "I saw you do the Espélugues Way of the Cross! It looked like you felt no fatigue, that its steep and slippery path didn't tire you!"

"Well, I am a little short of breath," admitted Evasio. "This Calvary is indeed steep."

The Italian farmer took on a look of feigned ignorance, as though he did not see what Isabella was driving at.

"But two days ago, you couldn't even stand up," exclaimed the stretcher-bearer. "I know it, because I took care of you on the train. You didn't even realize it, as your high fever was making you delirious."

With an affectionate gesture – Isabella reminded him of one of his daughters – Evasio took her by the arm and started walking toward the shrine again.

"I'll tell you," he finally admitted. "I arrived in Lourdes in very poor condition, you're right. I made the Way of the Cross effortlessly, or nearly so. There again, you're right. But in the meantime, something happened, a miracle: The Virgin Mary healed me!"

And so Evasio Ganora told Isabella his incredible story.

Just a few months before in December 1949, this Italian farmer, a father of five, found himself bedridden for days on end. A persistent high fever, heavy sweating, and nausea prevented him from returning to work and leading the life he knew. His condition worsened very quickly, and treatments proved ineffective.

"Last February 21, my doctor announced to me that I had Hodgkin's disease, a kind of lymphoma," he told Isabella. "He didn't say anything but, judging from his expression, I got the message that I would never recover."

Despite his precarious health, Evasio decided to go to Lourdes. His faith in the Virgin Mary was so profound that he wanted to go to France to pray to her – and (why not?) ask her to heal him. On the first day of his stay at the Marian shrine, he was taken to the pools in a little car. When he was dipped into the cold water of the mountainside, he felt something like a soft warmth invade his body.

"It was yesterday, June 2, 1950," continued Evasio, closing his eyes. "I'll remember that day all my life. The men in charge of the pool wanted to lift me to get me out of the pool, but I refused their help. I straightened up by myself and went to get dressed!"

"Holy Mother!" Isabella cried out, quickly making the sign of the cross three times in succession.

"From that moment," added Evasio with a smile, "I no longer suffered. I no longer have a fever. I can walk, and I feel great! After the pool, I went back to the patient welcoming center. Just think: I was on a stretcher only hours before…"

The man clutched the stretcher-bearer's arm a little tighter as his voice suddenly broke off. The memory was too emotional for him. His eyes were moist with tears.

Strongly impressed, Isabella dared not speak. They walked in silence, meditating on the complete change the Virgin Mary had just wrought in Evasio's life, and also, to some degree, in the young woman's life, too.

After some long minutes of silence, the Italian recovered his composure.

"Do you know what, Isabella?" he said in a joyful tone. "I think I will do what you do now."

"What I do?" she asked.

"I am no longer ill!" he proclaimed. "I shall therefore end my pilgrimage as a stretcher-bearer to thank the Holy Virgin!"

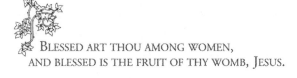

BLESSED ART THOU AMONG WOMEN,
AND BLESSED IS THE FRUIT OF THY WOMB, JESUS.

HOSPITALITY PERSONIFIED

Portrait of Étienne de Beauchamp, August 11, 1950

1950 The steam engine came to a halt with a noisy heave. Like an exhausted pack animal, it labored a few moments, sending its last plume of smoke toward heaven. The engineer got off his seat and leaned out of his door to see the passengers disembark. In his daily life, as well-regulated as the rails and switches under his engine, the arrival at the Lourdes station was always an exceptional moment.

Moving along the platform at low speed, he once again saw the figures gathered together to wait for the train, a little crowd armed with stretchers and first-aid kits. They were familiar to him, those hospitallers with their unusual suspenders[1] who would come and greet each convoy of the sick. Eager and warmhearted, they would climb aboard the cars to assist the ill and disabled who had arrived for their pilgrimage. The strength of their arms was not their only attribute, for their smiles and their readiness to help were legendary. They considered it a personal

---

1. These suspenders, now the stretcher-bearers' distinctive mark, are straps worn about the shoulders to help lift the sick people's stretchers.

honor to be able to welcome each pilgrim as though he or she were a brother or sister, as though he or she were Christ himself.

That is why the engineer liked to linger on his engine's running board a little while. Such an atmosphere was not to be found on any other train platform in France.

Not far from his engine, he noticed an old man standing very straight. The railway employee gave the old-timer a quick glance and a cordial smile, then returned to watching the stretcher-bearers. Little did he know that he had just greeted the one responsible for orchestrating this unique welcome.

Count Étienne de Beauchamp never tired of watching the pilgrims' arrival either. He had been president of the Hospitality of Our Lady of Lourdes for twenty-eight years. In spite of his ninety-one years of age, he personally choreographed the immense daily ritual that took place at the shrines – welcoming the convoys, distributing the crowds among the different welcoming centers, escorting the sick to the grotto and the pool. Beauchamp had directed thousands of hospital workers who worked together each year in Lourdes as a team to ensure that all these services operated properly. Discrete and efficient, he had been supervising everything for years. Despite his advanced age, he was often spotted at the station, at the basilica, on the esplanade, at the pools, and visiting the hostels. He also continued to spend many hours in his office, minutely organizing the daily schedule and selecting the service heads for that day. Retirement? The count did not give it any thought, for he was still needed at the shrines. Bishop Gerlier of Tarbes, with whom de Beauchamp was on intimate terms, held this friend in limitless esteem.

Though he was named president of the Hospitality in 1922, his presence in Lourdes far predated that honor. Originally from Poitou, he took up residence in the Marian city in 1906. The bishop at that time, Bishop Schoepfer, relied on him to render an immense service to the diocese. The anticlerical laws of the day had threatened to confiscate the grotto's domain from the Church. De Beauchamp, as one intimately familiar with the Lourdes pilgrimages, was in a position to save the situation by becoming a "lessee" of the venue, a legal fiction intended to prevent the expulsion of the chaplains.

Without a moment's hesitation, de Beauchamp accepted the bishop's request. Shaken by a string of family tragedies that left him without wife or children in a span of less than ten years, he needed to find new meaning to his life and its solitude. To consecrate it to Lourdes seemed to him a solution preferable to all others.

But de Beauchamp did not take up residence within his new walls so that he could be but a detached landlord, a dilettante spectator of the pilgrims coming to pray to Mary all year long. As an active member of the Hospitality of Our Lady of Lourdes, which was founded in 1885, he had the opportunity to dedicate himself body and soul to serving the sick. By 1907, he was promoted to vice-president of the foundation. He filled this position for fifteen years until the president's death left vacant a chair to which the bishop hastened to nominate him!

The count's long tenure at the helm of the Hospitality certainly did not lead this archconfraternity to stagnate in the routine provision of services. Quite the contrary! From the very outset, de Beauchamp fought to breathe a badly needed spirit of openness into the foundation. Until then, the Hospitality of Lourdes indeed held an absolute monopoly over the reception of pilgrims in the town. The volunteers from the different dioceses who brought the sick to the pilgrimage center were left without a job upon their arrival in Lourdes. For the entire duration of their stay, the Hospitality, jealously defensive of its prerogatives, took charge of the sick and returned them to their original guardian angels only at the moment of departure!

To de Beauchamp's mind, such exclusivity could not continue. After his years as vice-president, he applied his immense powers of conviction to encourage the birth of diocesan hospitalities in the four corners of

France. In 1925, after he had directed the archconfraternity for three years, he caused a stir by choosing the president of the Nord region's stretcher-bearers as his deputy! He could not have demonstrated more clearly the union between the venerable Hospitality of Lourdes and the diocesan organizations for the good of the sick and the service to the pilgrims!

The good of the sick, the service to pilgrims... Until the end of his earthly life, Count de Beauchamp would have this cause close to his heart. And because it coincided with the Church's most precious concerns – the ministry to the sick, one of the corporal works of mercy – the Hospitality president was rewarded with the highest distinction the Pope could offer to a layman. This dedicated man, who carried on his service in the background behind his army of hospital workers, was granted the Grand Cross of the Pontifical Equestrian Order of Saint Gregory the Great.

Born in 1859, a year after Bernadette witnessed the apparitions, Étienne de Beauchamp passed away in 1957, just as Lourdes was preparing to celebrate its centennial!

Holy Mary, Mother of God,

A WIFE'S PERSEVERANCE

Paul Pellegrin, Fifty-Sixth Miraculous Healing,
October 3, 1950

1950 Mrs. Paul Pellegrin rested her knitting on her knees. Through a half-open window, her sad eyes contemplated the Gave's icy waters as they calmly ran below the hotel. She remained pensive for awhile before turning her attention again to her husband, who was lying on a chaise lounge with a blanket over his legs, his face tensed up in a painful grimace. *How skinny he is!* she thought to herself.

"Paul, I would very much like you to go back for a bath in the pools," she whispered softly.

Colonel Paul Pellegrin slowly shook his head.

"Listen, I can't bear to remember yesterday's bath. Water at fifty-three degrees is really cold, and you wear only a shift," he told his wife. "Furthermore, dearest, let me remind you that we came to Lourdes only to take part in the Rosary Pilgrimage, not to expect miracles."

Mrs. Pellegrin insisted. "Paul, it's October 2, you've been sick for two years, you're in pain and no treatment has brought you comfort," she said. "I beg you to take another bath."

The colonel, feeling chilly, pulled up his blanket. In truth, he was tired of this permanent and exhausting pain.

It all started in January 1949. A sharp pain at the base of the thorax and a high fever ruined his health and forced him to check in to the military hospital in Toulon. Examinations, biopsies, and lung taps followed one another for days on end. The attempted treatments – emetine, because of his past service in the colonies, then penicillin – turned out to be completely useless. At wit's end, the colonel decided to check himself out of the hospital on February 14.

His health, however, worsened further still. In March, the physician treating him, Dr. Paul Berny, called upon a specialist, Dr. Pierre, to come for a consultation. He diagnosed an abscess of the liver.

The very next day, Paul Pellegrin was transported to a clinic for an emergency operation. His improvement was instantaneous – no more pain or fever. He believed himself to be healed. But, alas, the respite was short-lived. The abscess reasserted itself in May. He was hospitalized once again, but no treatment seemed to help. He was in pain and could no longer so much as feed himself.

The colonel ran his hand over his forehead to wipe off the tiny drops of sweat that endlessly beaded upon it. He watched the dust dance in the sunbeams just above the large blue pot decorating the round table in the hotel room. He liked these pots, the product of local artisanship. Made of the region's soil, clay, and a little sand, they were of a warm, deep, bewitching blue.

The colonel shut his eyes. He felt the burning sun of the African sand, the humidity of Indochinese nights; he saw bits and pieces of his long-ago military campaigns. He had been so strong then...

"Would you like us to take a blue pot back to Toulon, my dear?" he asked his wife.

Mrs. Pellegrin was startled, reawakened from her thoughts; she, too, often relived the unhappy past few months in her head.

"What do you think?" repeated the colonel.

"I sincerely think that only the Virgin can heal you, Paul," she told her husband. "Men have already done all that is in their power for nearly two years now."

"I came to pray to the Virgin, to honor her, not to solicit her," he replied. "I know that I am lost; nothing will ever be able to stem this tide of pus that is ruining me. I was telling you about the blue pot."

Mrs. Pellegrin was more than a little irritated.

"What does the pot matter, Paul, you're in pain! This catheter has been dripping for eighteen months now. I beg you to take another bath tomorrow."

"Understood," sighed her husband in resignation. "Tomorrow I'll take another bath, but it'll be the last."

On October 3, 1950, the colonel made his way to the shrine. He walked slowly, one hand clenched to his wound, as if to hold his bandage in place. He stopped at the Massabielle grotto to say a prayer to the Virgin, then walked along the Gave to the pools. There, a hospitaller took charge of him and roughly dressed his wound after his bath.

Exhausted, the colonel returned to the hotel and settled down in the chaise lounge near the round table. He stretched out his arm to stroke the blue pot.

His wife then noticed her husband's half-undone bandage. She took hold of a white enamel basin, a few compresses, and a little vial and came closer to her sick husband. "I'm going to clean your wound and change your bandage," she told him.

She then observed that the wound no longer dripped.

The next day, the bandage was still clean. As this had already occurred once or twice in the past, however, neither the colonel nor his wife gave any thought to a cure.

The couple returned to Toulon, and the colonel immediately went back to the Saint Anne military hospital to resume his series of shots.

The nurses there observed that there was no longer a wound, just a pink and perfectly healed spot. Suddenly realizing he had undergone a transformation beyond his hopes, Paul Pellegrin went home, shouting, "I'm healed, the Virgin has healed me! What a joy, what a miracle! You were right to push me into taking that second bath. Thank you, my dear!"

Being a reasonable man, however, he wanted proof, and so had himself examined by Dr. Pierre.

"What? You no longer have a bandage?" asked the astonished physician.

His amazement only grew when he noticed that the fistula had disappeared and was now replaced by a pink, supple, and painless scar.

"*What on earth have you done there?*" he exclaimed.

"*I'm just back from Lourdes!*" answered the colonel.

Three years later, a canonical decree of Bishop Gaudel of Fréjus and Toulon judged and declared that "*Colonel Paul Pellegrin's healing, which took place on October 3, 1950, is miraculous and must be attributed to a special intervention on the part of the Blessed Virgin Mary, Mother of God.*"

After his healing, the colonel became one of the most faithful followers of the Rosary Pilgrimage. He loved revisiting the Massabielle grotto, his heart beating with new life, and coming here to pray with his wife by his side.

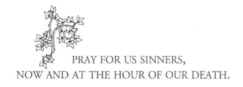

PRAY FOR US SINNERS,
NOW AND AT THE HOUR OF OUR DEATH.

DEEP IN A HEART

Anna Santaniello, Sixty-Seventh Miraculous Healing,
August 19, 1952

19
52 Terrible breathlessness! Why doesn't my heart help me, it should be so strong? Why does it abandon me, when my hands and my soul can still help, assist, and sustain those who need care? I did not become a nurse to be cared for, but to care for others. And all these children, too, that I cannot care for since I have become ill… It makes me so angry to have become an inert and useless burden.

Ah! The line is moving. I can see the entrance to the pools' changing room. Will I be able at least to get up, to bathe in the source's water with what is left of my will and hope? Holy Virgin, help me!

The people who leave after having immersed themselves in this freezing water seem serene, rested. Satisfied? No, that is not the word. In this place, it is not satisfaction that one seeks. So what am I doing here?

Anna, my girl, this is no time to waver. You know very well why you have made this arduous trip against everyone's opinion. They said you were risking your life. So what? My life has always been risky! Walking was perilous. Today, raising an arm is hazardous. Even breathing is now dangerous for me! I am here because nothing else has any meaning, because living in my state, completely dependent, a dead weight for my family, a burden for myself… living like this does not seem livable to me anymore!

My Lord! Have I become so self-centered that my physical healing alone is important to me? Is there nothing for me to do in this world besides become healthy? Is the universe really waiting for brave, good Anna to frolic on both legs, roaring with laughter? Who am I today that I should be owed a healing that others have not been granted?

See the length of the line to the pools. See the suffering, the fear of all these people who, like you, believe that Someone loves them, and that this love might help them, carry them, sustain them, perhaps even heal them? What have they got better than you, or not as good? Are they saints or criminals? Neither, to be sure. Yet here they are – on a stretcher, in a little car, unable to go to Mary by their own means, and yet so willing! They are just like you, your brothers and sisters in humanity, like these friends who came with you, like this poor Nicolino with his lifeless legs, so young and yet already broken.

Here we are. It does seem that these gracious poolside assistants are going to have to lift me up and carry me! I am incapable of the slightest effort – I who would love, on the contrary, to be in their place lifting up the sick, the infirm, the mountains!

"Relax, madam. We are here to help you. Think only of her and of your soul."

Yes, that's right, relax, Anna. Forget your powerlessness, your pains, your body. Forget yourself!

"There you are. The water is cool, but so pure! Do you wish to make the sign of the cross, to say a prayer? Do you have a specific intention?"

Yes, yes, an intention that all who need it may be healed in one way or another! A prayer for Nicolino who has everything to live for, every-thing to see, everything to love! Holy Virgin, you know the sorrow of losing a child. Look at this young man full of vigor, whom death will not take just yet but who cannot live much longer. Holy Mother, help him! Help me to help him, but whatever you can give me, give it to Nicolino. Mary, loving mother, clement woman, give him life and movement!

It's so cold, but it feels so good! What warmth in my heart! Come now, Madam poolside assistant, let me straighten up and get out of the water. I am too happy for having come here not to try to move my legs. They refused to carry me because my heart was unwilling, but I feel it has learned its lesson here. It has changed its mind, and henceforth it will do its best so that I can also do something for those who need it!

"This way, Madam, the changing room is right behind you. Would you like some help putting on your clothes? No? Goodbye, then."

Help? Why, I've got help, and more than I ever would have dared to hope! Get dressed quickly, Anna. Nicolino will need you later for his turn at the pools, and many others besides! It feels so good to stand alone! And my breath, coming back to me... I can even put my stockings on by myself! Oh! Holy Virgin, I dare not believe. You have heard me then, and you have given me the possibility of making myself useful again!

Anna, Anna, my girl, calm down! Don't get carried away like this, it's bad for your heart. And it may be a temporary improvement, a remission owing to the shock of the cold water. Bad for my heart? But that is all my heart is asking for now! Joy, enthusiasm, energy! Get up. Get up and walk, he said. Well then, do so! And go support Nicolino – he needs it. Thank you, Holy Mother! Thank you to him, for them, for all those I will be able to help!

Amen.

THE VIRGIN OF DUST

Our Lady of Lourdes in Oradour-sur-Glane, July 12, 1953

19 53 The village of Oradour-sur-Glane, located in the Limousin region of France, was the site of nightmarish atrocities of the German army during World War II. On June 10, 1944, a German Waffen-SS battalion on its way to fight the Allies in Normandy in the aftermath of D-Day entered the village, killed six hundred forty-two inhabitants, and razed the entire town. The men of Oradour-sur-Glane were executed by machine-gun fire; the women and children were rounded up into a church and burned alive. Only twenty-five or so citizens escaped the killing spree. Although a new Oradour-sur-Glane was developed at some distance from where it once stood, the original village was never rebuilt. Today it serves as a memorial to its victims, to the cruelty of the Nazi occupation, and to similar atrocities on civilians around the world.

On a summer morning, the little village of Oradour-sur-Glane put on a festive air. The villagers, dressed in their Sunday best, hastened toward the church in a long procession. The Glane River meandered gaily under the sun, beautiful and cool, just as Jean-Baptiste Corot had painted it so often in the last century.

Mrs. Mébu, clinging to her daughter's arm, trotted as fast as she could. She did not want to miss the beginning of the "baptism" of the bells – a blessing and dedication, really – by Bishop Rastouil of Limoges. Her old face lit up at the idea of once again seeing the statue of the Virgin of Lourdes – the new one, that is, the one that Miss Mébu, her daughter, offered to the diocese of Limoges after the massacre of June 10, 1944. Bishop Choquet of Tarbes and Lourdes had solemnly blessed the statue in the Massabielle grotto, a statue into which her daughter had poured her life savings.

The crowd entered the church. Hearts still were very heavy... How could one forget the day when the murderous insanity of the Nazi SS had transformed the old church into a human slaughterhouse?

Miss Mébu and her mother took the first place among the faithful. They sat very straight, their hands together. Near them, a young man fought back tears. Mrs. Mébu gently took him by the hand:

"You lost a dear one here?" she murmured.

"Yes," whispered the young man.

And he introduced himself very quickly, so quickly that she was able to make out only his Christian name – Guillaume.

In short, staccato sentences, he explained that his mother and sisters died in the church when it was set on fire. He only escaped the carnage because of his broken leg: He had stayed in his bed, and no one saw him.

"The next day..." he stammered, "the next morning I dragged myself through the streets all the way to the church. All was in ruin, corpses lying all over the place."

"Were you alone?" Mrs. Mébu asked. "Were there no other survivors?"

"Yes, there was, a lady from Paris and a handful of villagers," he replied. "The church was still burning, the high altar was shattered, the tabernacle bashed in; the bells, molten from the heat of the flames, were nothing but a foul mass spread on the ground, and everywhere, everywhere, charred corpses. I knew that my mother and sisters were among them."

Guillaume stifled a sob. Mrs. Mébu placed a maternal hand on his shoulder.

"Only the chapel on the left was spared," continued Guillaume, "that of Our Lady of Lourdes. The statues of the Virgin and of Saint Bernardette were intact amid the ashes."

"I know," interjected Miss Mébu. "That is why the first people to visit the ruins were called pilgrims, and it was a miracle that there were any survivors."

"But a few months later," Guillaume said, "when the pastor wanted to move the Virgin to protect her during the reconstruction, she fell to dust."

Miss Mébu sighed. "Yes, in the middle of catastrophe, the Virgin of Oradour remained *the guardian of the dead and the comfort of the living.*" she said. "*Once her mission was over, she disappeared.*"

Guillaume's tone changed a bit. "Happily, she has come back, more beautiful than ever! There she is, at her place in the chapel of Our Lady of Lourdes, facing Saint Bernadette, like before," he marveled with a glimmer of hope in his eyes.

Mrs. Mébu smiled. "My daughter offered the statue," she began to say before her daughter interrupted her.

"Please, Mother, the Virgin has regained her place, the way in which she came is not important, she is there once more," Miss Mébu said humbly.

"Hush, listen…"

A heavenly music rose in the nave as Bishop Rastouil entered, followed by the procession of the bells' godfathers and godmothers as custom demanded.

The ceremony was brief and moving. The bells started pealing, their high-pitched notes resounding throughout the valley, and they were "baptized."

Nine years had passed since the tragedy. With the sound of the bells of hope, the village could begin to emerge from its mourning, slowly, step by step.

Mrs. Mébu slipped her left hand under her daughter's arm and her right hand under that of Guillaume.

"Let us pay homage to the Virgin," she proposed.

Though the environment was no longer the same, though the modern church did not have the charm of the old burned-out Romanesque church, the Virgin was still just as beautiful and consoling.

On the church's doorstep, the old pastor explained to the faithful the origin of the name "Oradour."

"It comes from the Latin word *oratorium*," he said. "It indicates that, in Roman times, there had been an altar in a place of prayer for the dead, who at the time would be buried alongside the roads. Unfortunately, Oradour has not managed to escape its fate."

Mrs. Mébu shuddered. "It's terrible," she whispered.

Guillaume looked very pale.

"What do you intend to do now?" asked Miss Mébu. "Are you staying a few days in Oradour?"

"Oh, no! I'm going back to Paris as soon as possible," he replied.

"Someone's expecting you there?"

"No," answered Guillaume.

"Well, then," she pressed on, "why don't you come with us to Lourdes? We are leaving this very evening on a thanksgiving pilgrimage. You will see the beautiful Massabielle grotto."

Her kind insistence was difficult for Guillaume to resist. He felt as though he was no longer alone, and that he had found a spiritual mother and sister.

While Miss Mébu's little car drove off toward Lourdes, the newly baptized bells were still gaily chiming. Peace and serenity were indeed back in Oradour-sur-Glane, even in the midst of still strong and painful memories.

HAIL MARY, FULL OF GRACE.
THE LORD IS WITH THEE.

CHILDREN LIKE ANY OTHERS

The HCPT Pilgrimage, May 28, 1954

19 54 Like all great achievements, a pilgrimage to Lourdes for English-speaking children with disabilities was first the idea of one man, Brother Michael Strode, an English religious. In 1954, while working in a hospital for disabled children in the east of England, he proposed a pilgrimage to Lourdes for the children of his institution. He dragged a friend into the venture, and both of them – with the agreement of the children's parents – took four children to walk in Bernadette's footsteps.

Once in Lourdes, Brother Michael bucked the shrine's habits. This young thirty-one-year-old religious was convinced that disabled children must live among the others, without segregation. It was out of the question for him to let his young charges spend their week in the hospital, as was customary in the 1950s. Indeed, the sick and the disabled stayed at the hospital in the evening and came out only during the day, accompanied by their stretcher-bearers, to go to the shrine. They could neither walk in the streets nor enjoy the town's hospitality. Brother Michael, on the contrary, brought the children with him everywhere. He put them up at the hotel as if they were guests of honor; he took them for hikes on donkeys in the Pyrenees between celebrations, and even let them take part in the spectacular torchlight procession at night.

The children's joy was such that, upon their return to Sussex, the English religious decided to set up a charitable fund to allow more children to make the trip. Two years later, his vision became a reality in the form of an association he named Handicapped Children Pilgrimage Trust (HCPT). The young brother explained its principle as follows: *"Every child, whatever his origin and his parents' income, must be able to come. The trip is free of charge."*

Thanks to this organization, forty-three handicapped children and twenty-eight chaperons participated in the national pilgrimage of English Catholic schools the following year. But success was such that, in 1960, the pilgrimage of children with disabilities was separated from the school pilgrimages and become entirely independent.

Little by little, Scots, Irish, and Welsh joined in the project and created their own branches of the association. In every region, groups were set up comprising five to ten children, the same number of chaperons, a nurse, and a priest. All shared the same convictions and gathered the necessary funds to meet in Lourdes every year in an extraordinary explosion of joy.

"Once upon a time, pilgrims traveled in small groups to protect and support each other spiritually. Today, we consider groups to be real families," declared Tony Mills, national HCPT secretary in the 1990s. It was indeed an immense family of pilgrims whose fanciful and warm enthusiasm invaded the shrine, year after year, in the week after Easter. Each small regional team chose a distinctive sign for the pilgrimage – a hat, a badge, a scarf, a particular makeup – and put together its own banner. Everyone was allowed free rein for their often overflowing imagination, and the pilgrimage was always marvelously festive and colorful!

Sustained by this momentum, the number of participants down through the years has regularly increased. There were fifteen hundred children to celebrate the movement's twenty-fifth anniversary in 1981, and there were more than twenty-five hundred of them in 2006, fifty years after the association was created. Happily, Brother Michael was wrong when, after organizing the trip for one hundred and sixty-three children in 1963, that "*from both the financial and administrative points of view, I think we have reached our maximum capacity.*"

Since 1975, the HCPT also has had a house in Bartrès, a few miles from Lourdes. Groups of forty to fifty pilgrims stay there throughout the year. They are made up of handicapped teenagers or young adults who, as children, often participated in the yearly pilgrimage and wanted to continue to come in the same spirit – to pray, but also to spend the holidays in the heart of the Pyrenees. Over seven thousand people come in this way every year to the residence christened Hosanna House.

Despite the ever more complex organization, the movement remains faithful to its origins. It offers everyone both a time of pilgrimage and an enjoyable vacation in the Pyrenees – excursions into mountain villages and walks along the sea follow times of celebration before the grotto. "*We often tell the children that they are coming to spend the holidays with our Lady,*" explains Richard King, the present-day director.

The result meets expectations: "*Maddie has been to Lourdes twice,*" relates the mother of a little girl with a serious mental disability. "*During those two weeks, she made lightning progress. Her father and I believe that there is a link between the feeling of safety she feels with us and the joy and good humor she is in when she is in Lourdes. Last year, when she came back, she could even say her name. We had never dared dream that that might happen.*"

BLESSED ART THOU AMONG WOMEN,
AND BLESSED IS THE FRUIT OF THY WOMB, JESUS.

THREE SHOTS AT A MIRACLE

Marie Bigot, Fifty-Ninth Miraculous Healing,
October 8, 1953, and October 8 to 10, 1954

1954 Marie was thirty, a young Breton from a village in Ille-et-Vilaine. She was close to her family, oriented toward life and people, energetic, and eager. She ought to have been happy. The trouble was that for the past three years she had been in silence and darkness. She no longer could see or hear – cut off from the world she loved so much, isolated from people. She was living a nightmare.

The disease did not strike her suddenly. It had been chasing her down since her childhood, and it was relentless in its pursuit. Yet Marie never gave up. Despite her weak health, her skin diseases, and her hospital stays, she continued to believe in life, to seek out others so as not to isolate herself or descend into self-pity. As months went by and her condition worsened, her sight grew dimmer and dimmer without any hope of improvement. What she did not realize was that she had become an example of courage and tenacity for many.

Fate struck her an even harsher blow on April 3, 1951. She awoke that morning with a high fever and an intense migraine headache that felt like a pair of claws clamped onto her skull. The pain was so horrible that she could not get out of bed. The family doctor was called to her bedside and prescribed antibiotics, but the drugs met with no discernible success. Marie stayed in bed, crushed with pain and depression. As days went by, her fever rose even further. Two more physicians were called in but could do nothing.

On April 13, the young woman fell into a coma-like state. She was taken to the hospital in Rennes, but her symptoms were so violent and persistent that she was transferred to a specialized neurosurgical unit. On April 29, she underwent brain surgery. The problem was identified as arachnoiditis of the brain's posterior fossa, a cumbersome name for one of the gravest forms of meningitis.

Once back home, on May 23, Marie was but a shadow of her former self. Her entire right side was paralyzed, and she could barely move her neck. Migraines and dizziness plagued her. Her eyesight continued to decline and, as if that were not bad enough, she also became deaf. Months passed, and every day she was a little worse. Within one year, she had become completely blind, deaf, and hemiplegic in her right leg and arm. The doctors who dealt with her judged her case to be desperate and gave up all treatment. The young woman was virtually abandoned to her fate without sound, light, or movement.

Well… not quite. For deep within her remained a small glimmer of hope, a sort of unreasonable taste for life, a refusal to become discouraged. She began studying Braille. In August 1952, a hospital nurse proposed that she should participate in the next Rosary Pilgrimage in Lourdes. Marie accepted, but without much enthusiasm. She had never believed in devotional excesses. The trip, which was to take place in October 1952 with the Medical Service of the Rosary, represented for her the gift of life. No miracle took place that year, and she experienced no turn for the better. She actually got worse: Her paralyzed foot had twisted and become a clubfoot, *talipes equinovarus*, and she could hardly get around anymore. Marie did not express surprise at this development. She felt neither anger nor rage. She simply accepted it and waited.

The next year, in October 1953, she returned to Lourdes again with a thin thread of hope – that thread she clung to, come what may, and which she followed step by step toward the light that kept shining somewhere deep within her.

On October 8, 1953, Marie was in Lourdes on the great esplanade facing the Basilica of Our Lady of the Rosary. She participated in the Blessed Sacrament procession, following one step at a time, limping along with difficulty. Suddenly, at the very end, she was struck by a sharp pain. Marie stumbled, staggered, twisted the way a flame curls over itself... then relaxed, straightened up, and walked. Yes, she was walking normally! Her deformed foot was back in shape. Her right leg was working. Her arm moved. She once again felt energy coursing through her veins. Step by step, she walked toward the light. That was her first miracle.

The next year, Marie was on her way to Lourdes again. She was walking, but she still could neither see nor hear. For three years, she could not distinguish day from night. She could not hear the ticking of the clock, or the church bells that marked the time. Those three years seemed an eternity.

On the morning of October 10, 1954, the young woman was once again on the procession esplanade for the blessing of the sick. She was praying and completely focused. The words of her prayers echoed in her head. "*Ave Maria!*" They echoed louder and louder, like thousands of voices, singing and thundering. Marie raised her head, astounded. All these voices around her... and suddenly, the mighty tolling of the bells, like explosions of joy. She heard, she heard! That was her second miracle. All around her, excited whispers spread. "*Marie, do you hear?*" asked her neighbor. "Hush!" the young Breton answered. She wanted to go on praying.

The next day, she went back to the station to catch the train, delighted at being cured of her deafness. She did not ask for anything more than that. She would not stop praying to say thank you. All of a sudden, as she stood on the platform, there was a flashing light so bright it burned her eyes as though they were being torn out! Marie was carried into the sleeper car by nurses. Lying down, half unconscious, she heard the train start up, the rattling of the rails. She dozed. The light had softened to a cool white, crisscrossed with lightning. She opened her eyes. The lightning was the lamps of the stations as the train passed through. Marie saw! Marie heard! She got up, smiled, went to the window, and drank in the world to which she had just been reborn. She was healed!

Marie Bigot's total healing in three steps was verified at her return by all the doctors and was declared "*medically inexplicable.*" On August 15, 1956, after canonical investigation and judgment, the bishop of Rennes consecrated her the "fifty-ninth miraculously healed person of Lourdes."

At this writing, Marie has never had a relapse. She has recovered all her sight, her hearing, and her ability to move. Today a member of the Rosary Hospitality, she now devotes herself to helping the sick and restoring their hope. She continues to go to Lourdes every year. Now eighty-six years old, to this day she remains as active and as amazed by the gift of life as ever, steady in stride and steady in sight!

Holy Mary, Mother of God,

THE CITY OF THE POOR

The Creation of the Cité Saint-Pierre, August 1, 1955

19 55 *"What we want is to work at achieving the program outlined by Christ: the poor are evangelized."*

On the afternoon of August 1, 1955, on the side of the Béout Mountain, a few minutes away from the grotto shrine, Bishop Théas of Lourdes saluted the opening of the Cité Saint-Pierre construction site. Along with Father Jean Rodhain, founding president of the Secours Catholique, and Cardinal Lercaro, archbishop of Bologna, he had just blessed the ground upon which the Secours Catholique was to erect a building to house the poorest pilgrims. He had laid the first stone, which came from the grotto, within which a document recording the event was sealed.

The project had been carried out briskly. Fifteen days ago, Bishop Théas wrote to Father Rodhain: *"Desiring to make the Lourdes pilgrimage easier for the humble and for the poor, I thought that the Secours Catholique might undertake a project that is near to my heart and corresponds to the desire of Christianity. I should therefore be grateful to you for considering the organization, in Lourdes, of an Assistance-Center for poor pilgrims."*

It was not by chance that the bishop of Lourdes had turned to Father Rodhain. The previous year, Secours Catholique had opened two shelters for the poorest in Paris, the Myriam and Our Lady Assistance Centers. Bishop Théas knew this priest whose heart was ablaze with charity. He knew that if Father Rodhain would accept, he would go all out and turn the center into one of the showcase facilities in Lourdes, a witness to the Church's charitable works on behalf of the impoverished. Was that not a subtle message from Mary, who appeared not to a powerful man but to little Bernadette?

Providence also played a hand. At the very time that the bishop made his request, a Lourdes family, the Teillards, decided to put a forty-four-and-a-half-acre lot on the market. The bishop informed Father Rodhain who, with the consent of the board of trustees, visited the plot and bought it. This happened on the very morning of the laying and blessing of the cornerstone! He also met the archbishop of Bologna, who was accompanying a pilgrimage to Lourdes and, naturally enough, asked him to bless the grounds. His Eminence Cardinal Lercaro was a churchman well-known for his social initiatives. The request of Bishop Théas and Father Rodhain moved him. "*The poor must be loved fraternally so that God's justice may shine here below. I am glad to have been chosen to bless the beginning of this work,*" he explained.

From a vantage point on his new grounds, Father Rodhain contemplated Lourdes and the grotto's domain. He still remembered the hundreds of thousands of displaced persons who came to the pilgrimage he had organized here as general chaplain for war prisoners. He recalled that Sunday, September 8, 1946, and the Mass celebrated by Bishop Piguet of Clermont-Ferrand, who had been deported to Dachau, along with seventeen other deported priests, symbolizing all the Masses said clandestinely during the war years. He especially remembered the pilgrims assembled on the meadow before the grotto. They made up a living map where all were grouped according to their place of detention. Together they had welcomed the sick. They had heard the sermon of Father Riquet, preacher of Our Lady, who had been deported to Fresnes,

Compiègne, Mauthausen, and Dachau. Finally, they had welcomed the Blessed Sacrament procession. At dusk, the light of Bernadette's candle had been passed on to all the pilgrims gathered before the grotto. The immense expanse of light called to mind the words of the Gospel: "*Blessed are the meek, for they will inherit the land. Blessed are the peace-makers, for they will be called children of God.*"[1] He could see that gigantic torchlight procession as it got under way. It was faith lighting up the world and setting it ablaze; it was charity on the move.

Father Rodhain went back to the first stone of Cité Saint-Pierre. The charity that was needed to save the world was trying to speak through the Secours Catholique he had created in 1946. In order to launch this immense project, he had relied on his experience of family-and-friend networks established during the war. With a well-planned structure, with a will to use pedagogy and information, he organized volunteer teams who brought solidarity to life. He created the journal *Messages*, the circulation of which soon reached forty thousand copies, to fight against ignorance, the first obstacle to solidarity. *Charity is something other than an automatic distributor, however improved. Rather than having a gigantic distribution service, it is better to awaken, throughout Christendom, the notion of sharing.*

Bishop Théas, Cardinal Lercaro, and Father Rodhain looked at the stone, this grotto stone, this Gospel stone which was already, for them, the symbol of a charity at the heart of the shrine. Within the silence of their souls, they entrusted to God all those whom the center would soon shelter. They were far from suspecting that it would one day shelter twenty thousand pilgrims per year – twenty thousand of the poorest of the poor, for whom a hotel was out of reach, twenty thousand poor people to whom the Cité Saint-Pierre allows this "journey in hope" which they need so desperately to find a meaning for their lives. That

---

1. Mt 5: 5, 9.

August 1, 1955, the three men gathered on the Béout hillside could only feel a hint of the immense expectation of these poor men's hearts thirsting for a little hope and human brotherhood. Who better than they deserved a house in Lourdes? Perhaps, in the secret of their souls, these three men's thoughts turned to the One who found only closed doors at all the inns of Bethlehem. From then on, whenever his brothers and sisters arrived in Lourdes, there would always be an open door and an outstretched hand of friendship.

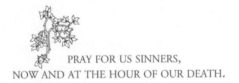

PRAY FOR US SINNERS,
NOW AND AT THE HOUR OF OUR DEATH.

THE MIRACULOUSLY HEALED WOMAN AND THE YOUNG PHYSICIAN

Alice Couteault, Fifty-Eighth Miraculous Healing,
October 11, 1956

1956 On the train, all are asleep. I am alone in the car's narrow corridor. It is four in the morning. I have spent a lot of time trying to sleep without success. I should go back to my berth and sleep, of course, if I'm to avoid being exhausted when we arrive in Poitiers tomorrow, but I do not have the desire. I am as overcome and excited as a child on Christmas morning. In fact, all that has happened to me in the past years up until yesterday seems just as mysterious and wonderful.

My aunt Alice made me take this long journey. I had only seen her once or twice before the war. I was a child at the time, and she was a distant relative, but life since then has profoundly brought us together, first through sickness and then through her unusual story.

Aunt Alice sent letters to my father rather regularly in which she would say – among other family news – that her limbs would sometimes feel weak and that she needed a walking stick. In 1949, the doctors spoke of multiple sclerosis, a serious illness without effective treatment. Perhaps because the symptoms came and went, perhaps also because of her profound faith in God, she kept up hope. That is how we began to draw closer.

Early in 1952, we received news that was very alarming. My uncle wrote to us that his wife had become terribly thin; she could no longer walk alone and could stay standing only by hanging on to the furniture; she was speaking with difficulty, and vigorous shaking kept her from writing and even got in the way of eating and getting dressed. The specialists they consulted were very pessimistic. Still, she found comfort in prayer. "You know that she has always been very pious," added my uncle. "She places her hopes in the intercession of the Holy Virgin. She even wants to go to Lourdes."

"That is her, all right, that idea," chortled my father, who deemed it sufficient to answer with a word of encouragement.

We were expecting to be notified any time about her inevitable death. We were therefore very surprised that June to receive a perfectly legible letter from Alice recounting her trip to Lourdes. She had experienced an intense reaction during her first bath in the pool, with palpitations and lightheadedness bordering on a fainting fit, but that evening she had been able to take a few steps in the room unassisted. On the next day, May 15, 1952, the "miracle" (that was the word she used) had taken place. During the Blessed Sacrament blessing, she had felt a burning sensation in her legs and feet and had sensed that her speech, which had been much impeded for the last few months, had suddenly been restored. At her return to the Sick People home, she had gotten out of her wheelchair by herself and had walked without help. The next day, she went to the Medical Bureau; her examination revealed no trace of the anomalies she suffered when she departed for Lourdes. The doctors were unwilling to speak of a miracle regarding a neurological complaint subject to growth and remission, so they had told her that she should be re-examined regularly for a long time to come. Yet she was writing to us that she was certain of having been healed through the intercession of the Holy Virgin, to whom she had been ardently praying for several months.

As for me, I had been baptized and had made my first communion, but I had abandoned just about all religious practice. I only went to Mass on Christmas, out of tradition, to sing the old hymns. So I did not for one minute believe in this unlikely miracle story. As far as I was concerned, it was a ridiculous belief from a bygone era. Furthermore, as a medical student, I had read neurology studies: They all mention the possibility of remissions, which could be complete and unexplainable. "The future, alas, will set her straight," I answered to my father when I gave him back the letter he had given me to read.

For four years, we regularly received enthusiastic letters from Aunt Alice keeping us up to date with her latest medical tests, which were always negative. Biological examinations, too, had returned to normal. Her case was under the scrutiny of a commission that she was sure would eventually consider her healing as miraculous. Yet she was amazed that such a great gift had been given to someone whose merits were as doubtful as hers. In any event, she now insisted on helping the sick on their way to Lourdes. She accompanied pilgrimages as a nursing assistant, and she would comfort the suffering by telling them her story. She would also tell us of her wish to see me someday go to Lourdes with her: "It would be good for a future doctor to see how much faith motivates all these sick people here and gives them hope."

In July 1956, Aunt Alice told us that the bishop of Poitiers had just declared her healing to be miraculous and had *attributed it to a special manifestation of Blessed Mary Immaculate, Mother of God.* My Cartesian mind was shocked. I decided to see for myself what had given such affirmations legitimacy. My aunt was to accompany a pilgrimage in October; I would go along with her, at least for the first few days.

So here we are. A few days ago, in the train from Poitiers, I was struck by the calm that reigned in the car; and yet there were people who suffer physically and mentally. I was getting the impression that the priest's words and my aunt's encouragements are more effective than my sedatives. When we arrived, my aunt took me to task with a smile:

"Bringing the sick here is one thing," she told me. "But you must also participate in the ceremonies if you really want to understand them."

Since I had made it that far, I figured I might as well sacrifice two or three more days to go to the Masses, the processions, and the prayer vigils. I accompanied my aunt wherever she dragged me – to the grotto, to the pools, to the basilica. Little by little, I feel in sync with all these people who prayed with confidence and whose eyes seemed to see infinity unfolding before them. I am quite impressed by the depth of this faith.

At the end of the second day, as I leaned against the ramp over-looking the Gave, I saw the procession of the sick advancing under the esplanade's plane trees, all loudly singing the *Salve Regina*. My aunt Alice broke out of the crowd to come and embrace me. She was so moved, her eyes were full of tears.

"See how, despite their illness, all these people are happy," she pointed out. "It is that happiness, more than healing, that they will take back from here!"

At that moment I understood what is, in truth, the miracle of Lourdes... and this night, on the returning train, I feel – I know – that my heart and my life have been changed for ever.

Amen.

"The Simpler the Better"

The Apparitions' Hundredth Anniversary, January 15, 1958

1958 Over the course of a century, the grotto's appearance had changed. The workmen busying themselves under the rock early in the year 1958 gave it a rejuvenation treatment. They loosened the venerable, richly – too richly – decorated altar, consecrated in 1908 for the apparitions' fiftieth anniversary. Anniversaries come one after the other, yet no two are alike! For the centennial, Bishop Théas decided to restore a simplicity more in harmony with the grotto's atmosphere in Bernadette's day. When the workmen left the completed work site, locals and pilgrims examined the new altar, offered by the mayor himself. It was a very simple table cut from the marble of the nearby Arudy quarries. Its blue-gray hue nicely matched the cliff's rock face. Bernadette surely would have given a nod of approval to its pure lines and simple design.

The former altar was not abandoned. In that hundredth anniversary year, the bishop of Lourdes sent it as a gift to Pope Pius XII. After it was transported to Italy, it would adorn the Vatican Gardens, where there was a reproduction of the Lourdes grotto. It would then receive the prayers of popes – once again, among many others, the sign of the bonds of affection that have united the city of Lourdes to Peter's successors for a hundred years.

The project of rejuvenating Lourdes, for Bishop Théas, would not stop at its physical appearance. For the previous hundred years, apparition stories had multiplied. These edifying readings often bordered on the whimsical and the fantastical. Like the grotto's altar, Bernadette's story needed to be trimmed of its excessive ornaments. The bishop of Lourdes wished to honor the truth, which is more beautiful than any gloss. In that centennial year, it had become urgent finally to grant the wish that Bernadette had expressed on her deathbed: *"The simpler what will be written the better."* In the rush to make something rosier, one often ends up corrupting it.

In order to bring his project to completion, Bishop Théas turned to a priest, a specialist in Marian theology named Father René Laurentin. With Dom Bernard Billet's help, Laurentin started analyzing and comparing all the archives of the time, which over the years had been scattered to the four corners of France. For example, Police Chief Jacomet's reports were found in Haute-Savoie, while that of the investigation committee that Bishop Laurence had established turned up in the diocese of Orleans.

It was to take more time for Father Laurentin to complete this gigantic undertaking than was needed to build the Saint Pius X Basilica, which had just been dedicated in 1958. Over twenty years, the historian-theologian would publish no fewer that twenty volumes! But the initial impulse had been given: The rigorous study of the sources would finally allow a true-to-life portrait of Bernadette.

Between projects and preparatory work, the date of February 11, 1958, had come, marking the centennial of the first apparition in Massabielle. That morning, fog and drizzle had accompanied Bernadette's steps to the grotto. A hundred years later to the day, the weather seemed to commemorate that sad wintertime, even adding gusts of wind that made the downpour dance. Yet Bishop Théas had a taste for risk: He went ahead with the scheduled open-air Mass in front of the Rosary Basilica. Resigned to the weather and smiling anyway, the sixty thousand pilgrims from around the world prepared to face the storm of the century – or rather, of the centennial. But just as the ceremony was about to begin, the sun pierced through the clouds and displayed a rainbow over Lourdes. Divine Providence, or a caprice of the weather? Whatever the case may be, the sun started to shine so brightly that the celebrant had to be sheltered under a canopy!

Soon it was noon. That was the hour at which the Virgin had appeared to Bernadette; it was also the time that the day's organizers set aside for a great appointment. Thanks to a radio set installed on the basilica's steps, the immense gathering suddenly received the Holy Father's voice. Pope Pius XII had insisted on participating in this anniversary and had been following the jubilee preparations for awhile. Already on July 2, 1957, he had published an encyclical, titled *The Lourdes Pilgrimage*, in which he keenly encouraged Christians of the world to travel to the French Pyrenees for this great occasion.

The Pope who joined the centennial opening ceremonies would not be there to bless its closure. Pope Pius XII passed away on October 9 of the same year, 1958. Less than three weeks later, at the Vatican, the conclave's white smoke signaled a new pope's election. Cardinal Roncalli, who adopted the name Pope John XXIII, was profoundly attached to Lourdes as well. It was Pope John who, that spring, had blessed the brand-new Saint Pius X Basilica with his own hands. Among the first gestures of his pontificate was to have the image of the Virgin of Massabielle engraved on his medallion, and his first apostolic blessing was directed to the bishop of Lourdes, to his diocese, and to all the jubilee-year pilgrims.

The centennial could end in an act of thanksgiving. There was a new Pope, but communion with Rome remained the same. Thanks to Pope

John XIII, another rejuvenation of unprecedented scope was being prepared. The Second Vatican Council would soon breathe a new spirit upon the Church.

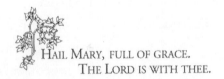

HAIL MARY, FULL OF GRACE.
THE LORD IS WITH THEE.

THE POPE'S MEDALLION

Pope John XXIII and Lourdes, June 29, 1959

19 59 The day had been a tiring one. The feast of the Holy Apostles Peter and Paul is important for the Church, particularly at the Vatican. In 1959, Pope John XXIII was in the first year of his pontificate. The celebrations had been long, as were his audiences, and within his papal apartments he did not begrudge himself the pleasure of finally taking a seat, in peace, alone. As he sat at his desk, he pensively contemplated the medallion of his pontificate's first year, which was stamped with his image. Cardinal Nicolas Canali accompanied by Monsignor Sergio Guerri, secretary of the commission for the administration of the Holy See's goods, had solemnly presented him with it today along with the pontifical engraver, Aurelio Mistruzzi.

Seeing his profile encircled by the customary Latin formula, *Ioannes XXIII Pontifex Maximus – Anno I*, he smiled. He felt like he was contemplating some ancient medal preserved in the stale air and dim lighting of a museum or curio room. After all, it may be that in a few decades visitors would lean over a display case to contemplate it. What legacy would he leave as Pope? He had no idea. The only thing he was sure of was that he would not like the Church to be spoken of as a museum. Some fresh air, some light – that was what he would like to give the Church during his pontificate.

The Pope played with the medallion absentmindedly. Emerging from his meditation, he contemplated the other side. In the foreground was the Virgin, her head surrounded by a halo of twelve stars. In the background, the cortege of pilgrims and of the sick evoked the hope of the faithful gathered in Lourdes. The Latin inscription encircling the scene commemorated the shrine's hundredth anniversary: "*In our presence the Marian year is celebrated in Lourdes.*" The Pope recalled the text he had written for this centennial's closing ceremony in February. He had explained his notion of the meaning of the apparitions: "*Popes consider it their duty, when, after an in-depth examination, they judge it to be opportune for the common good, to recommend to the attention of the faithful the supernatural lights that it has pleased God freely to grant to certain privileged souls, not to propose new doctrines, but to guide our conduct.*"

Pope John XXIII had no doubt that Bernadette belonged to those privileged souls, and he felt particular tenderness toward Lourdes. On March 25, 1958, while he was still only Cardinal Roncalli, patriarch of Venice, he had gone to the shrine to consecrate the Saint Pius X Basilica, which had been built for the apparitions' centennial. He remembered his arrival by Caravelle airplane at the Ossun airport, where he had been welcomed triumphantly by fifteen thousand people. He was particularly moved by this immense underground basilica with a capacity for twenty thousand pilgrims, and also by the personality and determination of Bishop Théas, to whom Lourdes owed these renovations. In his homily, after having compared the Saint Pius X Basilica to Our Lady Under the Ground of Chartres, he had paid homage to his perseverance in this basilica's construction, which had been difficult in a number of ways. "*I know that at the beginning of the undertaking of this temple, which is so vast and so unusual that one can compare it to an immense hall ready to greet numberless crowds running here from all points of the earth, there was no dearth of uncertainties and diversity of opinion. Today the reality is before us: and it is a cause of joy for our hearts [...] No, he who conceived and achieved the construction of this temple will not be shown up and has no need to blush."*

The Pope felt fond affection for Bishop Théas. They maintained a regular correspondence and even shared the same modest social origin, the same faith in the same burning desire to modernize the Church while remaining attached to tradition. He had entertained him several times in Venice and happily remembered those too-rare occasions when he was able to enjoy his hospitality at the bishop's chalet in Lourdes during vacation and rest stays, which he no longer dared hope for since his election by his brothers as Pope. He perceived a little better every day the magnitude of his task and the reforms needed for the Church to better meet the expectations of the men and women of his time.

Pope John XXIII had gotten up from his desk and opened a window to let in the June night air. He contemplated the sky and the stars that twinkled on the black backdrop. He wondered what the weather was like in Lourdes and tried to remember the landscape around the shrine. He hoped that his new office would allow him to go back there and once again to see those men and women who welcome to it all the diversity of the Church Universal. *Charity lived out,* he thought to himself.

Yes indeed, Lourdes was a beautiful place in the Church, a great shrine where the Gospel was lived out in its most radical aspect – the welcome, in the name of Christ, of every child of God, whoever he or she may be. To show his attachment to the shrine, he would send Bishop Théas a golden edition of the medallion of the first year of his pontificate, as well as several silver and bronze copies for him to distribute to those who, at Lourdes, contributed to the proclamation of Christ.

BLESSED ART THOU AMONG WOMEN,
AND BLESSED IS THE FRUIT OF THY WOMB, JESUS.

The Caravan of Hope

The "Iron Lung" Pilgrimage, September 28, 1963

1963 The convoy had been on the road for several hours already. Through the windows, one could see the changing clouds, the green and gold colors of the plains, the fiery leaves of the autumn trees, the harvest's bundled sheaves, the hills' purple curves, and, once in awhile, the shimmering of cities. In sleeper car number twenty-two, little Fernand, age nine, opened his eyes wide. It had been so long since he last saw these colors, these landscapes. He smelled the scent of cut grass, the heavy odors of the countryside, and even the sting of the factories' plumes of smoke, all of which imperceptibly seeped through the train's windows. He clung to all these forgotten sensations that were once again bubbling within him like fireworks. In just a few hours, the train would enter the Pyrenees foothills. Fernand would see the mountain again, and the torrents, too. Then he would arrive in Lourdes, the trip's destination. He did not know what awaited him there, but one thing was for certain: For the first time in many years, he felt free.

He no longer remembered how it all began. Was he two, three, four years old? No, he did not know anymore. He did not even remember ever having walked, or having run on the Doubs hills, having breathed the crisp air of his native Vosges, having made snowmen, having been to school, having sat on a chair like other children. For five years now, Fernand had lived in a hospital room. His frail body was locked up in a metal shell that helped him breath – an iron lung, a machine weighing over three hundred pounds without which he would die. He no longer could use his hands; he could only move his feet. All he perceived of the outside world was the nurses' white silhouettes, the doctors' grave expressions, the smell of drugs, the searing noise the machines made. In his room at the Maringer Hospital in Nancy, he survived in the company of other children who were also victims of the same disease, poliomyelitis. In the neighboring rooms, dozens of other patients were living through the same calvary – including some adults who had been locked up in their metal cages deprived of movement and fresh air for decades. With this prospect for the future, great courage was needed to hang on to the slightest hope. Many had already lost it.

That which was unhoped for, however, had occurred. One morning, Dr. Cattenoz, the hospital's head of service, with a victorious smile on his lips, burst into the rooms and shouted to everyone, "Do you want to go on a trip? Well, we're going to Lourdes!" Most of the patients were incredulous. How could that be possible with all this equipment weighing hundreds of pounds to which they were permanently hooked up and susceptible to the slightest interruption of power? Without electricity, they would surely die. And many had no faith, so Lourdes… Even the children had doubts, as the illness had long since taken away their wildest hopes and dreams.

But the doctor answered, "Nothing is impossible when you believe in it." Then he explained his struggle to them. He had been a stretcher-bearer at the Hospitality of Our Lady of Lourdes for several decades. He participated in the pilgrimage every year, accompanying handicapped and sick people. For six years, he had been struggling to achieve his dream of organizing a great pilgrimage to Lourdes for the victims of poliomyelitis – the most isolated and reclusive of patients.

After many refusals due to the dangers of the expedition – possible power outages, the transportation of highly explosive oxygen – the National Railway Company finally decided to equip a special train to transport the sick from Nancy to Lourdes, over nine hundred miles. A train was put together comprising ambulance cars and wagons containing electric generators. In every large station along the way, railwaymen were mobilized to hook up the electrical power in case of shortages. An army of nurses and doctors were on the alert. On site, in Lourdes, places of worship were equipped with electrical cables, and volunteers were getting organized in a hurry. He hoped that this one trip, even just a few days, would be time enough for his patients to recover their appetite for life. Cattenoz baptized his project the Journey of Hope.

Hours passed. In his sleeper car, Fernand had fallen asleep, rocked by the train's motion. Upon waking, the first thing he saw in the sky, above the mountain's jagged peaks, was a star… the shepherds' star, which was already shining alone. On the dark-green slopes speckled in white with sheep forming a sort of Milky Way, he saw shepherds assembling their flocks. Perhaps there were children running as fast as they could through the grass, with the scent of flowers filling their lungs. Suddenly, Fernand remembered his catechism – the shepherds at the crib, the Magi's caravan toward Bethlehem, the flocks, and the star as their guide. He was traveling by train, but what was the difference? He was moving toward hope. That evening he would hear the Gave roiling through town. Tomorrow he would see the Massabielle grotto, the white stone basilica jutting against the pines' deep green; he would listen to the hymns, smell the candles and incense; his heart would resonate in the middle of the crowd; he would live again in receiving communion with all the others in this fantastical place. *Thank you, Dr. Cattenoz,* he thought to himself. *And Lord, wherever you are, whoever you are, thank you for this rebirth.*

The first Journey of Hope, organized in 1963, was followed by a second of international proportions in 1968. Grouping thousands of polio patients from every country in the world – Christians beside non-Christians, believers mingled with nonbelievers – it had been renamed the Polio Pilgrimage. Today it takes place every five years, thanks to the great technical progress accomplished there, to the doctors' competence, and to efforts on the part of the National Railway Company. This pilgrimage, *a miracle of faith and generosity*, is the symbol of the integration of handicapped people, of their vitality in the world, a sign that they take *"full and active part in the concert of humanity,"* according to Pope Paul VI's speech on the occasion of the second Polio Pilgrimage in 1968.

HOLY MARY, MOTHER OF GOD,

FLAMES OF LOVE

The Fire at the Bernadettes' Home, November 26, 1964

1964 Sister Saint-Jean felt her glasses slide down her nose. She awoke with a start and tried to find the line of Saint Louis-Marie Grignon de Montfort's *Treatise on True Devotion to the Holy Virgin* that she was reading before she nodded off. Failing to concentrate, she decided instead to go on her night rounds in the dormitory. It was two thirty in the morning, and all the little "Bernadettes" were in a deep sleep. Sister Saint-Jean looked at them tenderly. Most of them were orphans – some sweet, some unruly – but at this time of night their chirping had finally come to an end.

The Sisters of Nevers founded this home for them to give them some instruction and professional training. Some of them were part of the *schola* and brightened up the shrine's offices with their young and beautiful voices. At the end of the dormitory, little Julie was sleeping peacefully. Sister Saint-Jean would readily admit her great affection for this child, who was abandoned at the age of five and would panic at the slightest provocation. Reassured that all was well, the religious prepared herself for bed.

Suddenly, she heard the sound of shattering glass. Hastening her step to the dormitory landing, she noticed strange glimmers on the second floor. When she opened the door, she had to take a step back, as she was literally blown away by a flaming whirlwind. The fire had already devoured the furniture and had started creeping up the walls.

Sister Saint-Jean rushed up the stairs in a flash, woke up the boarders, asked them to remain very calm, and took hold of the telephone receiver to call the fire brigade. The children, still sleepy, lined up among the beds without yet fully realizing the reason for this interruption of their sleep. The religious crossed to the other side of the room. There, too, the fire was blocking the exit staircase. Keeping her cool, she asked the girls to say the rosary.

At the fourth decade, the fire engine's bell resounded in front of the building. The sister made the sign of the cross and ran to the window. Three engines were posted in front of the home. The girls saw dark silhouettes running in the courtyard, unraveling hoses and hooking them up to the street's fire hydrants. Two teams of firemen, sent in as scouts, rushed into the smoke-filled rooms. In the two home-economics rooms, machines were on fire and were giving off highly toxic smoke. At the head of the party, Corporal Chief David Mazarès was exploring the building, but when one of the machines exploded, he had to be evacuated.

A few minutes, later the situation was clear: The fire had consumed the first and second floors, and the dormitory was accessible only through the windows. As one team attempted to extinguish the fire with its water hoses, Corporal Sébastien Mérigo started deploying the great ladder to create a gangplank to the windows. With his keen eyes, he picked the best spot. Corporal Romain Legaut and his assistant, First Class Christophe Monnié, were getting ready, pulling on their fire gear, the insulated respiratory apparatus, and their helmets. Other teams did likewise. All were local boys, and – believers or not – their hearts were set on serving and saving the young girls who were crying at all the windows on the third floor. Once the ladder was in place, they began to climb up.

Once in the dormitory, they briefly spoke to the sister and took stock of the thirty boarders they needed to take down. The first girls, wearing nightshirts and the bulky sweaters they had hastily pulled on, started climbing down barefooted on frozen rungs, protected by their rescuers. Sister Saint-Jean gave a moment's thought to her precious library, for which no rescue could be contemplated. Above all, she was impatiently waiting for her girls to be evacuated and refused to go down until they are all out of harm's way. She would like to have tried to reassure them of their imminent safety, but the fire had spread to the second floor and was burning so hot that the floorboards in the dormitory began to burn, forcing the girls to climb onto the beds.

Down below, the firemen of Tarbes arrived as reinforcement, and ambulances were ready to take in the first evacuees and to attend to them. News started to get around town even though day had not yet broken. Soon, the mayor, Bishop Théas, and several of the town's leaders were gathered at the foot of the home, hoping only to lend a helping hand. By three forty, twenty-one boarders had been evacuated. The dormitory was then completely filled with smoke. When Sister Saint-Jean, a cloth over her mouth, saw Julie cough, go pale, and faint, she shrieked with fright.

At that point, Corporal Legaut dashed in. He placed straps on the unconscious girl and lifted her up like a feather before the terrified religious. On the ladder, the child regained consciousness and opened her big frightened and shining eyes to find herself dangling in the frozen night air. The fireman reassured her very gently and soon laid her down, safe and sound, on a stretcher. Julie watched him walk away as though he were Michael the Archangel from her Missal.

Soon after the evacuations were completed, the dormitory windows were red with the glow of hell. At four fifty, the two flaming upper floors collapsed in a frightful crash before a terrified crowd. In the smoke that was covering the sky, Sister Saint-Jean and her little Bernadettes realized they had lost everything – books, clothing, and memories. As poor as they had been, they were then more indigent than ever. Yet, confronted with such a disaster, good things come; gifts of food and clothing arrived that very night. Monetary gifts soon followed and would continue to pour in during the following weeks to such a point that the home could be rebuilt completely.

In the pre-dawn morning, Sister Saint-Jean watched the fireman who saved Julie speak to the tiny girl and take care of her with tender kindness. By the new light shining in the eyes of her little charge, the religious understood that perhaps all was not lost in that terrible night. Pulling up the sleeves of her habit to lend her assistance, she smiled at the thought that, indeed, the Spirit blows where it will, even on the ashes of the Bernadettes' Home.

PRAY FOR US SINNERS,
NOW AND AT THE HOUR OF OUR DEATH.

IF LAZARUS WERE A WOMAN...

Marie-Thérèse Canin, Fiftieth Miraculous Healing, December 3, 1964

1964 In an orphanage in a suburb of Lyon, Marie-Thérèse Canin sat cross-legged on a carpet, surrounded by children. About fifty years old, she looked very much like Édith Piaf, the popular Parisian singer of sentimental ballads – same slight and bent body, same high forehead, same jet-black curly hair. She also had the same countenance, one in which a sometimes grave, sometimes sprightly, but never neutral expression could be read.

She had left her convent of the Little Sisters of the Assumption that day to speak to orphaned children, as she regularly did in other places and before equally rapt audiences. There were about ten children gathered about her, silent and captivated. She told them a story – her own – painful at first, miraculous at the end, with the simplicity of a peaceful virgin and the thick Marseilles accent of her native town.

"Already as a little girl, I had repeated bouts of bronchitis," Marie-Thérèse told the children. "I coughed all the time. I was out of breath at the slightest effort. I always had to guard myself from the cold. It got on my nerves, of course, but I told myself that someday it would pass.

And then, at the age of about twenty, I started feeling sharp pains in my spine, and losing a lot of weight, too. As I'm not very big to begin with, you can imagine! After many examinations, the doctor diagnosed tuberculosis."

"What's tuberculosis?" asked a towheaded boy. "Can I catch it, too?"

"It is a sickness that strikes the lungs, and that's very contagious," she replied. "Fortunately, there is a vaccine today to prevent it. But when my father came back from the war with tuberculosis in 1918, it hadn't been discovered yet. He died of it and, soon after, so did my mother."

That got the children's attention. "You don't have parents any more? You're like us, then?"

"Yes, like you!" replied Marie-Thérèse. "Poor people, they gave me the disease… Later on, the pains became more and more frequent and difficult to put up with. My back, stomach, hips, legs – everything was making me suffer atrociously. For ten years I alternated between stays at the hospital and rest periods.

"One day, after an effort, I couldn't get up and had to be operated on urgently. The Second World War had just ended, and my condition wouldn't stop getting worse. I no longer ate; I weighed seventy-seven pounds."

"Like me!" shouted out a little guy, showing off his biceps.

"For children," she continued, "that is a normal weight. Not for grownups. I was too thin, most of the time I had to stay lying down."

"Why, it's impossible to live that way!" exclaimed a little girl indignantly, welling up with tears, as if the action were taking place right in front of her.

"Yes, it's very difficult. You want it to stop; you wonder whether life still has meaning," said Marie-Thérèse. "In those moments, faith gave me a lot of strength, a lot of courage. God has always been by my side; he never abandoned me; he even did more for me. When I decided to leave for Lourdes, on the morning of October 7, 1947, my mind was very clear: Either I would die, or I would come back healed. There was no other solution."

"And then?" asked several children simultaneously.

"I got to Lourdes in a state of total exhaustion," she went on. "I was soon driven to the hospital. I had the bed under the great crucifix, the spot set aside for the patient who is worst off. And on the very first night I had a sudden urge to drink warm milk."

One child chimed in: "That's what I have every morning for breakfast!"

"Well you see, back then, I had spent a long time without even imagining it anymore," she told them. "The next day, at meal time, I took two pieces of bread with coffee. I felt something was happening in me. On the third day, I asked for permission to participate in the Blessed Sacrament procession. Back at the hospital, I felt a force lift me up off the bed, a sudden force that gave me back my breath and life."

"Like Lazarus when he comes out of the tomb?" asked one child who evidently knew his Scriptures.

"I was like dead, and now once again, without warning, life was coursing through me. For the first time in nine months, I was able to put my slippers on. I got dressed by myself, and I took a few steps in the hospital hallways, without any help," said the storyteller. "That evening, I ate my meal like everyone else. I was healed!"

"How is your story possible?" asked a skeptical but intrigued little boy.

"There is no explanation: It's the goodness of God," Marie-Thérèse said with authority. "That is how he decided it."

"Do you think you can make my parents come back?" one child asked.

"God is at our side in our trials; he helps us understand the worth of life, and to make the best of every chance we have," she responded. "He promises us that death will never have the last word. It sometimes happens that faith fortifies bodies, but it especially changes souls and binds us to one another. If you pray and think of your parents very hard, I am sure that they will hear your prayer."

Marie-Thérèse straightened her legs. She got on her knees, closed her eyes, and raised her hands to heaven. The children, having been drawn into the same sentiment through her story, adopted the same posture. They mingled their voice with Marie-Thérèse's, and with all the other voices, familiar still or forgotten, that death has stifled without snuffing them out: "*Hail Mary, full of grace...*"

AMEN.

GOD IN THE HILLS

Portrait of the Writer Francis Jammes, January 1, 1965

19 65 "Come in, I was expecting you. Sit down; may I offer you a cup of tea?"

Bernadette Jammes, eldest daughter of poet Francis Jammes, closed the cover of a collection of her father's poems. Squinting her eyes, she started reciting a few verses from *Glades in Heaven*: "*In the embalmed pallor of this maddened sun, the chapel in the fields, dressed in a small forest, encloses the mystery of clarity and joy.*" She looked kindly at the student as he sat timidly in front of her.

She had received a long letter from him regarding the research he had undertaken on the work of Jammes in Bordeaux University's literature department. The touching memory of her father, that patriarchal and fervently Catholic figure, always plunged her into a state of nostalgia in which joy and sadness would mingle. Yet she felt she must tirelessly tell her tale to every admirer of his poetry and to every Christian seeking comfort in this both simple and uncommon person.

On that beautiful morning, it was a spindly young man sitting before her. His untamed hair framed eyes worn out by reading. His fragility touched her; she imagined that her father must have had that lost and smoldering gaze himself.

Bernadette first told him about the infamous day in 1886 when Francis Jammes failed his university entrance exam. Upon finding out he was not among those having passed, the young man's mouth twisted into an irrepressible grimace, and he disappeared for days on end. That day, he decided to dedicate his life to poetry alone. He fervently swore never to give up his disdain for the charade of awards and artificial scales of merit. Despite his family's skepticism, he composed an extraordinary number of poems without letting up, which were promptly published in the press. He sought refuge in the Basque countryside; he had affection only for the intimacy of nature, for the soft hills' thrust, for the harmony of life in all its forms. His contemporaries' excessive symbolism and neuroses disgusted him. Above all, he refused to believe that poetry should give up something essential – the beauty of nature and the celebration of its sublime perfection.

Ignoring the pedantry of Parisian poets, he remained faithful to the Basque country's sweet savors. He compared himself to a young faun: His heightened senses remained ever on the lookout for the sensation he could procure by a simple stroll through the redolent forest with twigs and soil crackling under his feet. Everywhere he went, he would try to ferret out nature's grace. Deeply rooted in his native soil, his verses charmed Gide and Mallarmé.

Though taken up in her own narrative, Bernadette Jammes felt that the young student's mind was overtaken with admiration, envy, and a certain spirit of defiance. Not allowing these interior struggles to stop her, she recounted the release of *Jammisme*, Francis Jammes' literary manifesto. The poet had brandished it as an ode to voluntary simplicity, rejecting the contrivances of rhetoric. Many were those who scoffed at the naïveté of his writings, of his rustic country verses. Others were conquered by the freedom of his senses, the purity and tenderness of his outlook: "Jammes is my childhood recovered," writer François Mauriac once said.

In his own peaceful manner, the faun found his way back to the Catholic faith. In 1901, his manifesto proclaimed: "*The truth is the praise of God.*" Accompanied and supported by Paul Claudel, he converted in 1905.

The student interrupted Bernadette's narrative: "Your father was of Jewish ancestry, wasn't he?"

The question caught her off-guard. She had never thought about it. To her, her father had always been deeply Christian, and his conversion process was rather a celebration than a renunciation.

It was he who, in 1905, had brought Claudel to Lourdes. He knew the town's every nook and cranny, the bumpy aspect of the cobblestone streets, the heavy smells of warmth and of incense, the enchanting cradle of his country's hills. He had befriended Lourdes at the age of four, when he was still fastened to his mother's hand. At the time, he had rolled along with the flows of pilgrims and of the sick in procession. Nothing was more familiar to him than the mask of suffering on the infirm and the joy that lit up their faces as they approached the grotto. Lourdes was the holy place where the Virgin had spoken to the humblest, the place that welcomed endless waves of pain.

His conversion was a revelation. His childlike love of nature revealed itself to be a deep faith in God and in his creation. From then on his life as well as his art took a turn for the more fruitful. Francis Jammes married a woman from the north of France who gave him six children, of whom the first, the tireless narrator of his existence, was named Bernadette in homage to Lourdes. Jammes never ceased praising the image of a simple and humble God. He never stopped inspiring and guiding people who came to confide in him. Along with Claudel, he would in turn lead several young men to conversion.

Bernadette ended her story in a sigh. Her father died in 1938, the very day that one of his daughters was taking the veil. He had been the incarnation of the idea of a patriarch for his family, for a whole region, and for all those who wanted to purify themselves in his wonderment. Never did he turn away from Lourdes, the Catholic city of his childhood, the town that was, for him, a maternal invitation to enter into the Gospel's simplicity.

"Go to Lourdes as soon as you can, Sir," Bernadette told her visitor. "Listen to the hymns mingled with the groans. Feel the sweetness of the water that trickles along the blue-tinted Pyrenees mountainside. Bathe yourself in the warm and shortened horizon of a stormy day. Never will you learn anything truer about my father."

Bernadette took leave of her guest, clutching the collection of poems in her fingers, her eyes misty with emotion.

HAIL MARY, FULL OF GRACE.
THE LORD IS WITH THEE.

THE PILGRIM MONK

Brother Léo Schwager, Fifty-Seventh Miraculous Healing,
April 30, 1965

1965 In a train especially chartered for the pilgrimage of the sick from French-speaking Switzerland, Brother Léo Schwager was dozing. The few pilgrims who were still awake scanned the dark French night they were passing through that evening in late March. Lourdes was just a few hours away, and the sun would soon rise over the miracle shrine, the shrine of his own miracle.

As he did every year when he came with the pilgrims of his native town of Fribourg, Brother Léo could not help remembering the first trip he took just fifteen years ago, on April 20, 1952 – that long and painful journey, that journey of unhoped-for hope. He remembered the trust he had in God and in the Holy Virgin; he remembered his prayers during the trip, his pains, and especially his fatigue. Those three days remained seared in his memory. Perhaps that was because he had to relate his story so often – to doctors, priests, and bishops who questioned him – but especially to all those who, day after day, sought him out for a testimony to the love of God, the testimony of his encounter with the saving Christ. Everyone in that rail car knew his story. Whenever they came to see him, it was to speak to Brother Léo, the one miraculously healed in Lourdes. For all these infirm people, these pilgrims, for all the volunteers who accompanied them, he was, so to speak, "the proof" – the proof of the existence of God, the proof of the miracles of Lourdes, the proof that hope is not empty.

"Are you sleeping, Brother?"

Joseph's voice startled Brother Léo from his daydream. Brother Léo looked at him. Joseph was barely sixteen. His dark hair was still that of a child. He already had made the pilgrimage last year, and at the time he was the youngest volunteer. Brother Léo had agreed to bring him along despite his age because he had shown himself to be so tenacious and mature. His parents were pushing him, too. Once he returned from Lourdes, as he was on his way to school one morning, a car took a turn too quickly and knocked him over. The doctors saved his life after several hours in the operating room; nevertheless, he was not there as a volunteer this time, but as one of the infirm. His chest was wrapped tightly, and his legs were paralyzed; he could no longer walk, and had to get around in a wheelchair. Yet a smile lit up his face, which had lost nothing of its vitality.

Brother Léo answered him with a smile: "No, Joseph, I was just thinking..."

The boy's handicapped body reminded him of his own condition when, at the age of twenty-seven, he had taken the train for his own first pilgrimage. At the time, he could stand only for ten minutes at a time, and the doctors, after long examinations, had detected in him several symptoms of multiple sclerosis.

Once again, Joseph's voice broke the silence. "Do you think that Jesus and the Virgin Mary will perform a miracle for me in Lourdes?"

That was the question that all pilgrims asked themselves. How could he, Brother Léo, give an answer? It was a question he had been asking himself, too, for ten years, in a different yet similar form: "Why me?" Yet that healing had seemed so natural to him. He could still see himself in the big Our Lady Welcome Center hall where he had been greeted with the other pilgrims that April 29 after an exhausting twenty-four-hour trip. He recalled that first, cold night, during which sleep had been fleeting. He remembered every minute of April 30 – the first Office in the grotto, the Mass, and that incredible feeling of trust that had started to fill him. He could even still feel that same dull sensation in his leg, during his first bath, that sensation that already had made him believe in the miracle even before it happened. He remembered the afternoon recitation of the rosary at the grotto and his intense prayer for his own healing and that of the other sick. The only part he had forgotten was the sermon. Because of his suffering, perhaps?

Brother Léo was not in so much pain that day that he could not answer when, after the blessing of the sick, a stretcher-bearer asked him whether he had already been to the pools. He had been led there then and had taken his second bath that day. It was four o'clock in the afternoon, he recalled. Intense pains kept him from speaking, and yet, at the same time, a feeling of healing was beginning to overtake him. He felt the nearly total disappearance of the heaviness in his leg and his desire to go back to the welcoming center to rest. Unable to express himself, he allowed himself to be led to the Rosary esplanade for the blessing of the sick and he had intensely prayed: "My God, if it is your will, you can heal me. Holy Virgin, pray for me!"

"Why would they not want to?" answered Joseph, as if in echo to his prayer. The teenage boy, now saddened, returned to watch the darkened scenery through the train's windows.

Why? As he considered Joseph's sadness, Brother Léo was filled with pity. In ten years, not one miracle had struck any of the pilgrims he had accompanied. He sometimes felt guilty for having been chosen, guilty of having perhaps taken Joseph's place or that of so many others. No, God is not an accountant. He, Brother Léo, had not taken anybody's place.

He just touched Christ with his eyes and with his heart, just as the woman with the issue of blood had touched the hem of his coat and had been healed. Since his own miracle, he understood that Gospel better. Like her, he believed that God could heal him. Like her, in the midst of a crowd of other sick people, his faith saved him. He was certainly no better than others, but on that day, April 30, 1952, his faith got him on his knees as Christ went by, present in the Blessed Sacrament. His eyes followed it, without letting go, until the end of the procession. Only then, emerging from his prayer, did he know that he had been healed. His faith threw him on the ground, and Christ raised him up again, free of illness. "*Someone has touched me, for I felt a power going out of me,*" answered Jesus to his puzzled disciples. Brother Léo had experienced that power. He remembered the testimony of Professor Barbin, of the Nantes school of medicine, who witnessed the scene of his healing on the Rosary esplanade: "*I was noticing that, all at the same time, Brother Léo seemed oppressed, as if he had been struck physically or by a strong emotion, and that he was having trouble finding a deep inspiration.*"

Joseph's eyes were beginning to sag with sleep. Miracle or not, Brother Léo would pray for him with all his might, so that the boy might experience the power of God's love for him.

BLESSED ART THOU AMONG WOMEN,
AND BLESSED IS THE FRUIT OF THY WOMB, JESUS.

THE PRAYER OF THE DOMINICANS

The Rosary Pilgrimage, September 30 to October 7, 1965

1965 It was time for *Evening Words*. In the dark, the crowd was drinking in the words of the man in the white habit. Father Baron, of the Order of Preachers, was endowed with a natural eloquence that chroniclers do not shrink from qualifying as enveloping or even as "bewitching" – a somewhat inappropriate term to evoke these nighttime meditations spun out under the sky of Lourdes! In this gathering, witchcraft had no place. These *Evening Words*, nourished by the recitation of the rosary and molded by prayer, were as simple and unadorned as the rock of Massabielle. They went straight to the public's hearts just as they were. It was not magic at work, but grace.

Once again, in the autumn of 1965, Father Baron, Rosary Pilgrimage director, brought his large family to Lourdes – the Dominicans. Inaugurated in 1908, this yearly encounter became a well-established tradition. Even today, at the time of year when the entire Church is celebrating Our Lady of the Rosary, Saint Dominic's heirs and the lay people who are close to them converge in Lourdes with a crowd of sick people and hospitallers. For three days straight, they draw new strength in the contemplation of the sorrowful, joyful, and glorious mysteries. The large wooden rosaries hitched to the religious' belts and the chaplets emerging from everyone's pockets become instruments of common prayer. It rises tirelessly in the very place where Bernadette so loved to say her rosary.

Such quality of prayer did not leave the crowds indifferent. The few hundred people who initially answered the Dominicans' first call to prayer soon became a multitude, so much so that the bishop of Lourdes ended up granting them exclusive occupation of the shrines during the three days of their yearly pilgrimage!

As the *Evening Words*, which Father Baron would broadcast for the meditation of all, died down, the vigil of the encounter's first day was far from over. A torchlight procession then began under the cold light of the stars of the autumn sky. The Dominicans' white habits glimmered in the torchlight as they fraternally mingled in the crowd of lay people. This procession was followed by a holy hour, during which there was a rosary meditation before the Blessed Sacrament. Then came the time for Mass, which pushed adoration deep into the night by the time it was over, since communion took place at midnight.

Although the Rosary pilgrims were the last to go to bed that night in the shrine's vicinity, they also were the first ones to get up in the morning. By dawn, at five thirty, they were already crowding at the grotto or at the basilicas for a first Mass. The sick got some respite, since their Mass took place "only" two hours later at the very spot of the apparitions! Throughout the second day, they would be the heroes of the pilgrimage, the heralds of the suffering Christ. Indeed, they were the principal actors of the great Way of the Cross that would take place a few hours later.

For that occasion, the pilgrims gathered around an immense empty space prepared in the middle of the esplanade. At every station reading and meditation, a few of the sick were separated from the crowd and brought to the heart of this immense square. Lying on their stretchers, they progressively would form the shape, on the grounds of the esplanade, of the cross of Christ, the tree of life that conquers all sorrows. A few standing Dominicans outlined this human cross. At the moment of the prayer for the sick, they stretched their arms in the very gesture of Christ on the cross and interceded with all their souls for the distressed people assembled in the square.

That year, 1965, the Rosary Pilgrimage had to respond – as do all the Church's works – to new challenges: It had to adapt itself to the tremendous *aggiornamento* of the Second Vatican Council, which had just come to an end after three years of intensive work. For instance, the liturgical reform required a scheduling change for the pilgrimage: With the council's provision for concelebrated liturgies, the number of Masses celebrated in the morning at the various shrine chapels was reduced. Before the council, because so many priests accompanied their pilgrimages and because each priest needed to preside at his own Mass, one could count up to a thousand!

That, however, was but a practical detail amid immense spiritual evolution. Father Baron knew that a gigantic work – and an exciting one – awaited his team. How was he to respond better to the modern world's expectations? How was he to adapt the pilgrimage format to present needs? How was he to let himself be revitalized by a new spirit, to leave more room for the work of the Spirit in the hearts of men and women? The great Dominican family was ready to commit all its efforts to this enterprise.

As the years went by, the Rosary Pilgrimage serenely attuned itself to the times. Its organizers, who had always had a keen interest in aesthetics – of all the events that mark the rhythm of life in Lourdes, these Dominican encounters are reputed to be among the most beautiful – came up with novel ideas to allow the Spirit to breathe upon the rosary in all its beauty. In October 1998, for example, thirty-six thousand tricolored pennants flew above the esplanade, bearing the colors of the mysteries of the rosary – joyful yellow, sorrowful red, glorious white. Over forty-five thousand pilgrims had written their prayer intentions upon these flags, which they watched flutter at the whim of the wind. What a bouquet to gather for the Virgin of Massabielle! What a sheaf of supplications to lay in the heart of God!

In 2008, the Rosary Pilgrimage will celebrate its centennial. All can give thanks for a century of ardent prayers that continuously ascend to heaven and offer all our human suffering before God.

 HOLY MARY, MOTHER OF GOD,

Faith, Early in the Morning

Juliette Tamburini, Sixty-Second Miraculous Healing,
December 12, 1966

19 66 "I will stay with you awhile, if you wish," the nurse said. "Thank you, Juliette," replied Mrs. Millet. "The night will be less difficult, thanks to you."

Mrs. Millet liked this young nurse. Ever since she arrived at the Sainte-Marguerite Hospital in Marseilles late in 1966, the old woman appreciated her smile that joined her in the depths of her illness. Juliette knew how to find the words that lighten the heart's distress as well as the gestures that soothe the body's pains. Sometimes, when the dusk invaded her room, the old lady felt as though she was at the edge of an abyss of darkness and silence. The night of the sick can be so long! Was that why Juliette chose the night shift? Mrs. Millet often told herself that the young nurse seemed to guess what her patients were feeling.

Indeed, Juliette Tamburini was well acquainted with illness. She knew the body's pains and the hurtful stares of onlookers. She knew how long the day can be when one is bedridden, and she knew that apprehension that comes as evening approaches. She also knew the hope of remission as well as the despair of relapse. None of that was empathy; it was simply experience. But who would have guessed as much from seeing this young woman, bursting with energy, who spent her nights watching the sick, her weekends running through the woods with her Cub Scouts, her summers with camp children, and her winters serving the sick in Marseilles? Mrs. Millet would have had much trouble believing that her tireless nurse spent all her youth in the long calvary of an incurable disease.

Juliette was three years old when she became acquainted with hospitals. It was all because of a rare disease, an affliction so difficult to treat that it was highly improbable for a child to survive it. Against all expectations, the girl got better. By the age of twelve, however, her health had remained so fragile that she was believed to have had tuberculosis. A series of examinations resulted in a setting aside of that hypothesis. The dire diagnosis was that the bone of her left leg was being eaten up by an infection.

Thus began Juliette's long Way of the Cross. Between her bed and her wheelchair, she suffered martyrdom. The doctors tried all known treatments to alleviate her pain. The young girl began to go to hospitals the way other children go to school, because soon she was breaking out in nosebleeds so severe that they forced her to be hospitalized every ten to fifteen days.

As for school, she could only go when her suffering or surgical procedures allowed her the time. The infection persisted. It was not for lack of fighting it, though: In the course of twelve years, the young girl underwent eleven operations.

With every surgery, she could not help but hope that this latest intervention would be the last. The condition would better for a month, or maybe two months, or ten months, and everyone would begin to hope again. Then the abscess would reopen, and everything had to start over again. From one operation to the next, hope began to wear thin.

Juliette learned to go beyond despair despite some of her relatives' scorn. She was sometimes on the receiving end of looks that made her suffer more than the disease itself. She drew her strength from her parents' love and in her encounters with God every morning. Her parents had lost their faith long before, but the young girl continued to believe. When the dawn's light returned color to the world after the long nights of suffering in fitful sleep, she would always commit herself to the Father's hands. She would ask him for the strength to make it through one more day. It was her little time of grace and comfort at the start of her day.

Then came that day in 1959 when the verdict was handed down: The eleventh operation was a failure. The doctors admitted defeat. There was only one solution left: Amputate the infected leg. Juliette was twenty-three.

Her faith urged her to go to Lourdes to ask, not for her healing, but for the strength to face this last operation. In July, she was on the train bringing the sick on the diocesan pilgrimage toward the shrine. The journey took her to new lows of exhaustion. The pain was so strong that she could no longer sleep at all. Isabelle, her nurse, saw her strength decline and understood her fears of not being able to make it all the way to the pools. On July 15, she got an idea: If the patient could not make it to the grotto's water, perhaps the grotto's water might come to her? She therefore proposed to inject a little water into Juliette's sore with a syringe. Exhausted, the patient accepted on faith. A very fitful night passed. But when Isabelle changed the bandage the next morning, the wound seemed to have closed. By the end of the day, Juliette was finally able to go to the pools and finish her pilgrimage.

Immediately after she returned to Marseilles, she went to the hospital for the scheduled amputation. The doctors examined her. But... there was no more sore. The patient was sent for x-rays to help them figure out what was going on. Stupefaction ensued: The bone had repaired itself! Juliette's parents had trouble believing it. Nevertheless, the doctors counseled prudence: The girl had already had many remissions... and none had lasted.

Everyone kept Juliette's condition a secret for a year. But Juliette did not relapse and remained in perfect health. She returned to Lourdes in 1961, and then in 1963 for examinations. Every time, the conclusion was the same: The bone was intact; the nosebleeds had never resumed. Her healing was acknowledged as miraculous a few years later.

Mrs. Millet had just fallen asleep. Juliette contemplated this finally peaceful face. She was thinking of her own parents. She could see the wonder in their eyes before her overflowing energy after she was healed, and their astonishment when she announced her decision to become a nurse to alleviate the suffering of others, after having known it herself for so many years.

In the intimacy she had with God every morning, she gave thanks for her parents' journey as they rediscovered the faith – because, as she knew, the true miracle is the healing of souls.

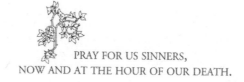

PRAY FOR US SINNERS,
NOW AND AT THE HOUR OF OUR DEATH.

A Royal Love at the Foot of the Grotto

King Baudouin of Belgium and Queen Fabiola,
July 8, 1968

19 68 Eight years ago to the day, King Baudouin was a man fulfilled. On this anniversary, July 8, he gave thanks to the Virgin Mary. His thoughts took him to Massabielle, where his marvelous story began in 1960 through the intercession of the Mother of God.

He could see the grotto where, incognito, he spent an entire night asking her for a spouse. He could still smell the ceaselessly burning candles as though he were there. He also thought of Bishop Suenens, who had recommended that February that he go to Lourdes, the city from which one comes back a different person! Enthused by the portrait of a sound lady, Veronica O'Brien, a pioneer of the charismatic renewal, that the bishop had drawn for him, he decided to meet her. Soon after, charmed by this uncommon personality who called him "Mr. King," he confided to her that, at the age of twenty-nine, he must think of giving to Belgium a queen who shared his religious convictions. He even told Veronica that, according to him, the woman he was hoping for lived in Spain, a Catholic land if ever there was one.

When she returned to see him in April, Veronica confessed to him that she felt that God had entrusted her with the mission of finding a wife for the king. Dropping all her other business, she went off to Spain to find his bride. In order to keep the mission a secret – after all, choosing a queen is no everyday affair – they decided that from then on he would be called "Luigi," she would be called "Grace," and Bishop Suenens would be referred to as "Michael."

Under the pretense of an investigation into the apostolate among Spanish aristocrats, Grace became acquainted with a certain Fabiola de Mora y Aragon to assist her in her quest. When she met the woman they would nickname "Avila," Grace immediately understood that her search was over. Indeed, the young woman – who was tall, thin, and sparkling with life, with intelligence, and high moral integrity – was the one she had come to seek. At the age of thirty-two, Avila, who took care of the sick and the poor with self-sacrifice and dedication, confided to her that she had entrusted her life into the hands of God, who *"perhaps is preparing something for her..."* Little did she know! Grace had no doubt when she discovered, in Avila's room, a painting she had seen in a dream the night before: Framed in red, it pictured a mother with a child in her arms. She enthusiastically hastened to write of her conviction to the king: *It is she!*

It is she, he thought in turn when he met Avila in Brussels some time later. At first contact, he was conquered by her vivacity and her humility. To think that everything nearly fell through when Grace mentioned their project to her! Persuaded that she had been caught up in a plot, the young Spaniard refused to see Grace again. It took the intervention of the apostolic nuncio in person for her to regain her trust and to agree to go to Brussels, under cover of an international congress in which Spain needed to be represented.

Soon thereafter, they decided to go to Lourdes together in early July 1960. The king secretly prayed to the Virgin Mary to guide him in this step. Unbeknownst to him, Avila had already done likewise by going to Lourdes some time beforehand. As soon as the king saw her get out of her car, charm and confidence were at work again. Their friendship had grown since the last time they met. He loved every one of her remarks and reactions. As he prayed next to her in the grotto, he acquired the conviction that God had chosen Avila to become queen of Belgium. Was it not she who would later tell him that as a child she was called "*Queenie*," the Little Queen? Completely enraptured by their happiness together, the two young people would not bring their conversations to a close until late at night as they walked in the esplanade along the Gave.

The next day, July 7, they attended a Mass in the crypt. They were so happy that they did not feel the time go by, and so they in fact attended two Masses, entrusting all their hopes to the Most Holy Virgin. During the rest of the day, they crisscrossed the region behind the wheel of a little yellow Renault Dauphine – which, as the king still remembered, had rather poor brakes! Avila wouldn't stop laughing. Baudouin felt in her *a joie de vivre proof against everything stemming from her trust in the Lord.* They closed their evening at the grotto by reciting the rosary.

The next morning, during the Office, as if struck by infatuation, Baudouin felt the impulse to write "I love you" in his missal for her. Nevertheless, he decided to wait another day to declare his love. But Avila surprised him once again when, after coming out of the church and having asked him to stop to say three *Ave Marias*, she turned toward him and said: "*This time it's yes, and I won't look back.*"

These words still echoed in his heart, eight years later, with the same emotion. On that July 8, 1960, Our Lady of Lourdes had performed a miracle. The happy couple had placed all their hopes in her. They had completely given themselves up to her mystery, and her answer went far beyond their expectations. A little later, Avila was to whisper to him, with her disarming humor: "*I knew that Our Lady is a Queen and a*

Mother, and has a good number of other attributions, but I did not know that she is also a matchmaker."

They were not, of course, spared all ordeals, since they had no children. Despite this heartbreak, they thanked the Holy Virgin every day for having brought them together. On the evening of their eighth anniversary, the king thanked her for having entrusted to him this precious pearl. His wife was able to cheer him up, even though, crushed under the weight of his responsibilities, he used to maintain a stoically serious countenance under all circumstances. Without ceasing, he asked the Holy Virgin *to fill them with holiness, to grant that they may intensely live the present moment and never to miss the opportunity of proving their love for one another in the smallest of life's gestures.*

AMEN.

A MAN WITHOUT HOPE

Serge Perrin, Sixty-Fourth Miraculous Healing,
May 1, 1970

19 70 Like every morning, the creaking of tires on the gravel let Serge know that his nurse had arrived. Stretched out on his bed on the second floor, he could hear his wife busying herself downstairs: the tinkling dishes, heels tapping on the entranceway tiles, the door creaking open — that darned creaking, for it has been months since he last was able to oil the hinges…

"Hello, Rosie. Come in, he is expecting you upstairs. Would you like some coffee?" In his bed, Serge Perrin, a forty-two-year-old accountant, a confirmed invalid, let out a long sigh. A new day had just begun.

Eighteen months ago, he had been profoundly happy. He had an adorable wife, three children, a good position in the local company, and pleasant surroundings. He had a well-regulated existence, like the lawn he mowed every Sunday and the well-oiled hinges of his front door. Then, suddenly… Fate? Bad luck?

On December 2, 1968, he woke up with an intense migraine. When he got out of bed, he noticed that his right leg and arm were not working well. But Serge Perrin, conscientious man that he was, nevertheless took his car and headed for work. On the way, fits of giddiness clouded his vision. Once he arrived at his office, he began on his accounts… and then collapsed into unconsciousness.

At first, his doctor believed it was caused by low blood pressure. Serge Perrin had had a similar problem in 1964, and everything had gone back to normal, thanks to his medicines. This time, however, days went by, and Serge Perrin was not getting any better. On the contrary, his right leg became more and more paralyzed. On February 2, 1969, he was sent to the neurosurgical clinic in Rennes, which Professor Pecker directed. The latter's diagnosis was one hundred percent certain: The right carotid vein was blocked, which also explained why his eyesight was diminishing. His condition was judged too advanced for surgery to be practical. Serge Perrin was sent home with a rigorous regime of treatment. Two months later, he returned to consult Pecker, but still there was no improvement. The doctor was not at all encouraging: "*There is nothing more that medicine can do for you.*"

Serge was staggered. What does this mean? He always believed in numbers, in facts, and in proofs. His world was tottering. Could science do nothing for him, then? So when, in April 1969, his wife suggested that he go on a pilgrimage to Lourdes to ask for the Lord's help, he answered: "Why not?"

The pilgrimage went according to plan, but without effect. The very rational Serge Perrin figured as much: What could one hope for?

Months went by, and the disease attacked him further. By June, Serge suffered eclipses of consciousness. Paralysis had reached his left side. In October, he was declared permanently and totally disabled. In January, when he went back to consult Pecker, the doctor noted that his vision troubles now bordered on blindness and that nothing could be done for his paralysis. When Serge heard the fateful word *incurable*, his morale took a hit. He felt abandoned. He was a burden for everybody else, useless and impotent. He was tired of it. He wanted to put an end to it.

On an April morning in 1970, Serge Perrin was at the end of his tether. The world had become unbearable to him. Above all, he could not put up with himself. He now cursed all that he had believed in – his routine existence, his habits, his lawn, and his front door. He blamed himself for not being able to get up, to kiss his wife, to play with his children, to make up for lost time. But it was too late: More than despair, he felt rebellion within himself. A new energy seethed within that he could express only by barking at his family.

"My dear?"

Serge opened his eyes. Among the room's shadows, he made out his wife's silhouette.

"Rosie is downstairs, she will be up soon," she informed him. "I wanted to speak with you first... You know, it's early April. We can still sign up for the yearly diocesan pilgrimage to Lourdes. I would like us to take part in it."

Serge was not open to that idea. "It's useless. I'm done for!"

"Don't say that," she replied. "You are angry, I know. What is happening to you is unfair..."

"No, on the contrary, it is quite fair!" he replied. "I am an idiot; I have wasted my life on stupidities."

"Listen, I would really like you to come with me to Lourdes," his wife asked again. "*If you do not do it for yourself, do it for me.*"

"I am unworthy of all this," he said, stammering a bit. "I... I... If you want to, let's go. I will do it for you."

On April 26, Serge Perrin arrived in Lourdes. The trip went poorly. His mood was ugly. For four days, he participated in the different ceremonies with no result. The night of April 30 was worrisome: He spent several hours in a semi-coma. The morning of May 1, upon waking, he knew it was his last day in Lourdes. In a jolt of consciousness, he said to his wife, "*I'd like to participate in the anointing of the sick at the Saint Pius X Basilica.*" She sighed; she knew what it meant. As the anointing ceremony was frequented by the most desperate cases, the majority of Catholics looked upon it as a ritual for those who are dying and believed the sacrament implicitly was about death anyway.

Within the basilica, Serge, leaning on his canes, attentively followed the ceremony. His mood progressively calmed down. The words of the bishop emptied him of his anger. At the moment of the anointing, he felt a great peace, and then a new sensation went through him. He thought he could feel blood circulating in the veins of his legs, which had been numb for many months. But he dared not part with his canes. That afternoon, he went to the grotto. And there, a surprise: He took off his glasses and noticed that he could see perfectly! There again, he dared not believe it. It was in the train on the return trip, which he boarded right afterward, that he received confirmation by the medical team: He walked, he saw, he had recovered the entirety of his physical capacities. He was healed!

This healing was later verified by Pecker, then by the International Medical Commission of Lourdes.

Serge Perrin returned to Lourdes every year to give thanks. On June 17, 1978, after the canonical investigation, the bishop of Angers declared Serge Perrin to have been miraculously healed, inviting "*Christians to discern in this healing a sign of the merciful love of the Lord who knows how to grant his grace even to those who have lost hope.*"

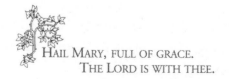

HAIL MARY, FULL OF GRACE.
THE LORD IS WITH THEE.

THE GRACE OF TIME

Ginette Nouvel, Sixtieth Miraculous Healing,
June 11, 1970

19 70 A body plunged into the pool's cold water. Little ripples disturbed a swollen belly as the skin suddenly stretched, as the heart fluttered. Then there was a wave of heat, a strange sensation of lightness at abdomen level, and the feeling of pain leaving gently, like the tide...

Ginette awoke with a start. For a few months, the pain had woken up too. A glimmer of tension lit up her dark eyes. Beads of sweat rolled down her temples. It was a hot and sunny day in the spring of 1970 – the weather forecast on the night before, for once, was not incorrect. Ginette, forty-two, was lying on her bed with wet sheets, next to her husband who was always on the alert, in their house in Carmaux that she had never left except for medical examinations or the operations that were performed sixteen years before in Toulouse. And, sometimes, to go to Lourdes.

"What is wrong?" worried her husband. "A bad dream?"

"A sweet memory... In the pool, in Lourdes, the day when..."

"Stop, my love. You'll do yourself harm."

"Oh, no," she replied, "I am doing myself some good."

Ginette suffered from a rare complaint that affects the region of the liver and requires the patient to undergo frequent punctures. This Budd-Chiari disease had struck her for the first time in 1953. She was twenty-five at the time. It was the era of Françoise Sagan, Juliette Gréco, and Brigitte Bardot. All over France, women were liberating themselves from social conventions, shattering the taboos of a straight-laced era. Ginette, for her part, in her Tarn countryside, with her swollen and painful belly, thought only that she was going to die. All the doctors agreed that the disease was incurable.

On September 20, 1954, despite pain and fatigue, the young woman nevertheless decided to make a pilgrimage to Lourdes. The next day, the first day of fall, after a long and trying procession, with her body plunged into the pool's cold water, that strange sensation...

Her husband helped Ginette get up out of bed. The sun was flooding the room. From the window, she could see the out-of-work coal miners making their way to the taverns, since the coal mines were closing one after the other. The patient felt dizzy and nauseous. Her stomach made her utter sighs of pain. She went forward as best she could through the room, one hand on her husband's shoulder, and suddenly stopped before her reflection in the mirror.

"I look like a pregnant woman," she said once again, surprised and with a disgusted grimace, as if she had just been made aware of her shape for the first time.

She and her husband had never been able to have children. That used to cause them pain; but later the mere chance of still being alive had dissipated their regrets. A rebirth was at least as good as a birth.

After her bath in the autumn of 1954 in one of the Lourdes shrines' pools, Ginette's fainting spells had vanished and her belly had gradually emptied out. She had recovered her young woman's generous figure and her determined look. The Virgin Mary, Mother of God, had granted her a reprieve. A miracle had taken place, acknowledged by the doctors and confirmed, in 1963, by Bishop Claude Dupuy of Albi. For sixteen years, Ginette was able to take full advantage of her extraordinary return to a normal life. For sixteen years, she continued to come to Lourdes regularly to bear witness to her disease's perfect remission. For sixteen years, she never stopped giving thanks to God for granting her life, and then granting her this time. For sixteen years... until that day in the winter of 1969 when she relapsed. Pains, dizzy spells, vomitings – and, once again, perhaps even harder to bear, the cruelly ironic "pregnant lady" look, as though she had to repay the benefit of her temporary healing. Of all those miraculously healed, she remains the only one ever to undergo a recurrence of her illness.

A burning pain went up Ginette's belly and pressed upon her throat. She was so weak that she nearly fell. Her legs could no longer hold her. Her husband helped her lie down. He drew the curtains to mitigate the heat and sat back down on the chair near the bed. His legs shook, too. With an expression that mingled rage with powerlessness, he stared at his wife's face twisted with pain After a few seconds, he dimly made out the young girl who danced on the day of the village fair, on the deserted town square, twenty years ago – her brown bangs half hiding her eyes, her slightly jerky movements, her yet-unfinished beauty, the immediate and unreserved certainty that she was "the one," so many promises lighting up the future...

Mr. Nouvel smiled at the memory. He held his now-sleeping wife's hand very tight. In a few days, Ginette would have to undergo an operation; she did not yet know that it would be fatal. Her body plunged into the pool's cold water, that strange sensation...

Blessed art thou among women,
and blessed is the fruit of thy womb, Jesus.

A Season in Lourdes

*The JOC (Jeunesse ouvrière chrétienne,
"Christian Worker Youth") in Lourdes, July 11, 1971*

1971 "Come on, Julien, come and have a glass with us!" my friends called to me.

"I can't. I'm going back to work," I replied.

"Join us later then! At the usual bar."

"All right," I said as I left the small group of seasonal workers with whom I am lodging for the entire summer season in Lourdes.

My name is Julien Crantec. I am nineteen. I live in the suburbs of Toulouse, and every summer I come and work in Lourdes. The hotels always need people and I always need money. My father, an airplane factory worker, has been on unemployment benefits for two years. He lives on the indemnity and odd jobs. My mother is gone. I was two. I never saw her again. I need to find money to help out at home and to finance my studies.

In Lourdes, at least, I have plenty to do. I am not idle! My schedule is organized to a tee. In the morning, from seven thirty to eleven thirty, I clean rooms at the hotel with a team of cleaning ladies. At lunchtime, I sell french fries in a little shack near the shrine. In the afternoon, I'm back at the hotel, where I function as a bellboy, a receptionist, or a linen-room keeper! Today, I carried to the station the luggage of a Swiss delegation due to leave by train tonight. I have never seen so many bags for such a short stay. It's eight thirty now, and I've just finished my service at the hotel. Now I'm going to serve ice cream in a hut downtown. It's the right time for it because people are finishing their day. It's when they return from the torchlight procession, too. Prayer builds up their appetite! My boss is so overwhelmed at the end of the day that he is glad to accept my help.

"A vanilla-coffee ice cream, please," asked a young girl who had looked at me funny the other night.

"Right away."

The customer looked at me insistently. She launched into conversation. "Do you work at the grotto hotel?"

"Why, yes!" I replied.

Her face lit up. "Me too. I'm a seasonal worker."

"Like me!" I said.

"Terrific!" she chirped. "Would you come with me for a drink at the JOC?"

This girl didn't even know me, but there she was inviting me for a drink with her! I won't be drinking with my other friends tonight. They'll understand, though: She's a girl, and what's more, she's pretty!

"Why not?" I accepted. "I'm off in an hour."

"So, I'll see you at 4 Arberet Street," she responded. "See you later! And thanks for the ice cream!"

Since I've been coming to Lourdes, I've gotten to know all the bars and cafés. But I had never heard of an establishment called "the JOC," and with good reason: The JOC is not a café, it's an association: *Jeunesse ouvrière chrétienne* (Christian Worker Youth)! By the time I realized it, it was too late to back out. The young girl saw me arrive and called out to me.

"It's here! Come in!" she invited me.

I was trapped! And what's more, we wouldn't be alone. Ten other youngsters were chatting over coffee. Not even booze... Coffee!

"Hello!" called out two young guys I think I've seen at the station.

"Hi," I muttered.

"You're at the grotto hotel, I hear?"

"Yes..."

"Are you making out OK financially?" asked a boy my age, point-blank.

It was none of his business! What nerve! I opted for humor and coolness.

"In Lourdes, there's nothing miraculous about the salaries!" I told him.

The girl who lured me into this trap smiled. She was really cute.

"For me, it's tough," continued the boy. "I got a raw deal at first, but thanks to the JOC, I'm beginning to get my rights respected."

I perked up my ears, interested.

"The JOC," interjected the girl who invited me, "is an association that is geared to young people to help them get work and lodging. Every year we meet in Lourdes for a seasonal presence. We welcome seasonal workers. They come here to talk, to swap good deals, to know their rights, to learn how to defend themselves, to make the right choices, to find direction..."

"Oh! It's a union..." I said.

"Not really," she stated. "We're not militant."

"A social association, then?"

"Better!" continued the girl, laughing. "We defend the workers at the legislative level, but we are also there to meet, to show that we are not alone, that we can take charge of our lives – in the sight of God," she added after a short silence.

I raised my eyebrows. It's silly, but I don't think anyone has ever mentioned God to me in all the years I've been coming to Lourdes – not my colleagues, nor my bosses, nor the other seasonal workers. The pilgrims, yes, a little. But with them, that's normal, and I don't really believe what they tell me.

I didn't see the rest of the evening go by. In the end, I let myself soak up the wholesome atmosphere reigning in the little association's meeting room. I bonded a little with the other youngsters and with the JOC members, the "Jocistes." I learned how to get the best value out of my work for my studies. I listened to the others, to Camille – that's her name – in particular.

And then, out of the blue, I let them drag me to the famous Lourdes grotto that I hadn't even taken the time to visit. I went out of curiosity, to please Camille especially. She was going there to pray pretty much every evening after her shift. When I discovered the crutches hanging from the grotto ceiling, I was staggered. I realized that I was not the only one to have a life I thought was kind of glum. I was not the only one, and I was not alone. Yes! There, in front of that grotto, next to a girl I'd known for only a few hours, I suddenly felt that I was not alone. So, I prayed as well…

HOLY MARY, MOTHER OF GOD,

THE BLUE JALOPY

Vittorio Micheli, Sixty-Third Miraculous Healing,
May 29, 1972

1972 As he tackled the ramp leading up to the upper basilica, Vittorio wondered whether he had overestimated his strength. In the "blue car" he was pulling there was a jovial, bearded, invalid, and… well, a very obese man! But the vehicle was in good condition, the ground good and smooth, and Vittorio's will unwavering, so the carriage made it safe and sound. Having reached the top, the stretcher-bearer, sweaty and happy, turned around toward his companion:

"Here you are, sir. Do you wish to go into the church right away? We're a few minutes early…"

"Call me Demetrio!" the man said.

"Right, we haven't even had proper introductions! My name is Vittorio."

"Well, Vittorio, you are an excellent stretcher-bearer. This ramp seemed steep, yet you climbed it in one try, and apparently without getting tired! Do you come to Lourdes often?"

"Nearly every year," Vittorio replied. "And every time as a stretcher-bearer. So I'm getting to know a few tricks! How about you, is this your first pilgrimage?"

"Why, yes!" Demetrio said as he launched into his story. "Last year, I had a serious car accident, and since then I've been paralyzed in the legs because of a spinal lesion. My wife pushed me into coming, with our pastor's collaboration. I'm a believer, and a practicing one... almost" – a sly smile formed at the mention of his reservation about the faith – "but I'm not sure I believe in miracles. Not, at any rate, as far as I'm concerned!"

Vittorio was a good conversationalist. "And yet you came! You took this step, which is ever so tiresome when one has lost all one's autonomy. So why?"

"I'm telling you, it's my wife's and the pastor's idea! I hadn't even thought of it before she mentioned it! Miracles... I'm not too sure that they're believable."

"Don't think that," Vittorio chided. "In Lourdes, there have been hundreds of astounding healings, and about sixty miracles duly certified by the Church!"

Demetrio took the statistical approach. "Out of how many millions of pilgrims who came with a heart full of hope and went home disappointed, whatever they may say? There are too many requests and too few who get healed for me to set one ounce of hope in them."

"Miracles are answers, signs addressed by God to the prayer of men," the stretcher-bearer explained. "One cannot draw up an account, for they occur in hearts and souls. But what is sure is that if you expect nothing, you will get nothing. Jesus said it clearly: *Ask and you shall receive.*"[1]

"That's why I'm not hoping for anything, since I haven't asked for anything!" Demetrio stated.

---

1. Lk 11: 9.

During this conversation, the chatty pair's cart had come closer to the upper basilica's entrance, but Vittorio took it upon himself to continue his journey toward the other ramp, which goes around the building and then down to the esplanade. Either he insisted on showing his companion how nimble he was at pulling the cart, or he wished not to cut short the discussion by entering the silent church prematurely. In any case, the paralyzed man did not react, thereby expressing his tacit and benevolent approval for continuing a stroll that wasn't displeasing to him.

"How about you, then? Why do you come to Lourdes?" asked Demetrio to revive the friendly exchange. "Why are you a stretcher-bearer?

"Because helping others is important to me," admitted Vittorio. "I make lots of encounters, like the one we are both now experiencing, enriching encounters from every point of view. And it has its physical benefits, too, as you were pointing out just a moment ago!"

"Don't try to convince me that that motivates you every year!" Demetrio replied. "Your way of speaking about the miracles interests me. Have you followed up on the question?"

"Pretty deeply, indeed. As for you, you're asking yourself a lot of questions regarding this miracle business. See, you do believe in them. At least, you'd like to believe in them, wouldn't you?"

"What cripple, what sick man, what unfortunate would not wish to believe?" Demetrio admitted. "Of course, I dream that, after a bath in ice cold water and a simple and sincere prayer, I go home on my own two legs. But it seems to me impossible, and, when you get right down to it, undeserved."

"What have you done, then, what unforgivable crime have you committed not to deserve an answer from God to a sincere request?"

Vittorio was getting deep into the conversation, and it was hardly the right moment as he had begun the ramp's downward slope, a time when he ought to have been focusing his attention on steadying the carriage and ensuring Demetrio's safety. Yet his desire to "convert" his passenger was as strong as the slope, and both threatened to drag him down whether he liked it or not!

"A crime!" hiccuped Demetrio to the rhythm of the jostling jalopy's jolts. "My Lord, I hope I've committed none!"

"Then have confidence," retorted Vittorio, braking with all his might to stop the vehicle, and turned to his passenger. "There is no such thing as fate, and all are called. Let me confide a secret in you: As a young man, during my military service in the Alpine troops, I had a terrible hip cancer. The doctors were so pessimistic that they barely attempted to treat me. I couldn't walk anymore. I came, like you, in a cart, to meet the Virgin, and I simply, respectfully, asked her to help me. To support me. Like you, I dared not believe. But I knew that she would listen, that she would be attentive and sensitive. I can assure you that these blue carts, symbols of my infirmity, of my impotence, I hated them before I took a plunge in the pool. Today, my greatest delight is in pulling them, hoping with all my heart that those I guide will obtain what I received. It may have already happened; I have no idea. If it happens once, just once, that would gratify me even more than my own healing, believe me. I had the good fortune of being miraculously healed, and the Church has recognized what happened to me; I actually know no more than that. What I'm sure of, though, is that it isn't just the healing of the bodies that counts – those aren't even the most important. A healed body sheltering a sick heart wouldn't find true happiness!"

Sincerity was so strong, so visible in Vittorio's sweaty face that Demetrio's shell of disbelief started to crack. He promised himself to consider a dip in the miraculous water in a humbler, more sincere manner. And he also started to see his little blue car from a different perspective; it suddenly revealed to him the conceited and prideful impotent man he had been, in spite of himself.

PAX ET BONUM

At the Tomb of the Capuchin Jacques de Balduina,
February 12, 1973

1973 In the early morning, two women painfully advanced in the snowy alleys of the foreigners' cemetery in Lourdes. This deserted place was that of the anonymous pilgrims from other countries – solitaries buried here, far from their family, from their region.

"How, Fernande, do you expect us to find your Capuchin's tomb in all this snow?" grumbled the frailer of the women, shivering.

"Don't worry, Sylvie. You can't miss it."

Fernande was a regular in this place. As a cleaning lady at the Grand Hôtel d'Angleterre in Lourdes, she was accompanying her friend Sylvie, who was visiting from Paris. Sylvie was very worried about the health of her daughter, who was visibly getting worse because of successive still-births. Fernande had suggested that she come to Lourdes for a few days of rest. But she also had her own little idea...

The previous night, she went to pick up Sylvie at the station; and, after a reinvigorating dinner, she told her of an unusual tomb, that of an Italian Capuchin who had died twenty-five years before but had the mysterious gift of hearing prayers and granting wishes. Sylvie was a believer, but as for miracles, she didn't believe in them all that much! Still, this morning, she agreed to follow her friend.

Having reached the middle of the cemetery, Fernande exclaimed, "There it is! Someone has come by before us and swept off the snow."

Indeed, a little further down the alley, Sylvie noticed a spot of color. Flowers! She went closer. The tomb was unpretentious, but decked with flowers. All around, there were marble squares bearing five little letters that told the whole story: "*Merci*" ("Thank you!")... She couldn't believe her eyes.

"Don't count them," interrupted Fernande. "There are nearly a hundred!"

Sylvie leaned over to read a Latin inscription on the tombstone: "*Pax et bonum*," and underneath: "*Père Jacques de Balduina, 1900-1948.*" When she straightened up, her face no longer expressed tension or boredom; just a sort of surprised wonder.

"Who is this man?!" she asked her friend.

"Oh, it's a long story!" Fernande replied before recounting the story anyway. "Benjamin Filon was born August 2, 1900, in Balduina, south of Padua. He was a patient, sweet child, always at the service of others. Contemplative and not very talkative, he preferred spending hours dreaming in the little church to playing. Mediocre at school, a whipping boy to his classmates, he often came home from school with bruises all over his head, yet he never complained. What a mystery this child already was! What gave him this peace, this kindness, this happy expression at every moment? Peace and goodness, *Pax et bonum*... Such is the motto of the Franciscan Order of Capuchins, those mendicant monks who have a convent in the village where his school was. He often saw them on the country roads, their rough brown habits tied with white cords, barefoot regardless of the season, to go begging and to care for the poor.

"At the age of fifteen," she continued, "Benjamin made up his mind: He wanted to become a monk. The First World War diverted him from his vocation, however. Called up as a recruit, he served as warehouse keeper and librarian in a Milan barracks. Freed from his obligations in September 1922, he immediately entered the monastery of Bassano del Grappa, where he took his father's first name. He became Brother Jacques de Balduina. Yet the novice master was skeptical: A year later, the day Jacques made his temporary vows, he confided in his mother: *'My dear lady, your son has me a little concerned, because he doesn't know how to do anything, except pray...'*

"Jacques did not lose heart. He shrugged off reproaches and bullying without batting an eye. The following year, he was off to the high school of Our Lady of the Elm in Thiena to undertake his theological studies. And there, a surprise: His grades took off, and his intelligence was discovered. Brother Jacques was making great strides toward ordination."

Fernande stopped speaking for a moment. A few snowflakes gently fell from the sky, and her voice started again, more gravely.

"In 1927, a shadow was cast upon Jacques' life. He could barely walk. The diagnosis was not long in coming: He had Parkinson's disease. Despite his pain, he continued his studies, eliciting his professors' admiration. With their support, he finally became a priest on July 21, 1929. Called to the monastery in Udina, he accepted the humble position of confessor.

"Tucked away in his little confessional for close to twenty years, he performed his duty discretely, content with listening to those who came to confide in him and to dispense words of comfort and forgiveness to them. Soon his reputation as a confessor spread to the entire region. Everyone began coming to see him – peasants, women, but also many priests. He knew how to calm anxiety, to say what is needed in a few words. His fortitude regarding his illness was exemplary: Without a word of complaint, he faced the pain every day to stay at his post.

"When he felt his end was near, he wanted to go to Lourdes to pay homage to the Virgin. The doctors advised against the trip, but he insisted. Leaving Udina on July 19, 1948, on the "purple" train for the sick pilgrims, he arrived in Lourdes on July 21 after a thirty-five-hour journey. Exhausted and laid out on a stretcher, he immediately asked to be taken to the grotto. The doctor forbade it. Transported to the hospital, he passed away at eleven at night singing the *Magnificat* in a low voice, nineteen years to the day after his ordination, without having been able to give thanks to the Virgin of Massabielle whom he had been carrying in his heart all his life. He was interred at the cemetery two days later.

"And since then, to everyone's astonishment, this tomb has been the only one in the cemetery always to have flowers. The faithful pour in from all countries to seek from him the same comfort he used to dispense while he was alive. The testimonials covering his tomb bear witness that the prayers addressed to him do not remain dead letters. To this day, he is nicknamed 'the saintly father'; his tomb is the object of an unofficial but constant pilgrimage. The Venetian Order of Capuchins is swamped with requests for a biography, for relics, for the story of Jacques de Balduina's graces."

That very morning, in February 1973, a new bunch of flowers adorned the monk's tomb, and a new prayer was addressed to him – that of a Parisian lady who had never heard of him before, but in whom he helped hope to be born again. This is how, by word of mouth, the humble Capuchin who used to go barefoot continues to bring souls to life.

AMEN.

THE CHILD WITH JET-BLACK EYES

Delizia Cirolli, Sixty-Fifth Miraculous Healing,
August 10, 1976

19 76 "Would you like me to help you?" a young man asked an Italian lady who seemed exhausted.

"No, thank you," answered the woman with a smile. "It's kind of you, but I prefer to take care of my daughter myself."

Gathering what was left of her strength, the dark-haired young woman lifted her child up on her shoulder and valiantly continued to walk among hundreds of pilgrims. In her arms, her daughter did not seem any livelier. She held in her shaking hand the little candle the hospitallers had given her at the beginning of the procession around the Marian shrine. In the flame's glimmer, her tired and thin face was a pity to see, but her jet-black eyes were lively and shining.

"Are you sure you don't want a stretcher for your daughter?" the young man insisted politely. "She doesn't look all that heavy, but still..."

"Fifty pounds," panted the mother.

She continued on her way, teetering under her meager burden. Sometimes the dark-haired girl nestled in her arms would groan, and her mother would hasten to reassure her. She covered her with kisses and whispered tender words in her ears. Then they bravely resumed their *Ave Marias* to the rhythm of the crowd all around them.

"She's fifty pounds," she suddenly repeated with despair, "and she is eleven years old." Whoever heard of an eleven-year-old weighing only fifty pounds?

The young man continued walking next to them in silence. He listened, aware that listening was perhaps what the woman needed most.

"The doctor wants to amputate her leg in order to try to save her and to keep the tumor from spreading to the rest of the body! Amputate her... never!" she cried, clasping her child a little closer in her arms. "I cannot allow that to be done to my little angel. And anyway, it is not even certain that it would save her..."

Her voice broke into a sob. It was the girl's turn to buck up her mother. Feeling her distress, the girl looked at her mother with her black eyes and smiled. Despite the pain that ravaged her features, the young man could still see that she was pretty and cheerful.

"I am sure that the Madonna will heal her," continued the young mother who was finding consolation in this conversation. "She will remove the tumor from the knee. She will get her back to us. I am sure of it! I believe it! *Maria, prega per lei*," she added in a strong voice.

As if to respond to her mother's ardor, the little girl clutched the candle with a firmer hand while reciting an *Ave Maria* that her mother joined in unison.

The fragile mother-and-daughter pair again walked on with courage and faith. The young man watched as they disappeared into the distance to follow the slow procession that was unfurling like a snake of light on the shrine's esplanade. *Poor women*, he thought with emotion. *May you hear them, Holy Virgin!*

For her part, little Delizia Cirolli's mother felt relieved. Having been able to tell someone of her anxieties did her some good. Tomorrow, August 11, 1976, she would bring her child back home to Sicily.

Certainly, she was exhausted, as was Delizia. But that pilgrimage to Lourdes had become necessary. *It's the only thing that can save my little angel,* she thought to herself, redoubling the fervor of her prayers.

As she made her way to her hotel after the last torchlight procession, Delizia's mother once again thought of this disease that had come to poison their very existence. So rapidly, too, and without warning! Within barely five months, her daughter's health had totally deteriorated. She had nearly stopped walking, brought down by the throbbing pain in her knee. She had lost her appetite, her *joie de vivre.*

"Virgin Mary, either you save her... or she dies," whispered the Sicilian lady as she tucked her sleeping child into her bed.

As for treatments, she didn't want any. Hospitals frightened Delizia, and her mother wanted to keep her close so that she could lavish all her love on her. An amputation? Her mother's heart could not face that. What was needed was a miracle!

But back in Sicily, she had to face reality: Her daughter was not healed. On the contrary, her condition continued to worsen. She was visibly losing weight. Delizia's mother, and her whole family along with her, ceaselessly prayed to Our Lady of Lourdes for the girl, but it came time to accept the obvious: Her child was going to die. And so, bravely, faithful to the island's tradition, the mother secretly chose her daughter's prettiest dress. That would be the one Delizia would wear in her casket...

After four months of unbearable anxiety and fervent prayers, the unthinkable finally happened. On a morning when the air was sweet, a little before Christmas 1976, the child asked to leave her room. She wanted to see the sun, to breathe in the seashore's briny air. So there she stood in the garden, watching the sea. Standing! Yet it had been so long since she last walked, as she lacked even the strength to sit up in her bed.

"Holy Virgin!" whispered the mother, her eyes brimming with tears.

The miracle that had been so long awaited, and desired with so much confidence, had finally arrived. Within a few days, Delizia recovered her health, started walking and even running again, and going to school. She resumed a normal life under the watchful eye of her mother, who never stopped praising Our Lady of Lourdes for this miracle.

The next year, Delizia and her mother returned to Lourdes to give thanks to the Virgin Mary. Together they went to the Medical Bureau to tell their story. But they would have to wait a long time for the girl's healing to be recognized as scientifically inexplicable. After six years of medical examinations, the bishop classed Delizia Cirolli's healing among the miracles. In her mother's mind, a few steps on a morning before Christmas had been enough.

Hail Mary, full of grace.
The Lord is with thee.

THE BISHOP OF THE RESISTANCE

Portrait of Bishop Théas, April 3, 1977

19
77

"He's dead!"

In the town, on the shrine's esplanade, in the churches, and at the town hall, the news spread like wildfire."

"He was no ordinary bishop."

"Isn't that the truth! He was a man of great character, that bishop of the Resistance. A great wartime figure."

"A holy man. A man of peace."

The citizens of Lourdes felt a little bit orphaned that April 3, 1977. The fact was that Bishop Pierre-Marie Théas had not only been their bishop for over twenty years; he was also a local boy, born in Barzun, a true Béarnais who spoke their language. When, in 1947, the mayor of Lourdes, Mr. Dupierris, had greeted the prelate, he had quipped: "*You're one of us. Consequently, you know us well. You know our virtues; you also know our few vices!*"

Despite his resignation a few years ago on his seventy-fifth birthday – a formality required of all Catholic bishops upon attaining that age – the former bishop of Tarbes and Lourdes left his mark on each·of them, just as he left his print on the shrines he had transformed to welcome the increasing number of pilgrims after the war. The Saint Pius X Basilica, with a capacity of twenty thousand people, was certainly his greatest building achievement. The shrine's financial business was difficult to manage, but it had turned out well in the end. He also asked the Secours Catholique to erect a welcoming center for the poorest pilgrims, the Cité Saint-Pierre. Lastly, it was he who restored the grotto and esplanade so that they might recover their former appearance – that of the days when Bernadette had had her apparitions – without the hundreds of testimonials, canes, crutches, and grilles. Plus, he had moved the pools and restored the Hospitality. Throughout his whole episcopacy, he did his utmost to extend Lourdes' influence throughout the world and to welcome new pilgrimages.

At the terrace of the Grotto Café, on the town square, everyone freely shared opinions and anecdotes. Memories abounded. An old man at the counter remembered the Mass said in the camp in Compiègne, that gateway to Buchenwald, Dachau, Neuengamme, and Mauthausen.

"The day before the Liberation, he said Mass along with a Protestant and an Orthodox beside him," the man said. "That unity in the face of barbarity moved me a great deal."

"Why was he in a camp?" asked a young waiter.

"Bishop Théas wasn't what you would call a friend to the Germans," the man replied. "You weren't born at the time, but he was one of the only bishops, along with Bishop Saliège, to announce publicly his hostility toward their conduct. As bishop of Montauban at the time, he had a letter read at Mass by all the priests in his diocese in which he denounced the way the Jews were being savagely hunted down and separated from their families. In 1944, he wrote to the Germans to complain of the arrest of several of his priests. Then it was his turn to be arrested."

"He played a great role in reconciliation and peacemaking after the war," added another man. "He met General de Gaulle and went off to Rome to see the Pope in the name of all the French bishops and of the new government. I remember that, upon his return, he came to Lourdes for the first pilgrimage of thanksgiving after the Liberation."

At one of the tables, a couple, members of *Pax Christi* – a movement he had founded and led right after the war – recalled memories of the man who had accompanied them in their prayer for peace. A true pastor who often mentioned that he had been a little shepherd: Before leading the people of God, he had pastured flocks in the fields near his village. Along with his native tongue, Béarnais, he had two things in common with Bernadette: He was simple man, sometimes a little short-fused like all true Béarnais, but very welcoming. He was also a man of prayer, deeply attached to the Virgin of Lourdes and to the shrines.

The conversation among the café patrons picked up.

"He loved truth," one woman said. "He's the one who gave Lourdes scientific credibility in the face of the many attacks on the part of medical circles who perceived superstition and hoaxes in the pilgrimages and miracles."

"That right!" said the first man. "Furthermore, he asked Father René Laurentin and his team to put together a veritable historical study on the shrines. As part of his brief, he apparently told him, 'Lourdes needs truth.'"

"Nor did the finished work disappoint him. I think Fathers Laurentin and Billet published something like ten volumes!" exclaimed another. "They spent years uncovering archives scattered throughout France, copying them, presenting them. Everything has been published. They did an enormous scientific work, setting down for the future the foundations for historical research."

The woman piped in again, "He also reorganized the Bureau of Medical Verification, so that every passing physician might give his opinion and that miracles not be claimed without rhyme or reason. He also organized a national, later international, commission composed of university professors and hospital chiefs, to verify on a case by case basis whether the healings presented by the bureau were 'miracles' or not."

"It is certain that, as regards unbelievers and even some Catholics who tended to think that Lourdes was the temple of simplistic belief, his work has been very useful, perhaps even salvific," concluded one of the diners.

"Yes, for the shrine, and also for Marian dogma," agreed another. "He encouraged theologians to study Mariology in Lourdes, as well as the messages that the Virgin delivered to Bernadette and during her other apparitions in the world."

The café owner, interested and moved by the conversation, showed his clients the morning newspaper. A long article was devoted to the bishop. It ended with an excerpt from his spiritual testament: "*The memories of my long life, especially the most painful ones, invite me to praise God and to thank Him. The Lord has loved me much. All the good in my life is a gift of God, only a gift of God, an absolutely free gift. Magnificat!*"

The Angelus bells rang. The little group of talkers split up, and the words of Bishop Théas echoed in each one of them to the rhythm of the carillon.

BLESSED ART THOU AMONG WOMEN,
AND BLESSED IS THE FRUIT OF THY WOMB, JESUS.

"*Rivers of Living Water Will Flow from within Him*"

Élisa Aloi, Sixty-First Miraculous Healing, August 13, 1978

19 78 "You've got some beautiful children there!"

The mother smiled and stroked the brown hair of her youngest, aged four. She certainly wouldn't contradict the old lady who just spoke to her.

"And they are so well-behaved," the elderly lady marveled.

Élisa Varacalli's four children silently advanced closer to their mother. Each one held in his hand a little candle in a paper cone on which the words of the *Ave Maria* and a picture of the Virgin of Lourdes were printed. One after the other, they followed the procession without the slightest hint of distraction. They were surprisingly calm.

The old lady looked at their faces, framed in dark hair, their lips moving speedily in a silent prayer. No, truly, she had rarely seen such well-behaved, devout children. Their mother, Élisa, noticed her procession neighbor's admiring astonishment. She whispered to her by way of explanation: "Without Lourdes, without the Virgin Mary, they wouldn't be here today."

The pretty Italian's family was no ordinary one. In a few bashful words, Élisa explained to the old lady that her family pilgrimage was the fruit of a miracle.

Nearly twenty years ago now, no one could have supposed that young Élisa – Élisa Aloi at the time – would someday be the happy mother of four magnificent children. The Virgin Mary surely had other plans for her.

When Élisa Aloi arrived in Lourdes in June 1958, her condition had been worsening for ten years. Struck with tuberculosis from the age of seventeen, the young Sicilian was caught as if on a dreary merry-go-round of infections, treatments, infections, hospitalization, and again more infections. Medicine was powerless to heal her. At the very best, it could only alleviate her pain a little.

The doctors did not view Élisa's trip to Lourdes with approval. The twenty-seven-year-old young woman was stuck in a plaster corset that encased her from the middle of her chest down to her feet. She was burning with fever, paralyzed in her lower limbs, covered in purulent abscesses. Any journey was complicated, even dangerous. This trip to Lourdes was insanity. Yes, insanity! For Élisa, as she had received ample proof the year before, was certainly not going to be saved in Lourdes! Indeed, a year before, she had already undertaken a pilgrimage, but without success. The healing she had so hoped for failed to materialize. Worse, her illness only worsened. The doctors did not appreciate her stubbornness.

But what the doctors doubtless did not know well enough was that nothing is impossible to God. It may well be that their patient seemed to be poised at death's door in every respect, yet in this battered body a little flame remained quite alive and burning. Faith? It is certain that therein, in that little thing that no medical equipment can measure, the secret of the young woman's future healing lay hidden.

"Doctor, dress my wounds with water, please," requested Élisa two days after her arrival in Lourdes.

The doctor who usually took care of dressing her wounds resisted.

"Water is insufficient! We have to disinfect!" he said.

But Élisa insisted, "Dress my bandages with water!"

One would think she didn't quite realize the condition she was in. A frightful-smelling liquid permanently dripped from her wounds. Water would be insufficient to clean them.

"Lourdes water," Élisa specified.

The doctor said nothing more. If it was the patient's will to be treated with grotto water, he did not wish to oppose it. During all the time he had been coming to Lourdes, he had been able to observe that the faith and abandonment of the sick to the Virgin Mary could sometimes move mountains.

And so the doctor sent a stretcher-bearer to fetch him a bucketful of Lourdes water. He needed a quantity sufficient to soak his patient's bandages as well as to inject water under her plaster and even directly into her abscesses.

As she was being treated, Élisa did not speak. No doubt she was praying.

A day went by, then another. And still, the doctor changed the bandages with Lourdes water. The results were not stellar, but at least the patient seemed to feel better for it.

On the third day, when the doctor took off the old bandages, he couldn't believe his eyes. The material was not soiled. As for the wounds, they seemed to have closed and to be clean.

Stuck in her immense plaster, Élisa smiled. "I can move my toes!" she said emotionally. It had been so long since she last could.

"I would like to have my plaster removed!" Élisa requested.

"I have to ask the head of staff," answered the doctor.

The head of staff was prudent. Though the healing seemed real, he preferred that Élisa's regular physician remove the young woman's plaster himself after she returned to Italy.

The verification of this unexplained healing therefore was passed to the doctor who had been following Élisa's case. He could not get over the sight of the young woman! *Miss Élisa Aloi returned from Lourdes completely healed and so healthy that one could not believe that it was the same person who had left in such desperate conditions,*" he would write to the Lourdes Medical Bureau that gives rulings on the miracles. "*I certify that Élisa Aloi is completely healed…*"

Her heart brimming with this story, the old lady looked at Élisa and her four beautiful children as they made their way to the fountains, where flows this sweet and blessed water to which all five owed their lives.

HOLY MARY, MOTHER OF GOD,

GROTTOES THROUGHOUT THE WORLD

Massabielle Replicas, May 12, 1979

19 79 Jean could almost hear the wind of his native Bigorre whistling in the bell tower of the Immaculate Conception Basilica and plunging into the mountains on the horizon. He could see it toying with the banners of the eucharistic procession, ruffling the hair of the faithful as they passed by. Yes, as he examined the walls that were covered in frescoes, he could imagine himself back home in Lourdes. Yet he was quite far away, for he was on vacation in Cuba. The crack in the rock in front of him in which a Virgin in a white dress and blue sash was smiling was located in the heart of Havana. The rocks of this grotto came from the Caribbean Sea. It was the first Massabielle replica to be built outside of Europe, and it was dedicated in February 1879 – two months before Bernadette's death.

The statue of Our Lady did not seem to suffer from the tropical heat. Cool and serene, crowned with a halo of festive lamps, she seemed right at home on the edge of the Atlantic Ocean, on that marvelous island where a communist regime as notorious as it was tenacious had not been able to stamp out the faith of Catholics.

Though it was the first chronologically, this replica of the Lourdes grotto is not the only facsimile of the site of Bernadette's visions to be constructed in other continents. Back in his hotel room, Jean opened his itinerary with amusement to examine the maps on which he had marked out the other Lourdes grottoes that exist around the globe.

Where should I start the survey? he wondered. *At the polar extremities, perhaps...?* Inuits have been spotted praying in a place called Paulaktuk, on the edge of the Arctic Ocean, where a Massabielle grotto has been erected by a missionary bishop. At its antipode, another statue of the Virgin graces the southern end of the globe with her smile in Punta Arenas, below the "howling fiftieth" (the fiftieth degree latitude south). That small Chilean town in Patagonia faces Antarctica, from which it is separated only by the Drake Passage and its terrible ice storms.

Brrr! Jean's finger returned to more clement latitudes. Not all statues of Our Lady of Lourdes are exposed to such extreme temperatures. The one in Oostacker, Belgium, enjoys a perfectly temperate climate. Yet that is not why that shrine, located near Ghent, received close to eight thousand pilgrims per day. When she had a replica of the grotto built in her residential park, the marchioness of Courtebourne had no idea of the religious fervor it would invite. But on April 7, 1875, a workman named Pierre de Rudder had himself carried to that grotto which, in the middle of the lowlands, evokes the mountain shrine of Massabielle. The poor, unfortunate man had been injured by a falling tree and was to have his left leg amputated. The operation, however, would never take place. The pilgrimage healed de Rudder from his injuries without any aftereffects! Ever since that event, crowds have thronged to Oostacker...

Having found himself taken back to Europe in his reverie, Jean remained there a moment. He knew that in Poland – in Debno, near Crakow – there exists a Massabielle grotto that attracted multitudes. The shrine even publishes a journal, the *Echo Groty*, which spreads

Bernadette's message in Polish! In the bordering nation of Slovakia, the Virgin of Massabielle is again represented in another very popular shrine.

Jean then turned his thoughts to the statue with perhaps the most ideal location in all of Europe – the one that stands in the gardens of the Vatican. When the popes kneel before the grotto erected by Pope Leo XIII to pray to the Mother of God, their hearts are as humble as that of all the anonymous faithful around the world who have built miniature grottoes in their back yards. They are all part of the countless millions who have prayed at the foot of a modest statue sheltered by a few rocks.

Jean once again let his thoughts escape to other destinations for more exotic horizons. In Polynesia, he had been told that the most flowery grotto in the world was in Bora Bora, where it basks in the luxurious scents of the region's flora. In Reunion, on the island of Mauritius in the Indian Ocean, grottoes built by Catholic missionaries have become an ecumenical crossroads where people of various local religions go to pray. In Saigon, Vietnam, the Massabielle replica survived the merciless wars that had shaken the country. In China, too, several grottoes have been built. The Christian religion might be just a relatively tiny and oppressed minority, but there are twelve million Catholics in that densely populated country, enough to create some rather large pilgrimages! Besides, the Massabielle replicas built in Shanghai, Canton, and Guiyang are not out of place in the traditional landscape. A priest of the area once explained it to Jean: The veneration of grottoes and waterfalls is quite common in Chinese culture.

From Singapore to Benin, from Australia to Mexico, from Canada to Argentina, and from the United States to Lebanon, other representations of the Lourdes grotto remind the faithful that Catholics can feel close to the banks of the Gave no matter where they are.

So many grottoes! Closing his itinerary and his map filled with little red crosses, Jean was torn between emotion and bemusement. For him, who had grown up near Massabielle, the imitation grottoes seemed a little tacky. Yet at the same time, how could one not marvel? From one shrine to the next, the graces that bloom in Lourdes have spread throughout the world and have multiplied exponentially. And everywhere, the Virgin Mary – the real deal, no mimicry there – receives the prayers of the crowds who walk by the inauthentic but moving effigies of her inimitable smile and tenderness.

PRAY FOR US SINNERS,
NOW AND AT THE HOUR OF OUR DEATH.

A GREAT MAN'S SIMPLICITY

Charles de Gaulle and Lourdes,
May 25, 1980

1980 Like every Pentecost vacation, I was on my way to Lourdes to visit my great-uncle, a former chaplain of the shrine, now retired in a rest home run by religious sisters. I have always loved the man, yet I didn't see him much in my childhood. Since my teenage years, though, I've been visiting him regularly. The old priest from another time, with his alabaster skin tone, ought to have rejected me, but we soon found we shared a common passion for history that dissolved our secular differences. This ninety-four-year-old scholar's intact memory has never ceased to amaze me all these years.

The streets of Lourdes were festive in the sweetness of the month of May as it ushered in the end of the university year. Pushing open the rest home's door, I smiled at the thought of discussing my future dissertation topic with my great-uncle. As usual, he was waiting for me, a steaming teapot carefully prepared by Sister Anne on his reading table. I found him rather pale, but the liveliness of his voice was reassuring.

After exchanging some family news, his eyes lit up with an inquisitive, "Well?" Thrilled at no longer having to wait before revealing my projects to him, I launched into the presentation of my topic: "General Charles de Gaulle, Religion and the State." I explained to him that I wanted to understand how mysticism can become a force of political impetus, how the General was an exceptional man precisely because he was sustained by faith. Giving way to my enthusiasm, I took out my notes and, with a trembling voice, read him the General's "prayer," the one he published in his *Egypt Journal* in April 1941: *I am a free Frenchman. I believe in God and in my Fatherland's future... I have but one goal: to liberate France.* To my great disappointment, however, I saw my great-uncle's white brow frown at my lyricism.

"Hmm. Yes, there are studies on that question, but what surprises me is the angle you are choosing, which is overly pompous. I don't believe that de Gaulle had that motivating force, at least certainly not in public. I think that it is a reality that deserves to be treated in greater depth, in the mystery of the soul, and not in grandiloquent sentences. True, he was marked with the seal of God from childhood in his devoutly Catholic family. For instance, we know that a statue of Our Lady of Faith stood over the house where he was born, in Lille, and that he received baptism five hours after birth even though his health was not in danger. He also was an altar boy, which garnered him a perfect mastery over the Mass that would surprise his aides-de-camp. Did you know that he came here, by the way?"

My feigned surprise visibly pleased my great-uncle, who began giving me all that his encyclopedic mind possessed on my topic by way of anecdote.

"De Gaulle was seventeen and, at the time, he was studying with the Jesuit Fathers. During his summer vacation of 1907, he went to Lourdes as a stretcher-bearer. In a letter to his mother, he related that he had witnessed the healing of a young woman who suffered from tuberculosis. The miracle did not receive official recognition, but de Gaulle would remain profoundly affected by it. In his political life, however, he remained discreet and tried not to receive communion in public. It was only after moving to Colombey that he would go to Mass with Yvonne, his wife, and that he would hear sermons, always sitting on the same chair scuffed over the years by the wear of his coat. Otherwise, when he was president of the Republic, he would have private Masses said at the Élysée by Father Louis de la Trinité, who was none other than his nephew, François de Gaulle, whose deep faith impressed him."

"He had a great spiritual ardor, didn't he?"

My great-uncle took off his thick, round wire-rimmed eyeglasses and cleaned them with the rough cloth of his religious habit.

"Ardor... ardor... You want him to be a hero, even in faith! I think that the heart of his relationship with God was neither to be found in his religious observance nor in his intellectual dialogue with Malraux, but rather with Anne."

"Anne?"

"Aha, you haven't done enough work, my boy, if you don't know who Anne is. Charles and Yvonne de Gaulle had a little girl in 1928 named Anne. She was born with Down's syndrome. For the General, this child, whom he loved deeply, was a great mystery."

Getting up with the difficulty typical of very aged people, my great-uncle fetched a book from his library, leafed through it with a sure hand and, after a few moments, read to me:

"Her birth was a trial for my wife and me. But believe me, Anne is my joy and my strength. She is a grace of God in my life. She helps me remain within the modesty of human limitations and powerlessness. She keeps me in the security of obedience to the sovereign will of God... She helps me believe in the possible meaning and end of our lives, in the Father's house, where my daughter Anne will finally find all her grandeur and all her happiness."

My great-uncle continued the story of de Gaulle.

"The General never left his daughter. Every night, he tried to teach her to say a few words of a prayer that never seemed to reach his child's lips. At Anne's death in 1948, he uttered this sentence to Yvonne: '*Now, she is like the others.*'

"But Anne is not quite dead, not even today, because the de Gaulles created a foundation that bears her name. And would you believe that the disabled and often indigent young girls who are received there come on pilgrimage here? They visit Lourdes to share the same wonder that the young Charles de Gaulle had known at the foot of the Massabielle grotto at the age of seventeen. Back in the old days, I accompanied them a few times during their visits. You're right, the General's path was that of faith, but you will surely find a greater treasure in the figure of little Anne than in any human heroism. Regarding Anne, Stanislas Fumet once said that '*she led her father in all his ways of responsibility and risk, solitude and courage, success and failure, which are all the paths of God.*'"

After a good long hour of conversation, there was a knock at the door.

"Sister Anne, you're coming to get us for dinner?"

I followed the two religious to the refectory, not without having been struck by the sister's Christian name and promising myself to remember this unexpected story about a great man transfigured by the simplicity of a child.

AMEN.

LIVES ENTIRELY GIVEN

*Planning the 1981 Eucharistic Congress,
July 16, 1980*

1980 This time, the ball was finally rolling: Father Marcel Mingam had just adjourned the first meeting of the French committee of the forty-second International Eucharistic Congress, of which he was the secretary general. The event he was preparing with his entire team was to take place three years later, on July 15 to 23, 1981, in Lourdes, a town for which he had a special affection. He had visited there often with the military pilgrimage as vicar general of the military chaplaincy. Lourdes had hosted a Eucharistic Congress twice already, in 1899 and 1914, with tens of thousands of people coming from many nations for the occasion. This time, however, it would be the centennial of the very first such congress, the one that took place in Lille in 1881 under the inspiration of a native of Tours, Émilie Tamisier.

"A hundred years," reflected Father Mingam. "The world certainly has changed in a hundred years!" Back then, the idea had been to demonstrate in a solemn, even triumphalistic manner, the Catholic belief in the true presence of Christ in the Eucharist, to a French society that was hostile to the Church and to her teachings. The Paris communards[1] had confiscated Church property in 1871 and had arrested priests; later, the Republican Jules Ferry had created "godless schools." As far as Émilie Tamisier was concerned, for her, a religious of Tours devoted to the perpetual adoration of the Blessed Sacrament that had just been instituted in 1856, the answer was in Christ himself, offered up in the Eucharist.

This time around, thousands of young people were expected to attend, and so the context was no longer anticlerical. Father Mingam and his team had just decided on the theme for the Congress: *"Jesus Christ: Bread Broken for a New World."* Far from seeking to make a show of faith in the Blessed Sacrament, this congress would be all about seeking to deepen the meaning and implications of the Eucharist in the ordinary world. Wasn't this bread of God offered for the salvation of all, to deeply transform the lives of Christians, so that they may be witnesses of the Good News throughout the world?

Conferences, exchanges, crossroads, vigils, concerts… and, above all, Masses, with an attendance sometimes exceeding a hundred thousand people, some of whom hail from different churches – everything must be provided for these pilgrims. For three years, Father Mingam gave himself up to the preparation of this Eucharistic Congress, which would have the unprecedented privilege of being honored by the presence of Pope John Paul II. The date was approaching, slowly but surely…

In the late morning of May 12, 1981, Father Mingam received, in his office of the Our Lady wing, the Vatican's definitive agreement to the congress program: He could breathe easier now. All would go well.

The next day, May 13, Pope John Paul II gave a general audience on Saint Peter's Square at the Vatican. As he stood in his white car and

---

1. The Communards were members and supporters of the Paris Commune. It is the name given to the local authority that ruled Paris from March to May 1871. It is generally presented as espousing an anarchist and/or socialist ideology.

greeted the enthusiastic people as it drove slowly through the square, a madman named Mehmet Ali Agça broke out of the crowd. Two gunshots rang out, and the Pope collapsed into the arms of his secretary. One bullet went right through his abdomen; the other hit his fingers. As the ambulance took off at high speed, the secretary heard the Pope's whispered prayer: "*Jesus, Mary, my Mother.*"

The sight of Pope John Paul II being carried out of the ambulance was reminiscent of Christ being taken down from the cross. Upon his arrival in the hospital, the doctors feared that he was dead. He was given extreme unction, the Sacrament of the Anointing of the Sick. The first blood transfusion failed; the second time, the doctors gave their own blood. Finally, after over five hours of surgery, the Pope seemed to have stabilized. During his convalescence, he spent many hours asking himself questions about this assassination attempt he had just survived. The date drew his attention: May 13, the anniversary of the first apparition of Mary at Fatima!

Later, when the Pope visited his assassin in prison, Ali Agça did not ask forgiveness, but rather asked: "*Why aren't you dead? I am sure my aim was true; the bullet was lethal.*" Ali Agça was not afraid of killing a pope, but now he was afraid of the Lady who had kept him from doing so. "*One hand pulled the trigger, and another guided the bullet,*" confirmed the Holy Father, convinced that Mary had protected him that day.

Fast forward to Lourdes, July 22, 1981. The Mass for the disabled had just begun in the Saint Pius X Basilica when Father Mingam heard a voice reverberating, broadcast by radio through the loudspeakers: "*God has permitted that I should suffer pain and weakness myself, in my own flesh. I feel all the closer to you. I understand your trial all the better. In my flesh I am filling up what is lacking in the afflictions of Christ on behalf of his body, which is the Church (Col 1: 24). I invite you to offer your trial with me to the Lord, who achieves great things through the Cross; to offer it so that the whole Church may know, through the Eucharist, a renewal of Faith and Charity; so that the world may know the benefits of forgiveness, of peace, of love."*

That voice belonged to the Pope! From his hospital bed, he offered the most beautiful of witnesses – the gift of self, united to the gift of Christ on the cross. Is that not the most beautiful Eucharist?

Father Mingam, too, gave of himself unstintingly. The Pope would come to Lourdes just two years later, but the priest would no longer be there to see him: On October 30, 1982, Father Mingam succumbed to a heart attack, dying *"from having borne the weight of the Congress,"* as his eulogist would say.

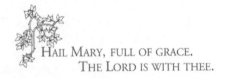

HAIL MARY, FULL OF GRACE.
THE LORD IS WITH THEE.

THE COAT OF LIGHT

The Art of Gemmail,
January 18, 1981

19 81 In the stillness of the early morning, Mathieu leaned over in his workshop to examine his newly colored sheets of glass. The great panes were sorted by hue: The blues ranged from that of a pale winter sky to that of the depths of a roaring sea. Nearby, the greens glimmered with sparks of linden tree, pine, or emerald.

Cold reigned in the workshop that January day, and the glass panes were slightly fogged by the apprentice's rapid breaths. The features of his face tensed up at regular intervals to the rhythm of the pincers cutting through the glass, which cracked and broke into jagged chips. Irregularly shaped strips piled up on the table like a strange monochrome puzzle, ready for assembly as images of light. Long minutes passed on this methodical preparatory work. Yet Mathieu's intensity was obvious, even to the blind old master *gemmiste*[1] sitting in a corner of the workshop,

---

1. Gemmiste: an artist of "gemmail," the process of combining pieces of stained glass to replicate an existing painting by superimposing colors to accurately match each shade in the original. The finished product is called "gemmaux." The art form was developed in the twentieth century.

who could hear with his ears what his eyes could no longer see. He left the young man to his work, but felt his tension.

As he reached for a new pane to cut, Mathieu suddenly shattered the silence with a ear-piercing shout: He had cut his hand by grabbing hold of the glass too quickly. That is one of the worst possible mistakes for a *gemmiste* to make. It is also one of his greatest fears, too – that glass, which would be colored, cut, and reassembled as a beautiful work of art, would turn on him and do violence to the most precious tool of his trade – his fingers, those nimble molders of sharp-edged matter.

Hearing the shout, the old master approached the apprentice with a confident stride.

"Well then, my boy, the day's not off to a good start?"

Mathieu, ashamed, answered in an inaudible murmur.

"Do you want to have a cup of coffee with me, and fix yourself a bandage?"

The invitation was insistent, and so the young artist complied. The two men sat in a window seat over steaming cups of coffee.

"Not too happy today, are you?"

Mathieu, taken aback by the accuracy of this judgment, was suddenly overcome by a need to speak openly that was uncharacteristic of his natural reserve.

"That's right, I slept poorly, and I've been on edge since I got up. It's these *gemmaux* for Lourdes! I don't have the faith, and it's getting on my nerves to be working on this pious claptrap."

"Ah… I see!"

A glimmer of understanding flashed across the old master's blind eyes.

"I was wondering what was irritating you so. The fact is, you don't know our work well enough yet. In six months, you've learned some rudiments, of course, but you mustn't have grasped the true mystery of our art. Remember that you wouldn't be here without the tenacity of three men who dedicated their lives to inventing this means of expression.

"Jean Crotti was the first to develop this art of light. His efforts ran into technical difficulties, though: His *gemmaux* didn't survive bad weather. He would have lost confidence entirely if Roger Malherbe-Navarre and his son hadn't picked up where he left off and discovered the famous secret 'binding agent' that we apply to our assembled glass pieces to join them before baking them. You couldn't even use the glass panes you were just now angrily cutting if those two men hadn't done their research. You are an 'heir' of this art, in a way. But those men haven't just left you their knowledge as a legacy; they've handed on their faith, too.

"Haven't you noticed what is written over the workshop's door? '*The specter of a disconsolate light wanders upon the world... but just a few whose homeland is both snow and summer are enough for day to break...' On our 'drunken boat,'*[1] *as long as artists, as long as souls who thirst for light, tenderness, beauty and love will yet be able to commune, nothing will be lost.* I find that sentence to be very beautiful, and it fits you very well. You may not have the faith, as you put it, but your soul is in love with beauty – it shows in the way you handle glass, like the most beautiful of fabrics – except this morning, of course! We are artisans of light, of human light... and of divine light.

"These *gemmaux* you are preparing for the 'way of light' of the Saint Pius X Basilica, according to Denys de Solère's cardboard patterns, will be an offering of beauty to the sick. They will find comfort and hope in them. Bishop Donze, over ten years ago, issued a call to *gemmistes*. He asked us to help the crowds from all over the world to perceive something of the mystery of light that revealed itself in a hollow of the rock at

---

1. From the title of a poem by Rimbaud, the "drunken boat" is a metaphor for life, in that, even as we pursue our life's journey, our path leads increasingly out of our control, thus forcing us to give up more of our self-determination.

Massabielle. You're not making 'pious claptrap.' Quite the contrary, you are offering to God a new face, an exceptional face. And if you do not know him, you will meet him in the *gemmail* by the way you overlay the glass pieces you have blown, molded, and scored to obtain the correct interpretation of a pattern by Agostini, Solère, Guitton and so many others. The great artists didn't fail to take note: Picasso, Braque, Rouault and Cocteau closely watched the birth of this singular new language of art and beauty.

"As for me, I'm going to reveal to you – before I let you get back to work – the conviction that guided my life and my vocation back when my eyes were able to see the light of day. We're like Saint Martin. We are traveling the path of artists, and along the way we pass by paupers – paupers in heart, in happiness, in health. We give them half of our coat, our *gemmail,* that unique one-off image in which we have patiently mixed color, care, toil, and talent. We offer what is best in us to warm the soul of one worse off than we. Perhaps someday we, like Saint Martin, will see Christ wearing this coat of light."

By the time they returned to the workshop, the sun had risen higher in the sky. Without a word, Mathieu was back at his bench. His hands gently caressed the glass, and his careful rubbing of the strips was the most beautiful answer to the old master's ears.

Blessed art thou among women, and blessed is the fruit of thy womb, Jesus.

THE PHILOSOPHER AND THE MYSTERY

Portrait of the Philosopher Jean Guitton,
October 1, 1981

1981 The man was not very tall. Despite the fact he was approaching his eightieth birthday, his eyes sparkled with youth through his big eyeglasses. With eyes filled with joy and good will, he scanned the faces of the graduates of the Lourdes International Biennial Event of Sacred Art *Gemmail.* He was there because his friend Roger Malherbe-Navarre, the event's organizer, had asked him to say a few words during the ceremony.

"Chance led me to meet Mr. Malherbe-Navarre and to discover *gemmail.* I then entered into the understanding of an art that goes beyond stained glass or enamel, and whose essence I should like to attempt to define."

Jean Guitton, the famous philosopher, friend of Pope Paul VI, is also a painter. As a young man just out of school, he had made a decision: He would take an interest in everything. He kept his word. The philosopher, who studied what is permanent and eternal and nourished himself at all the sources of culture, took an interest in all human questions and pursuits.

A few long rounds of applause, handshakes, and embraces later, the graduation ceremony was over. The participants then gathered around the buffet, cordially chatting about creation, Lourdes, and religious art. A lady journalist approached the small group that had formed around the philosopher.

"Maestro, would you be willing to answer two or three questions?"

Jean Guitton smiled at the young woman.

"I'm not the star today," he replied. "All these artists who seek to allow the mystery of God to appear through their works are the stars. They're the ones you should interview. Nevertheless, I wouldn't mind answering your questions."

Roger Malherbe-Navarre accompanied the philosopher and the journalist to a corner of the room where a table and some chairs had been assembled. They sat down and soon were joined by a few artists interested in their conversation.

"What is your interest in the *gemmail* technique, Mr. Guitton?" the journalist asked. "As a painter, have you every used it?"

"I tried to say so in my address. It seems to me that *gemmail* introduces depth into light. In passing through thin layers of glass, the light beam acquires brightness, phosphorescence, splendor. A while ago, I mentioned Solomon and the "brightness" of light of which he speaks in the Book of Wisdom – something that goes beyond human light to assimilate itself to God's light, that clarity with which Christ's transfigured body shone, the clarity we shall possess after the resurrection of the flesh. That is why I had created a *gemmail* representing the holy shroud of Turin for the Sixth *Gemmail* Biennial Event. The promise of eternal life seemed to be announced through the brightness that illuminated the image of the dead Christ. It was a little like the heavens passing from darkness to light behind the Golgotha scenes of the empty tomb in Italian paintings."

The journalist sought clarification. "So for you, *gemmail* is particularly adapted to revelation, in which religious art works participate."

"Quite," replied Guitton. "There is something in that technique that bonds light and matter, that gives a new and brilliant depth to the work, that reveals the true dimension of creation – its divine dimension."

"In that case," she proferred, "it is normal that *gemmail* should be the art of Lourdes and that this biennial meeting should take place in the town where the Virgin appeared."

"I don't know whether it's normal, but the image is indeed evocative," he answered. "In Bernadette's description, I believe, the Virgin is surrounded by light. She *is* light. Now, revelation is a new light shed on the world, an illumination of the world as it truly is, God's creation in the light of God's Spirit."

"You have written about Mary and have often spoken of God. Is Lourdes an important place for you?" the writer asked.

"Lourdes is important first of all because here we are in the presence of Revelation," was Guitton's response. "We were just talking about the light of *gemmail* and its link to Revelation. But Lourdes is also the place of little particular revelations that are most often discreet and anonymous. I knew a man who was healed during the Blessed Sacrament procession. He had had a terrible train accident and was healed. These unexplainable phenomena, these miracles one can live or glimpse at Lourdes, are revelations in the sense that they shed new light on our way of seeing and understanding the world."

The journalist put Guitton to the test: "One is always surprised when one hears an intellectual like you believing in miracles."

He had a ready answer. "You're reminding me of my friend, Pope Paul VI. At the time – it was in 1950 – he was only Father Giovanni Montini, and worked in the Vatican Secretariat of State. He wanted to meet to talk about my book on Mary. I had written that book after my five years in captivity with my cellmates – Jews, unbelievers,

Protestants – who were surprised to see me reciting the rosary. I still remember what Father Montini told me: '*You are an intelligent man, with that French, critical turn of mind... yet you have the same devotion as a woman from the illiterate people.*'"

A big burst of laughter coursed through the group, thus putting an end to the interview. As he was getting up, Guitton touched the journalist's arm and, looking at her half in earnest and half smiling, went on to say:

"You know, that quote makes you laugh. But putting me aside, it says something fundamental about man.

"All men have a need to find cracks of light in the darkness of their ordinary senses and of their finite minds. At times, we simply need to let go of our will, our reason, our analytical intelligence. Lourdes is the town where, at the end of the twentieth century, one can believe that a miracle is still possible.

"In that sense," the philosopher closed, "Lourdes is perhaps the most metaphysical town in the universe!"

HOLY MARY, MOTHER OF GOD,

THE MIRACLE-STRUCK WOMAN
OF THE COMPANIONS OF EMMAUS

Lucie Coutaz, Abbé Pierre's Secretary,
May 16, 1982

1982 From her bed, Lucie Coutaz watched Abbé Pierre and waved goodbye as he left her room. He, like her, knew she was living her last days, that she was preparing for the last journey, that "long vacation." He had to leave for Rome that May day of 1982, and she did not wish him to change his schedule on her account. She had been Abbé Pierre's secretary for forty years. For forty years, with him, she had been at the service of those who suffer. She watched him leave with great affection.

Lucie still remembered the first time she saw the abbé. It was in Grenoble, during the war. Their common friend, Father Henri de Lubac, had mentioned her to him, and he had come to meet her at her work, in the Social Information Bureau on Belgrade Street. At the time, the abbé was helping Jews who wanted to cross over into Switzerland. He was also the editor of a bulletin for young people who had gone underground – *L'Union patriotique indépendante* ("The Independent Patriotic Union").

She had received him at her house that very night along with one of his friends, a six-foot-six giant of a man, ironically named Little Louis, who was preparing to go underground. From that day on, she served as secretary for the bulletin, which she would type and prepare. After General Descours' visit, the abbé had joined the organized Resistance, and the Belgrade Street office had become a source of information for the local Resistance movement. Lucie was very lucky that she was never arrested. Since that time, she had never left Abbé Pierre.

She wasn't afraid of this last trip. She suffered and awaited deliverance all the more joyfully knowing that she would finally see the One who had been accompanying her for so many years. Christ was the companion who gave all members of the priest's Emmaus Community the strength to continue the struggle day after day. Christ remained alongside them, greeting, caring for, helping, and giving hope to all those who knocked at the door of these homes she had created with the priest known as the "pope of the poor."

The last journey... She remembered the first, and how painful it was. It was a journey she spoke so little of all these years, but one that remained with her every day. At the time, she wasn't yet the "Abbé's Lulu," whom the companions found rather difficult to deal with but in whom all acknowledged the personal qualities of a leader. No, at the time she was the daughter of a poor traveling salesman in the village of Trinité, in Savoy, France, laid out on a board all day as she was now, rendered motionless by a tubercular growth resulting from Pott's disease that blocked her vertebrae. Her only pastime back then was to embroider liturgical vestments that her parish friends had made, or decorative designs for the lady at the village delicatessen.

She owed her friends everything. They were the ones who, at a parishioner's suggestion, paid for the pilgrimage to Lourdes that was to change her life. They had collaborated to raise the necessary funds for her to seek her healing there rather than wait for it in prayer. They even gave her pocket money! Lucie still laughed about it.

The trip itself was horrible. It was September 8, 1921, the feast of the Nativity of the Virgin. She had to stand nearly the entire day. Leaving the station on foot, she walked three quarters of the way without being able to lie down, for the pilgrimage organizers forgot to arrange for a stretcher for her. Once in Lourdes, the pilgrims went directly to Mass, where she had to receive communion standing.

She could still recall that first night. She had stashed some cookies under her bed, but had neither the courage nor the desire to eat them. The next day and the day after that, she followed the usual routine – pool, grotto, Blessed Sacrament procession – by car, of course, with leg extensions because the seated position caused her too much pain. One of the stretcher-bearers from her own Saint Bruno's Parish was very kind and joked a little with her. Many of those with disabilities around her had just returned from the war. She was just about the only woman in the group.

On the third day, as Lucie emerged from the pool, she felt something. It was not a sensation of being healed, but rather an overpowering feeling of well-being. She felt herself filled with peace so strongly that it caused her to forget her pain. Her transformation must have been obvious because the stretcher-bearer looked at her with surprise when she got back into the car.

That evening, she related her story to the physician. Nevertheless, the disease had already reasserted itself. The doctor called her a "silly goose" and told her that the Virgin Mary would finish the job the next day.

The doctor may have been kidding, but he wasn't altogether wrong. The next day, after her trip to the spring water and her kiss to the Virgin statue, she went again to the pools. As she came out of the pool, she had the same feeling as the day before. Although she was prepared to receive the peace she felt, she still was not sure whether she had been healed. Yet that day she walked around the grotto alone, without assistance, and free of pain.

She could still recall her companions' faces. Since the night before, word had been circulating that she had been healed, and everyone looked at her with joy and astonishment.

In order to be sure of her healing, however, Lucie asked a friend to take her by car over a little stream on the way to the grotto. Although it was indeed a tiny, insignificant stream, it previously had caused her enormous pain at every passage because of the wheels' jolt on the uneven road. That day, however, her back no longer felt the shock. She had no more pain her body – only a great shiver in her heart. Now she was sure that this was a healing.

These memories returned to her as she lay on her bed awaiting that final journey. She often thought of that stream whenever she looked at the two little statues that stood on her night table, one depicting the scourging of Christ and the other a weeping Our Lady of La Salette. At the memory of her pain and deliverance, she prayed for all those she had taken in during her forty years by Abbé Pierre's side, since Georges, the first companion of Emmaus. Soon she would rest beside him, she hoped, in the soil of Esteville where he had once lived, in the shade of the great statue of the reclining Christ.

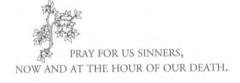

PRAY FOR US SINNERS,
NOW AND AT THE HOUR OF OUR DEATH.

A Bridge over the Iron Curtain

Czestochowa and Lourdes, Twin Cities,
August 26, 1982

19 82 It was never pleasant for soldiers of the Polish Communist Army to sniff the "opiate of the people," as Karl Marx characterized religion. Fortunately, their orders required them to park their armored cars at some distance from the Mass that took place in Czestochowa that summer morning. Perched on the turrets of their tanks, they watched the ceremony from afar, circling the town without besieging it. Just in case, their cannons were directed at the altar where Archbishop Józef Glemp of Warsaw and Gniezno, the primate of Poland, was officiating.

Religion! In Poland, more than in any other country in the Communist bloc, it was the nightmare of every leader and of every person devoted to Marxist doctrine. In a country that remained obstinately Catholic, the Church had not even had to bury herself in the catacombs: She remained standing, insolent, ever present. Every persecution seemed to make her stronger, more faithful. Seminaries had moved abroad, forming legions of future priests. Vocations crisis? In Poland, this expression had no meaning.

To be sure, the Church was peaceful. The soldiers assigned to watch this Mass that celebrated the six-hundredth anniversary of the Jasna Gora shrine, in Czestochowa, knew this. She was peaceful, yes, but she also was bound up with the agitators of Solidarity, a labor union led by Lech Walesa, who had become a thorn in the side of the Communist regime.

Two years before to that very day, Solidarity had wrested from the government the Gdansk agreements authorizing the creation of independent unions. The consequences of this liberalization were not long in coming. Demonstrations and political troubles erupted, so much so that in December 1981, General Wojciech Jaruzelski, the new head of state, declared a state of war in order to intimidate the people. He was wasting his time!

The volatile international scene did not help him either, to say the least. Since 1978, a Polish pope had been in residence at the Vatican. Furthermore, Karol Wojtyla, now Pope John Paul II, wasn't just anyone. The police had been gathering files on him ever since he had become the archbishop of Crakow, the system's irrepressible adversary. This dangerous individual now had the best possible pulpit from which to encourage dissidence against repression.

Pope John Paul II even succeeded in slipping a grain of sand into the agreement that had existed until then between Jaruzelski and the all-powerful Soviet premier Leonid Brezhnev. In 1979, the Pope asked to visit Poland. In spite of Brezhnev's directives, Jaruzelski did not dare refuse, fearing the Catholic people's indignation. From then on, Polish-Soviet relations were never quite as cordial as before.

This time, anyway, Jaruzelski had not repeated his gesture of openness to the Church. The Pope had wished to be present at the Jasna Gora celebration, but this new trip was forbidden to him. While Archishop Glemp was celebrating the Mass, the Pope celebrated his own in his chapel at Castel Gandolfo. His only consolation was that he was praying under the statue of the Black Virgin of Jasna Gora herself, which had been installed there by Pope Pius XI. In Czestochowa, on the seat that would have been for the Pope had he been there, a bouquet of flowers symbolized his presence.

Failing the Pope, another visitor received permission to go to Jasna Gora – Father Bordes, rector of the Lourdes shrines. He brought in his luggage the beautiful ceramic chalice that had been made for the preceding year's Eucharistic Congress. He offered it, with trembling hands, to Archbishop Glemp, for Czestochowa. On that day, representatives of the two Marian towns, Lourdes and Czestochowa, signed a pact of friendship by officially becoming twin cities! It is a double bond, because it involves both the dioceses and the municipalities. From that day onward, a bridge crossed the Iron Curtain to unite two towns that had everything in common – their history marked by the Virgin, the crowds of pilgrims they receive, their pride of place in the hearts of popes and of the entire Church.

The twinning is more than spiritual: It is also worth its weight in provisions and supplies. From the very beginning, Father Bordes entrusted the organization of a Polish relief committee to a shrine priest from Spain. At least once a year, Father de Antonio would go on the road with a truck containing thirty-five tons of foodstuffs. These expeditions – which, like all travels into occupied lands, were epic – wove solid and concrete bonds between the twin cities.

The pact forged under the watch of armored cars that August day in 1982 would come to an end a few years later after the liberation of Poland. The bishop of each diocese then reckoned that humanitarian aid had to come to an end, since the Polish population no longer needed assistance. It was up to the Catholics of each city, however, to remain united in prayer just as they were in the welcome of pilgrims. To this day, Lourdes and Czestochowa each receive about five million visitors every year.

The common history of the two cities is not over, for the twinning of the municipalities continues. In Lourdes, the Blue Star Association is in charge of maintaining, year after year, these privileged bonds with the Polish city. Trips are organized on either side. In 2004, the Poles were received in Lourdes as if in their own home; in 2006, it was the residents of Czestochowa who received the citizens of Lourdes with open arms. At every encounter, each prepared with brotherly care the programs, exchanges, and warm-hearted ceremonies that allowed all participants to deepen a relationship that everyone wished to perpetuate.

In 2008, as Lourdes prepares to celebrate the sesquicentennial of the apparitions, her friendship with her six-hundred-and-six-year-old elder sister is not about to fade. Despite the shrines' difference in age, the two cities feel like twins more than ever!

AMEN.

THE POPE OF FREEDOM

Pope John Paul II's First Visit to Lourdes,
August 11, 1983

1983 The explosion made the bedroom windows rattle and awakened Archbishop Gérard Defois in the middle of the night. The archbishop wondered for a moment whether the violent sound was just a nightmare, but the commotion in the adjacent rooms confirmed that the explosion was indeed real. He jumped out of bed in haste to find out what was going on.

He soon learned that Pilate's Station on the Espélugues Way of the Cross had just been dynamited. The Roman procurator's head was found on the Rosary esplanade. The damage was only material, fortunately, but Archbishop Defois was truly shaken by the vandalism.

The secretary general of the French Conference of Bishops had arrived in Lourdes just a few hours beforehand with a heavy responsibility – to ensure maximum security for the Pope's visit to Lourdes. The city of Lourdes, of course, is very familiar with mass gatherings, but this would be the first time that she would welcome a pope. A giant podium had to be erected, a press room had to be created, and direct telephone lines to the Vatican had to be installed. Above all, security had to be completely overhauled. Archbishop Defois and the organizers reviewed all the new installations as well as the timetable of the celebrations and of the movements of the Pope, who was to arrive two days later. And now a bomb had exploded in the shrine!

His efforts were clearly not in vain. Archbishop Defois was well aware that the Pope's visit did not elicit unanimous enthusiasm. A church had been set on fire in Saintes. Bomb threats had been received by telephone, announcing that the grotto itself was to be targeted. The bishops' secretary general felt the heavy burden of his responsibility. The awful Saint Peter's Square assassination attempt still haunted him. That had transpired just two years before, and the emotion he had felt at the sight of the Pope collapsing under the fire of a fanatic, the anxious wait during the hours of surgery, and finally the sense of relief at the news that Pope John Paul II was out of danger – it was all still fresh in his memory. He had been scheduled to visit Lourdes a few days later, but the assassination attempt had kept him from doing so.

In this month of August 1983, the Pope decided to accomplish this pilgrimage which he had been unable to do in 1981. His devotion to Mary was universally well known. *Totus tuus* ("All Yours"), which came from a longer prayer of entrustment to Mary attributed to Saint Louis Marie Grignon de Montfort, was the motto he had chosen upon his election.

Pope John Paul II wished to come before the grotto as a pilgrim, as a convalescent. The Saint Peter's Square assassination attempt ought to have killed him. The Virgin Mary – of this he was certain – had diverted the bullet that should have struck him full in the heart. This Lourdes pilgrimage was thus also the personal act of thanksgiving of a man who had miraculously survived his wounds. For the bishops of France and the event's organizers, this joy they shared with the Pope was mingled with concern.

On August 14, when the papal airplane landed at the airport of Tarbes just after three o'clock in the afternoon, the security detail was on maximum alert and the crowd was beside itself with joy. French President François Mitterrand, brushing aside the anticlericalism present in part of his constituency, greeted Pope John Paul II with these words: *"The institution that so deeply and intimately marked universal history, particularly the history of my own country, and which remains a living spring from which so many of our citizens continue to draw their reasons for hope."* The private conversation he had with the Pope at the prefecture of Tarbes immediately afterward lasted over an hour.

After the president's departure, the Pope reassumed his role as pastor. *"Blessed be God,"* he proclaimed from the podium before three hundred thousand pilgrims, *"for having prepared here, for Bigorre and the Pyrenees, for France, for the entire Church, such a place of prayer, of gathering for the faithful, of reconciliation!"*

"I had desired, with a great desire, this pilgrimage," he continued. *"God is now fulfilling me among you."*

He then went to the grotto where, in Saint Bernadette's footsteps, he went through the pilgrim's motions: He drank from the source, touched the rock, and kissed the ground. After lighting a candle, he entered into a long and silent prayer at the foot of the altar. Then he followed the usual itinerary of the torchlight procession, leaving it to the chaplains to lead the prayers and intone the customary chants that he continued, following their lead.

When the procession ended, night had fallen on the Rosary esplanade. The Pope stood out, a white, motionless figure on the basilica's terrace, before the crowd massed below. Archbishop Defois, standing three feet away from the small pulpit, felt the pressure of the crowd at his back. Seeing all these people so close to the Pope, he was struck with fear. With some effort, he redirected his attention to the Pope's address.

He had expected an exhortation to prayer, but he heard something quite different.

Pope John Paul II was addressing himself to the crowd and, through it, to all those listening to him on the radio, on television, beyond borders, and even behind the Iron Curtain that still heavily divided Europe. He evoked those pilgrims who were unable to come because they were oppressed by a regime, stifled for want of freedom. He encouraged them, hoping that, from Lourdes, his words might cross over all "iron curtains" and all walls. "*I knew that, at Lourdes, my speech would be free and that it would be broadly relayed by the media,*" he was to explain a few weeks later to the president of the French Conference of Bishops. Pope John Paul II, media pope? This wasn't an empty reputation, and he went on to play an active role in the collapse of communism in 1989.

The next day, August 15, the Pope celebrated the Mass of the Assumption on the meadow, facing the grotto. That afternoon, he met with young people in a great movement of enthusiasm. Then he spent some time among the sick, to whom he delivered a meditation on suffering.

"*Whatever its nature, be first clearly conscious of it, and then accept it, because the Lord can and wants to draw good out of evil,*" he told them. "*He is inviting you to be as active as you can despite your illness.*"

Twenty-one years later, the Pope would return to Lourdes, worn out by illness yet animated with a tireless will, living in his flesh what he had preached among the sick years before.

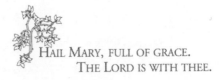

HAIL MARY, FULL OF GRACE.
THE LORD IS WITH THEE.

Making the Mystery Come Alive Again

Jean Delannoy, Filmmaker of the Apparitions,
January 18, 1987

19 87 Near a rocky channel, a young girl with an angelic face was sitting while others on the opposite bank were picking up dead branches and gathering them into bundles. On a felled tree trunk, the youth was gathering her strength, slowly doffing her clogs. A slight wind raised her woolen shawl. She gently lifted her face, which suddenly was beaming, and then she opened her eyes wide. A little farther off, facing her, a tight little crowd was observing without making a sound, massed on either side of some equipment that was complex and quite anachronistic in such a landscape. A camera was fixed upon a dolly, with microphones, and a whole apparatus of machines were poised in a studious moment: Mary's first apparition to Bernadette was being staged for the movies in the early days of 1987.

"Cut!" The little troupe dispersed, broke the silence, and got moving. At the riverside, the youth slowly got up. While the team was busying itself in an energetic ballet around the set, the director remained motionless in his chair for a moment. He was the one to give the signal, and yet the old man's gaze remained lost in contemplation of the young woman who lent her face to the little messenger and around whom the make-up artists were already at work. *I am Bernadette*, he thought, smiling at his aping of Flaubert regarding Madame Bovary.

The filming of *Bernadette* had just begun, and although Jean Delannoy – the great director of *La Symphonie pastorale* and *Notre-Dame de Paris* – waited until the twilight of his life to undertake this motion picture, the project had long been close to his heart. He was certainly not the first to film Bernadette's story or to bring his camera to the heart of the Marian town. Lourdes had quickly attracted the favors of the cinema after the apparitions first occurred, and Bernadette's destiny had often been filmed. Already in the silent era there had been many productions that had captured Bernadette and her native town, the apparitions, the miracles, and the pilgrimages in pictures. Many, in fact, had been screened on location, presented by the small Bigorre community's chaplains.

If Delannoy, at almost eighty years of age, decided to take his turn at dealing with Bernadette's destiny, it was not merely to give the sense of the sacred back to an age in which spirituality was sorely lacking. Rather than focusing on the saint's hagiography, it was Bernadette's determination that held his interest. It was the determination of a resolute young Lourdes girl, taken up in a destiny that was too great for her but which the ceaseless dance of skeptics and the powerful was never quite able to shake. He made this determination his own by seeking to stand as closely as possible to the little messenger's truth and candor and to draw the most accurate and most human portrait of her.

"*I am charged with telling you about it, I am not charged with making you believe it.*" It was these words of Bernadette's that Delannoy had in mind when he finally joined the actress. He had just realized in that moment that he had made these words his own, without even noticing.

Asking the make-up artists and the technicians to leave them alone for a while, Delannoy sat on the stump where, a little earlier, the young girl had been miming Bernadette's dazzled response. In a few choice words, the director reassured the young actress who was worried about her performance. The take was a good one; Delannoy was satisfied. Reassured but still trembling a bit, the adolescent calmed down a little.

Her task was not an easy one: Unlike *The Song of Bernadette* – the Hollywood portrait based on Franz Werfel's work, filmed forty years before by Henry King – Delannoy had decided not to show the Virgin appearing to Bernadette. It was only through the actress's eyes that the spectator would see, if he so wished. But observing the young Sidney Penny, for whom this was her first big role, the director felt his last hesitations vanish. He was Bernadette, but above all, she was Bernadette. In the gentle candor that never left the actress's features, Delannoy recognized, as he had always imagined it, the face of the little messenger from Massabielle. As if to reassure her completely, he once again confided his faith in her as the team was already setting up for the next scene.

It was only at the filming of the final scene a few weeks later at the Nevers convent that Delannoy would finally grasp what had always fascinated him about Bernadette's destiny. The scene was the arrival in the convent, and it was Sidney Penny's last line. Smiling at a sister who was stunned by her fragile appearance, Bernadette naïvely said: "*Yes, this is all there is to Bernadette!*" And the filming was over.

What Delannoy most wished to capture in pictures, from the first Massabielle apparition to the departure from Lourdes – and soon, in the sequel to his film, to evoke the passion of Nevers – was the story of Bernadette among men. It was the story of her innocence before prelates, the rich, the jealous; it was the story of her torment before the interrogations, the doctors' examinations and those of the episcopal commission. For this great reader of Victor Hugo, it was the eternal story of the little people against the powerful.

One last time, the director joined his young actress to congratulate her, and once again, she could not quite believe it. Touched, thanking the adolescent whose shy gaze looked downward as her cheeks blushed, Delannoy thought back to the day of the auditions. Sidney never stopped having doubts. And on that day, it had been precisely this reserve, this gracious innocence that had attracted him, just as it was Bernadette's innocence that had always overcome him. "*I give praise to you, Father, for although you have hidden these things from the wise and the learned you have revealed them to the childlike*": As he smiled on the young actress, it was those words of the Gospel according to Saint Matthew that came back to Jean Delannoy while the camera was being packed up behind him.

BLESSED ART THOU AMONG WOMEN,
AND BLESSED IS THE FRUIT OF THY WOMB, JESUS.

Under the Sign of the Rosary

Jean-Pierre Bély, Sixty-Sixth Miraculous Healing,
October 9, 1987

1987 It was October 1988. Alain Marchio, who was in charge of the stretcher-bearers attached to Saint Patrick's hall at the Our Lady Welcoming Center, checked that all the sick were comfortably settled on this fourth and last day of the yearly Rosary Pilgrimage.

His gaze lingered on a fifty-year-old hospitaller who was busy with a handicapped man.

"Is everything all right, Jean-Pierre?"

"Everything is all right, Alain."

Jean-Pierre Bély dedicated himself unstintingly. He looked after the most handicapped persons, helped the sick settle in, pulled the carts, and lent his ear to one and all. His experience as a nurse made him an excellent volunteer, quick to anticipate needs. Who could have guessed that this man, in full possession of his means, had been bedridden just a year before, laying on this very stretcher, his body broken by a multiple sclerosis that had nailed him to his bed? Had he not just been declared definitively a one-hundred-percent invalid by the Social Security Administration?

Marchio could still see him in bed, unable to sit up in his wheelchair, to such a point that a stretcher had to be fetched for the ceremonies in which Jean-Pierre was set on participating, after some hesitation, during the Rosary Pilgrimage, and of which he was to say: "*I discovered a feeling of love that liberates.*"

Liberation and confidence were the key words of the pilgrimage that Jean-Pierre undertook in October 1987.

Liberation was there from the beginning of the journey spent in song and in prayer, where the thought of Lourdes lessened the pains of his curled-up position. He found confidence when, as he went by the grotto of the apparitions, he whispered: "*Lord, you know me better than I do. You know what is good for me; you will know to give me the best you have.*" Surprise and confidence came when one of the ladies in white on the esplanade came to him and said, "*Don't be afraid! Have confidence! Mother Mary will put all of this to good order.*" There was liberation again when, on Thursday, he received the Sacrament of Reconciliation from a chaplain: "*And I absolve you from your sins in the name of the Father, of the Son, and of the Holy Spirit. Amen.*"

When the chaplain suggested that he take part in the anointing of the sick the next day, he joyfully accepted. From the very beginning, he felt as though he was growing wings. Nothing weighed him down, neither the need to get up early to attend the eight o'clock Mass, nor the pools, although he had anticipated them with horror. Everything seemed simple to him. Liberated from his apprehensions, he gave himself up completely to the mystery of Lourdes.

On Friday, the sky cleared. At the moment when the chaplain anointed his forehead and hands, everything around him reeled: "*Through this holy anointing may the Lord in his love and mercy help you with the grace of the Holy Spirit. May the Lord who frees you from sin save you and raise you up.*" A feeling of liberation and of interior peace such as he had never felt before overcame him. He felt himself alive again.

Spiritual liberation, forgiveness of sins: Is this not the true message of Lourdes, beyond physical liberation?

Entirely focused as he was on this inner renewal, he did not notice the vigor with which he crossed from the stretcher to the bed. Marchio, fearing this "healing" might be a flash in the pan, asked him to stay still and not to make any more excessively abrupt movements.

"Is everything all right, Jean-Pierre?"

"Everything is all right, Alain."

He had barely lain down on the bed than a strange feeling of inner cold gripped him. Nothing relieved the chill, neither the jacket he threw over his shoulders nor the blanket with which he was covered. Nothing helped either when, a few moments later, he started feeling a gentle warmth that grew in expanse and intensity. Starting from the toes, it crept up his spine and became like a fire moving through every part of his paralyzed body. Not understanding what was happening, he found himself sitting on the edge of his bed, feeling his skin, astonished and surprised to recover sensations he thought were gone for ever.

That evening, he fell into an untroubled sleep. A few hours later, he woke up. The clock struck three at the basilica. All was quiet. Yet he found it impossible to sleep. What happened to the person whose hand he felt on his hip? What was this firm yet delicate invitation he heard: "*Get up and walk?*"

In a state of agitation, he tossed and turned. When the night watch woman came to offer him help, he mentioned his intention to go to the toilet and refused help from a stretcher-bearer. Without actually realizing what was happening to him, he got up and, *like a child learning how to walk*, he staggered to the toilet and then went back to bed. Lying in the dark, he went over the story of the healed paralytic[1] who, once his heart had been healed – "*your sins are forgiven*" – experienced the healing

---

1. Mk 2: 1-12.

of the body – "*Rise, pick up your mat, and walk.*" Unable to calm down, he began to pray the rosary. Although he usually fell asleep before finishing the first decade, he recited a whole rosary until morning as an act of thanksgiving, the very rosary on the mysteries of which he would meditate, some time later, every last Tuesday of the month back in his parish.

Indeed, after this pilgrimage that witnessed his total healing, Jean-Pierre Bély would never cease giving back what he had received, helping his neighbor, tirelessly witnessing to the love of God – simply, in Bernadette's spirit. It was also to give thanks that, a year later, he would agree to have his case written up by the Medical Bureau of Lourdes, and that he would serenely assent to eleven years of medical examinations. These would lead to the declaration of Bishop Jean Pierre Dagens, on February 9, 1999, officially recognizing his healing as "*a personal gift of God and an effective sign of Christ the Savior, which took place through the intercession of Our Lady of Lourdes.*"

In his homily the same day, the bishop underscored the fact that the miraculously healed man was a living witness to two inseparable signs linked to Lourdes: "*The sacramental sign, the anointing with the oil of the sick, and then the physical sign, a healed and so-to-speak risen body.*"

Although he was in perfect health, Jean-Pierre Bély would never be able to return to his position as nurse at the hospital of Angoulême. Although he was officially recognized as the sixty-sixth miraculously healed person of Lourdes, he would for ever remain an invalid in the eyes of the administration.

Holy Mary, Mother of God,

Six Thousand Young People under Mary's Gaze

The Frat, April 2, 1988

19 88 "A good night's sleep, finally," sighed Christine contentedly, trudging over the few knapsacks cluttering the corridor in the train that would bring her back to Paris along with seventy young people from her chaplaincy.

The Frat – the gathering of Île-de-France high school students – was over, and, as Father Antoine, the chaplain accompanying them, saw it, 1988 was a good vintage. Hearing guffaws from the compartments, the young chaplaincy leader did not doubt it. Here and there, in the train that jostled them, small groups had formed around a guitar or a harmonica and the songbooks given out at the beginning of the five days of gathering. Features were drawn: Some eyes were puffy for lack of sleep, but smiles were beaming, and a festive feeling – a "foretaste of heaven," as Father Antoine put it so well – was in the air.

Sticking her head into each compartment, Christine again counted those present to make sure once again that no youngster had been forgotten on the platform. Anything is possible on the return of an assembly gathering close to six thousand people. She was also attentive to the comfort of those who were trying to sleep. The trip was to be long, and the chaplaincy leader had every intention of returning "her" young-sters in proper shape to their parents. The weather, fortunately, was more than clement for the month of March in Lourdes, and no one as much as caught a cold.

"Christine! Are you coming to vote in the contest?"

Boris, the seminarian who came to lend a helping hand to the chap-laincy for the high schoolers' supervision, called out to her, full of mirth, from the end of the corridor. Laughter erupted from the compartment.

"What have you come up with this time, Monsignor?" replied the young woman derisively.

"Your protégés have brought little souvenirs back from Lourdes. Now we have to vote to find out which is, indubitably, the most awful."

Within the compartment, four youngsters – Flore, Lucile, Guilhem, and Paola – were enraptured by their discoveries. They included glow-in-the-dark Virgins, plastic grottoes, and a candlestick Bernadette. The choice turned out to be difficult. The adolescents observed Christine, who feigned indignation.

"Ah, don't tell me that this is all you're getting out of Lourdes and from the Frat, now!" she said.

Laughter ensued. Then an awkward silence followed as gazes turned pensive. So much for the adolescent reserve of youngsters who, naturally, would not answer the question, which in any event required no response. Each one of them relived, in a flash, these five days, which were unfor-gettable for a young high school student.

This was the first Frat for Paola, a small fifteen-year-old brunette. She was supposed to have gone to Jambville[1] the year before, when she was at the middle school chaplaincy, but she had broken a leg just before the

---

1. The Frat of Jambville, in the Paris metropolitan area, has welcomed middle school chaplaincies from the Île-de-France every other year since 1979, thus alternating with the Lourdes high school Frat.

long Pentecost weekend. This Lourdes Frat, which took place during Holy Week, was her first experience of the great chaplaincy gathering.

Paola was a retiring girl. Her shyness, her modesty, had often prevented her from witnessing to her faith. She retained a moving memory of the Pascal Vigil two days before. The gathering in the Saint Pius X Basilica had been grandiose, but that was not what moved her heart. What marked her for life was the night of Easter: These dozens, hundreds of youths her own age were singing at the top of their voices in the streets of Lourdes, arm in arm, as they went back to their hotels: "Risen, Christ is risen, let us announce it in a thousand words to the whole world!"

Did this come out of a need to "party"? Certainly, thought Paola, but not only that. Since then, she felt less alone. Six thousand young people shared her faith in the resurrection that evening and were not afraid of singing it.

The girl's gaze met Lucile's, who smiled at her. A strong friendship had been born during those five days. Lucile, too, had been very impressed by the Pascal Vigil and by the celebrations as a whole. Full of life, the young high schooler often went to Mass grudgingly in her little suburban parish that was practically bereft of those under twenty-five years of age. Here, however, she had been overcome at the sight of several bishops and dozens of priests celebrating Mass together, in a liturgy so beautiful that she didn't even notice the time going by, a Mass organized by an extraordinary group, Bethel, that managed to bring together prayer and a festive spirit.

Flore, for her part, remembered her "crossroads" group. Lively and intelligent, she had dragged her feet a little when, the first day, she went to the gathering of small group meetings that numbered eight randomly chosen youngsters each. After the first meeting, she would not miss a single one for five days. The discussions were so rich, miles away from the idea she previously had of them.

Guilhem, though, was doubtless the most moved of the four. It was his first time in Lourdes. Contrary to his friends, who had no clear idea of this pilgrimage destination, this youngster had been impatiently waiting to go. His great-grandfather had gone on the very first Frat, in 1908, with the other twenty boys under Father Caillet's patronage. His father, too, went in 1958, to the great gathering commemorating the apparitions' centennial. In those days, the Frat was not coed: "Fratteux" (for the boys) and "Bernadettes" (for the girls) alternated every other year until the unification of the two branches in the early 1970s.

Ever since that 1958 Frat, Bertrand, Guilhem's father, had gone back to Lourdes every summer at the Assumption as a stretcher-bearer. Now Guilhem understood what motivated him. He, too, was profoundly touched by the faith of the sick who, despite their suffering and their weakness, retain their smile and their total confidence in the love of God. He decided to ask his father whether he could accompany him that summer.

Father Antoine, the chaplain, was quite right: Frat 1988 was a good vintage. That year again, six thousand young people went back home filled with the Holy Spirit to proclaim the Gospel and, like the Virgin Mary, to cast a softer gaze upon the world around them.

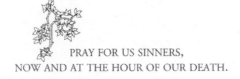

PRAY FOR US SINNERS,
NOW AND AT THE HOUR OF OUR DEATH.

Holidays in the Confessional

Confessions in Lourdes, August 22, 1989

19 89 For a brief interval of respite, Father Paul stretched his legs and rubbed his sore back. It was eleven o'clock in the morning. It had been two hours that the priest had been hearing confessions without a break, and his body recommended itself to his fond recollection, as if to remind him that he was not a youngster anymore. Yet already the confessional's door had opened again to let in a very young girl.

The old priest welcomed her with a smile. In simple words, he invited her to sit or to kneel. Discovering the old priest's lovable and loving face, the young girl relaxed. It was true, then, what she had been told that morning about the Sacrament of Reconciliation: The priests are not there to judge; rather, they are but the instruments of God's infinite mercy.

Father Paul tenderly observed the one who had just knelt before him. She was a little awkward, intimidated, doubtless not too used to coming to reconcile with God. In fact, she pulled out a little square paper that had been slipped deep into her trouser pocket.

"Bless me, Father, for I have sinned," she began to read.

Father Paul cocked his head toward her the better to hear her. His muscles started hurting again, but he soon forgot his discomfort. He was listening…

"Paul, when you hear confessions, don't just hear what the penitent is telling you. Listen to him!" his superior had taught him in major seminary. "Listen and pray! Pray that the Lord will whisper the words that will guide the Christian in his search for God, in his deep desire no longer to offend him. Pray the Lord to point out to you how to comfort the person who is coming to confide in him, to give him hope and to help him to leave fully aware of God's incredible mercy in his life."

The young girl stopped talking. She was waiting, watching the man pray at her side. Then, slowly, Father Paul raised his head. He smiled.

"Do you know the Act of Contrition?" he asked in a gentle voice.

The penitent seemed to have lost her bearings. She had not expected that! It wasn't on her little piece of paper! What is this Act of Contrition? Father Paul reassured her:

"Do you simply have a little phrase to beg the Lord's forgiveness?"

The young girl's features settled. So that was all! She reflected for a moment.

"Forgive me, Lord!" she simply murmured. "And change my heart!" she begged.

The priest was happy. These few spontaneous words were beautiful. He took his cue from them to speak to the girl and help her put her finger on God's mercy. Then he stretched out his hand over her and said:

"*May God our Father show you His mercy. By the death and resurrection of His Son, He reconciled the world to Himself and He sent the Holy Spirit for the remission of sins. Through the ministry of the Church, may He grant you pardon and peace. And I absolve you of your sins, in the name of the Father, of the Son, and of the Holy Spirit.*"

"Amen."

"Go in the peace and the joy of Christ!"

The young girl did not even take the time to answer; she got up, happy.

"Thank you, Father, thank you!" she stammered as she went to the confessional door. "Thank you, Father!"

The priest leaned back on his chair and once again stretched his legs. What an annoyance, these cramps!

Some time before the summer, when Father Paul had informed his sacristan that he was once again going back to Lourdes to hear confessions, he had received a lecture.

"I just don't understand why you're going back. You're tired! You yourself say that hearing confessions for hours on end hurts your back. And your legs! They can do without you this year, can't they?"

"Yes, but…"

"Don't look for excuses!" the sacristan interrupted. "No one is indispensable."

"You're right; they can probably do without me…"

"You see!"

"But as for me, I cannot do without hearing confessions!"

The sacristan had fallen silent. How was he to respond to that?

It was true, Father Paul could not do without hearing confessions. Offering the Sacrament of Reconciliation was too important. Of course, he was already doing so in his parish. But in Lourdes, things were a little different. Reconciliation was at the heart of every pilgrimage, at the heart of the Virgin Mary's message as well: *"Go drink at the spring and wash there!"* she had said to Bernadette. Yes, in Lourdes, the pilgrims came to wash, to rid themselves of their sins, and to go home with the desire to leave their old life behind.

To be sure, the two weeks the priest took out of his vacation to go to Lourdes every summer was not necessarily restful. As the years went by, his back caused him more and more pain, and he sometimes suffered even in his legs. Psychologically, too, some confessions particularly affected him. Some were simply hard to bear.

Nevertheless, every year, Father Paul would draw from one source or another, among the words of those who opened their hearts to him, to find small treasures of faith, of trust, and of love that deepened his own faith. He would also meet up with many priest friends, regulars of the Reconciliation Chapel – French, Polish, Italian, German, English, Spanish, and Dutch priests who responded to Lourdes' call. Like him, they came to offer God's forgiveness to their brethren. Whatever his sacristan might say, finding friends from every continent, all united in Christ, giving and receiving the profound and sweet mercy of God was a marvelous way of spending a good holiday. As long as God granted him the strength to do so, he would carry on!

Amen.

LIVES THAT ARE GIVEN

Maria de Jésus and Father Jean-Luc Cabes,
June 23, 1990, and May 10, 1991

1991 Leaning over her tiny desk, Maria de Jésus dos Santos wrote whatever crossed her mind in her little notebook. The young woman was writing more than a diary; it was a veritable collection of thoughts. There was only one constant in all the sentences, some of which were scribbled in haste – her love for the Lord.

From his earliest youth, Jean-Luc Cabes had also been writing. He commented on the different events marking his life in notebooks – his family life, his preoccupations as an adolescent, his commitment to the *Mouvement Eucharistique des Jeunes* ("Eucharistic Youth Movement," or MEJ), his questions as a student. Everything was there. In him, too, there was only one constant – his abandonment into the hands of the Lord.

Maria and Jean-Luc didn't know each other. Yet they lived only a few miles from each other.

Maria lived in Lourdes. She was a seasonal hotel worker who tirelessly worked for those around her. This life did not satisfy her completely because she wanted to enter the Carmel. At this point, though, it was still a secret, and nobody knew. "*I know where God wants me... at Carmel,*" she wrote in her diary on May 10, 1990. "*I know that's where it is, and that I shall be happy. I know there will be struggles, but I know that's where it is. I've been seeking for years, and now I have found. I know he had told me already, but I wasn't sure, and I wasn't ready. [...] God has called me; I answer straightaway: Yes.*"

Jean-Luc was in Tarbes. He was ordained a priest on April 16, 1989. He had felt for his entire life that he had been called by the Lord to follow him. How? Where? When? He needed a little time to discover his vocation, but after that he was certain he had made the right choice. "*If God wills it, if the Church wills it, if the Bishop calls me, I want to try to answer the Lord with all my might, to choose Him in turn, to offer my entire life to him, therefore to be a priest some day!*" he wrote in his journal on May 12, 1983.

Maria and Jean-Luc did not know each other. Yet they had much in common. Both lived near the Lourdes shrine. Both went there regularly to renew themselves in prayer. Both were concerned for others, for the young in particular. Both, above all, had a bright and happy faith. And both would give their lives to the Lord, completely.

On June 23, 1990, Maria was lighthearted. Elegantly dressed, she came home after an hour of eucharistic adoration. When her neighbor rang her doorbell to return a cassette tape of religious music, she opened the door smiling and welcoming as usual.

Unfortunately, the young man's intentions were not innocent. He probably had been attracted to this sweet, bubbly, and pretty brunette for some time. That day, he wanted to get physically intimate with her, forcibly if necessary. She refused, and she struggled. Crazed by rage, he strangled her.

A little earlier, Maria had written in her little notebook: "*There is nothing awful to death since, far from taking away life, it changes it into an infinitely better life.*"

On May 10, 1991, Jean-Luc was coming home from Lourdes, where he had just run a preparation meeting for a pilgrimage to Poland. The jovial thirty-two-year-old priest, whose face was swallowed up by an enormous pair of glasses, was nearly home when he noticed a group of youths attempting to steal a car. "*Thou shalt not steal,*" says the Lord. Jean-Luc intervened. In their panic, the youths stabbed him three times.

"*Our passage on earth is brief,*" he had written one day. "*Yet we are responsible for our share in the world's renewal. Every youth, every adult has a role to play in the Church. All the saints answered yes.*"

Did Maria and Father Jean-Luc know that they would die so early and that they would become models of faith for the pilgrims of Lourdes and for the faithful in general? The total gift of their lives for the Lord is an example to follow. "*We are walking together towards that beautiful country; we are walking towards heaven,*" Father Cabes had written to young people. By their witness, they show that holiness is still possible today and every day. By their prayers, they now intercede for those who turn to them.

These two young people's tombs nearly always have flowers, brought there by relatives or by anonymous persons who come to entrust intentions or to thank them for an intercession. For instance, Father Jean-Luc's brother, also a priest, is persuaded that his brother's prayers and those of young Maria have permitted the creation of the Gospel School, which today forms young people in Lourdes. The project had emerged a little before the month of June 1990; it materialized in October 1991. Coincidence of the calendar, or a fruit of the communion of saints?

Maria already had an opinion on the question: "*Our smallest pains, our lightest efforts can, through divine action, reach faraway souls and bring them light, peace, salvation,"* she wrote in her little notebook. *"Sacrifice and work are for us; for God is the action, near or far, that the least of our thoughts and actions will exert upon other souls... Nothing is wasted."*

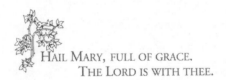

HAIL MARY, FULL OF GRACE.
THE LORD IS WITH THEE.

A Soul on Its Knees

The Alcoholics' Pilgrimage, June 14, 1992

19 92 Mary, tonight I am on my knees before you. The ground in the grotto is cold, but it seems far less hard to me that all the floors my body has sometimes collapsed upon to be left beaten, numb, and painful. I am on my knees, Mary, but I feel far taller than if I were standing. You've carved yourself a space in my chest as big as a cathedral, where all is silence, love, and peace.

Yet – you know this – these past years I have known only shouts, hate, and the night. I wasn't destined to bear pain, though. Born to a good family, I was fortunate enough to take over from my father in the family business. I got married. Above all, I made a lot of money. Too much, perhaps. I thought of my stocks, my real estate investments, and I gladly sacrificed a dinner alone with Françoise, my wife, for professional reasons. I also lied and thereby sacrificed some of my ideals, my convictions, because it was necessary to climb a few more rungs of what I thought was a ladder to success.

With deception and shady financial arrangements, I found myself suddenly alone. Françoise slept next to me, but we were more distant than two strangers: Estrangement, sad silences, and then scorn inexorably took over. When my troubles with the administration began and Françoise came to understand that, besides being absent, I was also two-faced, she left. I had no one.

As for you, Mary, I did not think for a moment that you could help me. I despised God, who seemed to block my projects. I lied even more. I sank deeper, and everything fell apart. What becomes of an exclusively materialistic man when he loses his house, his deluxe car, his expensive clothes, and his fancy watch? Nothing, Mary, nothing. He becomes an empty shell, a burden even to himself.

How I wanted to quiet the laughter of degeneracy that burst out at the corner of every street I wandered on – a window reflecting my sad and unshaven face; a storefront in which were displayed unaffordable shoes that I used to buy, unaware that they could represent weeks of food; couples going into fashionable restaurants while I was alone and sometimes hungry.

I wanted to disappear, Mary, to drown myself alive, and I did it. Alcohol became my only refuge. It numbed my mind and kept me from thinking about what had happened to me in that bottomless pit of waste. I drank with a death wish. Sometimes I drank because the first sips warmed me up or made me a bit happier. But there is always that moment when alcohol becomes a poison that makes a man even uglier, even dirtier. He loses his footing to such an extent that it is often in those times of lost moorings that he gets robbed and beaten. He wakes up with a bloody mouth and the certainty that nothing can save him.

But you were watching, Mary. And I did not know it. On one of those days of horror, I was wandering near Rue Saint-Denis. Amid the shady bars, I saw a church. The door was open. In the chancel there were votive candles around an icon. At a glance, I saw that there were homeless people like me. It so intrigued me that I went in and sat in a corner. Young folks were praying the rosary with street people, peace-fully. Once I got over my surprise, I felt my childhood memories return, memories of Sunday Mass with my grandmother, my mother's ivory chaplet.

But immediately rebellion came, mixed with sarcasm and spite for this God who allowed me to live in such degradation. A mad rage rose up in my throat; everything mixed together, my marriage, my failures, the prison of alcohol.

All at once I heard the very soft voice of a young girl say: "Let us trust Mary. She waits for us to put down our burden at her feet. She will take our souls under her mantle of tenderness and console us of all our afflictions." After that, I didn't hear anything, I was so disturbed... Those words were for me! I was a desperate case for everyone, except for you, Mary! You were waiting for me, and I poured out the flood of my woe into your silent heart. I came back every day. I handed everything to your gentleness – my failings, my misconduct, my regrets. You gave me friends, for the prayer group welcomed me like a long-lost son and helped me find work to get back on track.

A year after this deliverance, you gave me the greatest adventure of my life: I participated in the fourteenth *Eau Vive* ("Living Water") pilgrimage to Lourdes with over seven hundred other brothers who were once sick with alcohol, like me. It's the parish priest who told me about a lady physician, Dr. Marion Cahour, who created this wonderful movement in 1980. Convinced that alcoholism was a disease of the soul, she chose to help the spiritually sick. So she invites them to Lourdes every year, a symbolic place above all others, where a wellspring of graces and beauty flows from the rock, to receive the sacraments the Church offers, with their "compatriots" around them – wives, husbands, parents.

We are now at the last night of this pilgrimage, the last night, Mary. And I don't want to leave the grotto. I'm staying alone, on my knees on this blessed ground. I thank you for these four extraordinary days: I, a man of the world, was able to acknowledge my weakness by holding high a sign that read: "*Jesus, Savior, heal me from alcohol, thank You!*" I, a heartless man, was able to look at my sick brothers with love. I, a lost man, felt surrounded and guided toward the Massabielle spring as to the true heart of my recovered life. Tomorrow, Mary, I shall begin the very beautiful gesture of the Samaritan women that the *Eau Vive* pilgrims customarily make: I will fill a glass of water every night while reciting the Our Father, and every morning I will drink that water, which is like that which Christ offered to the woman at the well, the true water that restores to life.

I am not alone, Mary. You are there, my brothers are there, and most of all *I* am there, present to this life, seeking no longer to destroy it but rather aware of its worth in the eyes of God. I, the prideful, the arrogant, have never succeeded in life better than today, kneeling on my knees before you.

BLESSED ART THOU AMONG WOMEN,
AND BLESSED IS THE FRUIT OF THY WOMB, JESUS.

THE WORKERS OF LIGHT

The Feutiers *("Candlestick Cleaners") of Lourdes,*
August 14, 1993

19
93

Creak! Creak! Creak!

An unpleasant metallic sound made the few pilgrims raise their heads as they were praying at that late hour of the night. It was three o'clock in the morning. A few young people – who had stayed out late in cafés solving all the world's problems – had appointed a time to pray before going to bed. They had taken the winding path, which snakes its way from the top of the Massabielle rock all the way down. The hospitallers on duty in the medical reception areas had also left their posts, relieving each other so that each of them could pray at the grotto. There were at the most about fifteen people present to take advantage of the quiet night to kneel before the statue of the Virgin, which is continuously lit by a candelabrum of ninety-seven candles.

At night, the grotto is a haven of peace where it is good to stop awhile. The ceaseless ruckus that accompanied the passage of the pilgrims before the rock had ended. The heat of the month of August had cooled down. The moment was particularly well-suited to prayer... except for that unbearable scraping!

Creak! Creak! Creak!

The metallic noise picked up worse than ever. One young man, irritated, turned his head toward the intruders. Who dared perturb the silence thus?

"It's beyond belief!" he muttered between his teeth. "Can't they do this later?"

Creak! Creak! Creak!

Apparently not! Those responsible for these noises that broke the nocturnal calm had no intention of postponing their somewhat noisy occupation. They had only three hours for everything to be ready for the approaching new day that would begin at six o'clock with the grotto's first Mass.

The young man made an irritated sign of the cross, stood up, and went to the place from which the scraping noise was coming. He fully intended to make some remark to those who were bothering everyone within earshot.

The noise was coming from the burners, those racks set up next to the grotto for the pilgrims to place their candles. Two shadows were busy there. As soon as he saw them, though, the young man who came to protest knew that he wouldn't say anything unpleasant. The two workers were going about their work in silence, in a meditative sort of mood. They were gathering, sorting, scraping, transporting into their truck's bed – Creak! Creak! Creak! They were organizing, removing, scratching – Creak! Creak! – and returning to the truck's bed in a continuous choreography. They were the *feutiers* who are in charge of the continual maintenance of the flame in Lourdes.

At this point, irritation gave way to curiosity. The young man watched the scene with interest.

In Lourdes, light has a very strong spiritual meaning: There are fragile torches in the Marian processions, votive candles to ask for a grace, and finally tapers to express thanks for prayers granted. A brazier burns permanently near the grotto, patiently minded by these men in blue overalls who watch over the flame day and night. As one taper finishes melting away, another blazes up immediately, bearing a new prayer but the same hope.

The chain of light is uninterrupted in Lourdes. Fire burns there twenty-four hours a day. In the winter, when the shrine is less busy, the *feutiers* light the summer tapers that couldn't be lit at the time for want of space. In that way, prayers continue to rise to heaven without end.

The young man came close to one of the workers, who wore thin gloves to avoid getting burned. In order to clean out the grating of another burner, he moved over tapers that were still lit.

"You don't put them out before you move them?" asked the young man, very attentive to this back-and-forth motion.

The *feutier* raised surprised eyes to the man who had just posed the question. It was rare to have a conversation at this time of night. It isn't like it is during daylight! By day, near the burners, the *feutiers* are far more than workers of the light. They take care of the light, of course, but also direct the pilgrims and, above all, they listen. Around the burners, sometimes tongues come untied, or hearts open to share a joy, a sorrow, a prayer intention. So the *feutiers* are attentive and discreet. At the turn of a conversation, they try, in their own words, to comfort one person, to return hope to another. Every day, side by side with the pilgrims, they, too, are enriched. The total trust in God of some of the sick wins their admiration and deepens their faith. The prayers of children move them. Their interior life is ceaselessly strengthened by these daily encounters.

"We never snuff out a taper," answered the *feutier*. "To snuff out a taper, for us, would be like snuffing out a prayer. We let them burn to the end."

The young man would have liked to talk further, but already the worker had returned to his work. He had so much to do. The twenty-three sheet-iron squares that serve as burners had to be cleaned – Creak! Creak! Creak! – before the six o'clock Mass.

The pilgrim walked off and went back to pray at the grotto. Now the metallic noise that split the night no longer bothered him. He knew that these workers in the shadows who were performing their duty near him were, in fact, servants of light. The *feutiers* gather all pilgrims – men, women, children, those of good health, the sick, the poor, the rich, priests, laymen, Frenchmen, foreigners – into a single brazier that ascends to the Virgin Mary and to God.

The *feutiers* of Lourdes seem to have come into being with the shrine. They have watched over the pilgrims' brazier of prayers for ever. Better than anyone, they know the meaning of Pope John Paul II's words: "*Even a tiny flickering flame raises the night's heavy mantle. How much more light you will be able to make together if you are close to each other in the communion of the Church!*"

HOLY MARY, MOTHER OF GOD,

THE "LITTLE QUEENS" AND THE QUEEN OF HEAVEN

The Tour de France Stage in Lourdes, July 14, 1994

1994 One last flex of the legs, one last turn of the pedal in a dream, and the Tour de France cyclists woke up one after the other in their hotel rooms. The sun was already high in the sky, its rays covering the town's mountains and rooftops with a heavy caress. After eleven exhausting stages, eleven awakenings at dawn, what a joy to let oneself go in a well-deserved late morning in bed! The stop in Lourdes, on this July 14, 1994, was the only day of rest granted to the cyclists who had taken to their saddles in Lille, in the north of France.

Yet about thirty cyclists got up a little earlier than the others. After a healthy breakfast, they headed for the shrines, loitering a little like tourists on holiday... or rather on pilgrimage! Indeed, that morning, their bicycles were taking them to a particular destination: A Mass was to be celebrated especially for them in the Saint Pius X Basilica.

When they entered the subterranean basilica, they were greeted by the warm handshake of Dominican Father Henri Ponsot, who had wanted and organized this first Tour de France Mass. The idea had come to him after he had closely examined the composition of this traveling caravan, that nomadic village that follows the scrum from bar to barber. All the convivial places that make up a village were there. All? No, for the Church was missing!

Father Ponsot had wondered whether it would be possible to set up an absolutely free religious presence in the middle of this village. Although its population was somewhat seasonal, Lourdes nevertheless numbered no fewer that two or three thousand residents. His negotiations had failed to turn the caravan into a parish. On the other hand, the Tour's administration granted him its permission to prepare a Mass in Lourdes, where the river of cyclists was to mingle with the ocean of pilgrims.

Still a little surprised at being there in the church's shade after the bright sun of the Pyrenees slopes, the Tour cyclists examined the crowd around them. Indeed, they were not alone: Four to six thousand people had come to pray with them! The size of the crowd gladdened Father Ponsot: The large pilgrimage of the Community of the Beatitudes, which he had not expected, ensured a Mass prayed and sung with fervor.

Suddenly, just before the Mass, as the choir hummed a few last preparatory vocalizations, murmurs broke out in the basilica. The cyclists turned their heads to catch a glimpse of the important person thus announced and immediately smiled at his arrival with his snow-white hair.

Gino Bartali was like an older brother to them, an illustrious predecessor, a name written in letters of gold in the history of the Tour. In 1948, he had won the yellow jersey, and had left it in homage in the shrines of Lourdes. That year, when the Tour had come within its walls, the Marian city had been celebrating the Massabielle apparitions' centennial. Not only was Gino Bartali an ace at the handlebars, he was also a champion of the Catholic faith.

That morning, in fact, he had gotten out of bed even earlier than the others. The former runner who accompanied the Tour did not wish to enjoy his morning's rest. Let us rather say that he put it to good use by paying a filial visit: At nine-thirty, he laid an enormous bouquet of flowers at the grotto under the delighted camera lens of the *Dépêche du Midi*, which was only too glad to catch "Gino-the-Pious" red-handed in the act of praying!

Fully returning the smiles he was receiving from all sides, Bartali went to the first row, where he joined those in charge of the Tour who had clustered around Jean-Marie Leblanc, the general director.

Crozier in hand and mitre on head, Bishop Jean-Lucien Cadilhac made his entrance into the nave. Mass began like a welcome pause in the middle of this breathless race on the roads of France. Bartali, closing his eyes, was savoring the beauty of the chants and of the liturgy that seemed to him a foretaste of heaven: He whispered this to his neighbor, the lucky correspondent of the *Dépêche du Midi*, who quickly added the comment to his notes!

The recessional hymn was the last that Bartali was to savor in peace and prayer. Barely had the bishop left the nave – after exchanging a cordial handshake with the Tour's directors – than Bartali was assaulted by a crowd of admirers. Jovial, as was his usual demeanor, the former champion did not even give a thought to denying autograph requests. He signed everything, even missals and song sheets, exchanging pleasantries with his fans who were brimming with excitement!

Outside, in the streets of Lourdes, the runners who had just gotten out of bed graciously lent themselves to the same writing exercises. These included Miguel Indurain and Tony Rominger, the Spaniard and the Swiss, who were the two giants of this new edition of the Tour (Indurain would go on to win his fourth Tour in a row that year and would extend that streak to five consecutive victories in 1995); and Luc Leblanc, a Frenchman, winner of the stage that brought the cyclists to Lourdes through the formidable slopes of the Hautacam ski resort. Riders of every nationality signed kind words for pilgrims from every country without respite! For as long as a beautiful day of rest and recuperation lasted, bikes and stretchers passed each other while athletes and sick pilgrims smiled at each other, chatting for just a moment. At times, their concerns were the same. For instance, the Dutchman Marco Vermey insisted on filling a can with Massabielle water for his sick grandmother!

Along with the Tour, a blast of energy blew into the streets of Lourdes. This day of rest benefited everyone. The next morning, at the moment of departure of the "little queens" leaving the shrine of the "great" queen in a dash, Father Henri Ponsot found himself hoping that he had just created a precedent.

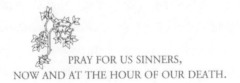

PRAY FOR US SINNERS,
NOW AND AT THE HOUR OF OUR DEATH.

THE LEAST OF YOUR BROTHERS

Portrait of a Female Hospitaller, August 12, 1995

19 95 *"Volet aver re gracia de vié t'aci pendent quinze dias?"*[1] Like Bernadette, I'm back. I'm a hospitaller: I made a promise, so I come back every year, each time with the same joy.

It's nearly six-thirty in the Lourdes train station, and the air is still cool. The humidity signals a hot day this August 12. The train just came to a stop in a deafening screech, waking all the sick. The hospitallers haven't slept much since they carried their invalid pilgrims aboard. Breakfast has been eaten; I had black coffee already an hour ago.

The stretcher-bearers on the platform are getting busy in their well-organized battalions. They're laying the sick on their dark blue stretchers and taking them to the various welcoming areas. Lourdes has a variegated and strong smell, a mingling of the smells of the Gave, the crowd, and the candles. I get a lungful as I arrive at the shrine. I run, I nearly fly in the day's first rain.

---

1. "Would you have the grace of coming here for fifteen days?" is what Our Lady had asked Bernadette during her third apparition.

As I arrive at the welcoming center, there are reunions and embraces. There are just under thirty of us in the room, from all sorts of different places, under the authority of our chief, Philippe. He's been coming with his family for twenty-five years; his son will carry the torch after him. I met up with "our" sick, all regulars. There's Georgette from Marseille, who has been coming to the National for thirty years; Pedro from Nice, who has been coming for so long that he no longer remembers his first time; and Gregory, a young autistic boy whose strikes you have to dodge and to whom the doctor alone can come near. Then there's Nina, the flirt: It takes four men to lift her, which delights her.

On this first morning of the pilgrimage, which is awaited and hoped for from one year to the next, faces are at ease. There no longer is pain or worry. Everyone is savoring the arrival with some excitement, even though Jean is absent, having passed away this winter. This morning prefigures the next five. Like many in Lourdes this August, our chaplain is an Assumptionist. He makes the sign of the cross to start a prayer. Everyone stops what he's doing and imitates him. A *Hail Mary* rises up, sung, gracious and halting, melodious and fragile, the first one of the *pélé* – as we commonly refer to the pilgrimage. I let the tears roll down my cheeks.

I'm in the hall, detached exclusively to the simplest tasks and to the basic care of the sick. I bandage, I wash bodies, I trim fingernails, I put cream on sores, I empty artificial bladders, I dress, I comb, I feed, I read aloud, I tuck in, I listen, I stroke, I comfort. Average age? Seventy.

I can see myself on that very first day, four years ago, hampered by my disgust and my awkwardness. With soiled hands, I would evaluate the damage with a sick stomach: Everything had to be changed, clothes, sheets, pillows, everything. I didn't dare ask for help, I didn't dare move, I couldn't look the patient in the eye. I hadn't been prepared for this. The task seemed insurmountable. Never again. Everyone has his own calling, and mine lay elsewhere. That's what I told myself.

"Raise your head, Georges, please. You're splendid! Did I shave you well?"

The man gratifies me with a satisfied smile worth all the riches in the world. My first patient four years ago was just like him. At the moment when I was closing my eyes to catch my breath, on that infamous first day, I had felt a calm hand cover mine. Opening my eyes, I was confronted with a clear gaze. It was my patient's gaze, simple and humble. It was a gaze of tenderness that came to my assistance – to me, the healthy one whom neither disease, nor the misfortunes of life, nor old age had yet struck. And I had seen the presence of Christ in it. *"Whatever you did for one of these least brothers of mine, you did for me."*[1]

I shall never forget that gaze because it made me what I am today – a hospitaller in the service of the sick, both hands in misery, waiting all year for this confrontation with charity, humility, the gift of self, this hospitaller who receives far more than she gives.

There are two of us now to wash up Georges, to respect his modesty when we rub his bruised and emaciated body. He hands us his cologne to perfume him before we dress him. Then I comb him with infinite delicacy and the fear that his few white wisps of hair may come out in my hands. Then he raises his chin and checks himself in the mirror I hand him. He's ready. Behind the walls of the Saint Bernadette Hall, Marie, his wife, awaits him. She, too, has made herself beautiful. They've been married half a century, but the look they give each other takes them back to their twenties. One can imagine them dancing on the feast of Saint John.

Before leaving, I draw up the sheets and set the covers in place. Under the bed there is an old cardboard suitcase, discolored in places, smelling of old pepper. I put away the comb and the pajamas, which I

---

1. Mt 25: 40.

fold with a mother's tender touch. "*Be servants to the poor*," Father Picard had said to the first hospitallers.

Shortly, in the shelter of the rock, under the basilica's imposing structure, I shall pray, my hands lit by a taper's little flame. The water of the Gave alone will fill the silence. Broken with exhaustion, I shall pray at the feet of *Aquéro*.

"*Lourdes brings me a kind of whiff of peace, trust and hope*," Father d'Alzon, one of the very earliest Assumptionists, used to say. In four days, I will get back on the train, regenerated. Lourdes is a renewed baptism.

I am a hospitaller, and for that I give you thanks, Lord.

 AMEN.

A CHILD, LOST AND FOUND

The Basilica of the Rosary, August 15, 1996

19 96 There was a big day crowd on the esplanade. A continuous flow of pilgrims slowly moved forward through the Saint Michael and Saint Joseph gates in a sort of spontaneous and shuffling procession animated by a common purpose. Here and there, along the sides of the four-hundred-yard-long immense avenue leading to the basilicas and to the grotto, priests in albs were granting absolution under a cloudless sky.

A few wheelchairs, a few "tringlots" – those stretchers on wheels, so to speak – and the "blue cars" typical of the Lourdes shrines rolled and stopped along with the crowd's movements, dictated by the lines to the open-air confessionals.

At the heart of this multitude that was wholly turned in the same spiritual and geographical direction were two people who seemed to walk against the current. They walked one direction and then another, passed to and fro, visibly seeking something or someone. It was a man and a woman, certainly a couple.

They would join each other occasionally, consult with each other, then leave in different directions again, periodically bumping into the pilgrims who, entirely absorbed in prayer, paid no attention where they were going. The more time passed, the more distraught the couple seemed.

Despite the throng, the woman, her eyes red with anxiety, continued her search around the information booths. For his part, the man went off toward the statue of the crowned Virgin around which he turned two or three times, stopping regularly to scan the crowd. He continued his way toward the Rosary Basilica at a quick pace.

Like a sympathetic mother opening her arms wide to comfort a sheepish child, the basilica extended its two immense entrance ramps, intended to facilitate access for tringlots and other wheelchairs, to the processing crowd. As the man's gaze fell only on little people, it was easy to determine that he was looking for a child – their child, probably, judging by the magnitude of their worry. At that point, the woman joined him, carried along by the flow of the procession that was slowing down as it approached the shrine's chancel. The child had not reappeared. The couple went in to search the Rosary Basilica.

Once within the darker interior of the basilica, they had to stop a moment to let their eyes adjust from the brightness outdoors. The pews were already occupied by many of the faithful at prayer. In the nave, pilgrims were visiting the church, holding guidebooks in their hands. By a tacit agreement, the man and the woman separated again to inspect each of the side chapels.

The woman went to the right, scanning even the confessionals. She discovered chapels that are richly decorated, adorned with splendid mosaics celebrating the mysteries of the rosary. Her mind was not disposed at that moment to contemplating these masterpieces of the faith, yet, with the emotions she was then experiencing, she could not remain insensitive to them. She thus discovered the joyful mystery of the Annunciation, which fleetingly reminded her of the moment she understood that she was pregnant with the very child she was so ardently seeking today. What Mary, the Mother of God, had felt at that moment must have been of an inconceivable intensity.

Then she moved on to the next chapel, though not without having turned around to look about the rest of the church to try to glimpse the man who was doing the same on the opposite side. This time, it was the joyful mystery of the Visitation, when the sweetest words a mother ever heard were uttered: *"Blessed art thou among women, and blessed is the fruit of thy womb."* Without being completely reassured, she felt that nothing serious could happen in such a place. She drew some serenity from it.

The chapel after that, with its Nativity mosaic, sheltered more people. Whispering their comments, many pilgrims were admiring the work, remaining in front of it for a long time, so that the woman spent some time attempting to glimpse the people in the first row, among whom she still hoped to see the lost child – in vain.

She had no success either at the chapel of the mystery of the Presentation, and it was with a broken heart that she contemplated the scene of that respectful and loving Mother who, without fear, entrusted her son to the hands of old Simeon. Could she, now that she knew the anguish of separation, remain as serene as Mary? Almost in spite of herself, given her haste to recover her child, she stood still for a moment of supplication that was as brief as it was pressing.

Her prayer was granted in the fifth chapel, where her husband had joined her, empty-handed. Indeed, it was in front of the image of Jesus at the temple before the doctors of the law after escaping his parent's vigilance that she discovered her son. He was sitting on the floor among other children attentively listening to the story told by an old priest, the story of a child whose parents thought him lost, though he had come to save all humanity.

HAIL MARY, FULL OF GRACE.
THE LORD IS WITH THEE.

A HARBOR OF PEACE

The New Our Lady Welcoming Center,
April 7, 1997

1997 At the new Our Lady Welcoming Center, the arrival of the first pilgrim closely followed the laying of the cornerstone blessed by Bishop Jean Sahuquet of Lourdes on February 11, 1996: The building's doors opened less than fourteen months later, on April 7, 1997!

It was an immense construction site, a project as vast as the heart of the people of Lourdes, a dream matching in size this city whose motto is "Lourdes, the Brotherly City"! Indeed, the construction of the welcoming center was managed by a society of mixed economic levels in a close partnership between the municipality and the diocese.

At the project's inception, the building on the architect's blueprint was of a size to give one pause. The center was to cover 216,000 square feet and offer 912 beds for the sick and the handicapped. These beds would be subdivided into units of 100, each independent from the other in terms of dining and recreation areas. Needless to say, the workmen who descended upon the site were attempting an achievement of ample proportions. Yet, when enthusiasm is added to professionalism, work goes faster than one might imagine. Workers of every specialty felt strongly committed to this construction with a "humanitarian" vocation.

The modern and elegant architecture also contributed to the interest that the builders felt for their mission. It was never a question of building a concrete block as ugly as it was utilitarian! For instance, the plans foresaw 29,700 square feet of glass surface to flood the center with light and give the sick a privileged view of the shrines. The building's fine, undulating lines would be capped with a roof made up of very beautiful slate from Lourdes' immediate surroundings. The whole vision was anything but stifling: It emphasized space, brightness, airiness. It was conceived to bid welcome to the pilgrims even before the words of welcome they would receive from the Sisters of Charity of Nevers, Bernadette's spiritual younger sisters, to whom oversight of this brand new edifice was entrusted.

On this day, then, the first pilgrim was welcomed within these walls that had so freshly risen from the ground. It was seven twenty-five in the morning. Sister Marie-Jo, the institution's directress, wore a radiant smile as she opened the door to him. Her face left no doubt that, although vast and functional, the center was not without a soul – quite the contrary! What was already breathing life into it was the presence of all the volunteers, hospitallers, stretcher-bearers, consecrated sisters, and priests who would all dedicate themselves to the service of the sick. These volunteers had preceded the pilgrims into the building.

For several days, countless skilled hands had been tirelessly busying themselves to ensure that the center would be welcoming from the very first hours it was in service. In fact, at their arrival, the first pilgrims – like those to follow – had the impression of having walked into a beehive, but a beehive whose activity was by no means noisy. It was like a beehive as serene as a harbor of peace.

A few days later, the dedication ceremony took place, gathering all the great movers and workers of this project that had been so masterfully brought to completion. The architect, with some emotion, presented the keys to the building to the president of the construction's management company, who in turn gave them to the mayor, who then gave them to the shrine's rector. "These keys," explained the rector, who finally handed them to Sister Marie-Jo, "are not the sign of power, but a sign of service."

The waves of pilgrims followed each other so quickly in Lourdes that the center soon was operating at full speed. It was already at capacity with its cargo of sorrows and smiles, distresses and hopes, personal stories and encounters, so many human treasures destined to be brought like prayers to the feet of the Virgin of Massabielle. In the hallways, one sometimes hears weeping, often laughter. One also sees countless flowers of friendship bloom.

How can one define the life of this Our Lady Welcoming Center? It is comparable neither to a hotel nor to a hospital. Indeed, the pilgrims who are lodged here are no more clients than they are patients. Though this house does not take in tourists, neither is it equipped with a medical infrastructure as such. Here, one does not turn away the healthy: All pilgrims can be accompanied by relatives who stay with them. It's a question of humanity, the center's managers would explain with a smile: Spouses are not separated, and a child is not separated from his parents. How could one let a sick person within the walls while politely asking the person who brought him here to find himself a room in town?

In April 2007, the Our Lady Welcoming Center blew out its ten birthday candles, figuratively speaking. A million pilgrims had stayed there, including Pope John Paul II, who stayed overnight in August 2004. The beehive was as animated as ever and as peaceful as ever. There was the peacefulness of the general wake-up call when the hospitallers join the pilgrims at their bedside to say morning prayers with them; the friendly race to the elevators that the volunteers from the different pilgrimages "fight over"; the stretchers' intense comings and goings in the foyer, where kind hands gently place blankets around the sick; the laughter of the children who have so many opportunities for play that they never have time to be bored.

The center is enriched with all the prayers that ascend from within its walls, and with all the generosity extended there. Anchored in the land of Lourdes at a stone's throw from the grotto – just a walk across a bridge from the Gave's left bank – the immense institution continues its mission of welcome under Our Lady's loving gaze.

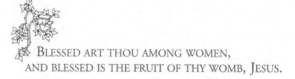

BLESSED ART THOU AMONG WOMEN,
AND BLESSED IS THE FRUIT OF THY WOMB, JESUS.

FIFTY YEARS OF HAPPINESS

Jeanne Frétel, Fifty-Second Miraculous Healing,
May 25, 1998

19
98

There were so many candles that the "Happy Birthday" written across the cake was barely distinguishable: Ninety-four flames flickered, celebrating ninety-four years of life. Who would ever have guessed that Jeanne would be blowing out nearly a century's worth of candles, when she had received the Sacrament of the Anointing of the Sick three times at the age of thirty-four?

Surprise! The small flames lit up again by themselves, as if by magic. Magical candles were all the rage. *A resurrection*, she thought to herself, watching these lights return to life again in the dark. There on the cake was a reflection of her life…

One has to go back to 1938, when it all began. Jeanne liked telling her story, especially on her birthday – another year that sublimated the insane, the inexplicable.

"I was twenty-four at the time, and a nurse," she began. "Seemingly sturdy, I was in fact as weak as a lamb. I had an appendicitis attack, and I was taken to the Hôtel-Dieu hospital. I thought I would leave it soon enough, but do you know how long I stayed there, my friends? For the entire war!

Exclamations of surprise rose among the guests.

"While Hitler was invading Europe, disease was invading my body! Well, I was hoping that the destruction of the Third Reich would be a question of weeks, and I wished the same for my healing. That was without taking into account the stubbornness of my infectious demons – an ovarian cyst, then a tuberculous peritonitis followed by complications, the last of which left me with three teeth on top and six on the bottom. Even Hitler had a more beautiful smile than I did!"

There was a little humor in the midst of the retelling of this tragedy because Jeanne had learned detachment since her recuperation. Yet at the time, nothing would have made her laugh, especially not her cauldron-sized belly in which she could feel her bowels seething.

"You must've been terribly weakened."

"Annihilated, my little Thérèse! I was so skinny I would have frightened a wolf! I could not walk, I could not eat, I could not sleep. My temperature ran 104 degrees at night, 96.8 in the morning. Believe you me, this was no little bout of indigestion! And it only got worse."

At this last recollection, her fingers tensed up, crinkling the gift-wrapping resting on her knees. For a brief moment, she examined them from the corner of her eye. To think that for years it was not her birthday but her morphine shots that marked the rhythm of her calendar...

"I wound up going to the Pontchaillon Hospital. *There to die...* Now, three years earlier, they had instituted the Mass for the sick in Lourdes, where the healthy came to support those suffering with their prayers. So, as I lay dying, I was taken with the Rosary Pilgrimage. Other than my continual vomiting, I was aware of nothing. I could have been told I had just been elected Miss Brittany, and I would not even have batted an eyelid. Then came October 8, 1948. That is when I... when she... when he..."

Jeanne hesitated as she searched for the right words. Father Jeannin smiled. As a historical figure of the Rosary Pilgrimage, he knew the story of the fifty-second miraculous healing of Lourdes quite well.

"You were transported on a stretcher to the Mass celebrated in front of the Saint Bernadette altar," Father Jeannin said, picking up the story. "The pilgrims were thronging around the sick, and Father cut a path to you. He did not dare give you communion, but the stretcher-bearer insisted, so he gave you a small piece of the host. Thereupon..."

"Thereupon, I felt very well!" exclaimed Jeanne, who still could taste the miracle in her mouth. "*I asked to be taken to the grotto. Once there, I had the sensation that someone was taking me under her arms to help me sit up, then that the same invisible hands were taking my fingers to place them on my belly: it had gone back to normal!* And, incredibly, I could have eaten a horse!"

"Ten years since you'd had a big meal!" Father Jeannin interjected.

"I didn't deprive myself: veal with mashed potatoes, two helpings, three pieces of bread, jam and cookies," she replied.

"And you managed to swallow all of that?" asked Thérèse.

"Why yes, the appetite of an ogre!" said Jeanne. "That afternoon, I took a dip in the pool, standing, without feeling tired. The doctors from the Lourdes Medical Bureau were staggered! Back in Rennes, my doctor was just as stupefied: I had not a single symptom left, not even morphine withdrawal. His patient, who was about to leave this world, was now gaining over two pounds a day! I went back to my nursing job, working from 5:30 a.m. to 11 p.m. *My doctor was not a believer; I gave his scientific self-esteem a terrible blow...* Also to the unbeliever among the twenty physicians of the Lourdes Medical Bureau who examined me a year later. My healing *escaped the laws of nature*; that was their conclusion."

"What about the Canonical Commission?" someone asked.

Jeanne drew out of the little pocket above her heart a wrinkled piece of paper, yellowed with age. She unfolded it and, slowly, weighed her words, or rather those of Cardinal Clément-Emile Roques, archbishop of Rennes:

"The case of Miss Frétel belongs in the series of extraordinary, scientifically inexplicable events in the presence of which one can only repeat: 'The finger of God is there.' We recognize that Miss Jeanne Frétel, suffering from tuberculous peritonitis with signs of meningitis and in a critical state of cachexia, was instantaneously and radically healed on October 8, 1948, at the moment when she was receiving communion at the St. Bernadette altar in Lourdes, and we judge and declare that this healing was miraculous and must be attributed to Our Lady of Lourdes."

Those who were gathered watched Jeanne in amazement. Until her death five months later, she would have an infinite gratitude toward God and Our Lady of Lourdes in her eyes. For fifty long years of perfect health, the visits of the frail spinster from Rennes to the esplanade had witnessed to her faith.

"'The finger of God,'" repeated Jeanne in a murmur, as she mischievously dipped hers in the thick chocolate frosting of her birthday cake.

 HOLY MARY, MOTHER OF GOD,

NINE MONTHS TO FIND ONE'S WAY

The Gospel School in Lourdes, November 7, 1998

1998 The weather was exceptionally mild that fall. In the walkways of the house of the Sisters of the Assumption, at the entrance into Lourdes, Pierre and Chelo sat on the bench, warming up in the noontime sun.

"I hope I'll be worthy of the trust you put in me by picking me to accompany you, Pierre. Did you know that before I was an accompanier, along with my husband Jean-Michel, we were students at the Gospel School? In fact, that's where we met."

"I didn't know," Pierre replied. "Was that long ago?"

"In 1991, the year the school opened," Chelo explained. "We stayed nine months; nine months to listen to God, nine months to learn to live out the Gospel; nine months of reflection before committing ourselves to a professional or spiritual life. You'll see; it goes really fast. Amid the Christian formation classes, pilgrim assistance, hospital stays, prayer and community life with twenty young people our own age, I didn't notice the time passing by! But enough about me. What pushed you to leave everything behind to spend nine months here?"

Pierre told his story. "I experienced all sorts of failures these past few years, and I wanted to take a step back. Also, I'm an only child; I want to learn how to live in a community. When I met Father Cabes and he told me about his school, I felt right away that I had to go. I'm hoping it will help me learn what God wants from me – to leave on a foreign mission, to get married... The month I've been here, everything has been turning around in my head, I don't really know where I'm at."

"That's normal; everything is new and so dense," assured Chelo. "You'll see, soon everything will be clearer. Some find out they want to raise a family, others aim for the priesthood, and still others wish to remain lay persons and to commit themselves to the service of the Church."

She used herself as an example. "Look, who could have imagined that I, the little Spanish girl from Saldaña, would marry a Frenchman from Rodez, in southern France – especially since, when I first arrived here, I was already engaged to someone else?"

Chelo was silent for a while, overcome by the memories that were returning. She could see Father André Cabes and his brother who was also a priest, Father Jean-Luc, telling her eight years ago about their wish to create a formation school for young people eighteen to thirty years old.

It caught her interest, so she decided to leave her family and pursue this adventure. Her fiancé would wait. After all, nine months go by so quickly.

What she had not foreseen was that one of the boys at the school, Jean-Michel Feral, was to have a sudden epiphany after he had gone to confession in January 1992: Chelo was the woman of his life. Chelo, who already was realizing that the life she had intended to live was not completely in harmony with what she had been learning and living for the past few months, received his declaration with surprise but confidence. As Father Cabes recommended, they let life go on as if nothing were the matter, trusting in God's will.

Once back home, Chelo understood when she saw her fiancé that everything was different now. She would make her way with Jean-Michel. Yes, God gave them a sign to live, through their love, the love of God. Engaged in June 1993, a year to the day after the end of school, they married in August 1994 – she overcome with emotion in her long white dress, and he serious-looking in his black suit and blue bow tie.

A slight cough from Pierre brought her back to reality.

"I'm sorry, Pierre, I was lost in thought," Chelo apologized. "When we married, Jean-Michel and I immediately wished to thank the school by becoming accompaniers. Being accompanied is indispensable to mature one's spiritual progress, to go beyond difficult milestones, to find one's way. So tell me, where are you at?"

"At the beginning, I had trouble, because the rhythm is so sustained: up early for prayer, studying without breaks, participating in community life with young people from all backgrounds, helping others," Pierre said. "I didn't feel comfortable. These past few days, though, it's gone better. I'm going with the flow. Parish visits, helping the sick, studies, discussions with others, everything is becoming more meaningful. I feel like I'm learning how to love."

"I like to say that to love, you have to die a little to yourself, to others, to your activities," Chelo responded. "Here, we die one year to be born again to life. Stopping for a year to start listening to God, in this fast-paced society where one has to know what he or she wants to do very early, demands patience and trust. We must trust in the mission to which God is calling you and have patience for the time necessary to discover it and to bring it to a successful conclusion."

"How about you, Chelo," Pierre asked, "have you found this mission of yours?"

"Yes, everything became clear when I got married," she replied. "Living marriage as a true vocation by living out, every day, the 'yes' of the first day's commitment – having children, teaching them to grow in size and in wisdom, being a Christian every day, building on a foundation of rock thanks to prayer – that is my mission. That is what makes Jean-Michel and me progress, what pushed us to become an accompanying couple, to get involved in the life of our parish, to try every day to apply what the school taught us. That is also why, since 1995, we have lived in Lourdes, near Mary, who allowed us to meet and to whom we pray every day."

"What is it that most helped you to see things clearly here?" Pierre asked.

"Though the fifteen weekly hours of classes taught me a lot, I preferred the 'fraternities' that gathered us into small teams on Thursday nights," came Chelo's answer. "I can still see us talking, regrouping, each helping the other to learn in truth. You, too: I'll help you grow in truth. You can count on me."

"Thank you, Chelo," Pierre said gratefully. "With your support and that of all the others, I feel that I'm going to find my path."

Chelo and Pierre walked back toward the school. They looked at the scattered leaves and silently prayed: *Lord, help me every day to learn in truth. Amen.*

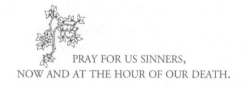

PRAY FOR US SINNERS,
NOW AND AT THE HOUR OF OUR DEATH.

THE TOMB OF A THOUSAND COLORS

Portrait of Giandomenico Facchina, Mosaicist,
June 12, 1999

1999 A ginger cat, its whiskers twitching and its tail bolt upright, was prowling about among the tombstones of the Père Lachaise Cemetery. It went down the second row, stopped, and stood squarely in front of the little chapel adorned entirely with mosaics. He lifted his head a little, as if to make sure he was at lot 41, then sat and began to groom his fur with an expert tongue.

"Ah! There you are, you little rascal!" exclaimed a bent old lady with a weather-beaten face enlivened by two bright blue eyes.

She caught the cat and held it tight.

Cemetery guide in hand, a couple of young tourists, looking for famous tombs, looked at her with a smile:

"Is that your cat, madam?"

"Yes, that is my cat, his name is Gaston. I live nearby, but I have no garden, so he comes into the cemetery to play," the elderly lady said. "Every night I find him in front of this chapel. He knows I always come here; it is my favorite."

"It's true, it's very beautiful with all the multicolored mosaics," said the young man.

"That is where the great artist Giandomenico Facchina rests," the old lady explained with pride.

She added a note of confidence, "He is my great-grandfather. Have you never heard of him?"

"His name rings a bell, but I must admit that I do not quite know what he did," the young woman acknowledged.

"He created mosaics all over the world: in the United States, in Algeria, in England, in Argentina, in Brazil, in Japan... He received multiple gold medals at the Universal Expositions of Paris and Amsterdam," the lady explained. "Ah! He was truly a great artist! He was the son of a laborer from the north of Italy, and he probably would have been a laborer himself if he had not fallen in love with the mosaics in the Cathedral of San Giusto in Sequals, when he was participating in restoration work. From then on, he had only one wish – to become a mosaicist."

The cat meowed and moved about a little in his mistress's arms. The old lady let him go and continued her narrative, allowing him to saunter around the chapel.

"My great-grandfather then took up residence with his uncle, Monsignor Giuseppe Facchina, canon of the San Marco Basilica in Venice. He hired himself out as apprentice to two Roman artists in charge of restoring the church's mosaics. Then he renovated several mosaics, including those of the château of Princess Baciocchi, Emperor Bonaparte's niece. He felt more skilled at handling tesseras and came to France, to Montpellier, and then to Béziers.

"That was when he invented his famous restoration method, putting an end to the old method that consisted of destroying everything to rebuild it afterward. He called this method '*extraction and setting of ancient mosaics without alteration*,' and patented it on March 23, 1858.

From that date on, the most delicate restorations were entrusted to him. He was truly acknowledged as a master by his contemporaries."

"What you are telling us really makes me want to see some of his mosaics!" exclaimed the young man enthusiastically.

"Go and visit the Garnier Opera House!" the cat lady recommended. "Its floors and ceilings are covered with mosaics in shimmering colors."

"Created by your great-grandfather?"

"Yes, he had a revolutionary technique that allowed for considerably reduced costs and delays. He would prepare his mosaics entirely in his workshop, and then would place them on the walls needing to be decorated. You can imagine that with such advantages his success was immense. He received orders from all over the place, even as he continued to beautify the capital – the Town Hall, the Petit Palais, the Discount House, the Printemps and Bon Marché department stores, the Louvre and Carnavalet museums, the Sacré-Cœur. Oh yes, you can see my great-grandfather's mosaics all over Paris!"

"He must've had his workshop here, then?"

"Yes, he had a big one that he left to my grandfather. France was his second homeland; he received citizenship in the 1890s. He was very well respected for his art and received a medal when he was named to the Knights of the French Legion of Honor."

"Didn't he go back to Italy anymore?" one asked.

"Less and less," the lady answered. "He had turned over his Italian factory to his great friend and associate, Angelo Orsoni. In fact, it was with Orsoni that he undertook the greatest project of his life – the mosaics of the Rosary Basilica in Lourdes. Unfortunately, he did not see their completion. Orsoni continued alone after Facchina's death in 1903. And it was Angelo's great-grandsons, notably, who restored these mosaics with the Facchina method."

This indeed rang a bell with the younger cemetery visitors. "Why yes, we saw a documentary on those restorations. Fabulous mosaics. They made us dream! And the history of this Orsoni family, how marvelous!"

"The Orsoni were great artists and worthy individuals, kind and generous."

The young tourist turned to her companion. "Why don't we go to Lourdes to finish our vacation?"

"Excellent idea!" answered the man warmly.

"Then I have only to bid you a good stay," the old lady said. "Above all, make sure to marvel at the mosaics of the Rosary Basilica. You must see their many colors. They're enchanting!"

"Thank you, Madam, for sharing this beautiful story with us."

"Bon voyage," said the old lady with a smile.

She leaned towards her cat who, feeling dinnertime coming, was purring and rubbing against her legs.

"Come on, Gaston, let's go home."

She waved goodbye and walked off limping, with Gaston tenderly nestled at her heart.

AMEN.

A SPIRITUAL JOURNEY

The American Pilgrimage to Lourdes, September 18, 1999

19
99 Sheltered from the sun by a parasol on the terrace of the Grand Café in Lourdes, James Lee Murphy was writing an article. An American journalist at the *Washington Post*, Murphy had always believed that the city of the Immaculate Conception was synonymous with rain, like Brittany or Normandy. So it was with some pleasure that he experienced a bit of the long, hot summer there that continued to bake the pavement in mid-September 1999. It was a kind of Indian summer, like in his native Minnesota.

He had arrived from Paris, where he was a correspondent for the *Post*, just the day before to cover the forty-fifth American pilgrimage that had already begun a few days earlier. This was a change of pace from his usual work. In Paris, he was more interested in reporting on French politics than on religion, but he accepted this assignment as a kind of weekend break.

He took advantage of his arrival at the airport of Lourdes to meet the communications director. After a very friendly one-hour interview, he decided to complete his article with a passage on the development of this airport. Indeed, ever since the airport opened in 1958 for the centennial of the Virgin's apparitions, the number of pilgrims coming by air had steadily increased and had reached six hundred thousand the last two years. The original airport was designed to welcome only half a million travelers every year, so it had to be modernized. The authorities had dedicated the new equipment on July 19 of the previous year, officially opening a renovated airport that was now capable of receiving a million visitors per year. But the principal and remarkable characteristic of the Lourdes airport had to do with the destination and the state of the travelers – pilgrims and religious tourists from all over the world, a great part of whom are ill or handicapped.

"Even before reaching the city and the shrines," he wrote, "the airport of Lourdes turns our usual standards on their heads by placing at the heart of its operations not the healthy man, but the sick man. Everything is designed to avoid useless detours for persons with reduced mobility: separate entrances, platforms making elevator access easier, ramps, special wheelchairs to move along airplane aisles… But most striking are the two resting halls located at the arrival and departure levels, each containing twenty-five beds and a special infirmary where the sick can receive care. In Lourdes, the first-class are the handicapped coming from the whole world, not businessmen."

A shadow glided across the table. Lifting his head, Murphy found the tall figure of a Dominican priest with a broad smile and cheerful cheeks.

"I am Father Joseph Allen, prior of Saint Dominic Convent and Priory in Youngstown, Ohio," the priest introduced himself.

"Hello, Father. I'm writing up an article on the airport of Lourdes and the welcome of handicapped pilgrims. Pleased to meet you," Murphy replied. "Like I said on the phone, my newspaper assigned me an article on the forty-fifth American pilgrimage to Lourdes. Thank you for agreeing to meet me. Would you like something to drink?"

"I'll have a beer," said Father Allen. "And I'm the one to thank you for this interview. Regarding the airport, did you know that the first

American pilgrimage to come by plane was led by a man who had been miraculously healed by Our Lady of Lourdes? It was in July 1947. In those days, of course, the airport didn't exist. They'd landed at Orly before putting in a day to make it here."

"Who was the miraculously healed guy who accompanied them?"

"It was Father James Cox, pastor of a parish in Pittsburgh, Pennsylvania. It's an important city spiritually: You may recall that it was from Duquesne University in Pittsburgh that the Catholic charismatic renewal movement was born in February 1967. Father Cox came to Lourdes for twenty years, the last two times by plane. In fact, he was not healed in Lourdes itself, but his ulcerated eye, from which he had suffered for three years, was cured after he poured some imported Lourdes water on it and prayed to the Virgin. Three hours later, he had no more pain, and the ulcer was completely healed. I guess he was ten or eleven years old at the time. What a beautiful gesture of faith for a child."

"A long-distance miracle that led to his desire to come to Lourdes," interjected Murphy.

"Yes. He accompanied many pilgrim groups," said Father Allen. "But that first airplane pilgrimage affected people more than the other ones. I remember several shrine directors who talked about it as a great event. Today, of course, coming by plane seems very normal, but in 1947..."

"I suppose that these pilgrims come to Lourdes as part of a vacation in France?" asked Murphy. "I'll bet they take advantage of Lourdes to stay over in Paris."

"No, not at all. Actually Father Cox insisted that this pilgrimage be consecrated only to prayer and to the Virgin of Lourdes," the priest replied. "I don't think there was even a day of sightseeing in the surrounding area, although the region is well worth the visit!"

The Dominican spoke highly and enthusiastically of the tourism and culinary merits of Bigorre. His simplicity and good nature surprised the journalist.

"But let's get back to you and to the forty-fifth Rosary Pilgrimage from the United States," continued Murphy. "How long have you known Lourdes?"

"I first came here in 1975, for the Holy Year, and I have been accompanying the American rosary pilgrims since 1977."

"Is there a particular theme?"

"Yes, vocations. I am very attached to the theme of the family, for it is in the heart and grace of the family that priestly and religious vocations are born. During the pilgrimage, couples renew their wedding promises by presenting roses to the Virgin."

"Thank you, Father," said Murphy. "I'll come to your celebration tomorrow. I'm eager to see what such a gathering looks like. I haven't been back to Mass since middle school."

Highly impressed by Father Allen's natural friendliness, the journalist gathered his notes and quickly pocketed them. Yes, he was eager to be at the next day's Office. He who had not posed himself the question of God for so long felt intrigued by all that was going on in this town. "Am I becoming bewitched by Lourdes?" he wondered with a smile.

Hail Mary, full of grace.
The Lord is with thee.

Thousands of Healings

A Bureau for the Miracles, March 13, 2000

2000 There I was in front of the door on the third floor of the John Paul II Welcoming Center. I was a little disappointed. I thought this door would be a little less simple, a little more grandiose. And yet, alone in front of the plaque that says "Medical Bureau of Lourdes," I felt small. A real miracle has just taken place in my life, and I felt like telling everybody! But will anyone even believe me?

I took a deep breath and knocked.

"Come in!"

After a hesitation, I walked into a room flooded with light. Behind the reception desk was a young woman who smiled at me.

"Hello!"

"Hello," I said, looking at the tip of my shoes. "This is the place to declare miracles?"

"Indeed."

"I am here to declare one."

I ventured a glance at the desk. The young woman was not laughing at me; she was just a little surprised, that's all.

"Tell me all about it!" she said, pointing out a seat for me.

"The fact is, I would like to be sure that you are indeed the person to whom I am supposed to speak."

The secretary gave me a hard stare for a moment, then picked up her telephone.

"Dr. Theillier?" she asked into the receiver. There is someone here who would like to declare a miracle."

"He is on his way," she told me as she hung up the phone.

A side door opened, letting in a man with a white beard. He stopped for a moment, surprised to see me.

"Dr. Theillier," said the secretary right away, "this young man would like to speak to you."

The doctor's eyes lit up.

"Come in, my boy," he invited me, opening his office door.

Intimidated but reassured to see that these grownups were treating me seriously, I went into the doctor's office.

"Take a seat," he told me, moving a chair toward his desk. "For starters, can you tell me who you are, and how old you are?"

"My name is Martin Renaud. I am twelve."

"And you came to the Medical Bureau all by yourself?"

"Yes, my parents are so overcome by what has just happened that they are still in front of the grotto," I said. "I told them I was going to declare a miracle..."

"Do you mind if I call the shrine welcoming center?" inquired the doctor.

"What for?" I asked.

"I would like to tell them that you are here," Thellier said. "Your parents will be looking for you."

The doctor left a brief telephone message, then turned toward me again: "Now, I am listening!"

I began my story.

"Here goes. Ten days ago, my parents told me that they were going to get a divorce. It hurt me so much that I told myself that the only way to stop this pain was to ask for a miracle from the Virgin Mary. So I told my parents that I wanted us all to go to Lourdes, as a family, one last time. We live close by.

"We arrived this morning, and I took them to the grotto. I prayed and prayed... and the miracle happened. Dad took Mom's hand, and he started to cry. She did not stop whispering in his ear: 'I love you! I love you!' It's a real miracle! That's why I came to declare it."

The doctor set down his pen with a smile.

"You are right, Martin. I am happy for you! To reconcile the way your parents just did can be considered as a true miracle due to the Holy Virgin. I believe it. You can thank her and never forget this marvelous grace.

"Unfortunately," he added, "I cannot write down what you just confided to me in the list of miracles."

I looked at him, taken aback. "Why not?"

"You saw what is written on the door: 'Medical Bureau,' You see, I am here to verify healings that have to do with medicine. When someone is suddenly and without reason healed of a serious disease that was gnawing him up, I am in charge of studying his case for a later acknowledgment of a miracle by the Church."

"But my parents?"

"You see, lad, I know that there are hundreds of miracles like yours that happen every day in Lourdes," the doctor explained. "The miracles of Lourdes are all miracles of healing – healings of the heart, of the soul, of life's wounds that hurt us. Parents reconciling, young people who recover their faith, people who suddenly feel loved and no longer want to die... The graces of Lourdes are far more numerous than anyone knows, because they take place most often in people's hearts. And it is a rare person who then comes here, as you did, to declare his miracle.

They go home, healed on the inside, carried by a new faith, without telling anybody."

"Who comes to see you then?"

"Those who reckon they have been physically healed in an unexpected way. You know, since the creation of this bureau, the Church has acknowledged only sixty-seven miracles! And yet, our archives contain hundreds of testimonies of extraordinary healings. And that's leaving aside all the 'miracles' like the one you have just told me about."

"How do you recognize a true miracle then?" I asked.

"As far as medicine is concerned, we first verify that a patient has indeed been healed by studying his or her medical file and all the documents that attest to his or her condition before coming to Lourdes. Then, the most difficult task remains to be done – to conclude that the healing is truly extraordinary. This demands several years to verify that the patient does not have a relapse and that science cannot explain this improbable healing one way or the other. And even then, after receiving the opinion of the many doctors of the International Medical Committee of Lourdes, after declaring that this healing was unexplained, the final decision is not up to medicine. It is the bishop of the diocese of the former sick person who must give the ruling. If this healing has borne fruit around itself, if it has strengthened the faith of this or that person, then, maybe, he will publish an acknowledgment of a miracle with a capital 'M.'"

I remained quiet.

"You know," added the doctor, "it is a very delicate thing to speak of a 'miracle.' Many do not believe in them. The Church must surround herself with many precautions so that no one can contest the truth of these miracles. That is why she created this Medical Bureau. She wanted doctors to study the healings from a scientific point of view, and not simply with the eyes of faith. Otherwise, she might be accused of not being honest. That is why the acknowledgment of a miracle involves a long and delicate procedure. But this does not mean that what just happened in your life isn't one, in its own way. It is a grace from the Virgin Mary. It is one of the countless ones that she sends to men and women here, in Lourdes, and everywhere in the world."

I thanked the doctor and left the bureau. As I went outdoors, I caught a glimpse of him at his office window, watching me as I ran toward the grotto to join my parents. He was smiling as he reflected, I'm sure, on the blessing of the Massabielle spring, on the acknowledged miracles, and on the whole procession of inner healings and miracles of grace of which he has been the objective and happy witness.

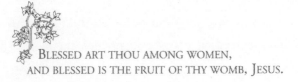

BLESSED ART THOU AMONG WOMEN,
AND BLESSED IS THE FRUIT OF THY WOMB, JESUS.

"Drink the fountain's water and wash in it"

The Story of the Lourdes Pools, June 30, 2000

2000 "Look Daddy, it was Grandpa's great-grandfather who built these pools."

It was nearly two o'clock in the afternoon. Taking advantage of the beautiful weather, Pierre and Marie had decided to take Jules, their seven-year-old son, for a walk along the Gave. They had arrived from Lyon the night before to entrust him to his grandparents for vacation. Marie's father, like his entire family for generations, lived in Lourdes, and it was a joy for him and his wife to take care of Jules, whom they adored.

Jules' finger proudly pointed out to his parents an arrow-shaped sign indicating "Men's Pools." Next to it, a placard records the words of the Virgin to Bernadette: "*Go drink the fountain's water and wash in it*," and lists the hours it is open. Under the trees along the building, pilgrims, sitting on benches or leaning on the barriers set up to organize the wait, peacefully chatted as they waited for the opening. A man in a wheelchair was telling the story, with an accent and an exaggeration typical of Marseille, of his first arrival in Lourdes and his first bath ten years earlier. Pierre stopped, gripped by the story.

With his parents otherwise occupied, Jules found someone else to talk to. An old priest in his cassock, sitting on the bench, hands leaning on his cane, smiled at him when he heard his voice, and they were now chatting as though they'd known each other for ever. As the priest told the little boy that the buildings were far too recent to have been built by his grandpa's great-grandfather, Jules embarked on the explanation of the story that his grandpa had told him the year before during the vacation.

"My grandpa's great-grandfather, he is the one who built the Lourdes pools, a long time ago, with several friends," the boy said with confidence. "My grandpa, he told me that Saint Bernadette was still alive, and that the pilgrimages had just begun."

The old priest knew the story of Lourdes well. Nearly thirty years earlier, he had even written a guidebook for pilgrims from his diocese. After a quick calculation, he understood that Jules was talking about the very first pools, the ones built in 1864, two years after the promulgation of Bishop Bertrand Laurence's *mandamus* instituting the cult of Our Lady of Lourdes.

Pierre and Marie joined their son and greeted the old priest, apologizing for his prattle. But the latter stopped them and spoke to Jules.

"You are right. Your grandpa's great-grandfather built the first pools of Lourdes," the priest told him. "But these are not the ones. You know, as more and more pilgrims started coming, bigger pools had to be built to receive them all. At the time you are telling me about, before the first pools were built, there were fewer people coming to the grotto, but still there were some pilgrims. Maybe your grandpa's great-grandfather was one of them, and it was also him who built the stone basin where the first miracles occurred."

Jules was fascinated by the gentleness of this man's voice, this priest who seemed to know the story of his ancestor so well.

"I don't know," the boy said. "Grandpa told me of a mommy who gave her child a bath when he was going to die."

"That is right, that was one of the first miracles, in July 1858," the priest explained. "And it took place in the stone basin where the spring water came to the surface. The child's name was Justin Bouhort. He was two years old and was wasting away. His mom, nearly despairing, had come to pray at the grotto. And she made this kind of crazy gesture, but full of trust in the Virgin Mary, of bathing him in the basin's water. They say that some of the pilgrims around her tried to keep her from doing it. You know, the water must have been like today, fifty-four degrees Farenheit. I don't think your mother would be very happy if she saw someone putting a baby in that chilly water!"

Marie was listening to the priest, standing, her hand on Jules' shoulder as he sat next to this marvelous storyteller. She smiled in agreement. She'd never understood how pilgrims could bathe in water so cold. She knew the pools are only half full and that people bathe in them only for a very short time, and generally without being completely immersed. She never had had the courage of going herself, though. As it was, she had trouble bearing the temperature of the water in Brittany, so fifty-four degrees…

Her son's voice interrupted her meditation. "So the pools didn't exist then?"

"No, your grandpa's great-grandfather built them in 1864," said the good priest. "They looked like the pools of the spa towns in the region, like those of Bagnères or of Cauterets. Since then, they have been enlarged very often in response to the demands of the more and more numerous pilgrims who wanted to come here. The buildings you see today are not in the same place as the first baths. They date from 1955. It was the bishop of that time, Bishop Pierre-Marie Théas, who had them built for the apparitions' centennial. But they were renovated again twice, in 1972 and in 1980, making a total of seventeen bathtubs today. Here, for the men, there are six; a little farther down that way, there are eleven for the women. And in each of the two buildings, there is a smaller pool for children."

A young priest joined the group and interrupted the old priest to tell him that it was his turn to go into the pools. With a half-surprised, half-sad expression, the child asked them if they were sick and were going to bathe to heal. The two priests reassured him: The old priest explained that although he was much older than Jules, he was in the pink of health. They were accompanying a group of pilgrims and were expected to take over the spiritual direction at the pools for the day. They were going to help the sick pray to God and the Virgin before their baths.

Jules watched them move away toward the entrance to the pools among the pilgrims and the sick. He was eager to find his grandpa to explain to him what the old priest told him. And since his grandpa was not doing so well, he was going to offer to accompany him someday to the pools so he could bathe in them.

HOLY MARY, MOTHER OF GOD,

THE WEAK WILL SHAME THE STRONG

The Faith and Light Pilgrimage, April 12, 2001

20
01
It is Easter 2001 in Lourdes. The opening celebration of the fourth Faith and Light Pilgrimage was about to begin. Jean Vanier was standing in the middle of the crowd that had gathered on the Rosary esplanade. A few minutes later, it would be his turn. On the podium, the microphone was waiting for him. For the time being, his gaze scanned the assembly of his pilgrims and friends. He remembered the days when he was a Navy officer, and when he taught philosophy: Those were good times, but none matched the happiness that had filled him since Easter 1971 on the first pilgrimage of persons with mental disabilities which he had organized in Lourdes with his associate, Marie-Hélène Mathieu. That was a high point in his life that gave birth to the Faith and Light Association, an accomplishment that followed several years after his founding of the first L'Arche communities of group homes for the mentally disabled.

Once again, his heart led him to mingle with these handicapped people who are his treasure. Up until 1968, it was believed that they had no place in this pilgrimage because they were too handicapped, too unable to experience the proceedings, too disturbing for the other pilgrims. Since then, Vanier had proved that the opposite was true: Thinking had evolved and hearts were opened, allowing the mentally disabled to come to Massabielle at the feet of the Virgin.

Vanier now entered more cheerfully into this communion, attentive to the atmosphere reigning around him – music, voices, a kind of effervescence, but above all, laughter. "It is a great mystery that those who bear such heavy daily burdens are capable of so much joy," said Cardinal Carlo Martini in Lourdes in 1991. This memory made Vanier smile: Today, the mystery remained intact.

Still, he remembered the precious discovery that he had made one day: the radical cry of these suffering people is a call to love. There is no question of asking for the healing of the mind, but for that of the heart.

During the 1971 pilgrimage, a child had left a psychiatric hospital to go to Lourdes. At his return, the nurses had asked the friends who had brought him whether they had been bothered by his perpetual drooling. "But he did not drool for a second!" they had exclaimed. Jean was now remembering the obvious: There are plenty of things that happen when the heart feels loved and welcomed just as it is.

Once near the crowned Virgin, he came upon two mothers deep in conversation. One only needs to see the familiarity binding two mothers of handicapped kids, to catch the way in which one of them readjusts the other's son's sailor hat, to understand that the Faith and Light communities that bring them regularly together are wells of energy in which they find the strength to listen to each other, to share common activities, to pray in unison. The concept had borne fruit.

A little further down, other scenes filled him with joy. Sylvie was leaning her head on the shoulder of the teacher who accompanied her because he had warmed up her hands. Geneviève was giving somebody a kiss because he had pushed her wheelchair all the way to the esplanade. If he had not seen these little miracles all around him for thirty years, Vanier would have wanted to cry. As it was, he just felt joy in his heart.

A woman approached him, a young boy at her side.

"Let me introduce my son, Alexis. He survived sudden infant death syndrome, and today he is sixteen. He still has a long way to go, but we have learned that joy and suffering can live together. Thank you."

Vanier gave her an encouraging smile: "Make the best of this pilgrimage! Lourdes is the heart's rest. Leave behind daily routine to refresh yourself at the spring. After that, you will be able to continue walking through the desert."

The founder of Faith and Light was intimately convinced of this: These people who have come to Lourdes feel at home. As Bishop Henri Donze of Tarbes and Lourdes once said, "*How could they not feel at home in this place sanctified by Bernadette Soubirous, an ungifted little girl and, as people used to say, good for nothing, like them?*" Without a doubt, on this day, everyone had a place here.

At that moment, Vanier noticed a banner that said in large characters: "Every life, even for a disabled person, has value."

"Yes, the Virgin also welcomes the smallest of her children, the most beloved; they are limited in their intelligence, but in no way in their heart, their faith, and their hope," Vanier said with a smile to the two who carried the banner.

A little farther down, a heated exchange grabbed his attention:

"It's true, the look other people give a mentally handicapped child is not always easy to bear for the parents, but trust in your own judgment. A handicapped person is first a human being, with his duty and his simplicity. He is called to live as a son of God, and he, too, is capable of fulfilling the mission on earth... *He's a prophet of love!* Think, for example, of young Hirotada Ototake, who was born with neither arms nor legs. He wrote a splendid book, *Nobody is Perfect*, that sold four million copies. In it he affirms that the handicapped will come to the rescue of our dehumanized society. All you need is to trust yourself..."

His gaze filled with tenderness, Vanier took his leave. It was time for him to speak. As he walked up onto the podium, he saw floating in the air the symbol of Faith and Light made by Meb, a Down's syndrome painter. It depicted twelve people on a small boat under a sky filled with a sun and clouds. As he faced the crowd, he saw hundreds of Faith and Light communities from the whole world, sailing under his eyes like so many little sister boats. Moved, he cleared his voice:

"*God chose the weak of the world to shame the strong*, says Saint Paul in his first Epistle to the Corinthians. *For, to become truly human, the strong need the weak, so that they may discover their heart.* I hear them from here: Five thousand hearts of mentally handicapped people and ten thousand hearts of parents, friends, and educators, beating as one. It adds up to a lot of love in this happy Easter. I am sure that, under the maternal gaze of Our Lady, this pilgrimage will be one of joy!"

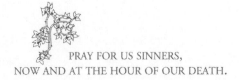

PRAY FOR US SINNERS,
NOW AND AT THE HOUR OF OUR DEATH.

THE FLUORESCENT VIRGIN

The Bondieuseries *("Religious Souvenirs") of Lourdes,*
July 1, 2001

20 01 "This time, I can no longer refuse," sighed Father Alain, fastening his suitcase. Until now, he had skillfully avoided the invitations of his dear cousin Christian, a priest in Creuse, to lead youth camps in the summer. This time, though, he did not have the heart to find a solid excuse, such as a music and liturgy colloquium in Sicily, theological formation in Rome, family obligations... He had run out of reasons; perhaps he had used them all up in the past years!

Arriving at the Gobelins' crossroads, looking for the bus that was to bring him to Montparnasse Station, he was still grumbling. If there only were the camp, there would be no problem. But the kicker was that it was taking place in Lourdes! For this young and brilliant priest of the Archdiocese of Paris, that was not his cup of tea. He did not know the shrine, but from afar it resembled to him a rather disastrous stereotype. His parents, who had been there several years before, confirmed his aversion to the rampant mercantilism there. Father Alain was a cultured man: His knowledge of art history was rich and broad, his studies in Italy had made him infinitely sensitive to the luminous representations of the mystery, and of the grace that only such painters as Cimabue or Fra Angelico were able to convey. So the petty trinkets gussied up in pink and blue that were sold at the market in Lourdes could only provoke his mockery and disdain.

To add insult to injury, there was pandemonium on the train. Three youths fell victim to the gastroenteritis epidemic that was raging through Paris at the time; the dinner car had nothing left for those who were still hungry; and a teething baby decided to let the entire car know about it. Father Alain was about ready to vent his frustration, but he managed to suppress his irritation enough to kindly and gently take care of the young people.

When they arrived, they encountered the stifling heat typical of the Pyrenees, but the shelter where the group was to set down its luggage was not air-conditioned. "No matter," proposed Father Christian, "a stroll along the Gave will settle everyone's emotions!" The twenty young-sters and the two priests went down the main street that snakes among the stores, streets filled with vendors of religious articles of all stripes! Virgin-shaped bottles with a crown for a cork lay side by side with Christs whose hearts dripped with blood, and snow-globe Bernadettes. On the right, they were hawking glow-in-the-dark statues, while on the left one could find chaplets that smelled like roses.

The further Father Alain went down the street, the more visibly he laughed. Having arrived at the shrine's door, he could no longer contain himself and left his group for a few moments. He thought he absolutely had to bring back to his Parisian friends some of these rare specimens. His eyes fell on a small store that was so filled with lit-up articles that it resembled a firefly. Father Alain grabbed a basket with a resolute hand and began his shopping.

First, a bestseller – a plastic Bernadette at the foot of a plastic grotto, with a flask of Lourdes water, the whole thing encased in a beautiful plastic block engraved "Lourdes." "Now that is a must," thought Father

Alain. Then he peered at the fragrant chaplets, the Mary and Jesus holo-gram key rings, and the Lourdes water lozenges with "a taste of miracle." When he stumbled across a piece of "the true cross," he could not keep from bursting into laughter. An elderly gentleman raised his eyes from behind the counter and came near him. He could see the irony shining in the priest's eyes and his impeccable Roman collar, so he very kindly offered him a cup of coffee.

"All the pilgrims are at the grotto, Father. I would not mind having a little chat with you," the vendor said.

Feeling guilty about his outburst of laughter, Father Alain dared not refuse. So there he was, introducing himself to a gentleman he knew nothing about. After a few moments, his natural outspokenness brought him to admit his aversion for the objects around them.

"No offense, but these pious knick-knacks are so far removed from the face of God," the priest said. "They caricature him, they reduce him to laughable realities, they turn him into a made-up doll, whereas he is the infinite. I am sorry, but the history of the world contains so many beauties striving to get at the mystery that here I cannot help being amused."

"Oh, granted, Michelangelo would have a heart attack if he saw all of this!" the vender admitted.

At that comment, Father Alain gave a good-natured smile. *At least he's lucid,* he thought.

"I thought exactly the same as you for a long time; I found all this piety ridiculous," the man explained. "I'll bet you think I am making money off people's faith, right? Well, Father, no, that's not quite it. I lived in Paris once, under the Louis-Philippe Bridge. I was homeless. I had lost everything – family, love, money, house… Anyway, you get the picture. I was left with only a lot of contempt for my fellow man. When you live so close to the Seine, it is not very difficult to put an end to it all.

"One night, a homeless lady, Monique, saw by the look in my eyes that I was planning to take that final leap. We all know each other, you see. She didn't want to let me, and after a long night of discussion, she gave me a little plastic Virgin statue like one of those. It was filthy all over, but it glowed in the dark. You can laugh, but I owe my life to that trinket. I got back on track, as they say, and one day it became clear to me that I wanted to be surrounded with these objects.

"I've heard a lot of testimonies about these *bondieuseries* that sustain the faith of the simple or powerful. We are naked in the faith, Father. You seem well-educated and cultured. Yet you also have that untouched part, that childhood of your faith, underneath all your diplomas. And you know as well as I do that God takes any shape he pleases to help us believe in him, to keep us near him. I'll grant you that these objects are but a few pebbles on a spiritual path that must go far beyond. But do me a favor: Take this little Virgin, and don't mock the faith of the simple, for it touches God's heart just as much as the faith of the saints does."

Unable to do anything but smile with tears in his eyes of shame and gratitude, Father Alain headed for the grotto, this grotto he didn't know yet and which had just offered him a treasure for his life as a priest.

AMEN.

FROM THE ROCK TO CONCRETE

The Marseille Bernadette Community, August 3, 2001

20 01 The sun was beating down on Marseille. The city was buzzing and smoking with the thousand activities of a great metropolis despite a heavy heat that the nearby sea was unable to alleviate. North of town, the sun cast its beams directly upon the big city apartment buildings clinging to the slopes of the Étoile mountain range.

Between the projects, there were scorching parking lots peopled with stationary and tightly sealed cars within which the air must have been boiling. There were burned-out or rusted carcasses without wheels, flat tires without a chassis, abandoned exhaust pipes, and and all kinds of other forgotten auto parts.

It was a day of blinding light, crushing temperature, a silence punctuated with the shouts of children and a few blaring TVs.

Not a living soul was out and about. People stayed in the uncertain shade of their overheated apartments, poorly protected from the blazing sun.

Yet Faara didn't hesitate. She crossed through those abandoned lots we still call "parking lots" out of habit. Her stride was sprightly, defying the general torpor. She had on a light, inexpensive dress and her dollar-store "flip-flops" that gaily clattered on the burning asphalt (no need to waste your money on fine clothes here). Her quick pace served as much to speed her away from the overheated atmosphere as it did to avoid nasty or dangerous encounters, a daily risk for these young women who live in a neighborhood where human respect is not a common value.

Faara was going to the folks in Block E. The elevator had been broken down for a long time, so she did not hesitate for a moment as she bounded up the staircase four steps at a time.

In the sun-filled apartment, she met up with Aymeric O'Neill and his wife, Christine. From their time in Brazil, where they had lived for five years in a shantytown, they maintained a very extroverted joy. The auxiliary bishop of Salvador de Bahia had sent them to this Lauriers project to serve as a "*hinge of grace.*" The few young people who were already there were in a good mood, and each one contributed a humorous comment or a smile. The atmosphere presented a strong contrast with the heavy silence of the projects.

The couple had gathered several "newbies" who were to participate in the life of the Bernadette Community. While offering Faara some coffee, Christine explained how their spiritual adventure began when they were sent as missionaries to the Brazilian shantytowns. With a gleam in her eyes, she quoted the Gospel phrase: "*I was a stranger and you welcomed me.*"[1]

"'*We are going on a visit like poor people, empty-handed, to avoid establishing a material relation, to remain in the image of God, free. The poor are our masters,*' said Saint Vincent de Paul," Christine told Faara. "And what better example than Bernadette, the very simple and most wretched in the village, like all those girls in the *favelas* we've met? God trusted that unassuming and unknown little girl. The Bernadette Community

---

1. Mt 25: 35

tries to look at the young in the projects from the same perspective of trust. Sometimes to remind them of what a share of the marvelous they have within themselves is enough to keep them from drifting."

Aymeric enthusiastically continued:

"*The solution is to give back their dignity to those who suffer. Through our presence, we wish to bear a message: We live here, with you, because you are worth it.*"

He also explained that in order to devote themselves truthfully and completely to this task, his wife and he had made the choice not to have any work outside the project and to live very modestly.

Faara could not help but wonder about the difficulty of dialogue between Christians and Muslims, the latter being in the majority in this project. Christine, who knew that the young woman, after a long period of searching, was on her way to baptism, gently answered:

"*Muslims have a real respect towards believers, and we wish to give testimony freely. Love cannot be imposed, it is lived. Conversion belongs to Christ. What belongs to us is to live in Jesus and to speak of God.*"

Aymeric then outlined the program of activities, explaining the different ways of getting involved in the community's life, which had no other goal than to put a little balm on the project's wounds. To fight failure at school, the community had organized a tutoring system: Over seventy high schoolers and older students helped other younger students every week by having them come over and study with their families. To combat rampant street violence, Aymeric offered afternoons of fun by taking out tables, board games, and paint for the children. He spent time sharing emotional ups and downs with regulars and drop-ins. Finally, to ease loneliness and all forms of despair, the committee organized hikes and summer camps where young people could go to the countryside to experience silence, to learn, to play, and perhaps also to pray.

The meeting was at its peak, and every youngster felt called to a different activity. With so many willing souls before him, Aymeric concluded by confiding to them the conviction that lit up his life since they arrived in the projects: "*You can find beauty at the feet of apartment buildings.*"

Faara went back across the parking lot in the golden light of the late afternoon. The young catechumen thought intensely of Bernadette, the hideous "dungeon" where she lived for a time bathed in love, the obscure and plain grotto where she had met the infinite, and her hidden life in the Nevers convent. She knew that the couple in Block E was like the leaven in the dough, and that its gentle and persevering presence could change lives, starting with her own. Something within her had been illuminated, and from now on it was to dance in the depths of her eyes, even when the projects brought its share of hostility and ugliness.

It was hope.

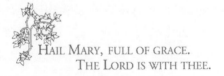

HAIL MARY, FULL OF GRACE.
THE LORD IS WITH THEE.

OUR LADY OF ASIA

The Propagation of the Message of Lourdes,
February 9, 2002

20
02
I was adopted. My parents had two children, and then they decided to welcome a third. The adoption services asked them if they would accept an Asian child, and they said yes. They promised themselves that they would let me discover my country and my roots when I turned eighteen.

I am now nineteen. I am also a seminarian, and providence so willed it that, while on an apostolate with *Lourdes Magazine* during vacation, I was given the responsibility of speaking on the links between Asians and Lourdes! This happened on the eve of what promised to be a life-changing trip to India.

While waiting to leave, I stayed with the Handmaids of the Sacred Heart of Jesus. Since their arrival at the shrine in 1995 with Sister Hélène in the leadership role, they have been opening wide their arms to welcome their Asian compatriots and devising a Lourdes pilgrimage program for them so that every moment might bring its own faith experience. In their white house with green shutters, all is warmth and devotion. The atmosphere there is conducive to prayer. Founded in 1923, the congregation numbers close to six hundred religious in 2002. These kind sisters are not short of work, considering that the group welcoming service in Lourdes records that nine percent of its visitors are Asians.

In the foggy early morning, Sister Hélène drove me to the Tarbes airport. My destination was India and the "Lourdes of the Orient." My adventure had just begun.

After hours on a plane, a bus, and a car, I finally arrived at my last stop in the Pondicherry region. To my very great surprise, the Marian Shrine of Vellangany looked almost like an exact copy of the Rosary Basilica. The resemblance was striking! It was February 11, the feast of Our Lady's first apparition to Saint Bernadette.

I sidled through the hundreds of people who had come to celebrate the Tenth World Day of the Sick. Brown-skinned children with shaven heads were praying the Way of the Cross on their knees in the sand. To my right, a woman in a turquoise sari was making her confession in the open air; to my left, Muslim families were lighting up tapers, and Hindus in variegated garments were honoring the Virgin of Good Health with a rain of flower petals. You would think it was an interreligious shrine! Our Lady, global Mediatrix of interreligious dialogue?

"A nice lesson in love, isn't it?" said an old man behind me.

"It's Our Lady's work, for sure!" I said, impressed.

"Everything started here when a beautiful Lady came to heal a lame orphan," the man said. "After that, she sent him to ask for a chapel to be built. Moved by these apparitions, everyone congregated in this fishing village: Christians, non-Christians, many of the oppressed, the *Dalits,* as we say. These days, the road conditions are bad enough to burst many a tire, and yet people come from all over India to gather around the statue of Our Lady of Good Health. Look at how beautiful she is with her fairy lights!"

The old Hindu never tired of contemplating her. A Tamil edged in between us. We were all gathered as one heart to honor Mary.

Night was falling, and I went to sleep, rocked by the Indian *Ave Maria* melody heard from the shrine. Early in the morning, the shrine priest who took me in gave me an article from the local newspaper. Aided by my English studies, I could make out an excerpt of the pilgrimage diary of Father Angelo Pelis, an Oblate of Mary Immaculate. Incredibly, he was talking about the feast of Our Lady of Lourdes, but in Laos!

Father Pelis wrote: "*I'm going to Paksane, one hundred and four miles from Vientiane, where a flourishing missionary district is located. Ten adolescents are baptized, then the evening yields a torchlight procession, quite simply, just as in Lourdes. A small group of girls in colorful skirts and arrayed with the traditional silk scarf accompany the Virgin. The statue, normally venerated in her grotto near the church, is adorned with light, candles, countless flowers… Massabielle, the Gave, the basilicas, everything is so far and yet so close tonight!*"

That was exactly what I felt the day before! This Father Pelis and I were living the mystery of Lourdes thousands of miles from the shrine. The end of the article left me speechless: The cornerstone of the North Laos Seminary is a piece from the Massabielle rock. A piece of Lourdes at the end of the world – that made me want to hit the road across India in the footsteps of the missionaries!

Since 1860, Bernadette's story has been circulating by word of mouth. Father Tarbes brought the message from Lourdes to Pondicherry; Father Peyramale – a relative of Bernadette's pastor, born in 1844 like the saint herself – created a grotto dedicated to Mary in his village lost in the Indian countryside, and Father Darras has done as much, even adding the building of a chapel in Chetpet. I am amazed at this irresistible propagation of the message of the Immaculate.

When I told Father Aman all of this, he smiled at me. He then explained that in India there is a profusion of the first names Lourdes-Raj, Lourdes-Mary, Lourdusamy, given to Indian children as a sign of devotion. But that's not all: All of Asia has faith in Our Lady of Lourdes. He told me about Taiwan, where representations of Mary outnumber family portraits! And in Vietnam, west of Qang-Tri, there is a place called the "Vang" where the Vietnamese gather every three years; it is where the Virgin appeared to comfort persecuted Christians and to encourage them to persevere in the faith. Father Aman had a lump in his throat when he told me about China and his brother missionaries who live in clandestinity.

My return to Lourdes two weeks later might have been disorientating due to jet lag and cultural changes, but I actually readjusted very smoothly. That was partly because it was time for the yearly pilgrimage of the Tamils of France! I ran to join Sister Hélène amid the celebrations, glad to rediscover the offerings of incense and flowers, the joyful songs and graceful saris celebrating the happy encounter of Indians and Sri-Lankans.

"So, young man, what about this Asian trek?" someone asked.

"The Virgin has made an immense family for Bernadette... and for me, too!"

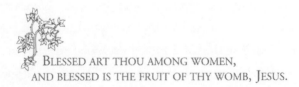

BLESSED ART THOU AMONG WOMEN,
AND BLESSED IS THE FRUIT OF THY WOMB, JESUS.

THE RAINBOW OF SCARVES

Scouts and the Youth Village in Lourdes,
July 16, 2002

2002 *Village, V-I-L-L-A-G-E: Seven letters like the colors of the rainbow, the seven gifts of the Holy Spirit or even the seven notes in a scale – V for a vivifying life, I for intensity, L for length of time, L for luminously, A for amity, G for growth, E for entirely together.* The words of Father Yves Chalvet, Youth Village director, still echoed in Yann's head. He had heard them on the day of the site's inauguration, when "his" dear youth camp was renamed "Village" to help with translation – for this place now welcomed Scouts and youngsters from the world over!

On that evening, the words of Father Chalvet took on all their meaning. July 16 was the day of Mary's last apparition to Bernadette. But it was also the feast of Our Lady of Mount Carmel and of the Village's chapel dedicated to her. This evening, it was the Scouts who ran the procession from the chapel.

For Yann, it was a special day, a day that took him back a few years to 1993. He was only fourteen at the time and was already in the Scouts of France, but he was still far from ever imagining that he might become chief! No, at that time he was just a little Scout like the others. He even was right in the middle of a teenage crisis and had done everything in his power to avoid this famous Lourdes camp.

Alas, his efforts were all in vain. Instead of going to a roller-skating and surfing camp with his middle school friends, he had ended up, seething with rage and bad will, in this little town way up in the mountains to build… a chapel!

The tall twenty-three year-old Yann smiled when he thought back to the rebellious kid he was at that time. He could still see himself stepping onto the Lourdes Station platform, his scarf all askew, with the firm determination not to grant a single smile during the entire camp. He remembered the exhausting trip to the youth camp. The heavy sack on his back, the tent weighing on his shoulders, and that interminable journey under a sweltering heat. As in a fog, he could see the setup in the middle of a tide of tents, the smiles, the words of welcome bursting forth in every language. Despite this prevailing good mood, he had grumbled until bedtime.

By the next day, his state of mind had completely changed. That day, Yann had discovered the construction site. The chapel rose a little above their campsite, like an empty shell. Only the framework was finished – the earthworks, pillars, roof – while the rest remained to be done. This would be a real challenge! Working together on this construction site were two hundred Scouts from all over.

From that point on, Yann could only remember moments of joy. There was the uncontrollable laughter with the Scouts from La Rochelle while sorting out the pebbles in the slate quarry; the pride he felt seeing the walls slowly rise; the unforgettable late nights when the sun set over the Pyrenees; conversations under the stars in which all shared their camp memories; and their projects, their dreams of a more beautiful world.

He who in his fourteen years had always regarded Scouts from other movements with a certain disdain was slowly realizing that all these "scarves" shared the same sense of service, the same ideal. He had had a conversation with Rover Scouts from the Scouts of Europe at the end of their traveling camp in the Pyrenees. During a pause, older Ranger Guides from the Unitary Scouts of France had told about a camp project in Peru for the next summer, a month of service in an orphanage. He had even made an exchange – in rough English – with some Romanian Scouts, extraordinary in their simplicity and able to perform miracles with next to nothing.

But those who fascinated him the most were the "white scarves," the Scouts of all movements who came to serve the sick. These young people had shown him a path of openness to and respect for others that he wanted to imitate. The days went by, the chapel had been raised, and Yann had felt more than a friendship, a true fraternity, growing within him.

Finally, the last stone was set just in time for the inauguration. Three months to build a chapel! It had been a true performance. For the first time, he had understood the beauty of working for God. For a month, he had worked on this site without asking himself any questions. For him, these were stones piling up to form walls. But these were not just any walls. They were there to help young people pray, to tell of the greatness of God. Yann, who had always found Masses to be a little too long, participated in the inauguration Mass with all his heart.

That was nine years ago. This evening, July 16, 2002, Yann was watching "his" kids, his little pioneers in the first row. He could sense their emotion and pride at having organized the procession in honor of Our Lady of Mount Carmel. From his location, Yann was struck by all the colors that enlivened the procession in the torches' glow. His pioneer group's red shirts blended in with the green shirts of the Lille companions with whom he set up camp, with the blue sweaters of the Scouts of Europe Rovers from Paris, with the white shirts of the Unitary Scout Ranger Guides from Bordeaux. And if you looked at the scarves, it was a veritable explosion of color! Clearly, Father Chalvet got it right with his rainbow.

Yann would never tire of watching these Scouts who were gathered in the same spirit of service, these young people with whom he was sharing far more than a campsite. He knew that all followed the same ideal, the same thirst for living to the fullest without leaving anyone by the wayside. That is why he had chosen to bring his young people here this summer of 2002 – to immerse them in this fraternity that taught him to live to the fullest. *A Scout is a friend to all. He is a brother to other Scouts.*

HOLY MARY, MOTHER OF GOD,

Saying "Yes" As Mary Did

Two Vocations in the Light of Lourdes,
May 12, 2003

2003 On that late morning in Nantes, the sky was a cheerful blue. The city was coming alive. On the sidewalks, the terraces were filling as lunchtime approached. Two young men were sitting at one of them. Florent and Adrien were in their twenties, happy to share this springtime moment like the other students on the terraces. If one perked up one's ear, Florent's and Adrien's conversation might be surprising. They, too, were laughing and recalling fond memories, but one could hear unusual words there, too.

"So, you've made your decision?" asked Adrien.

"Yes, it's settled, I'm going to the seminary next September," affirmed Florent.

"I'm happy for you. What a beautiful decision!" said Adrien. "I admire you. I envy you a little, too. As for me, I don't feel ready yet."

"Don't worry, everyone's path is different," said Florent reassuringly.

"People think that vocations arrive like a revelation," said Adrien. "They have a romantic idea of it, but that's false! In fact, it's rather a feeling that matures, slowly. I can remember, when I was little, Masses where I was an altar boy, the organ, the priest's gestures. All of that filled me with wonder, and I could see it wasn't having the same effect on my pals. I experienced that fondness as a call, a sign sent to me. I wasn't thinking; it was spontaneous. *In a little corner in my head, I had said 'yes' to the Lord, not too aware of where I was treading, flying blind!"*

"I hear you," acquiesced Florent. "I, too, have been thinking about it since I was a kid. I can't even remember how it all began – maybe at First Communion. That shows how long it's been!"

He burst into a big echoing laugh, an infectious bit of mirth that was his trademark.

"I love your laugh!" exclaimed Adrien. "It reminds me of the first time I came to Lourdes with the youth pilgrimage two years ago. You were part of the leadership team and led the vigils, remember? Your infectious laugh impressed me a lot. We spent some really good times together; it meant a lot to me."

"Of course I remember! You were new, discovering Lourdes with wide open eyes!"

At this recollection, the two friends smiled, recalling those wonderful moments spent together.

"How about you, when did you come to Lourdes for the first time?" continued Adrien.

"With my family, when I was younger," said Florent.

"How did it strike you?"

"*It was like an invitation…*"

Florent's expresson became thoughtful, and he continued:

"In fact, I was already thinking of becoming a priest, *but I lived all of that in my own little corner. When I came to Lourdes, I truly was aware of belonging to a pilgrimage. Not just anywhere! For me, there was something extraordinary in this place where the Virgin had appeared to Bernadette, a child like me. Thanks to this apparition, I understood that God was anxious to become known. Besides, in Lourdes, his presence is palpable everywhere*

– in the grotto, with all its tapers lit by pilgrims, *and especially in the adoration tent: That's where I had the concrete feeling of meeting Christ.* Lourdes truly is a place of encounter! It's an encounter of thousands of pilgrims from all countries, all languages, all spiritualities, all united in prayer. It's the *encounter of a Christ with a thousand faces. And it is that encounter that convinced me to say 'yes' as Mary did, to accept the incredible as Bernadette did."*

"Crazy!" smiled Adrien. "That's pretty much what it did to me. I was seventeen at my first pilgrimage. I was a senior in high school. There was a dynamic atmosphere among all the young. *It was a real change from the Sunday morning Masses where I always found myself isolated. In Lourdes, I had the sense of belonging to a community.* When I arrived in town, at first I was shocked by all the hotels and businesses. Then I went into the shrine, and there everything changed. *I felt peaceful, as if I were leaving all my cares behind.*

"When I entered the grotto, I had a very strong feeling. It was unforgettable. There was this gathered crowd, and yet there was an incredible atmosphere of prayer. *At the time, I had a lot of questions… I had already had feelings for a girl, and I thought I was at a crossroads, having to make a decision. In the grotto, I went to touch the Virgin's rock. And then, everything became clear: I understood that I had to accept myself in my searching, that I didn't have to impose a brutal choice on myself. That's not how things work! Lourdes helped me see myself more clearly and entrust myself to God as I was,"* Adrien said. *"I felt accepted, and so I accepted my faith better."*

"You're right," Florent responded, "but I also think that it's *the fact of being with other pilgrims that allows one to accept oneself as a believer and to make courageous choices."*

"Of course! Being with all these young people gave me an incredible self-confidence. I realized that *it wasn't all that silly to believe in God in the year 2000,* that it allowed one to experience beautiful things," Adrien replied. "To have encounters while having the Encounter. Yes, *it's an invitation to say 'yes,' to open up to life...* When I got back to my classes in high school, I tried to share what I had felt with my classmates. It wasn't easy. Then I wanted to go back to Lourdes to share my faith with others. That's why I've been investing myself, like you, in the leadership team since last September. Too bad it's your last year!"

"Hey! I, too, fully intend to go back to Lourdes every year. The seminary is not a convent!"

And, once again, he exploded in a big laugh.

Florent entered Saint John Seminary in Nantes in September 2003. In September 2007, he began his fourth year, still with the same infectious passion. Adrien, meanwhile, honored his commitment to lead the youth pilgrimages while continuing his studies in humanities at the university. In 2005, after completing his master's degree, he chose to go to the school of faith in Coutances to deepen his search. That inner journey has confirmed him in his vocation. He joined Florent at the seminary in September 2006 and now he, too, in all confidence, walks toward the priesthood.

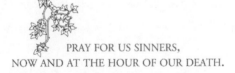

PRAY FOR US SINNERS,
NOW AND AT THE HOUR OF OUR DEATH.

A THOUSAND FORMS OF GRATITUDE

The Ex Votos *of Lourdes, July 2, 2003*

2003 In those first days of the summer of 2003, the sun was lighting up the grand esplanade of Lourdes. Miss Odette Vignoux, her flawless bun framing a finely wrinkled face with a bone china complexion, was going to the grotto at a brisk pace. A few days earlier, during a friendly cocktail party that her students had organized for her retirement, she had received a gift from her colleagues in the Department of Letters at the University of Marseille. It was a week in Lourdes in one of the town's fancy hotels. This had been a dream of hers that she had often mentioned to them when fantasizing about the day when she would have some time to herself. She wanted to take a moment to give thanks to the Lord for the joy that her years of teaching literature to hundreds of students had given her.

After Mass, Odette stopped awhile in front of the hundreds of little dark marble plaques engraved with gold that lined the crypt's hallway. They reminded every passer-by of God's actions for men and women, the old and the young, who for nearly one hundred and fifty years have been coming to pray to the Virgin Mary in the shrine. She could not help but find these *ex votos* and their accumulation nearly oppressive.

The short texts did not, for the most part, explain why the donor thanked God or the Virgin. Yet, through the "thank you" notes, the "for a healing" testimonials that seemed so cold and so distant, she felt something of the joy and fearful gratitude of the pilgrims who wanted to leave a mark of their request having been granted *ex voto* ("according to a vow," as Odette, a distinguished Latinist, remembered). This marble wall also reminded her of the work of Christian Boltanski in memory of the workers of the Grand-Hornu, in Mons, Belgium. That work had been commissioned from the artist by the director of the Contemporary Art Museum that had opened a few years ago in that industrial center. A whole wall made up of iron boxes, each one bearing a worker's name and sometimes his photograph, and containing written fragments of his life found in the archives. It was the same cold commemoration, and the same aggregate of persons, but also the same possibility, through imagination and faith, to enter into the innermost depths of a life by focusing on one of the parts of this great puzzle.

In the grotto, the *ex voto* testimonials have disappeared. Yet Odette remembered that the last time she came – with her parents, over forty years ago – crutches hanging from a stretched wire recalled the miracles experienced by sick or handicapped pilgrims who had recovered the use of their limbs here, the joy of freedom and life. As a child, that image had struck her. She had remembered it not long before when she was working with one of her students on the latter's doctoral thesis on the writer Rainer Maria Rilke. She started to recite slowly, in a quiet voice, focusing on the grotto and on the pilgrims who were slowly crossing it, absorbed in their prayer:

> "*Which one of my sick limbs shall I hang beneath thine image,*
> *Thou who didst stay mute to my long and slow appeals?*
> *Shall I affix my hands that fell down from my heart*
> *Or that very heart from which these hands departed?*

Wilt thou, then, heal my foot, that arduously walked the path
Up to the wretched chapel? Dost thou want my bended knee?[1]"

The remainder of the poem was lost in her memory while her gaze stopped upon a very young girl in a wheelchair who was accompanied by a couple and a young child. *There must have been a row of empty wheelchairs in front of this grotto,* she thought. They would have indicated that healing that came from God, like the litter carried by the paralytic in the Gospel, near the pool of Bethesda, or the empty tomb of Christ calling all men to believe that death does not have the last word. But the *ex votos* have become stones where writing alone is present. No more hanging crutches, no more little paintings, images, or objects that are so common in Marseille and in Odette's beloved South. All of these works, often quaint, which, in their own way, told of the encounter of man with God – through an event, a shipwreck, a broken leg – all that is left are stones where today faith alone can make out echoes of the Gospel.

On her way back, Odette thought about the painting by Philippe de Champaigne, "*Ex-voto*." The painter represented a reclining religious sister, a single beam of light falling upon her. That simplicity and austerity suit the mystery of Lourdes and of young Bernadette. It was the mystery of a visit, that of Christ, born of his Mother, causing all men who recognize him as the heart of the world to shudder. In the last analysis, the very grotto of Lourdes is an *ex voto*. That is perhaps why it has been copied in so many places: It is the *ex voto* of all men and all women who thank God every day for coming to meet them through his Mother, an *ex voto* that welcomes all the marble plaques and all the crutches in the world.

---

1. Rainer Maria Rilke, *Ex-Voto. Späte Gedichte,* Insel Verlag edition. Translated and quoted by René Creux, *Les Ex-Voto racontent* (Paris: Flammarion / Switzerland: Fontainemore, 1979).

Back at her hotel, Odette smiled. She could imagine herself laying a copy of each one of the theses she had directed before the grotto by way of thanks for the happiness she had felt teaching literature to her dear students.

Amen.

THE PILGRIMAGE OF SMILES

Lourdes Cancer Hope, May 12, 2004

2004 The word fell like a guillotine blade, brutal, raw, and irremediable. Nearly incredulous, Thomas nevertheless felt something like a dagger piercing his heart. It was cancer. He was thirty-four, and he had cancer.

Since that bad news, weeks had passed, and it was difficult to bear treatments as well. But the hardest thing to accept was the averted or pitiful look of others, that distance that many now put in their relationships with him. It was as if the illness were contagious, as if it were a curse, as if he did not have an urgent need to be looked at, listened to, loved, esteemed today as much as before, today more than yesterday.

Despite his parents, who supported him as much as they could; despite his girlfriend who was as attentive to him as ever but who could not come to grips with the sickness, he felt alone. He would have liked to fight against his cancer, but he needed others to fight with him. Alone, it was beyond his weakening strength.

Thomas was discouraged when he walked into the waiting room at the hospital of Tours where he was to have a scan. A man was already waiting for him. The man raised his bright eyes, put his book aside, got up, and stretched his hand out to Thomas. His name was Barnabé, and he was in a relapse of a cancer he thought had been healed. A calm and luminous strength radiated from him, however. Thomas did not understand where it came from. Questioned about it, Barnabé answered in three words – "Lourdes Cancer Hope" – which the young man received like an electric shock:

How can one associate cancer and hope? Thomas thought. *The former destroys the latter, gnaws at it, leaving nothing of it! These words cannot be uttered in the same breath, it's…*

But the revolt that Thomas wanted to let explode ran out of steam by itself. So he asked questions. He wanted to know what was hidden behind that name. Barnabé explained:

"Lourdes Cancer Hope ("Lourdes Cancer Espoir"), LCE as it is called, was born in 1985, spearheaded by a man with cancer. The next year, three hundred and fifty people participated in the association's first pilgrimage. Since then, it has taken place every year in September, and it now brings together forty-five hundred people who are either sick or confronted with cancer. Beyond the pilgrimage, the association is organized in delegations that work everywhere in France to support specific activities. These initiatives, though simple, change everything – telephone calls, visits, letters of encouragement, days of friendship… These small actions are rays of hope that light up the often dark daily lives of the sick."

Hope! The word was uttered once again. Silence set in between the two men. This word was still empty, nearly shocking for Thomas, whereas it was filled with strength and light for Barnabé. The latter continued then, with a quiet yet surprisingly firm voice:

"What I am about to tell you will surely scandalize you at first, but I cannot remain quiet. I hit the same depths as you, the same dejections, the same hopes and jolts of energy that come to nothing, the same temptations to give up on everything, and once again the desire to fight in spite of everything. I met other patients, some who had been healed, some who had not. I met hurried doctors, and others who took the time to speak to me. I met sympathetic friends, and others who were embarrassed at being with me with their good health. I relied on some to hang in there, and I tried not to begrudge the others.

"I had forgotten God a little in all of that, but he had not forgotten me. He was waiting for me on the Lourdes Cancer Hope Pilgrimage, to which my brother insisted on bringing me. I did not expect anything specific from it... You may not believe me, but what I found there was the impossible become possible. I thought I would encounter the sadness of cohorts of the sick; what I found was the joy of crowds loving life! Joy was evident on all faces, from cancer-ridden children all the way to women who came instead of their sick husbands. There was laughter about to break out on all lips, a holiday atmosphere in which pretense had no place. Besides, LCE is nicknamed 'the pilgrimage of smiles'; that takes the cake, doesn't it? I thought I would be annoyed by pilgrims more superstitious than animated by a true faith. I was amazed by the simplicity of the prayers and ceremonies, everyone's prayerful attitude, and the truthfulness and freedom of the exchanges. I was overwhelmed by Bernadette – so small, so simple, yet so great and so genuine. Sickness, pain, relapses, incomprehension, destitution... she knew it all, bore it all, accepted it all in peace, trust in God, hope. Yes, hope!

"I also met Mary's smile, her maternal goodness. I felt I was somebody for her, someone who counted. And she brought me to Jesus, her Son, whom I had somewhat written off in my life. He showed me that he had undergone pain before me, and that he could talk to me about it. And he gave me sick brothers and sisters so that we might be stronger together.

When I left Lourdes, I still had my cancer, but my heart and my soul were healed. And that's the more beautiful healing! I went back on pilgrimage several times to draw courage from there once again, to see the members of this incredible LCE family. I did not choose to be sick and to suffer; no one ever does. It isn't easy every day, and yet I thank God who, through all these trials, made me discover his love for me. He opened my eyes to fraternity, to the beauty of life, to the deep joy that even cancer will never take from me.

"Yes, as shocking as it may seem, I have never been as happy and at peace as today! It is because I am no longer alone, because I know that I never again shall be alone, and because I have understood what counts: God bears the weight of my pain with me; beyond cancer, Life with a capital L is promised to me. That's what hope is! And that's the true miracle of Lourdes."

The waiting room door opened, and a doctor invited Barnabé to follow him. The man got up, gave Thomas a warm handshake, and wished him to discover what he had discovered for himself. Before going away, he turned around and called out with a smile:

"I may have bored you with my tale, but you know, the Lourdes Cancer Hope Pilgrimage is not told, it is lived!"

Thomas remained lost in thought. In his heart, a little flame had been lit, tenuous and fragile yet. But he sensed that it was that of hope, and he now knew where that flame could grow.

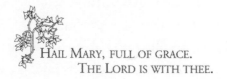

HAIL MARY, FULL OF GRACE.
THE LORD IS WITH THEE.

The Pope of the Sick

Pope John Paul II's Second Visit to Lourdes,
August 15, 2004

20
04 *I would like to hold you in my arms.* Jacques, from his blue cart, was listening with all his heart. The words of the old man in white reached him in the depths of his illness. These were not the words of a healthy man, nor of a powerful man of this world. No, these were the words of a sick old man who was burning with love – a humble, weak, exhausted man. Yet when Jacques caught his eye, he read all the strength of an inexhaustible love in it. He who had come to Lourdes to ask a miracle of this almighty God hidden up in the heavens had just received far more in one single moment. This old man – who, like him, was sitting in a wheelchair because his legs could no longer support him – gave a father's gaze, so close that Jacques was overcome. In a few seconds, Pope John Paul II had just revealed to him a face of God he had not suspected – the luminous mystery of an infinitely loving Father.

The Pope had arrived at the shrine that very morning. Twenty-one years after his first pilgrimage, he had wished to celebrate the one-hundred-and-fiftieth anniversary of the proclamation of the Immaculate Conception in Lourdes. What place could be more fitting? It was in

Lourdes that "the Lady" revealed this name of Immaculate Conception to the young Bernadette. *The Immaculate Conception*, as Bishop Renato Boccardo, organizer of the Pope's travels, recalled, *is the beauty of human life created in the image of God.*

The Pope had carried out this pilgrimage as a sick person, as had so many before him. Every word he uttered left him breathless. He no longer walked, allowing himself to be led around in his wheelchair instead. His health left the organizers in a state on uncertainty until the very end. The Vatican authorities had postponed the confirmation of his visit as long as possible. Once it was announced, everyone stepped into action to prepare, from the VIP security service to the emergency ambulance service and the hospital. The latter was readied in light of Pope John Paul II's health, which was so precarious. On the ground, the infrastructures necessary to welcome three hundred thousand had to be set up in record time. That would include sound, video, and screens and the stage for the celebrations, and also water distribution, lavatories, guardrails, and the housing of pilgrims.

When the Pope arrived in Lourdes that morning, he was cheered by the crowd through which he moved sitting in his car, the famous "Popemobile" that went with him on his trips. It had been a long time since the old man last stood upright in it. Even now, he remained sitting in his seat, his face tense with pain but also with an indestructible will. Before such courage, emotion reached its zenith among the pilgrims. Many of the sick, like Jacques, were moved by the state of this pope who resembled them.

Once at the grotto, Pope John Paul II wished to kneel at the feet of the Virgin's statue. He received some assistance, but after a few moments his body sank, and two assistants helped him to sit his seat at once. After recovering, his first words were for the sick to whom he felt closer than ever: "*I am with you, dear brothers and sisters, I am sharing with you a time of life marked by physical suffering, yet no less fruitful in God's admirable plan."* The suffering Pope added: *"I would like to hold you in my arms, one after the other, with affection, and tell you how close I am to you and in what solidarity with you."* Unable to make further speeches as he had during his first trip, he then entered into a long silent prayer before the grotto, his face deep in his hands. Behind him, several French bishops in the first row could not withhold their tears.

After a rest, Pope John Paul II was back at the grotto that afternoon in better shape. He introduced the five "luminous mysteries" he had proposed in his apostolic letter *Rosarium Virginis Mariae* in 2004, at the beginning of his pontificate's twenty-fifth year. These new mysteries invited the faithful to contemplate the great steps in Jesus' public life. The Pope continued his pilgrimage in the shrine as he meditated on these five mysteries.

For the first mystery, the baptism of Jesus, some of the sick and some hospitallers awaited the Pope near the pools, just as the crowds, gathered along the Jordan River, awaited John's baptism. The meditation on the second mystery, the wedding at Cana, took place on the meadow, before the adoration tent. It was families, symbolizing the wedding feast, who welcomed the procession. As for the proclamation of the kingdom that constitutes the third mystery, Pope John Paul II meditated among the sick. Is it not to the poor *par excellence* to whom the joy of the kingdom is announced?

After a time of prayer, the procession made its way to the reconciliation chapel near the statue of the Curé of Ars for the fourth mystery, the Transfiguration. Dozens of priests in purple stoles were hearing confessions and receiving pilgrims who sought them out. *"Reconciliation is the transfiguration of our sinful lives,"* Bishop Jacques Perrier of Tarbes and Lourdes commented to introduce the prayer time. Meditation on the fifth mystery, the Eucharist, took place in front of the Rosary Basilica with a thousand altar servers, boys and girls, cheering the old man.

Because of his frailty, it was impossible for the Pope to participate in the traditional torchlight procession. Nevertheless, he addressed a message of peace from the Our Lady Welcoming Center, where he wished to lodge like all sick pilgrims. The next day, celebrating the Mass of the Assumption before two hundred and fifty people, knowing full well that he was inescapably approaching death, the Pope concluded his homily with these vibrant words: "*The Virgin of Lourdes has a message for you; here it is: Be free men and women! Walk with Mary on the paths of your humanity's full actualization!*"

Blessed art thou among women, and blessed is the fruit of thy womb, Jesus.

AT THE SERVICE OF THE SICK

History of the Our Lady of Salvation Hospitality,
December 1, 2004

20 04 Miss Simonot, a teacher at Massabielle High School in Lourdes, crossed the courtyard with a brisk stride on an October afternoon. She had volunteered to take charge of a few religious culture classes about the town where she was born and even whose climate, as unforgiving as it is, she cherished. She was happy that the history of the shrine was not getting lost and that her students could at least have an acquaintance with the miracles of fraternity that take place there every day. Once in her eighth-grade class, she cleared her throat.

"Today we are going to talk about the Our Lady of Salvation Hospitality," Miss Simonot said. "Of course, as I tell you every time, do not hesitate to interrupt me if there is something you don't understand.

"By 1870, the Lourdes pilgrimages had undergone a surge in the number of participants, and it was becoming difficult to welcome all those who wished to come. In 1872, the Assumptionists created the Our Lady of Salvation Association, whose goal it was to work for the salvation of France through prayer. Yes, Thomas?"

"Ma'am, who are the Assumptionists?" asked Thomas, interrupting as the teacher had asked. "Does it have something to do with the feast of the Assumption on August 15?"

"It does," the teacher replied. "They take their title from the word 'Assumption,' from the Latin *assumere,* meaning 'to take with oneself, to take away.' The Blessed Virgin was indeed 'taken away' to heaven. The Assumptionists are consecrated men and women who live communally and are committed in the name of Mary to fight against exploitation and exclusion. The association is notably in charge of organizing the national pilgrimage every year. Do you know when it takes place?"

"Around August 15, Ma'am," another boy offered. "My parents are volunteers every year."

"That's it, David. The choice of that date is relatively recent, though," Miss Simonot explained. "The first national pilgrimage, subtitled 'of the banners,' took place in October 1872. It would only be a century later, at the request of the bishop of Lourdes, that the decision was made to organize it always around August 15.

"But let's backtrack a little. Beginning in 1876, the Little Sisters of the Assumption had taken care of the pilgrims. As the number of pilgrims grew more numerous each day, however, they could no longer handle the responsibility. So, in 1881, the Our Lady of Salvation Hospitality was created. Composed of lay persons, it placed itself at the disposal of the sick who were participating in the national pilgrimage organized by the Assumptionist Fathers.

"At this point I should like to make an aside on a word we mentioned during a former class – 'hospitality,'" she said. "Does anyone remember? Lucile?"

"We had talked about the story of Abraham and Sarah, who granted their hospitality to three visitors," Lucile recalled. "You had also had us read the passage in which Jesus said to his disciples, '*Whoever receives you receives me.*'[1]"

"Well done, Lucile. That quotation illustrates the spiritual meaning of hospitality that the Our Lady of Salvation Hospitality makes its own. Just a moment ago, David said an important word – 'Volunteers.' They are also called 'hospitallers.' Without them, the national pilgrimage, which takes in seven thousand pilgrims every year and up to thirty thousand on August 15, could not take place. Today there are four thousand who have committed themselves, among whom two thousand are young people.

"Lay persons, men or women, young or not so young, single or married, give of their time and money – for they pay their own way for this trip and during their stay – to take care of the sick. They put into practice the sentence of Jesus that goes, '*It is more blessed to give than to receive.*'[2] Do you know how to recognize them, David?"

David knew the answer. "Every year, my parents stitch a little woven red cross on their clothes."

"That insignia was given by Pope Pius IX to the pilgrimage leaders in 1873," the teacher explained. "Their motto is *Christo Domino servire*, meaning "To Be at the Service of Christ the Lord." Let us now try to enumerate the different services in which the hospitallers participate. Christine?"

"I think they accompany the sick on the trains," Christine offered.

"Yes," said Miss Simonot, "and as soon as they arrive in Lourdes, at the Our Lady of Sorrows Hospital or at the Our Lady Shelter, they assist in the wake-up calls, meals, and bedtimes. Anything else? Antoine?"

"They work as stretcher-bearers during the processions and the celebrations, and help the pilgrims to bathe," came Antoine's reply.

---

1. Mt 10: 40.
2. Acts 20: 35.

"Yes, in those cases they are pool attendants. Don't forget their role at the grotto where they take on policing duties to regulate and discipline the immense crowd. Sophie?"

"They participate in caregiving," added Sophie.

"That's right. Volunteers in the medical profession constitute the community of health-care givers, and they are assisted by all the other volunteers. They care for handicapped and sick people, young or old," the teacher explained. "What is important to keep in mind as well is that the work of the hospitallers is not only material. Though they are helping 'hands,' they are also 'hearts.' Listening, comforting, entertaining the sick, who are often so lonely for the rest of the year, is part and parcel of their role. Ah, there's the bell ringing, it's already over! François, as usual, your head is in the clouds..."

Miss Simonot had it wrong. François hadn't missed a bit of the presentation. Later, he would become a hospitaller. By six o'clock in the morning, he would help Marcel get cleaned up, lovingly and patiently, joyful just to be together. Every year, despite the niggling desire to go on vacation, he would answer Our Lady of Lourdes' call during the five days of the national pilgrimage. On the esplanade, he would place a blanket around Monique and hold Georgette's hand very tight. For hours on end, he would listen to Franck talk about his grandchildren who make him forget his multiple sclerosis. He would not forget to bring Christophe his verbena tea and, in the evening, despite his tiredness, he would sing out the hospitallers' prayer: *Mary, mother of Jesus, we offer thee all our strengths to build a better world, seeking not to be served, but to serve, to serve our sick brothers... Amen.*

"François, do you hear me? Off you go, it's time for your next class. Off with you!" the teacher said.

The lad left the classroom in a daze. Miss Simonot smiled and murmured, just for herself: "And you, François, will you love serving?"

HOLY MARY, MOTHER OF GOD,

A Crown of Nine Gems

The Shrines around Lourdes, August 10, 2005

2005 "Let's go!" Despite the few rainclouds lingering on the Pyrenees mountain peaks, the dynamic team joyfully got going on the little pebble path.

"*Hail Mary, full of grace!*" intoned the lead walker. "*The Lord is with thee...*" continued the four strapping lads as they fell energetically into step behind him.

The five youths would not miss this yearly meeting for the world. These hiking days were privileged moments among the cousins: They represented three days of freedom during which they would be alone, without their parents. These were three hiking days during which they would have to fend for themselves and surpass themselves, too. Best of all, these were three days during which their faith would be refreshed!

It all began in 2003, a little before the feast of the Assumption, August 15. For the first time, the boys' parents would allow them to go alone, for a day, on a hike. They were each thirteen, and each saw the world as their oyster. On vacation at their grandparents' house, the five cousins began with a long study of their itinerary before setting their hearts on a small village a few miles away – the village of Héas.

With packs on their backs, solid hiking boots on their feet, and walking sticks in hand, they set off from their vacation home, nearly running in order to reach their goal by nightfall. Everything had been organized: Their parents would come and fetch them in the early evening after they had enjoyed a dinner under the stars!

The five cousins walked with a good stride all day, sometimes stopping to drink a little or munch on one of the granola bars their grandmother had slipped into their pockets. Their itinerary was relatively short, but tough. They had to scale a few crests, walk down slippery slopes, and climb badly maintained footpaths. Yet nothing dampened their spirits. Quite the contrary, the difficulty of the excursion galvanized them.

It was only five o'clock in the afternoon when they reached Héas. Their parents would arrive around eleven at the earliest. At that point, one of them suggested visiting the church.

It was no sooner said than done. The five youngsters entered the small granite building. The chapel was neither very big nor particularly beautiful. Yet, without warning, it submerged the five boys with emotion. They allowed themselves to be overcome by the place's serenity, and without even realizing it, they started to recite a rosary out loud.

The rest of the evening wasn't how they had imagined. To be sure, they picnicked like trappers, but they spoke neither of girls nor of friends. Rather, they devised plans for the next year.

Leaving the chapel, transformed by this improvised time of prayer, they learned from an information board that the church of Héas belonged to a "crown of shrines." "Everyone knows Lourdes," said the yellow pamphlet that had been hanging there for years, "but who knows the crown of shrines that surrounds it?

"Well before the apparitions to Bernadette in 1858, the Virgin was venerated in nine shrines set on the slopes of the Pyrenees: Héas, Piétat,

Saint-Savin, Poueylaün, Bourisp, Nouilhan, Médous, Bétharram, and Garaison," the brochure explained. "These places do not have the impact of Lourdes, but to ignore and forget them completely would pretty much serve as an implicit denial that the Virgin Mary had prepared her coming to Lourdes through them."

As they read this piece of paper, the five boys made a firm decision: Every summer, they would walk to one of these nine pilgrimage sites.

The first year, in Héas, they saw the little chapel consecrated to the Virgin Mary, where the shepherds could attend Mass on Sundays when they would lead their flocks to graze in the mountains. The following year, in Bourisp, they prayed in a church erected on the very place where an ox had discovered a statue of the Virgin – a statue which, though moved several times, always returned to that spot miraculously.

This year, the third, the five cousins were on their way to Garaison. In time, their little trek had taken on the air of a pilgrimage. They prayed and sang as they walked. Some people took the road to Compostella, and in doing so they walked along the "crown of shrines." The cousins' road is shorter, of course, but the exercise is none the easier for all that. Walking in the mountains requires real endurance and great tenacity.

With a glance at the map in their hands, the boys thought about the history of the Garaison shrine they had read about before taking off.

About 1515, a young shepherdess, Anglèse de Sagazan, was keeping her father's flocks near a spring at Monléon, in the Garaison valley. Suddenly a lady dressed in white appeared to her and introduced herself as the Virgin Mary. She asked the shepherdess to have a chapel built in that place. No one besides her father believed Anglèse. It was only on the third apparition, when the young woman presented herself to the lady with her family and a few village people, that the population opened its eyes and began to believe. To convince them, the Virgin Mary had transformed the black bread that Anglèse was holding into a fresh white loaf... An oratory was built, crowds came on pilgrimage, and the water from the spring performed miracles.

As they read this history, the boys noted the striking resemblance of these apparitions with those of Lourdes – the shepherdess, the miraculous spring, the crowd... This little spiritual trek certainly had many marvelous discoveries in store for them in the years to come!

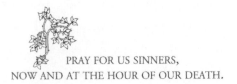

PRAY FOR US SINNERS,
NOW AND AT THE HOUR OF OUR DEATH.

AT THE SERVICE OF LORDS

The Order of Malta in Lourdes, April 30, 2006

20 06 The young woman tenderly wiped little Kathie's mouth with a handkerchief. The child smiled at her. The volunteer's heart tightened. This smile was without a doubt the most beautiful she had ever seen.

The little girl was certainly not a great beauty. She was quite the opposite. In the street, people often averted their gaze from the face of this child deformed by disease. Her mouth was huge, always gaping and rimmed with drool that never stopped dripping. Her eyes seemed to bulge a little. They shone with a disturbing intensity. But when Kathie smiled, her face would suddenly light up. Forgotten were her eyes, her mouth, and her deformities. She would become beautiful, infinitely beautiful, for in her smile one read all the joy and love that were hidden in her child's heart. One could guess all the trust she put in those who took care of her.

"Ju... Ju... lie!"

Kathie tried to articulate the name of the young woman who patiently had been watching over her for four days.

"Yes, sweetie, it's me!"

The girl smiled all the more, showing all her teeth.

"What is making you smile?" asked Julie.

"Ju... Ju... Julie!" repeated Kathie with contagious joy.

"Seems she likes you," noted a neighbor, lying on a stretcher.

"Yes, indeed, we have become friends."

Kathie came close to choking with joy hearing Julie speaking of their new relationship in this way.

"I know Kathie pretty well," continued the neighbor. "She's like me; she comes every year. A regular! Eh, Kathie? You recognize me, it's Gisèle."

The girl turned her eyes sparkling with mischief toward the sick lady.

"Gi... Gi... sèle!" she articulated, with nearly no trouble.

"Have you been coming for long?" asked Julie, piqued by curiosity.

"For twelve years," Gisèle said. "The Order of Malta never forgets. They always come and get me for their annual pilgrimage. It is my yearly outing, my breath of fresh air, my vitamin!"

The sick woman pulled up to her chin the black blanket completely covering her thin body. There was a white eight-branched cross on the material. All the sick people around her, including little Kathie, had the same blanket on them.

"It's the first time I've come," confided Julie.

"Are you a member of the order?" asked Gisèle.

"No, I'm just beginning to discover it. I met some members of Malta at the social emergency ambulance service where I volunteer," replied Julie. "I liked what they told me about their order. They've been perpetuating their hospital mission at the service of the weakest for ten centuries. From knights of the Middle Ages to today's knights, from Jerusalem to the whole world, they have given ten centuries of charity, faith, and devotion. It's extraordinary! I wanted to know more, and they invited me to their yearly pilgrimage to Lourdes. I didn't think it would be so intense," she added, tenderly looking at little Kathie.

"I understand. They are our lords," answered a voice behind her.

The voice belonged to a lady who was about fifty years old. Like most of the ladies there, she was wearing a long black cape lined in red. On her shoulder was the same white eight-branched cross. She was holding Gisèle's stretcher.

"Excuse me?" hesitated Julie.

"The sick are our lords," continued the hospitaller. "Each one of them resembles Christ, and we must serve them. Do you know the motto of the Order of Malta?"

"Um, no, not yet," said the young woman, excusing herself.

"It is *Tuitio Fidei et Obsequium Pauperum* ('Defense of the Faith and Assistance to the Poor')," the hospitaller said.

Julie meditated on these words for a moment.

"Do you come here often?" she finally asked the woman.

"Every year for fifteen years now. For me and for many members of the order, Lourdes is a an inexhaustible source of newfound energy. Here, the service to the poorest is at the heart of the pilgrimage. At the same time, our spiritual thirst is ceaselessly fed and renewed by prayer at the grotto, the Masses, the immersion in the pools, the teaching. Lourdes is in perfect harmony with our order's *raison d'être*."

Julie scanned the crowd around her. There were several thousands gathered on the esplanade waiting to hear Mass. The sick, lying on stretchers or sitting in the blue cars pulled by hospitallers, were lined up in the first rows. A volunteer was busying himself gently among the weakest. Most of the women were wearing the same long black-and-red cape as Julie's neighbor. The men often were dressed in black with a beret on their head. Some were walking between the rows to distribute a little water to the sick who had been waiting for awhile under the sun. Others were reciting a rosary with the persons for whom they were caring..

Hail Mary, full of grace… le Seigneur soit avec vous… Bendita tú eres entre todas las mujeres… und gebenedeit ist die Frucht deines Leibes, Jesus…

Santa Maria, Mãe de Deus... ora pro nobis peccatoribus... now and at the hour of our death. Amen."

They had come from the four corners of the globe for this annual pilgrimage of the Order of Malta. All of them believe in the same ideal – to defend the faith in a world where impiety is ceaselessly gaining ground and to take care of the poorest among them.

"Ju... lie!"

Kathie's call drew the young woman from her thoughts. She turned her head toward the child. Gisèle and the lady hospitaller accompanying her did likewise. All three looked at the smile that was again lighting up the girl's face. At the sight of these four women, able-bodied or sick, one could guess that each would go home strengthened by this pilgrimage.

Gisèle and Kathie would stock up on loving care. Julie and the hospitaller of the order would receive a lesson in courage and humility. All four would be bathed in the love of the Virgin Mary, who watches over the smallest and the most destitute.

"You... you... will... re... turn... next... year?" asked Kathie with a hint of anxiousness.

"I think so, yes," answered Julie. "In fact, I am sure. Yes, certainly, I shall return!"

AMEN.

THE ALGERIAN WAR VETERANS IN LOURDES

The AFN Pilgrimage, June 9, 2006

20 06 I am ready.

I am over seventy years old. It is time for me to make my peace with the past, with history, and with myself.

In 1988, I received an invitation for the first pilgrimage of North Africa veterans in Lourdes. That year, the president of the ACAFN[1] association, Gabriel Nivel, and the spiritual director, Father Pierre Leborgne, had gathered only three hundred people. My guess is that at that time the immense majority of us were against the idea of such a display.

That was eighteen years ago. We thought we had the strength to struggle against our demons alone. But little by little, with the perseverance of these two men and a handful of others, the gathering increased in number every other year to such a point that it became unavoidable for many war veterans, including me, even though I had promised myself never to bring up those grievous years. Between fifteen thousand and eighteen thousand people were expected this year, each one with his own story and his own war wounds. I will be among them for the first time.

---

1. Anciens combattants d'Afrique du Nord, "North Africa War Veterans."

Up until now, I have not been able to face my Algerian War companions. Their eyes would have rekindled pains, reopened certain blocked-off doors. I could not have spoken to them; I was not ready. Sickness and the urgency of age convinced me to close that chapter of my life once and for all.

I had time to go over questions, images, smells, and faces during the journey. Yet, as I got off the train, I went straight to the station café out of a persistent apprehension rather than the heat of the month of June. I needed to take a break, to catch my breath before diving in, before beginning the program: In a couple of minutes, I was going to meet with vets from my regiment. Cheating would be out of the question. We're all North Africa vets, with all that it means in terms of fraternity, ideological struggles, and nightmares. We dare to speak of war, not of a pacification mission; we speak of fanaticism and nationalism, of our share of atrocities, violence, death, and sin. All of us here know what it was like. So does the café proprietress, who has served me a lemonade. She watches her customers with a particular tenderness, and for that reason she can guess the fear and torment that many of us are feeling at that very moment. Programs have been set up here and there on the tables. I took one last look; I already knew mine.

First of all, I want to make the Way of the Cross. I need to thank the Virgin for her protection during those years of conflict. She is the one who allowed me to keep hope deep in the Arab villages when my morale was at a low point and my health was failing. I have been praying to her since 1952, and today, finally, I am visiting her land to walk by her side.

Of all the stages in this pilgrimage, this one seems to me to be the easiest, the most obvious. It was the next one I was looking forward to as much as I was dreading it – the meadow with its huts listing every regiment. That is where I will find my comrades. Our friendships are undiminished even though we have not seen each other since then. I have never been closer to anyone than to those guys. We lived, fought, and slept together. When some lost their lives to an enemy who is no longer ours, we were still together. And still today, we continue to bear the same burden: It is the burden of remembering all those we left back there and the remorse we have been dragging around since then. Fighting a war stays with you for ever, but at least we were side by side, and that is enough to make brothers of us.

We would like to know what each of us became. The rest, all that our lives could neither hide nor erase, I know we will be able to read between the lines. Between us there will always be something unspoken, like some wretched bandage hiding a raw scar. As much as we try to persuade ourselves that all we did was obey orders in Phillipeville, Algiers, or Constantine, nothing can make the hate, the impunity that guided us, go away. A war turns bad even the most gentle, even the most innocent of men. It has to, if you're to survive.

Together, we will pay homage to the dead. More than forty years after the fact, we will pray for our comrades and for the others, too, those unknown guys – all victims, no matter what side they were on – all those whom their family and friends saw disappear one day. Lourdes is surely the only place in the world where politics does not estrange people's hearts. I know that several of us will cry out of love as much as out of guilt. That is when it will be best to be together.

This evening, we will go to the vigil at Saint Bernadette Church. We will pray and sing, and maybe we will go and have some drinks at the station café, or maybe both. The most important thing will be to avoid getting separated. I do not know what the others are coming to find here; I do not even know myself – pardon, peace, friendship, compassion? But I am certain that together, thanks to the Virgin Mary, each one of us will find it.

Tomorrow I intend to go on the torchlight procession. Marching next to veterans from Algeria, from Morocco, or from Tunisia will give me the necessary strength to find the light and to get rid of the feeling of shame that has been clinging to me for so long. And I will pray for the Virgin that I may obtain pardon and that my wounds may be healed.

I am just now realizing that I am really expecting a lot out of this pilgrimage. Maybe I should have responded to the call sooner. I had chosen to try to move on, and then, like anything that you try to forget or make disappear, it ends up catching up with you someday. That someday is today; it is this pilgrimage.

I have finished my lemonade and thanked the proprietress. I can go out now.

I am ready.

HAIL MARY, FULL OF GRACE.
THE LORD IS WITH THEE.

A Day in Bernadette's Footsteps

Day Pilgrims, July 12, 2006

2006 I turned fifteen a couple of months ago, and I still cannot really get used to the idea. Until this year, I hadn't yet asked myself too many questions. But this year, I don't know, it's different. Fifteen years old! At my birthday celebration, between the candles and a chocolate cake, my father whispered to me:

"You'll see, fifteen is a fabulous age. It's the age when everything is possible!"

Even my grandfather got on the bandwagon. He gave me his "special fifteen-year-old present": a trip to Lourdes! He decided to do this for each of his grandchildren. Grandparents sure have crazy ideas, as if a trip to Lourdes could get a fifteen-year-old teenager excited! I thought he was still living in another era.

So there we were, two months later, a teenager and his grandfather, waiting for the train to Lourdes at the Biarritz Station. I wondered what the trip was going to be like. "Lourdes": The very word conjures up images of the Blessed Virgin, a grotto, churches – not very exciting, to be honest. Grandpa would surely insist on visiting the church and reading the region's tourism guide to me. The morning could be pretty long, but after that, we would have lunch in a nice little restaurant and, anyway, it would be a lovely day, and the mountains are not far away. Maybe I would be able to rescue the afternoon...

At that point in my planning, Grandpa interrupted me:

"You know, I came here with your father when he was a child, forty years ago. I do understand that a pilgrimage is not necessarily the present that a youngster dreams of today. But you'll see, Lourdes is a special place."

"Umm... you bet, Grandpa," I told him.

The next day, an enthusiastic grandpa woke me up at seven thirty. An hour later, I found myself still a bit dazed in front of my hot chocolate.

"We have an appointment at nine o'clock in front of the Virgin's statue, so let's not be late," he urged me.

An appointment? With whom? So we arrived in front of the square. To my great surprise, hundreds of people already were jostling each other – young people, not-so-young people, alone, in couples, in small groups, from all nationalities... They were gathering under big yellow signs: *Day pilgrims, Pellegrini di un giorno, Pèlerins d'un jour, Peregrinos de un dia, Pilger für einen Tag...*

We wound our way to the French sign. Grandpa stopped for a moment and contemplated the crowd:

"Things sure have changed. The first time I came with your father, there was only a handful of us. It was in 1966, I remember. That was the first year they proposed this kind of pilgrimage; it was called a 'one-day pilgrimage,' if I remember correctly. Father Gourron invited all the tourists and solitary pilgrims to join in so that their stay in Lourdes would not be a simple curiosity visit, but a real pilgrimage! We were even able to meet the movement's initiators, Bishop Théas and Father Point. They walked among us; they came to talk to us. Look, forty years later, there are thousands of us from all continents. It is quite simply extraordinary!"

And then we were off. Grandpa placed his arm on my shoulder:

"We are going to the grotto. You'll see, it's a special place."

I could not help but be struck by the prayerful attitudes of all these pilgrims. The celebrant told us about the message of Lourdes, about the gestures and words that the Virgin and Bernadette Soubirous exchanged, right here, in 1858. There was something moving in the story of this girl who was so simple, in these words that were so intense. There was a truth here that struck me as something obvious.

Around ten o'clock, we left the grotto to go on the Way of the Cross. Meditation and a prayerful attitude tangibly increased at each of the fifteen stations on the way until we reached the upper basilica. Grandpa said next to nothing; he simply stayed near me. But I needed no words to feel that we were sharing the same emotion.

After Mass, our group split up. We picked a spot on the meadow among the many pilgrims.

"So, your impressions?" Grandpa asked me as he unpacked the sandwiches.

"It's weird," I replied. "I thought we were going to Lourdes, you know, just to see… In fact, there are hundreds of us, with a reception, a guide. It is a real pilgrimage!"

"So much the better," said Grandpa. "Afterward, we'll take a walk around. There must be forums in which we can participate."

We very soon found ourselves in a discussion circle. Everyone told his or her story, shared ideas, and listened with interest. The sincerity of these exchanges surprised me. I usually did not like talking about God, but I went for it there. Between questions and testimonials, I discovered that the other pilgrims were not that different from me. They, too, had many questions in their heads. But they were progressing; they were trying to live out their faith in their everyday lives, a faith that was simple and alive.

I was beginning to understand the reason for this gathering. What would I have done if I were visiting here alone? I might've breezily read a pamphlet with the description of the city, its history, and a few dates. Here, however, I am walking in the Virgin's footsteps and facing questions that I had never asked myself.

The day was far from over. We later saw a video montage on Bernadette Soubirous, her complete destitution at the time of the apparitions, and Mary's message. At about four o'clock, we joined the sick for the Blessed Sacrament procession.

We advanced along with them, silently, as far as the Saint Pius X Basilica. They exuded so much humility, so much serenity. I felt like sharing, helping, benefiting from this pilgrimage. I wanted to join them, even a little bit.

The day continued with the torchlight procession. The procession formed at dusk, the torches were lit, and we found ourselves in the midst of the hospitallers. I was a little embarrassed, because I felt like a curious intruder. Suddenly, one of them took my hands and placed them on a young girl's wheelchair. She turned around and smiled at me. I smiled back.

Never would I have thought that a gaze, a smile, might take on such importance.

I shall not forget.

BLESSED ART THOU AMONG WOMEN,
AND BLESSED IS THE FRUIT OF THY WOMB, JESUS.

FRIENDS IN THE LORD

The Ignatian Family Jubilee, July 27, 2006

20 06 Xavier arrived in Lourdes among the last. In the Saint Bernadette Church, filled with young people, he was given a spot in the first row. He hated that. He wasn't too convinced when he came and would rather have stayed at the back. A student in Paris, he had met Béatrice, one of the chaplaincy girls whom he liked. She belonged to a prayer group of the Ignatian Youth Network, and on Sunday nights she went to a strange Mass, "the Mass that takes its time."

Xavier, for his part, preferred expeditious Masses, but he went a few times to accompany her. One day, she mentioned a kind of pilgrimage to Lourdes. Xavier did his best to tell her that pilgrimages were not really his cup of tea, but Béatrice retorted: "But you must come! It's in honor of your patron saint and his friends. What, doesn't Saint Francis Xavier mean anything to you?"

He did go to Lourdes, and that is how he found himself in the first pew of the international youth Mass that inaugurated the great "Manresa 2006" jubilee. This jubilee, as he now knew, was that of Saint Francis Xavier and of the Blessed Peter Favre, who were both born in 1506, and of Saint Ignatius of Loyola, who died in 1556. These were the first three of the ten founders of the Society of Jesus, and they were being honored in Lourdes – the former five hundred years later, the latter four hundred and fifty years later – until August 4, and all year pretty much everywhere else.

Xavier would have liked to have been able to show Béatrice everything he knows now. Among the hundreds of strangers who were singing around him, however, he felt quite alone: The pretty young woman had stood him up, as he learned on the station platform. Who in the world comes down with chicken pox at the age of twenty-three?

It was at that same age – Xavier made a note of it as he was reading in the train – that Francis Xavier and Peter Favre met a former soldier who was already approaching his fortieth birthday. His name was Ignatius. As a student in Paris on an October evening in 1529, Ignatius burst into the "Paradise," the room he was to share with Peter and Francis Xavier at Saint Barbara College.

Xavier, who also had a roommate, could not help but like this aristocrat from Navarre, this Francis Xavier, or rather Francisco de Jassu y Javier to give him his full name. He was a man who liked sports and gambling dens. He held the coveted and comfortable position of canon of the Cathedral of Pamplona. Xavier admired how he was able to get along with Peter, that rather timid peasant from Savoy and, more difficult still, how he could put up with Ignatius, that intruder who once had fought against his family and thought it necessary to convert him.

In Francis Xavier and in his resistance to grace, Xavier fancied he saw himself. He wondered what might've happened for Ignatius to win over Francis Xavier's confidence and drag them both along the path that he was to follow as an apostle to the Indies, to Japan, and to the outskirts of China. How did he get to the point of allowing God to conquer him? And how did the clear and consistent antipathy of Francis Xavier for Ignatius yield to the point that, along with Peter, all three liked to call themselves "friends in the Lord"?

"Friends in the Lord," was precisely the theme of the "Manresa 2006" gathering. Xavier saw it repeated everywhere around him on the jubilee logo. He could also make it out on the faces around him, although he was not yet ready to admit that to himself.

The next day, he went to the Saint Pius X Basilica for the morning Office. This time, he took care not to place himself in the first row so that he would have a better position as an observer. The gathering was more diverse that morning. He saw gray-haired Jesuits looking all around them. And young people, thousands of young people just like Xavier were there!

Later in the day, during a forum, he met Philippe, who was in charge of logistics. Philippe helped him find his way in the Jesuit crowd, where he was not the only one to get lost. Visibly, the jubilee was an historic event in that for the first time it brought together all the members of the Ignatian family, so to speak.

"Let's see," said Philippe. "There are about ten thousand people here, among them four hundred fathers of the Society of Jesus, the Jesuits; a good thousand religious sisters from forty female Ignatian congregations; and four thousand lay members of the Community of Christian Life (*Communauté vie chrétienne*, or CVX). Add to that about a thousand joyful children, and that's not all. The Eucharistic Youth Movement, the Ignatian Youth Network, the alumni from Jesuit schools, those from the Madeleine Daniélou centers, the Christian Movement of executives and directors, the New Way... Even I have trouble identifying all the groups that are represented here!"

Xavier asked him whether he knew any "Xavières" groups and why there were no "Xaviers." Philippe smiled and called a certain Sandrine, a short-haired woman dressed in jeans and a blue sweater who got right down to business.

"Where do you live?" she immediately asked this curious young man. Xavier thought to himself, *So it is true that the Jesuits always answer questions with other questions.*

Sandrine then exclaimed: "No need to become a Xavière or a missionary in the Moluccas! You have everything you need right there in Paris to be on a mission. Many of us live there, and believe me, it's not necessarily any easier than with the cannibals in the days of Francis Xavier!"

So Xavier took comfort in the idea that he could be a "solo Xavier," but with a capital X. For the time being, he had an abundance of choices among Masses, forums, concerts, processions, vigils, the giant picnic, films or expositions, and diverse workshops. He chose to sign up for an initiation retreat in the *Spiritual Exercises*, those retreat meditations that Ignatius wrote for his disciples and for all those who wish to learn to pray contemplatively in an intimate encounter with God.

The next morning, Xavier entered a little oratory where a reproduction of the Christ of the Abbey of Javier awaited him: With a raised hand, Jesus asks Thomas to put his finger in his wound. Xavier read the passage from John on which his spiritual accompanier suggested he meditate: "*Do not be unbelieving, but believe.*" Jesus seemed to look Xavier straight in the face, and Xavier could not, would not, avert his eyes from it.

HOLY MARY, MOTHER OF GOD,

A History of Passion and of Service

The National Pilgrimage, August 15, 2006

20
06

The church bells were still vibrating on a warm August 15 day. Bordeaux was calm, and only a few children's cries and honking cars interrupted the heavy and humid silence of lunchtime. Yet 2006 was not the favorite year of Aude-Amélie de Brimont Saint-Ferrières. For the first year since she was twelve, she did not participate in the national pilgrimage to Lourdes, the one sponsored by the Assumptionists. Instead she sat alone in her great living room, in her pleated blue skirt, on the edge of her Louis XV damask covered seat, with the shutters closed to protect her from the heat and windows slightly ajar for air circulation. The countess of Brimont Saint-Ferrières, her back straight and her gaze unfailing, watched a television set that her irreligious but loving great-grandchildren had given her for Christmas.

No, it would not have been reasonable to go this year except as a sick person. But Aude-Amélie felt healthy enough not to make herself a burden on anyone. She said as much to the good Fathers who were urging her to come, and to her parish priest, whom she dryly eyed up and down when he began his little set piece about true humility. Although she was slowly nearing her eighty-eighth birthday, she did not wish to be treated as a child. Her legs were tired, certainly, but her brain was fine, thank you very much.

On television, a thirty-year-old man, responsible for one hundred fifty volunteer stretcher-bearers on the national pilgrimage, was being interviewed after the broadcast of the Mass. He happily mentioned the priests who were accompanying them: "*These religious, rooted and open, recall the source and end of our service.*" The countess watched this young man tenderly. He could have been her grandson. She would have liked so much for her children and grandchildren to have remained faithful to the family tradition by becoming volunteers at the Our Lady of Salvation Hospitality, which was celebrating its hundred and fifty-fifth year of taking care of the sick on pilgrimage that day. Despite the respect they have for their mother and grandmother, these days the grandchildren preferred to spend the month of August in the cool air of Brittany's beaches or in Arcachon rather than serving the sick on pilgrimage in Lourdes.

For her, the national pilgrimage, the Our Lady of Salvation Hospitality, were above all her grandmother, Duchess Margueritte, and her great-uncle, Father Hubert-Vincent de la Mortandière. Both of them were present at the first pilgrimages, in La Salette in 1872 and in Lourdes in 1873. They were friends of the Assumptionist Father François Picard. When Aude-Amélie was still a little child, they would tell her of the troubled times in which the pilgrimages began, of a France that had been ready to abandon its Christian roots after her defeat to Germany and the bloody events of the Commune.

In those days following the First Vatican Council, the first order of business for Father Emmanuel d'Alzon, founder of the Assumptionists, was to fight against modernism and against Gallicanism[1]. He had

---

1. Gallicanism usually refers to the belief that the power of monarchs is independent of the power of popes, and that the church of each country should be under the joint control of the pope and the monarch.

entrusted the development of the Catholic League for the Defense of the Church to Father Picard. During a meeting in Auteuil on January 24, 1872, with the foundress of the Little Sisters of the Assumption, Mother Marie-Eugénie Milleret de Brou, and a few society ladies, including his young and energetic grandmother, Father d'Alzon had created the Association of Our Lady of Salvation, a reference to the sweet smile of the medieval statue of the Virgin that stood in the room.

At the very same time, as her older relatives told her, a Parisian priest, Father Thédenat, had spearheaded a national pilgrimage to La Salette for the month of August 1872. But the enterprise was having trouble getting going, and, in the month of June, the priest had made an appeal to Father Picard to avoid a stinging failure that would have been grist to the mill of the anticlericals. Father Thédenat, after receiving permission from Father d'Alzon and with regrets that this pilgrimage was not going to Lourdes, had worked so doggedly that he managed to gather hundreds of pilgrims – including many priests, religious brothers and sisters – from all over France despite the criticisms of certain people.

The pilgrimage of La Salette, therefore, had indeed been a national pilgrimage. Father Picard had made arrangements with the railways and organized the encampments. Under his direction, the first pilgrimage infrastructure was born in the heat of action. On August 22, the day after the pilgrimage, the National Council of Pilgrimages had been founded to organize and promote national pilgrimages. By the next year, in July 1873, that national pilgrimage had gathered more than thirty thousand pilgrims at the foot of the Lourdes grotto.

In the years that followed, the histories of the national pilgrimage and of the shrines of Lourdes were written in parallel, even though Lourdes was not the only destination of the pilgrims who traveled to Rome in 1873 and to Jerusalem in 1892. In July 1873, the Assumptionists had created *Le Pèlerin*, a simple information bulletin that had developed over the years into a true Christian newspaper. As early as 1875, the first ambulance wagon had been dedicated, allowing the Little Sisters of the Assumption to take care of the sick at their departure for Lourdes. In 1881, to carry the sick in their stretchers from the train station to the grotto, the permanent work of the Salvation Hospitality and the hospitallers was founded. It was this foundation whose hundred and twenty-fifth anniversary was being celebrated that day, which the countess was watching at that very moment on her television set.

What history, she thought. *What a beautiful history of passion and observance. How many personal histories, too,* she thought with a laugh. Like many of her friends, she had met her husband at the national pilgrimage. True, this pilgrimage had a conservative image for some people, especially its detractors. But one should not exaggerate. Last year, when God had granted Aude-Amélie the grace of being able to participate in it, she had found the gathering rather colorful and diverse. The countess got up, absentmindedly smoothed the pleats of her skirt, and turned off the television set. On the inside, she only had one dream – to get better so as to be able to go on the National again the following year.

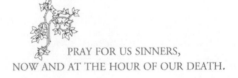

PRAY FOR US SINNERS,
NOW AND AT THE HOUR OF OUR DEATH.

SITTING UNDER GOD'S GAZE

*A Pilgrimage of the Teams of Our Lady to Lourdes,
September 16, 2006*

2006 Claire and François were sitting. Certainly, the seat made of greenery could be a little more comfortable, a little less hard, but they had time. They had the entire afternoon before them, and the Lord was there. Besides that, he was everywhere, wherever they went. But since the couple was in Lourdes that week, coming into his presence would surely be even easier. All the conditions were there for them to be able to do what the Our Lady Teams, to which they belong, called the "duty of sitting." It simply consists of meeting two by two, as couples, to talk under the watchful eyes of God.

The principle is simple to articulate, but far less simple to carry out. Claire and François were fully aware of this. They had not been able to sit down to speak peacefully together for several months now because of work, overburdened schedules, children, worries, both good excuses and bad. Though they had been members of the Our Lady Teams for several years, they felt at a dead end. They hardly ever talked anymore, and they no longer prayed together – or at least not often, anyway. They also fought a lot and were growing distant from each other. For them, this pilgrimage could well have been their last chance.

"Let's all go to Lourdes," one of the couples from their team had suggested during the previous year's reunion.

"Bah!" François had sighed.

"I don't know if I feel like it," Claire had admitted.

"Well then, do you think it's useful for you to come back next year?" their friend had asked, trying to shake them up a little.

At these words, Claire had felt a sinking sensation. Leaving the Our Lady Teams would have meant the end of her marriage. Sometimes she had felt that was not far off, but these monthly encounters had allowed her to keep her head above water in spite of everything. She and François had joined the teams one year after their marriage. "The duty of sitting, personal prayer, concrete effort, reading the word of God, prayer as a couple, family prayer" – the program had attracted them right away. During the first years of their marriage, the teams had been a vital place of sharing, of encounter, and of prayer for them as a couple. Then François had changed jobs, and Claire had taken care of the kids, no longer giving any thought to herself or to him. The Our Lady Teams alone had encouraged them to meet together at least once a month. Leaving the team was something quite impossible!

"All right, we'll go," she had consented then.

François had been surprised at first, and then he, too, had accepted. What was there to lose?

So there they were, sitting on the immense meadow facing the grotto, on the other side of the Gave, for their "duty of sitting." They had not necessarily thought of sitting in that particular place and at that particular time, but the Lord willed it so – they were convinced of that. Indeed, a few minutes ago, they had gone before the grotto for a Mass among team members. Each had looked to the Virgin of Massabielle expecting a sign, a glimmer, some hope. Suddenly, their hearts had abruptly moved, and they had felt the need to talk to each other. François had dragged Claire toward the meadow, and she had gone along with it.

"Shall we pray?" she suggested.

"You're right, yes, let's pray."

The couple knelt to pray a decade of the rosary and to beg the Virgin Mary and the Lord to bless them and to accompany them.

"Shall I begin?" asked Claire after their prayer.

"No, me first," answered François. "I have more to let go of."

"You don't know that," retorted Claire.

"Yes, I swear. Listen to me…"

What Claire and François said to each other was their business alone. One thing is certain: Their "duty of sitting" lasted a long time, a very long time. François spoke slowly while Claire lowered her head, wiping a tear every so often. Then she began to speak, and it was her husband's turn to listen. Both were sitting cross-legged, one facing the other; before long, they were sitting next to each other. Soon, François tightly hugged his wife. He had not done so for an eternity.

When the couple finally got up again, they burst into laughter. Claire's face was smeared with mascara, while François' back hurt and his legs were stiff from sitting on the ground so long. Their pants were streaked with green stains from the grass. François took his wife's hand. Those two were not saved just yet. Their marriage remained fragile, for such difficulties cannot be fixed within a few hours. Nevertheless, the hardest part was surely over.

Before returning to the hotel where the other team members were waiting for them, François and Claire went back to the grotto for a long time. François intensely observed the Virgin's face raised toward heaven, and he suddenly smiled. He was remembering his wife's enthusiasm after the information meeting on the Our Lady Teams after their wedding.

"It's wonderful!" she had cried out after the testimony of a couple that spoke of how the teams had allowed them to get out of a rut and to make a renewed effort to reaffirm and grow in their love. "That is what I want, helping others to save their marriages!"

"Don't you think you could do us some good, too?" François had asked teasingly.

"Why yes, of course," she had answered without conviction. "But it's obvious that we'll never need it!"

François smiled to the Virgin, who had given him a little of her gentleness so that he would have the strength to forget the vexations and the misunderstandings. He knew that when they went home, she would still be smiling and that he would be able to draw from that source to remain a loving, patient, and faithful man throughout the rough patches of life.

Amen.

LIKE THE APOSTLES AT THE FEET OF MARY

The French Conference of Catholic Bishops,
November 5, 2006

20 06 On that Sunday morning, there was much agitation around the Our Lady of the Rosary Basilica. The France Television buses and those of the *Jour du Seigneur* were parked nearby, and technicians were getting busy, finishing up the preparations for the live broadcast of the Mass. It was barely ten o'clock, and already a crowd of pilgrims was gathering as they stepped over the cables. It was the usual landscape of the shrines' sacramental life: One could make out small groups of men dressed in black or gray. Big crosses were hanging from their necks and resting under their Roman collars.

All the bishops of France had been together since the previous evening for their plenary assembly. For the forty years since the end of the Second Vatican Council, they have been meeting in Lourdes every year. Formerly, they had met in Paris, at the *Institut Catholique*, or in Rome during the council. Lourdes had been chosen for its capacity to welcome all the bishops and their many meetings, but especially for all that the shrine had represented for nearly one hundred and fifty years.

In front of the basilica, a few journalists were commenting on the beginnings of the session. They appreciated finding themselves in Lourdes with the totality of the French bishops and the conference's various service chiefs. During these few days, they could interview all the bishops. Each one had his own style, but in general all were ready to have exchanges with them on the important subjects of their annual agenda. Catechesis, priests, the liturgy, the proclamation of the faith, the reconfiguration of parishes, the number of Masses, the role of laymen – all these subjects were broached. There was no miracle solution. As the Spirit blows and under the eye of Mary, however, the debate was rather free and reflected each pastor's concern for finding new paths for the Gospel in his own diocese. The ardor of the younger bishops was sometimes tempered by the wisdom of the older, and the rigidity of some by the openness of others.

At eleven o'clock in the morning, the tolling of the bells interrupted the journalists in their conversations, and all headed to the interior of the basilica for Mass. Above the altar, the Virgin Mary, surrounded with angels, seemed to welcome the procession of bishops and to envelop them in her prayers. It was hard not to think of Mary and the apostles as they prayed together awaiting the descent of the Holy Spirit at Pentecost.

By meeting in Lourdes under Mary's watchful eyes each year, the bishops bear witness that their assembly is far more than a mere administrative meeting where they deal with arcane business matters. It is rather a meeting of the successors to the apostles, who pray together to pursue, in the Church's communion, the commission entrusted to them by the Lord. Just as in the emerging Church, opinions are sometimes opposed and discussions are lively, yet unity prevails.

After the Mass, pilgrims and journalists contemplated the family picture of the bishops of France who, in procession, had returned to the square in front of the church. There were over a hundred bishops in alb and chasuble to pose under a blue sky speckled with clouds. Jokes abounded, and it was in a general good mood that small groups formed and perpetuated the joy of the celebration in the pleasant noonday heat. The journalists took advantage of this to gather the bishops' first impressions and a few bits of inside information to feed their newspapers the next day. Some pilgrims were attempting to recognize the more media-friendly bishops or to catch a glimpse of their own.

One bishop joined a few pilgrims from his own diocese, among whom he recognized the lady responsible for catechism along with her two children and her husband, whom the bishop had ordained a permanent deacon two years earlier. He good-naturedly kissed the children and asked them if they had been to the grotto. The conversation inevitably settled on the subject of Mary and the pilgrimages. The bishop gently answered the barrage of questions from Juliette who, with all of her eight years of age, wanted to know everything. Yes, the bishops ask for the help of God and of the Holy Spirit to make their decisions. Yes, like all other pilgrims, the bishops go to pray to the Virgin in the grotto. As in the Gospel or in the first community of apostles after Pentecost, Mary is discreet, but very present. She is the Mother of the Church; she helps them in their work.

As the parents looked on, embarrassed that their daughter was asking so many questions, the bishop agreed to reveal the prayer he had addressed to Mary. It is a prayer that Pope John Paul II had offered for the bishops gathered in Puebla in 1979: "*May Mary obtain for you from her Divine Son the audacity of the prophets and the Gospel prudence of Pastors; the clear-sightedness of masters and the assurance of guides, the greatness of soul of witnesses and the gentleness of fathers… The future is in God's hands, but in a certain sense, God puts it in your hands, too.*"

A little further down, the communications director for the French bishops was exchanging a few words with the journalists at hand. By way of conclusion, she reminded them of the motto of the archbishop of

Bordeaux, who was president of the French Conference of Catholic Bishops – "Fraternity and Trust." Then each of them went back to his lunch arrangements.

Soon, the area in front of the basilica was again empty. Only a few technicians were finishing up putting away the camera equipment that had served to record and broadcast the Mass live on the *Le Jour du Seigneur* program. In this way, many more people were able to see the Eucharist being celebrated live by the entire French episcopate.

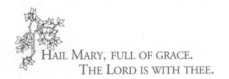

HAIL MARY, FULL OF GRACE.
THE LORD IS WITH THEE.

THE STATION MASTER'S GRANDSON

The History of the Trains to Lourdes,
January 1, 2007

20
07
"Choo-chooo!" shouted the little boy, squatting over his miniature railway set.

His grandfather, lying next to him with his hand as headrest, corrected him:

"Not choo-choo; toot-tooot! That's the sound the steam engine made on its way into Lourdes."

For a retired station master in the city of miracles, there is no sweeter retirement than to play trains with one's grandson.

"*City of Béziers*, that was its name. The first special pilgrimage train organized by the *Compagnie du Midi*! It arrived on July 16, 1867. And do you know how many passengers it brought with it?"

"Seven hundred!"

"Oh… did I tell you already?"

Giving himself a quarter turn, the grandfather grabbed the steam engine and made it climb the last few yards.

"It's climbing the ramp, blowing its last cloud of steam, and then comes the complete halt. The travelers are getting off, looking for each other, and gathering into groups. Soon they're off on procession, crossing the town to Massabielle and offering the homage of their long trip to the Immaculate."

Wishing to add his own touch to history, the little boy placed his caped and armored super-hero figurines, who would function as proud substitute pilgrims, around the grotto.

"After the apparitions," continued the grandfather, "the train company gave up its project of a Pau-Tarbes via Ossun line. The more winding option through Lourdes was far more judicious. In 1909, three hundred and six special trains ferried two hundred and ninety pilgrimages – one hundred seventy thousand people in all! At the time, it was a real shambles: Four lines had access to Lourdes, some sections of track were one-way, and Lourdes lacked side rails. Several trains had to ask for shelter in neighboring stations!"

The grandfather started piling up the cars, one on top of the other. Ten seconds later, his grandson clapped at the inevitable "crash!"

"Imagine the organizational difficulties in 1958 for the apparitions' centennial: One thousand and twenty-two pilgrimage trains arrived in Lourdes, including thirty-six special convoys on the busiest day! Not to mention the regular trains…"

"Wow!"

"And in the cars, what an atmosphere! You don't forget passengers like those. The pilgrimage's spiritual preparation began during these journeys. On the train, prayers competed with the noise of the rails, and sometimes the mood reached its zenith to the rhythm of guitars."

Rummaging about in his shirt pockets, the little boy took out two characters in armbands. The former station master then adjusted his imaginary present-tense narrative:

"In the train, the stretcher-bearers are speaking with the sick. It isn't time for intimate conversations yet, but introductions are behind us now. In the early morning, sleepy faces yield to thrills of excitement. All who are able are at the windows, on the lookout for the as yet unseen grotto.

From their berths, the sick want the landscapes rolling by described to them. Say, you know what you should put at your station's entrance? A banner that says, 'Pilgrimage World Center.'"

"Here?"

"*Ja, mein Freund!*"[1]

"What?"

"Yep! The people alighting on the platform are from all over the world! Every language is spoken at the Lourdes Station."

A figurine in blond pigtails took her place in the first car. Next to her, a man with a big moustache gave her a broad smile. Proud of the effect, the little boy turned to his grandfather, who enthusiastically continued:

"In 1998, five hundred and forty special trains transported three hundred and thirty-two thousand pilgrims from France, Italy, Belgium, Germany, Spain, Switzerland, the Netherlands, Great Britain, and Austria! And I can assure you that when you go to the international Mass or to the torchlight procession, you see all those nationalities on parade, and it's an extraordinary communion! But... what are you up to?"

"I'm putting it all away!"

"We're all done playing? So you, too, are abandoning ship... I mean, the train? You know that within ten years, between 1978 and 1988, traffic decreased by twenty-five percent!"

"Why? No more pilgrims?" asked the boy, who at once stopped putting away his train set.

"Not at all! But the national train company and the diocesan directors quarreled over the price increases, the out-of-date equipment, the late arrivals, and the often defective air conditioning and sound systems. The bottom line is that the national railway company committed itself to

---

1. "Yes, my friend," in German.

regaining the pilgrim's trust. Special TGVs [high-speed trains] came out in 1995. In 2000, the company renovated the Lourdes Station especially for the thirty thousand sick people who would arrive there, installing elevators to transfer them from the arrivals platform to the reception hall, underground passages to keep them from having to cross the tracks, and renovation of the station hall and the parking lots. And in 2006, the city and the shrines of Lourdes had the idea of transforming the railway cars into ambulance cars!"

"With revolving lights and everything?"

"No, young man, no revolving lights, but on the inside, you can choose to set up seats, beds, or wheelchairs. The clients will only have to ask! Do you realize that, if it works, then in 2009 you'll be able to add a new train model to your miniature railway system?"

The little boy cast a glance at his set, already imagining the brand-new cars' arrival.

"And if you want to see what it looks like for real," continued the grandfather, "you need only become the train company's Mr. Pilgrimage. He's the one who checks the quality of services."

"I can have that job when I'm bigger?"

"Why not? But when you're at your post, don't advertise trains too much, OK?"

"Why not?"

"Because I think that the national railway company would be in quite a fix if all six million yearly visitors came by train!"

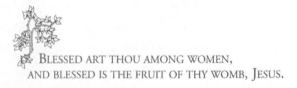

BLESSED ART THOU AMONG WOMEN,
AND BLESSED IS THE FRUIT OF THY WOMB, JESUS.

A Survivor's Dream

The Founding of a Dialysis Center in Lourdes,
June 6, 2007

20 07 On a cool summer morning, a woman was leafing through a diary bound in worn leather. She found the following entries.

April 21, 1954

My name is Bernard Hay. I am a lieutenant in the Eighth Airborne Chasseurs Battalion, volunteer, parachuting instructor in the airborne troops of Pau, and I am twenty-four. I don't know why I say that: Shells kill indiscriminately, regardless of age or rank. Hell spares nothing and especially no one. The day breaking over Diên Biên Phú was blood-colored, in a sad sort of way. The Viet mortars were pounding Éliane II, which we had retaken under the cover of night. Three hundred died in two hours, and I came away with a body riddled with shrapnel, those "decorations" that the enemy pins deep in your flesh. Two of my men evacuated me in a tent canvas, but a machine gunner took aim at us and downed them both. I got an explosive bullet fragment in the right kidney. Nailed to the ground, I fainted.

The same day, Viêt-minh troops took the peak overlooking Diên Biên Phú. With their bayonets, they plumbed bodies strewn on the ground, making sure they were corpses. A blade perforated my posterior, but I remained stoic, as my lower body was numbed by the shrapnel along my spine. Night brought a glimmer of hope: A Legion battalion's counterattack once again dislodged the enemy. A doctor leaned over me: "*Good God, he's not dead…!*" The surgical unit did what it could with the means on hand. Outside, soldiers did what they could with their last strength, but in vain: The vise is tightening around the camp.

May 7, 1954

Overrun, we capitulated and faced our fate as prisoners. I left my pain in the hands of Geneviève de Galard, the only nurse prisoner of the Viets. Our enemies make no distinctions: wounded or not, prisoners receive two hundred grams of rice per day. I'm losing weight visibly; I weigh about as much as a sparrow's feather.

June 1954

Hanoi. A surgical operation doesn't give me the use of my legs back. I am now a flightless sparrow.

July 21, 1954

The Geneva Accords are signed. I'm repatriated by sea. Thirty-one days by boat, six hundred wounded in the hold, one porthole for forty, and no cold storage for the bodies of those who die…

I've made up my mind: *if I make it, I'm going to Lourdes.*

May 1956

I was in front of the grotto pools, lying on my stretcher. It was my first military pilgrimage. Paralyzed, I was trying to regain my taste for life. *What better place than Lourdes can appease spirits and bodies bruised by war?* I thought to myself…

Just then, the accident happened: My stretcher slipped from my bearers' hands, and my spine hit the lip of the granite basin. The fall produced what no doctor was able to do: The veterbrae that had been stuck fell into place and decompressed the spinal cord! Besides cherishing the Virgin, I have only one thing left to do: Relearn how to walk...

April 1962

I have gradually regained confidence and stability, standing on my own three feet. With my cane, I'm returning to Lourdes to serve the sick. Five months a year, I'm in charge of the grotto's security team.

August 13, 1975

It has been thirteen years since my healing in Lourdes. My left kidney has just given out on me. Eight days after my wedding to Anne-Marie, I have been placed on dialysis. Because there is no dialysis center in Lourdes, we have no choice but to rack up the miles, traveling alternatively to Pau, Tarbes, and even Bayonne, one hundred and seventy-two miles round trip, three times a week!

May 1976

I'm coming back from Pau with Father Lhomme, who is also on dialysis. We're so tired from our hours of extra-renal purification that we almost didn't make it! "*We're idiots,*" he tells me. "*Why don't we create a center at Lourdes?*" No money, no land, no authorization from the Ministry – the project is totally foolish! But foolish and faith start with the same letter...

1979

We're having a lot of trouble. Still, Anne-Marie is never discouraged: "*There's no rose without thorns,*" according to her. And once you've charged Éliane II, you don't give up so easily. Our tenacity is paying off:

Doors are finally opening before us. At the same time, we hear of Father Lhomme's passing. We had not heard from him in a long time. The truth leaps out at us: He's beginning to achieve his project from up there!

September 29, 1981

The APDL[1] is born, and money is raining from heaven – ten million francs in donations. It's incredible! Books are written about wartime heroic deeds often enough; there should be books about human generosity. Its heroes are legion…

April 21, 1986

Drum roll: The Saint John the Baptist Dialysis Center is opening in Bartrès! The beds face the basilica's bell tower. Bishop Charles Renfrew, auxiliary bishop of Glasgow, admitted to me that *he prays far better in his dialysis patient's bed than in front of the grotto, where there is too much noise!* What fills me with joy is that this center is a genuine place of prayer.

1994

The Legion of Honor and the Cross of Saint Gregory the Great vie for space on my lapel – in homage to my courage and dedication, they say. I'm proud of one thing – that of seeing the faces of my partners in pain smiling because they no longer have to pick between pilgrimage and dialysis.

The rest of diary's pages were blank. The woman picked up a fountain pen and started to write:

---

1. *Association des amis des pèlerins dialysés à Lourdes,* "Association of Friends of the Lourdes Dialysis Patients."

June 6, 2007

My Bernard, it's been twelve years now since you left us, but your fight carries on as intensely as ever. I, your wife, your little Anne-Marie, have great news to tell you: Twenty years after the center's creation, our son will dedicate the first international pilgrimage for kidney patients tomorrow!

Do you remember that day when, in the dialysis center's courtyard, we removed a vine that was choking the chestnut tree you so loved? We found a little glass Virgin there, encased in the trunk facing the Massabielle grotto, transparent and purple because of the vine's sap. Well, when I see how what you created has been developing, I am convinced of one thing: The Virgin is watching over you. After the war, you had promised to go to Lourdes. I think that Mary made you a promise that never ends, even now that you are gone.

HOLY MARY, MOTHER OF GOD,

WWW.LOURDES-FRANCE.ORG

The Web Site and Webcam of the Lourdes Shrines, July 25, 2007

2007 "Simone, are you coming?"

"Yes, yes, here I come…"

Bundled up in her blanket, Simone dragged her feet to the desk where Martine was sitting. Her eyes riveted on the computer screen, her sister had assumed the role of well-informed Web surfer.

"I'm telling you, it's really good!"

"I would have preferred being in Lourdes, like last year…"

"I know, but you're too weak now. Better for you to rest than to get sick during the pilgrimage. And with the new technologies, we can go to Lourdes virtually!"

"I know, the webcam…"

"You'll see, it's really simple."

"Like the Ariane 5 user's guide?"

"No, no, it's child's play, try!"

Martine made some room for Simone in front of the screen. At a typist's speed, she typed out the site's address, *www.lourdes-france.org.*

One click later, she was on the page of the programs transmitted by the sanctuary's two webcams.

"Shall we begin with the broadcast rosary?"

A little window opened and a male voice was heard by way of introduction: *To deposit your prayer intentions, dial 0 892 46 00 12*, followed by a repeat, a female voice this time: *0 892 46 00 12, 34 cents per minute, we will deposit it for you at the Massabielle grotto…*

"You'd think it was a draw for a game show on TV."

"Simone!"

Finally the message was in the priest's voice. He bid welcome to the surfers joining the local pilgrims for the holy rosary. Then he began the prayer. Simone, who was busy readjusting her blanket on her shoulders, slowed down her movements and became suddenly more attentive.

Lord God, in the Virgin You gave us a perfect model of charity and humility. Grant that Your Church may follow as she did the new commandment by dedicating itself to your glory and in the service of men, and in being the sign of Your love for all peoples. Through Jesus Christ our Lord, Amen.

"Amen," Simone caught herself answering, in unison with the virtual assembly.

At that moment in the rosary were heard the prayer intentions recorded by telephone that would join those dropped in the box at the Virgin's feet. Simone and Martine were silent, in communion with the messages' authors. Suddenly, Simone was rooted to her spot. Among those voices, she just recognized Martine's: "My most holy Mother, I would like to pray to you for my sister Simone who has cancer. These past few months the disease is hitting her very hard, she can't get up, and she can't eat any more. Could you grant her a little respite in her suffering? Thank you infinitely."

Simone looked at her sister, who visibly had not expected to hear her prayer on the *Présence Lourdes Pyrénées* airwaves, either. Tears shone in her eyes, and her lips trembled.

"Thank you," she managed to articulate.

Then she added in a little sniffle:

"The site isn't all bad, after all…"

That was the very moment that the Internet connection chose to stop unexpectedly.

"Oh no!" exclaimed Simone who was beginning to acquire a taste for the Lourdes site's potential.

Martine quickly reconnected and set up the grotto feed. Located on the Gave's right bank, the webcam was facing the apparition site. Simone was pleasantly surprised, although she probably wouldn't recognize Roger, Joséphine, and her other friends if they walked in front of the camera. On the other hand, she did make out the great tapers' candelabrum perfectly, at the grotto's entrance, and the Virgin perched on her rock. As she was observing the parade of pilgrims, one thing ended up intriguing her: It had been three times that a wheelchair passed in the foreground pushed by a lady bedecked with the same straw hat.

"Is it always the same film?"

"There are new grotto shots every fifteen minutes. Every three minutes there is a new thirty-second sequence. Meanwhile, it's on a loop."

Suddenly Martine was excited.

"Simone, look! The Chartres Hospitality is arriving in front of the grotto!"

"How do you know that?"

"See those red and white caps? I had asked Roger and the others to wear them, so that you could recognize them."

Simone gave her sister a look filled with gratitude. For a whole hour, she was engrossed in observing the hospitallers accompanying the sick.

Martine had time to make some tea and to return with shortbreads, which Simone devoured without even noticing, although she hadn't had any appetite for weeks. At nine forty-five, the two sisters were still in front of the computer, this time connected to the Rosary Basilica esplanade. At the moment when the torchlight procession was beginning, the site unexpectedly shut off! Martine re-established the connection.

"There, I can see those red and white caps again!"

Simone let out a breath. Once again, she was in communion with the Chartres pilgrimage.

"My pilgrimage!" she blurted out, moved.

Onscreen, daylight was fading, gradually plunging the basilica into a twilight atmosphere. Simone shuddered, as if the breeze whistling on the esplanade were blowing on her back, but her eyes were smiling. Martine had not seen such a happy face on her for months. She said a silent prayer, not really knowing to whom she owed these modern marvels.

"Shall we go see what's happening around the crowned Virgin?"

"I get to click!"

It was getting late. The camera caught two or three stray pilgrims just like on the procession esplanade.

That evening, Simone fell asleep better than she usually did. When, at midnight, Martine got up for a glass of water, Simone was back in front of the screen.

"What are you doing?"

"I'm watching the Virgin…"

Martine leaned over her sister. On the screen, only two sources of light penetrated the grotto's obscurity – the candelabrum tapers and the Virgin in her light. On the night backdrop, she seemed to be floating in the air, supernatural and yet so present.

"It's wonderful, you know. She'll never leave her rock. Whatever my condition, I'll be able to seek refuge in front of this screen to pray to her!"

PRAY FOR US SINNERS,
NOW AND AT THE HOUR OF OUR DEATH.

THE SONS OF THE WIND

El Pelé and the Gypsy Pilgrimage to Lourdes,
August 22, 2007

20 07 Entering the shrine – where the two processions leaving from the Gypsy reception grounds of Paradise and Abadie are destined – El Kéti was deeply moved: He had been coming here for fifty years! One day in September 1957, his father had decided to go with his clan to the first Gypsy pilgrimage to Lourdes, organized by Father Fleury, and the tradition took root.

It was kind of a curious call to come and pray at the feet of her who watched over the sons of the wind: Roma, Manuche, Sinti, Yeniche, Ciganos, all Gypsies. And then there had been those intense words of Bishop Pierre-Marie Théas, which his father had recalled to him on every pilgrimage until his death: "*For a hundred years, Our Lady of Lourdes has been waiting for you and desires your visit. You too, and as much so as the others, are children of the Blessed Virgin.*" Mary the vigilant, Mary, the mother of travelers, who humbly wandered with the Christ Child between Bethlehem, Egypt, Nazareth, and Jerusalem – so faithful to the Gypsies, those people of the wind and the road!

El Kéti was living a unique, unforgettable day. To give thanks for this fiftieth pilgrimage of faithfulness to Mary and to the ancestors, he had been picked to carry a banner of honor in procession. It was that of Blessed Ceferino Giménez Malla, nicknamed El Pelé, who died a martyr in 1936, rosary in hand, under the bullets of Spanish militiamen. In El Kéti's heart, he was the first and best of Gypsies since Pope John Paul II declared him blessed on May 4, 1997, in Saint Peter's Square in Rome!

His heart beating fast, moved and conscious of his responsibility among his own, El Kéti held high the embroidered banner. He remembered with tenderness his grandfather, wise José Giménez, witness to the blessed's wedding on February 3, 1912, and he smiled at a grace that is so able to weave strong and patient bonds across generations.

El Kéti pondered the humble greatness of faith, which sometimes makes its way in a man for a long time, like an invisible river, before it resurfaces all at once with the mysterious brilliance of deeper waters. It's a bit like that, the story of El Pelé who all traveling people honor today for his courage and dignity.

Born in 1861, in Spain, in a Gypsy family, he grew up as a true son of the wind – traveling, begging, weaving flat-bottomed wicker baskets to transport straw. He was tossed between hunger and cold, having encounters good and bad, like that with the famous bandit La Cucaracha – "the cockroach" – who stole from the rich to give to the poor. In keeping with Gypsy tradition, his father, El Tics, married him to Teresa Giménez Castro at the age of eighteen. A short while after that, overtaken with madness, El Tics ran away with another woman, abandoning his entire clan. From then on, in his kindness, El Pelé would welcome everyone. He settled in Barbastro, capital of Aragonese Piedmont, in a neighborhood where two Gypsy families already were living in peace.

That is where the humble and quiet life of El Pelé – now a horse trader, though still illiterate – turned more and more toward heaven.

Around 1910, he adopted Pepita, one of Teresa's nieces, as he and Teresa were not able to have children of their own. He married his wife, in the Catholic sacramental rite this time, in 1912. Since then, he had been like the anointed of God, always praying his rosary, participating in processions, tapers in hand, and taking care of the poor. El Bomba, an old neighborhood Gypsy, saw him every day coming and going to Mass.

One day, at a street corner, El Pelé found Raphaël Jordan, former mayor of Barbastro, who suffered from tuberculosis, vomiting blood in the street. He picked him up and comforted him with the simplicity of a brother. The lives of the saints are sometimes as smooth as the palm of your hand, and all would have gone well if the devil hadn't got involved.

When he went to sell his mules at the Vendrell fair, El Pelé was accused of having stolen one of them. He was thrown in prison and, after a long time, was finally declared innocent. With a single voice, all those who knew him proclaimed his innocence. But he, simple and peaceful, gave thanks anyway, making his Way of the Cross, on his knees in the dust, toward the Chapel of the *Holy Christ of miracles* who had restored his freedom and his honor. He had been humiliated and deprived, but that was how much God had honed in him the faithfulness of the workman of the first hour and the ardor of the workman of the final hour. All this would later help him find peace as he neared death.

In 1922, at his wife's death, he became even more prayerful, reciting the rosary every day and drawing crosses with a crayon on children's hands to teach them the charity and love of Christ. He became a lay Third Order Franciscan, spent one long nocturnal vigil each month in adoration of the Blessed Sacrament, ridding himself little by little of life's baggage.

Then, on July 25, 1936, everything came to a head. On that day, the city of Barbastro experienced the madness of civil war. El Pelé, now seventy-five years old, defended a priest who was being manhandled by militiamen and was arrested because of the rosary he was carrying. Because he refused to abandon it during his imprisonment, he was executed on August 9 along with the other condemned men in the town's small cemetery and thrown into the common grave, his rosary beads still clasped in his hand.

El Kéti knew that the "sons of the wind" on pilgrimage in Lourdes had a saint in heaven who humbly has prayed his rosary for them and led them on the roads. He heard the breeze singing in this banner and felt himself pushed toward the grotto by the *Ave Maria*, by the guitars and all the beauty of these faces lit up with hope. His eyes did not leave the Lady who was inviting them to drink the spring water, the water of heaven. And he thought of the first Gypsies, about the year 1500, centuries before the apparitions, who had come in their carts to the Massabielle grotto. They had not guessed that their children and grand-children would continue to visit this place in such large numbers, on foot, by car, and in caravans. Filled with the joy of the Catholic faith, there were nearly ten thousand that year, mingling their chants from the past and from the present in homage to the Lady of tenderness, "the Saint," as they say among themselves.

Amen.

VATICAN AIRLINES

A Bridge in the Sky between Rome and Lourdes,
August 27, 2007

2007 The airplane was already maneuvering on the tarmac of Rome's Fiumicino International Airport. Sitting in the window, Flora watched the wing flaps open and close for the last check before takeoff. There was nothing angelic in the flapping of these wings: The aircraft in which Flora was sitting was a run-of-the-mill Boeing 737. And yet, the charter that was about to take off had something unique about it: It was the first airplane to fly a regular route for the Vatican between two cities newly united by a celestial thread – Rome and Lourdes, the Eternal City and the Marian town.

For this inaugural flight, celebrity passengers had taken their seats aboard the Boeing among simple pilgrims like Flora. Cardinal Camillo Ruini, vicar-general of the Diocese of Rome, accompanied the first users of this very Catholic link. Smiling and happy about this unprecedented event, he commented to his neighbors on the original sentence that adorned the aircraft's headrests: "I seek your face, Lord." Just like the aircraft's yellow and white cabin, painted in the Holy See's colors, the interior decoration of the plane expressed in a visible way the airline's vocation.

Although the ticket prices were ten percent cheaper than the competition's lowest fares, this was not simply a low-cost enterprise. It offered its passengers an atmosphere quite conducive to pilgrimage.

This airline, already humorously nicknamed "Vatican Airlines," is the fruit of a five-year agreement between the Roman pilgrimage works and Mistral Air, which belongs to the Italian Postal Service. That is why the company does not offer simple flights for independent passengers. The ticket prices are part of a global formula of spiritual travel offered as a monopoly by the Roman pilgrimage works.

Though the company bore a sacred imprint, its primary goal, of course, was to ensure for its passengers the professionalism and safety that must accompany any trip by air. But beyond that, its in-flight crew was entirely committed to its specific mission – the transport of pilgrims on their way to great religious centers.

It was about eleven thirty in the morning when the control tower gave the Mistral Air flight authorization to take off. The airplane roared, gathered momentum, and ascended to the heavens. Through the window, Flora soon was admiring the shimmering Mediterranean, which reflected the azure above with a mirror's limpidity. Soon there was Corsica, "the island of beauty," set snugly in its maritime case. And half an hour later – hardly time to admire these grandiose landscapes fashioned by the hand of God – the airplane began its descent over the Pyrenees and landed without a hitch on the tarmac of the Tarbes-Lourdes Airport to deliver its passengers to the land of Bernadette.

Having arrived at the shrines, Flora and the other passengers of the Mistral Air flight joined those of their fellow countrymen who had arrived by more traditional means. Indeed, it is in these late August days that the Diocese of Rome's yearly pilgrimage takes place, gathering about three thousand Italians in Lourdes.

A few moments later, a Mass united all the Roman pilgrims around Cardinal Ruini in the Saint Bernadette Basilica. For these Christians used to living in the shade of the dome of Saint Peter's, the two basilicas seemed suddenly very close, linked by a short hop in the European sky!

Along the Gave, the hours passed quickly. As the sun started to set on the mountains, it was already time to think about going back to the Tiber's waters. This first "Vatican Airlines" flight had been scheduled to make a lightning-quick round trip, and it was to land on Italian soil at midnight. The Boeing's passengers, therefore, were making their way back to the Tarbes airport, bringing back to the grandeur of Rome the simplicity of Bernadette's message.

At the airport, some of the excessively hasty pilgrims had a comical surprise. Having failed to take the time of checking in the Massabielle water bottles they were bringing back from Lourdes, they found themselves stopped by the security inspectors. It was a reminder of temporal restrictions and safety precautions brought on by the unsettled world situation of terrorism, a stark wake-up call after the atmosphere of sacredness, the momentary glimpse of eternity that they had lived for a few hours. Vials containing more than three ounces of liquid were not authorized in the cabin, and even the water from the spring dug by Bernadette cannot be made an exception in international law when it comes to air safety. Half-dismayed and half-amused, the pilgrims had only one solution left: They drank their water on the spot before boarding the plane!

The last glimmers of the summer dusk were barely lighting up the Pyrenees when the aircraft took off for its destination. Tired and happy, Flora fell asleep, clutching in her fingers the chaplet that she had bought in Lourdes. In her slumber, she was still thinking of Bernadette, who so loved praying the beads of hers in the Virgin's company.

Cardinal Ruini, who had stayed in Lourdes, was also happy and satisfied. He knew that this inaugural flight was to be followed by many others: The company was now providing three or four trips per week to Lourdes. He also rejoiced at the idea that the other great Christian pilgrimage destinations would soon be served by "Vatican Airlines": In a few months, about thirty aircraft would be streaking through the airways of the world to link Rome to such shrines as Santiago de Compostela, Fatima, Czestochowa, and even Guadalupe, Mexico. This program is expected to be in full swing starting at Easter 2008. At the time when the Pope will pronounce his traditional *Urbi et Orbi* blessing from the balcony in the Holy See, this should be another way for the Eternal City to be "for the world"!

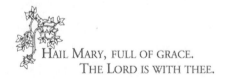

HAIL MARY, FULL OF GRACE.
THE LORD IS WITH THEE.

SILENCE IN THE MEADOW

Maria de Faykod's Way of the Cross, October 1, 2007

2007 "How about going to the Way of the Cross?"

Lucie looked at her husband with surprised tenderness: "Now? It's not even seven o'clock!"

Pierre wedged himself as well as he could against the back of his wheelchair and smiled with a little bit of gentle mischief. At the age of seventy-seven, he considered it a privilege to still be able to surprise his wife with his unpredictable whims.

"The world belongs to those that rise early!" he answered. "I've heard a lot of good things regarding this new Way of the Cross. I would like to walk through it in the quiet of dawn, rather than among the crowds moving about here at more 'Catholic' times. Furthermore, we're leaving tomorrow and won't have the time."

Lucie understood. She acquiesced, also impatient to discover these monumental stations that had been gradually delivered to the shrines of Lourdes over the years since 2004. She knew, by reputation, the sculptor whose hands produced in marble the narrative of Christ's last hours.

That was Maria de Faykod, born in Hungary of a Swedish father and a Hungarian mother. A graduate of the Beaux-arts of Paris, she had settled in Aups, in the Var department of France, where her workshop was right next to an open-air museum that displayed her works, which were famous beyond French borders. That is where her chisel was fashioning in Carrara marble the forms for the stations of this Way of the Cross, which she had conceived through her sensitivity as an artist as well as a believer.

With Lucie pushing Pierre's wheelchair, and the two spouses made their way toward the meadow facing the grotto. The sculptures stood very tall, like beacons above the waves of pilgrims, guiding the crowd's prayer. But Pierre was right: In the early-morning peacefulness, nobody had yet trod the Way of the Cross. His wheelchair could get very close to the first station: Everything here is geared for the sick, and the Way of the Cross is accessible to all handicapped people.

When they came to Christ's arrest, Pierre and Lucie long looked at this Jesus in the humble posture of the captive. In their hatred, his enemies had already crowned him with thorns. With eyes lowered under that painful sign of mock royalty, he was holding together his fettered wrists. His hands, thus joined, formed a heart. Christ's heart! That heart gripped with anguish at the approach of death and at the idea that some might not allow themselves to be touched by him. They would not be touched with that heart overflowing with love that brought Jesus to the supreme sacrifice, that heart which the resurrection would grant eternity.

Through these white marble hands, Pierre and Lucie had entered into prayer. It only remained to continue their way along the stations that followed one another. Everywhere, on these gigantic blocks, details would stop their eyes and feed their meditation. There was the hand of Christ, crushed under the cross, running the risk of breaking. There was the wondrous face of Mary stopping for a moment her Son's advance in a tête-à-tête in which human pain and theological hope arose. There was the fallen Christ, his fingers brutally planted in that ground from which the tree of the cross would soon rise. There was the infinite gentleness of Veronica, wiping the condemned man's face.

For Pierre and Lucie, minutes went by without their noticing it. In front of each station, they spent a long moment of contemplation, plunged in prayer and forgetful of the passage of time. When one is making one's way with Christ towards Golgotha, one cannot be in a hurry. Pierre knew it well, since his illness had been slowly making him ascend Calvary for years.

They reached the last stations, those of hope, for Maria de Faykod had not laid down her chisel after the laying in the tomb. She sculpted three more blocks that bring the faithful into the proclamation of the Good News: Mary's wait on Holy Saturday, the resurrection of Christ, and the meal with the disciples of Emmaus. From the heart of darkness, the seventeen stations lead to the Light.

Lucie and Pierre had finished their prayer. The sun was flooding with its brightness the Way of the Cross, still empty, facing the basilica. Soon it would be time to go to the pools. Meanwhile, the husband and wife were holding each other by the hand, happy and serene.

"The Way of the Cross is so important for us," murmured the sick old man. "What a good idea to have made one accessible to us."

Lucie and Pierre let their gazes wander in the direction of Espé-lugues, the hill marked by the Way of the Cross built shortly after Berna-dette's time. Steep and awkward, climbing it was an impossible challenge for most of the sick or handicapped pilgrims. Pierre could never have gone there.

"Think about it, Lucie," he said. "Millions of pilgrims come here every year. They speak all sorts of languages, they come from every horizon. They bring many of this earth's pains with them. A real congress of cripples! And these millions of people are going to follow Christ step by step, just as we did. What a procession to accompany his ascent to Calvary!"

Once again, the spouses contemplated the statues lined up on the meadow. Monumental and bare, expressive and sober, grandiose without grandiloquence, this Way of the Cross is apt to touch every pilgrim. It is beautiful. It is true. It is universal.

BLESSED ART THOU AMONG WOMEN,
AND BLESSED IS THE FRUIT OF THY WOMB, JESUS.

HEAVEN UNDER EARTH

The Saint Pius X Basilica, December 8, 2007

2007 With a hand that, for the occasion, was not trembling, the old man caressed the concrete pillar. His rough and wrinkled palm gently slid along the gray surface, confirming by his touch what his failing sight had guessed: This smooth and hard, inert and pure matter, at least, had not aged! His wrinkled and smiling face betrayed the intense emotions that gripped him – pride and nostalgia.

He could remember those interminable nights calculating, by hand, resistances, compression efforts, rupture tensions, the length of load-bearing walls. Fifty years later, nothing had moved. The concrete was just as it had been on the first day. Mr. Freyssinet, mentor of the young engineer he was at the time of the subterranean basilica's construction, had gotten it right. Semi-arcs, rising from the ground, joined and buttressed each other at the center of the arch, on either side of a long umbrella beam, much like a fish bone. At each end, the semi-arcs rested upon a V-shaped double pillar – a kind of "crutch," the limbs of which transmitted the arch's weight to the ground, the other one on the contrary "dragging" it upward. The two forces nearly canceled each other out, and the structure's hundreds of tons and grass-covered roof rested on little articulated elements absorbing any possible deformations.

This simple and bold technique, combined with prestressed concrete, that Freyssinet had invented brought together three otherwise incompatible qualities in construction – an immense enclosed, simple, and wide-open space. That engineer was a visionary who had perfectly understood that a church is more than a building. The Saint Pius X Basilica, with its hollow and curved forms, resembled a shelter protecting the encounter of the human soul with the divine presence.

The old man turned toward the middle of the edifice, where the high altar is located. How far away it seemed! The altar servers were getting busy. They were preparing for the High Mass that would open the jubilee of the apparitions' hundred and fifty years on this feast of the Immaculate Conception. The crowd was dense. The imposing size of the building created a slightly unreal feeling of immensity, nearly of infinity.

From his location, an almost complete view of the basilica opened up to him who had seen it, bit by bit, during its construction, in the years 1956 to 1958. It was a real masterpiece, conceived in hope, excavated in pain, and achieved in joy.

This reflection reminded him of the ups and downs that preceded the opening of the construction site. The bishop at the time, Bishop Théas, wanted to build a shelter capable of protecting the crowd of pilgrims from the abundant Pyrenees rain and to have it ready for the apparitions' centennial at the latest. The great shelter soon became a church, then a basilica. The poor bishop had to put up a fight. At the outset, everyone had applauded the idea. Then the difficulties that arose – water seeping into the basement, swelling cost estimates, shrinking timetables, donations too slow in coming – got the better of this beautiful unanimity. The old engineer clearly remembered the worried face of Mr. Vago, the head architect, every time he visited Bishop Théas with a satchel full of new bills, and the bishop's often sad expression when he contemplated the still uncertain construction site.

The basilica's atmosphere was dry. This observation amused the old man, and not without reason. Problems of soil humidity, stemming from the fact that the site was situated at the bottom of the valley right next to the Gave, crisscrossed by tumultuous and corrosive subterranean waters, had seemed insurmountable. Providing proper drainage and building an underground dam to protect the structure had been epic enterprises. The final flooding of the excavation,[1] though planned and inspected, had nonetheless impressed even the public works specialists. As a commentator of the time wittily observed, the waters of Lourdes had spilled a lot of ink!

The former engineer's gaze took in the chancel, which rose in a gentle slope so that the central altar might receive the pilgrims' prayers like a precious vase. It was another sensational idea, this slight convexity of the floor, corresponding to the arch's concavity. As a result, the view of the massive and elevated altar from any point in the church would be clear and direct.

He could still see the images, for ever engraved in his memory, of the basilica's consecration celebrated by Cardinal Angelo Roncalli on March 25, 1958. At the end of the ceremony, the future Pope John XXIII had not been afraid to admit that at the outset he had misjudged the project.

No, the old man did not regret this last pilgrimage, in the footsteps of his youth, to one of his first professional adventures – a technical adventure, a human adventure, and also a spiritual adventure. He had discovered that technology could and should always be at the service of humanity, and never against it. He had learned the virtues of

---

1. After making it waterproof against the subterranean streams, the engineers flooded the excavation to check its resistance to water. Then they emptied it.

perseverance and of hope. He had understood that there was, between God and man, a covenant, and that the monuments built to God's glory were its seals.

Yes, the old man had understood many things at the time. And today, standing in the heart of what was the work of his life, though he had been only one of its many cogs, he realized that in reality, it had molded him more than he had shaped it.

Moved, he reflected that, decidedly, Lourdes would always be the work of God more than the work of man.

HOLY MARY, MOTHER OF GOD,

THE SHRINE'S VOICE

Lourdes Magazine, *a Self-Portrait, January 8, 2008*

20 08 *[An anthropomorphized journal speaks for itself:]*
In her office where my articles are still scattered and decked out with colored notations, Martine is busy at work. Two days before my files have to be sent, her telephone is ringing off the hook: Between the proofreader who warned that she'd be over around three, the translator who wished to change a word, and the photo editor who is having trouble finding the requested photograph, the copy editor does not have a minute to lose.

"No need to panic," she murmurs. "Even if Luisa only receives the lot on Thursday, I'm sure she and Gianni will manage a miracle."

Luisa is the one who scrupulously takes care of the layout for all of my issues. And Gianni Giachetti is my printer. For him, printing *Lourdes Magazine* is participating in the Marian city's pastoral outreach. Thanks to him, we get exceptional rates. When I arrive in their offices in Casale, a charming little town located between Milan and Turin, it is as if I were arriving in my second home.

"There we go; it's beginning to take shape. Once again, Bernadette has given me a heck of a hand!" smiled Martine, ever calm and confident.

The fact is that ever since the copy editor has been working here, she has had a chance to get used to our constant pace. Besides, she's quite right not to be worried: I've been placed under the patronage of Saint Maximilian Kolbe, who already read my ancestor journal, *Le Journal de la Grotte*, in 1930; I was blessed in 1991 by Pope John Paul II, and entrusted to Mary's care from my very first issue. What could possibly go wrong?

Here is my story: I have existed since the very beginnings of the shrine, as it was important that I should be the echo of the intense life at the heart of Lourdes. At the start, in 1865, I was but a meager weekly brochure of four pages. Then, as I grew older, I put on weight and moved on to about ten pages twice monthly. At that time, I was still called *Journal de la Grotte*. In 1987, I filled out with a magazine supplement which, in 1991, officially became *Lourdes Magazine*. From twice monthly, I moved on to eight issues per year; my layout improved – at the advice of an experienced editor, Pierre-Marie Dumont – and my distribution never stopped broadening. Translated now into five languages, I travel to over one hundred and thirty countries. You can see that I lead an exciting life. I benefit from the knowledge of people who know everything about the shrine, like Dom Bernard Billet, our trusty historical advisor.

Here I am now on the desk of François, the managing editor. Martine laid me right next to Bernadette's picture that sits enthroned on his desk.

François is the moving spirit behind the paper. Since 1991, he has overseen my destiny like a *journalist in Paradise*, in his own words. He joined the team in 1997 and found the family he had been missing, since he had to leave behind many of his own in Algeria. He sees to it that I am *understood by the little people, and I that invite every pilgrim to bring Mary back home, like the apostle John, to live of the Holy Spirit through Her and in Her.* He makes of me *a refreshing spring* ceaselessly repeating the Good News, *a solid rock* in which one finds a word of truth, a *light* for the readers, and evangelization tool open to all religions. I am waxing poetic, but I must admit that it is Bishop Jacques Perrier who spoke of me in those terms in 1996, for the fifteenth anniversary of *Lourdes Magazine*. I feel flattered, just as I am happy to land among thousands of pilgrims – young ones, old ones, sick ones, healthy ones, people of all nationalities and all conditions. With a print run of up to sixty thousand issues, I travel all around the world.

Daniel has been in charge of my promotion since 1991. Endowed with an incredible sense of humor, always in a good mood, he spreads the Good Word among the advertisers and heads up the team of vendors who work in the shrine kiosks. He says that through all the encounters he makes, he receives more than he gives. The true wealth of Lourdes, and of *Lourdes Magazine* in particular, is indeed the encounters. People, spontaneously, do not hesitate to let you know how much you mean to them and they tell you, as if they had always known you, their joys and their sorrows.

But I am still the luckiest one! One day, I made Pierre's day. He had come to Lourdes especially to bring me back to his family who couldn't make the trip. Another day, I arrive with the mail into the hands of Josephine, who awaits me like the Messiah and devours me from cover to cover. On yet another day, I am translated into Spanish to be understood by Paquita, a faithful reader who regularly thanks the editorial staff for always taking the time to answer her letters by hand. On the fourth day, here I am on Gilles' bedside table. The night before, when he had gone to buy a magazine to read on the train, he found me in a kiosk. His life is about to be changed for ever. Already bowled over by the "readers' letters" section, which largely comprises prayers and testimonies, each more moving than the next, he is now reading the section entitled "Parole," devoted to a Lourdes confessor's reflections. What he does not know yet is that once he reads the "Grotto Journal" section, in which the abbé Pierre tells his secret link to Lourdes, then the "Forum" that relays the news of the Montfort pilgrimage, he will never be the same again. His revived faith will henceforth make him the most faithful of readers and pilgrims.

I have made so many encounters that the pages that have generously been granted to me to speak of myself would not suffice to tell them all. What could be more beautiful? I owe this fabulous fate to all those who make me what I am. I wanted to pay them a tribute here; just as I wanted to tell all my readers how proud I am of being a daily support to them.

So, I'll see you in the next issue!

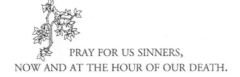

PRAY FOR US SINNERS,
NOW AND AT THE HOUR OF OUR DEATH.

THE 2008 JUBILEE

The Apparitions' One Hundred Fiftieth Anniversary, January 17, 2008

20 08 The church's door had opened. As light as the flutter of wings, a rustling of fabric skimmed the silence without troubling it, and Clémence continued her prayer in perfect peace. In front of the granite baptistery of a church "just like the others," she was praying with her eyes closed better to imagine the scene that took place here on January 9, 1844. On that day, the city of Lourdes, numbed in the mantle of winter, was brightened by peeling bells. A baby, born two nights before, was being baptized – the tiny Marie-Bernarde Soubirous.

The parish church of Lourdes, the first step in Bernadette's spiritual life, has become the first stop in the path that all pilgrims are invited to take in this year 2008, for the one hundred fiftieth anniversary of the apparitions. In front of the baptismal font where Bernadette underwent her second birth, Clémence was thinking about her own baptism, on that life of sanctifying grace that she had received by water and the Holy Spirit.

The rustling of fabric stopped behind the young woman, and a scent of jasmine perfumed the air. Distracted, Clémence's imagination flew from the baptistery in Lourdes and brought her back to India, to that humanitarian trip last summer. She associated that smell with the hair of the women she spent time with over there, near Pondicherry. Everywhere, bunches of white jasmine were affixed to black hair. What a memory! Unable to bear it any longer, Clémence turned around and opened her eyes wide with surprise. A gracious figure in a sari was standing behind her, and a big bright smile answered her befuddled expression.

In response to Clémence's mute questioning, the young Indian woman explained the reasons for her presence in this unexpected place. In this early 2008, she had come to prepare the Tamil pilgrimage, which was to gather in Lourdes in August, comprising a few hundred Christians and Hindus who had settled in the four corners of Europe.

"I have never been baptized," said the young woman, pointing to the granite basin. "But I feel good here."

Clémence nodded. Interreligious dialogue often seemed impossible. Would this be one of the benefits of the jubilee? In Lourdes, in this festive year, it seems almost self-evident! Clémence apologized to the young woman for her indiscreet surprise and related her trip to India in a few words. In a common agreement, the two visitors decided to go together on the visit suggested by the shrines, which is marked through the town. Unbeknownst to them, they were thus participating in one of the twelve missions that the diocese had outlined for Lourdes in this jubilee year: the encounter between religions, in addition to service to the sick, prayer for peace, and the welcoming of the excluded.

At a few streets from the parish church, the two walkers entered into the "dungeon" where the Soubirouses used to live. Clémence, without daring to say it to her companion whose caste she did not know, thought of the Indian "untouchables." In this place, grace bloomed in such a poor family. What universality in that message!

Next they came to Saint Michael's Gate, then the esplanade. A joyful atmosphere reigned among the basilicas. Everything was decorated with the care one gives to adorn the walls for a family party. And the analogy is apt this year, as every pilgrim must feel at home in the city of Mary, and everyone must know that he or she is welcomed as a very dear guest. That's quite a feat when one remembers there are millions of visitors expected this jubilee year!

As soon as she entered the Marian domain, Clémence felt enveloped by the warm atmosphere. Leaving her spiritual baggage at the feet of the Virgin, she had the feeling of being at home, even though this was her first visit to Lourdes.

She knelt down and got to work. Indeed, like all visitors this year, she had come to participate in a vast construction site. During the last jubilee – the centennial, in 1958 – the construction site had been entrusted to workmen: They were building the Saint Pius X Basilica. As the years progressed, public works continued. Lourdes created welcoming centers, built bridges, and restored monuments. This time, the organizers have decided to enlist all pilgrims in a somewhat peculiar construction enterprise. It is the erection of a "basilica of prayer" along the Gave. The basilica built in 1958 was subterranean; the one being built in 2008 is done so with the heart and soul of every pilgrim!

At the moment when Clémence was kneeling at Massabielle, this spiritual shrine was just beginning: Crowds of pilgrims had yet to go there to bring their own "stone." Yet, how beautiful it was already! Clémence closed her eyes and opened her heart. The invisible basilica around her was inhabited. The young woman felt a presence there, without yet grasping who it was. Standing next to her, the Indian woman was praying, deep in her own meditation.

A moment later, the two young women set out again: The Jubilee circuit was taking them beyond the grotto. Crossing a bridge, they went up the Gave, followed the markers, and finally reached the former hospice of the Sisters of Nevers, which was the end of the walking tour. This is where Bernadette had made her First Communion in 1858. Entering into the chapel where a very sober cross adorns the white wall, Clémence understood: The presence lighting up the inside of the jubilee "prayer basilica" was none other than that of Christ. The diverse events of the year have as their only goal to invite the crowds to come and contemplate in Lourdes along with Mary, the marvel of marvels, God's presence among the sanctuaries, through the rustling of the Holy Spirit in the transfiguring love of Christ, who promised us that he would be *with us always, until the end of the age.*

AMEN.

APPENDIX

TIMELINE

DATE	NATURE	EVENTS
1830	*Political history* *Marian apparition*	• Beginning of Louis-Philippe I's reign. • July 18 and November 17: Apparitions in the rue du Bac.
1844	*Lourdes history*	• Bishop Laurence named to Tarbes diocese. • January 7: Birth of Marie-Bernarde Soubirous, a.k.a. Bernadette, daughter of François Soubirous and Louise Castérot, at the mill at Boly. • January 9: Bernadette is baptized. • November: Bernadette is given to nurse with Marie Lagües in Bartrès.
1846	*Church history* *Marian apparition*	• June 16: Pope Pius IX is elected. • September 19: Apparitions at La Salette.
1848	*Political history*	• February 22-24: Revolution in Paris and abdication of King Louis-Philippe. • February 25: Proclamation of the Second Republic. • December 10: Louis-Napoléon Bonaparte is President of the Republic.
1851	*Political history*	• December 2: Coup d'état by Louis-Napoléon Bonaparte and reestablishment of the Empire.
1853	*Political history*	• Crimean War.
1854	*Lourdes history* *Church history*	• Bernadette is evicted from the mill at Boly. • December 8: Pope Pius IX proclaims the dogma of the Immaculate Conception in his bull *Ineffabilis Deus.*

1856	*Lourdes history*	• November: The Soubirous family goes to live in "the dungeon".
1858	*Lourdes history*	• February 11: First apparition. Bernadette sees a Lady all dressed in white in the Massabielle grotto. • February 14: Second apparition. Bernadette sprinkles the Lady with holy water. • February 18: Third apparition. Invitation to come to the grotto for fifteen days. • February 19: Fourth apparition, in the presence of eight people. • February 20: Fifth apparition, in silence. • February 21: Sixth apparition. Police Chief Jacomet interrogates Bernadette. • February 23: Seventh apparition. • February 24: Eighth apparition, in the presence of two hundred to three hundred people. The Lady calls for prayer and penance. • February 25: Ninth apparition. The miraculous spring gushes forth. • February 27: Tenth apparition. • February 28: Eleventh apparition. • March 1: Twelfth apparition, in the presence of fifteen hundred people. Catherine Latapie is healed. • March 2: Thirteenth apparition. The request is made for a chapel. • March 3: Fourteenth apparition. • March 4: Last apparition of the fifteen days, in the presence of eight thousand people. • March 25: Sixteenth apparition. The Lady gives her name in the local dialect: "Que soy era Immaculada Concepciou". • April 7: Seventeenth apparition. Miracle of the taper. • June 3: Bernadette receives First Communion. • June 10: The civil authorities close off the grotto. • July 16: Eighteenth and last apparition, in silence. • July 28: Bishop Laurence institutes an Episcopal Investigation Commission for apparitions and miraculous healings. • October 5: Napoleon III has the grotto reopened.

1860	*Lourdes history*	• July 15: Bernadette boards with the Hospice Sisters.
1861	*Lourdes history*	• August 22: Bishop Laurence purchases the grotto land.
	Political history	• April: American Civil War begins.
1862	*Church history*	• January 18: The Lourdes apparitions are officially recognized.
	Lourdes history	• January 18: Bishop Laurence recognizes the miraculous healing of Catherine Latapie, Louis Bourriette, Blaisette Cazenave, Henri Busquet, Justin Bouhourt, Madeleine Rizan, and Marie Moreau. • August 29: Ministerial authorization is granted to build a chapel at Massabielle. • October 14: Construction of the Chapel of the crypt.
1863	*Lourdes history*	• First torchlight procession. • First draft of a statue of the Virgin by Fabisch.
1864	*Lourdes history*	• April 4: This statue is blessed. • July 25: Loubajac pilgrimage. • The first pools are installed.
1865	*Lourdes history*	• The *Journal de Lourdes* is launched.
1866	*Lourdes history*	• May 17: Arrival of the Garaison Fathers. • May 19: Bishop Laurence blesses the Chapel of the crypt. • May 21: Solemn dedication of the grotto cult. • June: Lourdes is connected to the railroads. • July 8: Bernadette arrives at the convent of Saint-Gildard in Nevers. • July 8: Bernadette's last account of the apparitions to the religious community. • July 19: Bernadette takes the habit and becomes Sister Marie-Bernard.
1867	*Lourdes history*	• October 30: Bernadette's religious profession.

1868	*Lourdes history*	• April: The *Annales de Notre-Dame de Lourdes* is launched.
1869	*Political history*	• November 17: The Suez Canal opens.
	Lourdes history	• November 24: Bishop Laurence acquires the Mont de Piedebat.
1870	*Lourdes history*	• Bishop Pichenot is named to head the Tarbes and Lourdes diocese.
	Church history	• July 18: Proclamation of papal infallibility.
	Political history	• July 19: The Franco-Prussian War is declared.
		• September 4: The Third Republic is proclaimed.
		• September 20: Rome is taken by Victor Emmanuel's republican troops; the Pope's temporal authority is in jeopardy.
		• December 2: Battle of Loigny.
1871	*Marian apparition*	• January 17: Apparitions in Pontmain.
	Political history	• May 10: Treatise of Frankfurt, loss of Alsace-Lorraine.
		• August 31: Adolphe Thiers is elected president of the Republic.
	Lourdes history	• June 28: Pilgrimage of General de Sonis.
		• August 15: Bishop Pichenot dedicates the Upper Basilica.
1872	*Lourdes history*	• October 6: First banner procession.
1873	*Political history*	• May 24: Thiers falls; Mac-Mahon is elected president of the Republic.
	Lourdes history	• Bishop Langénieux is named to the Tarbes and Lourdes diocese.
		• July 12: The *Pèlerin* is launched; it becomes *Pèlerin magazine* on January 3, 1877.
		• July 21: First French national pilgrimage.
		• September 6: Dedication of the organs in the Immaculate Conception Basilica.
1874	*Lourdes history*	• April 6: Laying of the cornerstone of the Our Lady of Sorrows Hospital, a.k.a. Marie Saint-Frai Welcoming Center.

1875	*Lourdes history*	• Bishop Jourdan named to lead Tarbes and Lourdes diocese.
1876	*Lourdes history*	• July 3: Crowning of the statues of the Virgin on the esplanade and in the basilica.
	Marian apparition	• February 14-December 8: Apparitions in Pellevoisin.
1877	*Lourdes history*	• September 8: Father Peyramale dies. • Construction of the first Pilgrim Shelter begins.
1878	*Church history*	• February 20: Election of Pope Leo XIII. • *Quod Apostolici muneris* encyclical on modern world.
1879	*Political history*	• January 30: Mac-Mahon resigns. Jules Grévy is president of the Republic.
	Lourdes history	• April 16: Bernadette dies in Nevers.
1880	*Lourdes history*	• Creation of the Our Lady of Salvation Hospitality.
1881	*Political history*	• June: Law on freedom of assembly. • July: Law on freedom of the press.
	Church history	• *Arcanum divinae* encyclical on the Christian wedding.
1882	*Political history*	• March 28 and June 16: Jules Ferry law on free, obligatory, and secular primary education.
	Lourdes history	• Bishop Billière named head of the Diocese of Tarbes and Lourdes.
1883	*Lourdes history*	• July 16: Laying of the cornerstone of the Rosary Basilica by Cardinal Desprez, archbishop of Toulouse.
1884	*Church history*	• *Humanum genus* encyclical condemns freemasonry.
1886	*Lourdes history*	• The *Journal de la Grotte* is launched.
1887	*Lourdes history*	• August 22: First eucharistic procession to the grotto.

	Political history	• Jules Grévy resigns from the presidency of the Republic; Sadi Carnot succeeds him on December 3.
1892	*Church history*	• February 11: Pope Leo XIII dedicates the feast of Our Lady of Lourdes.
1894	*Political history*	• June 24: Sadi Carnot is assassinated. • June 27: Casimir-Perier becomes president of the Republic. • Zola's *Lourdes* is published.
	Lourdes history	• The grotto's printing press is built on the site of the Savy mill.
1895	*Political history*	• January 15: Casimir-Perier resigns; Félix Faure succeeds him.
1898	*Political history*	• Dreyfus affair: Zola publishes *J'accuse* in the *Aurore*.
1899	*Political history*	• February 18: Émile Loubet is president of the Republic.
	Lourdes history	• Bishop Schoepfer is named to lead Diocese of Tarbes.
1900	*Political history*	• July 19: The metro is dedicated in Paris.
1901	*Lourdes history*	• October 6: Cardinal Langénieux dedicates the Rosary Basilica.
1902	*Political history*	• June 7: The Combes cabinet is formed. • Three thousand Catholic schools are closed over the summer.
1903	*Church history* *Political history*	• August 4: Election of Pope Pius X. • April 9: Religious congregation chapels are closed. Lourdes is in jeopardy.
1905	*Political history*	• December 9: Law of separation between Church and state. • December 29: Decree on Church property inventories.

	Church history	• April 15: *Acerbo nimis* encyclical on the teaching of Christian doctrine. • December 20: Pope Pius X's decree on daily communion.
1906	*Lourdes history*	• Joris-Karl Huysmans *Les foules de Lourdes* is published.
	Church history	• February 11: *Vehementer Nos* encyclical, followed on August 10 by the encyclical *Gravissimo officii* condemning the law of separation.
1907	*Political history*	• March 28: Law on the freedom of religion.
	Lourdes history	• February 11: Bishop Meunier of Évreux recognizes the miraculous healing of Father Cirette. • October 27: Bishop Renou of Lourdes recognizes the miraculous healing of Jeanne Tulasne. • The Feast of Our Lady of Lourdes is extended to the whole world.
	Church history	• September 20: A collective letter of the bishops of France criticizes the state schools' neutrality.
1908	*Lourdes history*	• Fiftieth anniversary of the apparitions. • First Rosary Pilgrimage. • February 4: Bishop Williez of Arras recognizes the miraculous healing of Élisa Lesage. • February 5: Cardinal Andrieu of Marseille recognizes the miraculous healing of Sister Maximilien. • February 11: Cardinal Luçon of Rheims recognizes the miraculous healing of Marie-Thérèse Noblet. • March 25: Bishop Meunier of Évreux recognizes the miraculous healing of Sister Sainte-Béatrix. • April 25: Bishop Heylen of Namur recognizes the miraculous healing of Joachime Dehant. • May 1: Bishop Douais of Beauvais recognizes the miraculous healing of Aurélie Huprelle. • May 10: Bishop de Ligonnes of Rodez recognizes the miraculous healing of Sister Saint-Hilaire. • June 6: Archbishop Amette of Paris recognizes the miraculous healings of Clémentine Trouvé, Marie Lebranchu, Marie Lemarchand, Esther Brachmann, Rose François.

- July 1: Bishop Dubourg of Rennes recognizes the miraculous healing of Father Salvador.
- July 2: Bishop Bougoin of Périgueux recognizes the miraculous healing of Johanna Bézenac.
- July 25: Bishop Waffelaert of Bruges recognizes the miraculous healing of Pierre de Rudder.
- August 15: Bishop Delamaire of Cambrai recognizes the miraculous healings of Sister Marie de la Présentation and of Marie Savoye.
- August 30: Bishop Meunier of Évreux recognizes the miraculous healing of Sister Eugénia.
- October 10: Bishop Douais of Beauvais recognizes the miraculous healing of Sister Joséphine Marie.
- November 1: Bishop Douais of Beauvais recognizes the miraculous healing of Clémentine Malot.

1909 *Lourdes history*

- September 22: Bernadette's body is found intact.
- December 8: Bishop Gibier of Versailles recognizes the miraculous healing of Cécile Douville de Franssu.

1910 *Lourdes history*

- July 30: Bishop Catteau of Luçon recognizes the miraculous healing of Marie Biré.
- August 5: Bishop Rumeau of Angers recognizes the miraculous healing of Aimée Allope.
- September 8: Bishop Walravens of Tournai recognizes the miraculous healing of Amélie Chagnon.
- November 6: Bishop Henry of Grenoble recognizes the miraculous healing of Antonia Moulin.

1911 *Lourdes history*

- June 4: Bishop Gely of Mende recognizes the miraculous healing of Marie Borel.

1912 *Lourdes history*

- March 7: Bishop Nègre of Tulle recognizes the miraculous healing of Sister Julienne.
- July 2: Bishop Bonnefoy of Aix recognizes the miraculous healing of Élisa Seisson.
- September 8: Bishop Cezerac of Cahors recognizes the miraculous healing of Marie Fabre.

- September 14: The Espélugues Way of the Cross is blessed.
- November 25: Bishop Maillet of Saint-Claude recognizes the miraculous healing of Virginie Haudebourg.

1913	*Political history*	• January 17: Raymond Poincaré is elected president of the Republic.
	Lourdes history	• September 8: Bishop Catteau of Luçon recognizes the miraculous healing of Juliette Orion.
1914	*Political history*	• August 3: Germany declares war on France.
	Lourdes history	• September 3: Pope Benedict XV is elected.
1916	*Political history*	• February-December: Battle of Verdun.
1917	*Marian apparition*	• May 13-October 13: Apparitions at Fatima.
1918	*Political history*	• November 11: The Armistice is signed.
1919	*Political history*	• June 28: Treaty of Versailles; France recovers Alsace-Lorraine.
1922	*Church history*	• February 6: Pope Pius XI elected.
		• Beginning of the Poincaré cabinet.
1923	*Political history*	• French troops occupy the Ruhr.
1925	*Church history*	• June 14: Pope Pius XI beatifies Bernadette.
		• July 18: Bernadette's body is set in a reliquary in the Nevers convent chapel.
1926	*Lourdes history*	• The Foulards Blancs (hospital scouts) are founded.
	Political history	• Second Poincaré cabinet.
1927	*Lourdes history*	• First pilgrimage of the Scouts of France.
		• Bishop Poirier is named to head the Diocese of Tarbes and Lourdes.
1928	*Lourdes history*	• The *Bulletin de l'Association médicale de Lourdes* is launched.

1929	*Lourdes history*	• Bishop Gerlier named to head Tarbes and Lourdes diocese.
	Political history	• The Maginot Line is built.
1930	*Lourdes history*	• July 27: Mariology congress.
1933	*Church history*	• December 8: Pope Pius XI canonizes Bernadette.
1934	*Lourdes history*	• International Combat Veterans' Pilgrimage.
1935	*Lourdes history*	• April 28: Year of Redemption closing ceremonies.
1936	*Political history*	• The Popular Front comes to power: Léon Blum cabinet.
1938	*Lourdes history*	• Bishop Choquet named to lead Tarbes and Lourdes diocese.
	Political history	• September: Munich Accords.
1939	*Church history*	• March 2: Pope Pius XII is elected.
	Political history	• September 3: War is declared on Germany.
1940	*Political history*	• May 10: Germany invades France.
		• June 22: The armistice is signed.
1941	*Lourdes history*	• April 20: Marshal Pétain visits.
1944	*Political history*	• June 6: Invasion of Normandy.
		• August 15: Invasion of Provence.
		• August 25: Liberation of Paris.
	Lourdes history	• December 10: First international military pilgrimage.
1945	*Political history*	• May 8: End of World War II in Europe.
1946	*Lourdes history*	• May 20: Cardinal Roques, archbishop of Rennes, recognizes the miraculous healing of Sister Marie-Marguerite.
		• September 10: Pilgrimage of prisoners and the deported.
	Political history	• November 23: French Indochina War begins.

1947	*Lourdes history*	• Bishop Théas named to lead Diocese of Tarbes and Lourdes.
	Marian apparition	• December 8-14: Apparitions on Île-Bouchard.
1948	*Lourdes history*	• Creation of the "Fire and Clan of the Our Lady of Lourdes Hospitaller Scouts". • First Pax Christi pilgrimage. • March 18: Bishop Lacaste of Oran recognizes the miraculous healing of Gabrielle Clauzel.
1949	*Lourdes history*	• May 31: Bishop Provenchères of Aix-en-Provence recognizes the miraculous healing of Francis Pascal.
1950	*Lourdes history*	• November 20: Cardinal Roques, archbishop of Rennes, recognizes the miraculous healing of Jeanne Frétel.
1951	*Lourdes history*	• December 14: Archbishop Feltin of Paris recognizes the miraculous healing of Louise Jamain.
1952	*Lourdes history*	• June 6: Bishop Delay of Marseille recognizes the miraculous healing of Marie-Thérèse Canin. • July 13: Archbishop Richaud of Bordeaux recognizes the miraculous healing of Jeanne Gestas.
1953	*Lourdes history*	• December 8: Bishop Gaudel of Fréjus recognizes the miraculous healing of Paul Pellegrin.
1954	*Political history*	• May 7: France defeated at Diên Biên Phu; end of French occupation in Indochina.
	Lourdes history	• May 28: First HCPT pilgrimage. • July 21: Geneva Accords. • November 1: Algerian insurrection.
1955	*Lourdes history*	• May 18: Cardinal Innitzer, archbishop of Vienna, recognizes the miraculous healing of Edeltraud Fulda. • May 31: Bishop Angrisani of Casale-Monferrato recognizes the miraculous healing of Evasio Ganora. • August 1: Laying of the cornerstone of the Cité Saint-Pierre.
1956	*Lourdes history*	• First pilgrimage of the Order of Malta. • May 12: The new pools are blessed.

		• May 30: Saint Pius X Basilica construction site is blessed.
		• July 16: Bishop Vion of Poitiers recognizes the miraculous healing of Alice Couteault.
		• August 15: Cardinal Roques, archbishop of Rennes, recognizes the miraculous healing of Marie Bigot.
		• September 8: Dedication of the Cité Saint-Pierre.
	Political history	• March 2 and 20: Independence of Morocco and Tunisia.
1957	*Political history*	• March 25: Treaty of Rome and creation of the EEC.
	Church history	• Pope Pius XII encyclical on "The Pilgrimage of Lourdes".
	Lourdes history	• First Gypsy pilgrimage.
		• June 4: Archbishop Rémond of Nice recognizes the miraculous healing of Henriette Bressolles.
1958	*Lourdes history*	• Centennial of the apparitions.
		• March 17: Bishop Rémond of Nice recognizes the miraculous healing of Rose Martin.
		• March 25: Dedication of Saint Pius X basilica.
		• August 5: Bishop Guyot of Coutances recognizes the miraculous healing of Lydia Brosse.
	Political history	• June 1: Charles de Gaulle returns to power.
		• October 4: The Constitution of the Fifth Republic is adopted.
		• December 21: Charles de Gaulle becomes president of the Republic.
	Church history	• October 28: Pope John XXIII is elected.
1959	*Lourdes history*	• November 14: Cardinal Feltin, archbishop of Paris, recognizes the miraculous healing of Yvonne Fournier.
1960	*Lourdes history*	• June 2: Cardinal Montini, archbishop of Milan, recognizes the miraculous healing of Maddalena Carini.
		• December 18: Bishop Charrière of Lausanne recognizes the miraculous healing of Brother Léo Schwager.
1961	*Lourdes history*	• *Recherches sur Lourdes* is launched (to 1984).
		• June 28: Bishop Théas of Tarbes and Lourdes recognizes the miraculous healing of Théa Angele.

1962	Political history	• March 18: Évian Accords and independence of Algeria.
	Church history	• October 11: Second Vatican Council begins.
1963	Lourdes history	• May 31: Archbishop Dupuy of Albi recognizes the miraculous healing of Ginette Nouvel. • September 28: First polio pilgrimage.
	Political history	• Franco-German friendship treaty.
	Church history	• June 21: Election of Pope Paul VI.
1965	Church history	• December 8: Pope Paul VI closes Vatican II.
	Lourdes history	• May 11: Archbishop Lallier of Marseille recognizes the miraculous healing of Juliette Tamburini. • May 26: Archbishop Fasola of Messina recognizes the miraculous healing of Élisa Aloi.
1966	Church history	• First plenary assembly of the bishops of France.
	Lourdes history	• Creation of "Day pilgrims".
1968	Lourdes history	• May 1: Dedication of the Saint Joseph chapel. • September 30: First international polio pilgrimage.
1969	Political history	• April 28: General de Gaulle resigns. • June 15: Georges Pompidou becomes president of the Republic.
1970	Lourdes history	• Bishop Donze is named to lead Diocese of Tarbes and Lourdes.
1971	Lourdes history	• First "Faith and Light" pilgrimage.
	Political history	• June 13: François Mitterrand becomes first secretary of the Socialist party.
1973	Lourdes history	• The *Bulletin de l'Hospitalité Notre-Dame de Lourdes* is launched (renamed *Lettre de l'Hospitalité Notre-Dame de Lourdes* in 2002).
1974	Political history	• May 19: Valéry Giscard d'Estaing becomes president of the Republic.
	Lourdes history	• First "Eau Vive" pilgrimage.

1976	*Lourdes history*	• May 26: Archbishop Gottardi of Trento recognizes the miraculous healing of Vittorio Micheli.
1978	*Church history*	• August 26: election of Pope John Paul I. • October 16: election of Pope John Paul II.
	Lourdes history	• June 17: Bishop Orchampt of Angers recognizes the miraculous healing of Serge Perrin.
1979	*Lourdes history*	• Pilgrimage of one hundred thousand ex-prisoners and deported persons.
	Political history	• First European parliamentary elections.
1981	*Political history*	• May 10: François Mitterand is elected president of the Republic.
	Lourdes history	• July 16-23: Forty-second Eucharistic Congress.
1982	*Lourdes history*	• August 26: Czestochowa and Lourdes become twin cities.
1983	*Lourdes history*	• August 15: Pope John Paul II visits on pilgrimage.
1985	*Lourdes history*	• *Lourdes aujourd'hui* is launched.
1986	*Lourdes history*	• April 21: Foundation of a dialysis center. • September: First pilgrimage of the Lourdes Cancer Hope Association.
1987	*Lourdes history*	• January 18: Jean Delannoy's film shooting.
1988	*Political history*	• May 8: François Mitterand is re-elected president of the Republic.
	Lourdes history	• March 25: Bishop Donze of Tarbes and Lourdes dedicates the Church of Saint Bernadette. • First pilgrimage of Africa war veterans. • September 19-23: First gathering at Lourdes of the Our Lady teams. • Bishop Sahuquet is named to Tarbes and Lourdes diocese.
1989	*Lourdes history*	• June 28: Bishop Bonmarito of Catania recognizes the miraculous healing of Delizia Cirolli.

1990	*Lourdes history*	• The shrines' general services are reorganized.
1991	*Lourdes history*	• *Lourdes Magazine* is launched.
1993	*Lourdes history*	• First World Day of the Sick. • Creation of *Radio présence Lourdes Pyrénées*.
1994	*Lourdes history*	• July 14: Tour de France stage.
1995	*Political history*	• May 7: Jacques Chirac elected president of the Republic.
1996	*Lourdes history*	• Creation of the shrine's Internet site.
1997	*Lourdes history*	• April 7: Opening of the new Our Lady Welcoming Center.
1998	*Lourdes history*	• Bishop Perrier named head of Tarbes and Lourdes diocese.
1999	*Lourdes history*	• February 9: Bishop Dagens of Angoulême recognizes the miraculous healing of Jean-Pierre Bély.
2000	*Lourdes history*	• Opening of the Pope John Paul II Welcoming Center.
2002	*Political history*	• January 1: European currency comes into force.
2004	*Lourdes history*	• June 19: Blessing of the first station of the Way of the Cross sculpted by Maria de Faykod. • August 15: Pope John Paul II's second pilgrimage.
2005	*Church history* *Lourdes history*	• April 19: Pope Benedict XVI is elected. • September 21: Archbishop Pierro of Salerno recognizes the miraculous healing of Anna Santaniello.
2006	*Lourdes history*	• July 27: Jesuit pilgrimage.
2008	*Lourdes history*	• One hundred fiftieth anniversary of the apparitions.

INDEX OF THE PROPER NAMES

French Authors

Composition and typesetting : FACOMPO, LISIEUX

Printed in September 2008
By Transcontinental (Canada)
Edition number : MGN08014